The Politics of Tragedy and Democratic Citizenship

THE POLITICS OF TRAGEDY AND DEMOCRATIC CITIZENSHIP

By
Robert C. Pirro

continuum

2011

The Continuum International Publishing Group
80 Maiden Lane, New York, NY 10038
The Tower Building, 11 York Road, London SE1 7NX

www.continuumbooks.com

Library of Congress Cataloging-in-Publication Data
Pirro, Robert Carl.
The politics of tragedy and democratic citizenship / by Robert Pirro.
p. cm.
Includes bibliographical references and index.
ISBN: 978-1-4411-6525-1 (pbk. : alk. paper)
ISBN: 978-1-4411-6653-1 (hardcover : alk. paper)
1. Tragic, The Political aspects. 2. Political psychology. I. Title.
JA74.5.P54 2011
320.01–dc22

2010032424

ISBN: 978-1-4411-6525-1 (PB)
      978-1-4411-6653-1 (HB)

Typeset by Newgen Imaging Systems Pvt Ltd, Chennai, India
Printed and bound in the United States of America

Contents

Acknowledgments

This book culminates a twenty-five year intellectual journey. An encounter with Nietzsche's *Birth of Tragedy* in the summer after my junior year in college first got me to think about the links between tragedy and politics. By then, I had already read, and puzzled over, the closing passage of Hannah Arendt's *On Revolution*, in which tragic choral verse (in Greek script, no less) serves as the coda to a work on modern revolution. What had originally seemed to me merely to be a poetic flourish would become, under the influence of Nietzsche's iconoclastic work, the foremost piece of evidence for my later claim that Arendt's understanding of the nature and significance of politics was shaped by a theory of the political significance of tragedy. In the years after I tried to vindicate that claim in my book, *Hannah Arendt and the Politics of Tragedy* (2001), I could no longer pass over without a second thought the many allusions to tragedy or ordinary language uses of "tragedy" to be found in scholarly works, news articles and broadcasts, and personal conversations. This book explores the significance of these allusions and examples of usage in the works of some contemporary political thinkers, activists, and creative artists and maps out the larger significance of selected instances of the politics of tragedy, laying a claim for a new sort of democratic political theory founded on an appreciation of the multifaceted legacy of the oldest sort of democratic political theory.

The various debts I have incurred over the years of working on this project are too numerous and varied for me completely to list, or even fully to remember. Let me single out a portion of them. For their making themselves available (in person or via email) as valued interlocutors and critical readers over the years it has taken for this project to find its final form, I would like to thank William Astore and Josef Chytry. For their thoughtful comments on parts of this book manuscript as well as their valued suggestions about getting the manuscript to press, I thank John McGowan and Louis Ruprecht, Jr. I am also grateful to Dan Latimer and Allen Dunn for making space in the journals they respectively edit, *Southern Humanities Review* and *Soundings: An Interdisciplinary Journal*, for small parts of this project. Thomas Greven kindly arranged an opportunity for me to present a paper on the politics of tragedy in comparative German-American perspective in his Politics Research Colloquium at the Free University's John-F-Kennedy Institute in Berlin, for which I thank him. Rich Pacelle's commitment as chair of Georgia Southern University's Department of Political Science to foster faculty scholarship is also much appreciated, as is the friendship of fellow theorist and faculty member, Steve Engel. My wife, Julia Schmidt, has been an invaluable partner in this project, offering intellectual fellowship, emotional support, and patient encouragement. I can only hope to be as helpful to her scholarly activity as she has been to mine. This book is dedicated to her and to our two boys (another shared project to which we have devoted a bit of our time and energy).

Sources

An earlier version of Chapter 2 was originally published as an article in *Political Theory* (30:2) under the title "Václav Havel and the Political Uses of Tragedy."

An earlier version of Chapter 5 was originally published as an article in *Soundings: An Interdisciplinary Journal* (LXXXV:1–2) under the title "Nelson Mandela and the Ordinary Uses of Tragedy in Private and Political Life."

An earlier version of Chapter 6 was originally published as an article in *Thesis Eleven* (98) under the title "Tragedy, Theodicy and 9/11: Responses to Suffering and Their Political Significance."

An earlier version of Chapter 7 was originally published as an article in *Southern Humanities Review* (43:2) under the title "Goat Song in a Democratic Key: Tragic Legacies in German Culture and Politics."

Earlier versions of Chapters 8 and 9 were originally published as articles in *German Politics and Society* (22:1) and (26:3) under the titles "Situating a German Self in Democratic Community: Greek Tragedy and German Identity in Christa Wolf's Mythic Works" and "Tragedy, Surrogation and the Significance of African-American Culture in Post-unification Germany: An Interpretation of *Schultze Gets the Blues*," respectively.

CHAPTER 1

The Politics of Tragedy: An Introduction and Overview

For those of you who are black and are tempted to be filled with hatred and distrust at the injustice of such an act, against all white people, I can only say that I feel in my own heart the same kind of feeling. I had a member of my family killed, but he was killed by a white man. But we have to make an effort in the United States, we have to make an effort to understand, to go beyond these rather difficult times. My favorite poet was Aeschylus. He wrote: "In our sleep, pain which cannot forget falls drop by drop upon the heart until, in our own despair, against our will, comes wisdom through the awful grace of God." (Robert Kennedy, after receiving news of the assassination of Martin Luther King Jr.)

On April 4, 1968, Robert Kennedy was scheduled to address a campaign rally in a Black neighborhood at what his semi-official biographer would later describe as "the heart of the Indianapolis ghetto."[1] Organized by civil rights leader John Lewis, the event was intended formally to kick off Kennedy's campaign to win Indiana's Democratic Party presidential primary. He had announced his candidacy two-and-a-half weeks earlier in the midst of a presidential election season roiled by contention over President Johnson's war policy and rocked by antiwar candidate Senator Eugene McCarthy's unexpectedly strong performance against the incumbent in the New Hampshire primary. Notified of King's shooting as he boarded a plane in Muncie, Kennedy learned of King's death upon his arrival in Indianapolis. Rejecting the advice of the city's mayor and police officials to cancel the out-of-doors event, Kennedy proceeded to the rally.

Lacking the polish and rhetorical ease of his brother John, Robert Kennedy was a speaker capable of greater emotional self-exposure who was usually at his best in extemporaneous settings. Improvised at the last minute, Kennedy's speech from the back of a flatbed truck to the predominantly Black crowd on that windswept Indianapolis lot was, by all accounts, one of his best. Ordinarily very reticent about his brother's assassination, Kennedy chose this night to evoke that painful memory and establish a bond of shared suffering with his listeners, who had, only seconds earlier, let go cries of affliction upon hearing Kennedy's report of King's death. (Later, at his hotel, when Kennedy was confronted with weeping campaign staffers, it may have been that same memory that reportedly led him to say to one of his top aides, in an apparent tone of rebuke, "After all, it's not the greatest tragedy in the history of the Republic."[2]) Kennedy followed up his quotation of Aeschylus with a call for understanding and compassion across racial lines. Asking his listeners to return home and pray for King's family and for the country, Kennedy concluded his speech: "Let us dedicate ourselves to what the Greeks wrote so many years ago: to tame the savageness of man and make gentle the life of this world. Let us dedicate ourselves to that, and say a prayer for our country and for our people."

To anyone who was not an intimate, Kennedy's evocations of the tragic wisdom of ancient Greece might have seemed puzzling additions to a speech fashioned at the last minute and under the pressure of terrible events. In fact, Kennedy, whose achievements as a student in prep school and at college were far from illustrious, had made the Greek tragedies and, in particular, the verse from Aeschylus's *Agamemnon*, intellectual and emotional mainstays in the time since his brother's assassination. (Aeschylus's words would eventually serve as one of the two epitaphs on the marble slab positioned across from his grave at Arlington National Cemetery.[3]) His reliance on the Greeks for spiritual sustenance began during a stay at a Kennedy family friend's Caribbean vacation home in the early part of 1964. Jackie Kennedy had brought along a copy of classicist Edith Hamilton's, *The Greek Way*, a masterful survey of classical Greek literature, written for non-specialists, in which lessons about the dignity and tragic limits of human agency are powerfully evoked through the stories and words of Aeschylus, Thucydides, and other canonical Greek writers of tragedy and history. While his sister-in-law and her family and friends mustered what good cheer they could, Kennedy mostly remained in his room, poring over Hamilton's narrative and underlining passages of special interest (including the Aeschylean verse from *Agamemnon*, which appears twice in her book).

The encounter with *The Greek Way* marked the beginning of a self-directed program of intense study of the classics, particularly the Greek tragedies, as well as other works by Hamilton. Deriving comfort from the tragic wisdom of the Greeks, Kennedy kept their works close at hand and transcribed many of their consoling passages into his daybook. Senate aides recalled how he would often recite tragic verse from memory.[4] The effect of this intellectual immersion on his temperament was so marked that his sister, Jean, told Arthur Schlesinger that, "after 1963 he found consolation in Greek tragedy rather than religion; this was the expression of his character."[5] The depth of Kennedy's engagement with Greek tragic wisdom was also clear to Maxwell Taylor Kennedy decades later when he compiled a book of passages from his father's writings and from the words that his father chose to record in his daybook. Included in the work are many allusions to the Greek spirit and quotations from the works of the Greek tragedians. Especially significant are the Greek touches from Kennedy's April 4 speech, which are the sources for the book's title, *Make Gentle the Life of This World*,[6] and for M. T. Kennedy's characterization of his father as the kind of person who "would quote Aeschylus when he spoke to the poorest audiences that a presidential candidate had ever bothered with, and they cheered."[7]

The claim about the audience's cheering response to Kennedy's recitation of Aeschylean verse raises questions about the meaning and impact of his engagement with Greek tragedy. Without a doubt, this engagement was highly meaningful *for him* as he confronted the devastating loss of his brother and the premature end of the Kennedy Administration. Aside from the terrible shock and sadness that follows upon the violent death of a close family member, Kennedy had to deal with a shattering blow to his sense of purpose. Having devoted himself as campaign manager to winning the White House for his brother and then becoming a mainstay in his brother's administration as attorney general and White House confidante and factotum, Robert Kennedy felt especially adrift in the wake of the assassination. Burdening Kennedy as well may have been a sense that the murder of his brother was payback for Kennedy Administration policies, including the assassination efforts against Castro that Robert Kennedy had been urging on the CIA, as well as his investigation and prosecution of Mafia bosses, some of whom were connected to the anti-Castro CIA campaign. Edith Hamilton's encomium to the classical Greek spirit of striving in the face of life's harsh and sometimes self-inflicted blows—"All arrogance will reap a rich harvest of tears," was a phrase from Aeschylus he had underlined. "God calls men to a heavy reckoning for overweening pride"[8]—introduced him to a literature of redemptive poetry in which the ironies of action and the devastation of loss is fully acknowledged, that acknowledgment then becoming a spur to renewed, if also chastened, effort.

For the people gathered before Kennedy on that cold April evening, unwilling recipients of the news of Martin Luther King Jr's assassination, what meaning might Aeschylus's words have held? One cannot know for sure, although Kennedy's biographers almost universally credit his six-and-half minute speech with helping to maintain peace in Indianapolis on a night that saw rioting break out in most American cities. Baring his most terrible pain, Kennedy can be seen as offering to his audience what, years earlier, his first reading of *The Greek Way* had so compellingly promised him—a form of solace grounded in a belief that great suffering could bring forth a larger wisdom. That this sort of offering, articulated as it was in the language of tragedy, could find receptive ears at a campaign rally in "the heart of the Indianapolis ghetto" may not be as farfetched as it might sound. For, according to a line of thought pursued by public intellectual and critic Cornel West, it would precisely be in an audience composed of underprivileged African Americans that one ought to expect to find the most heightened American receptivity to an appeal based on tragic wisdom.

A rare figure in American intellectual life for his longstanding engagement with notions of the tragic and for his linking of the prospects for advances in social justice to the wider diffusion of a tragic sensibility throughout American society, West has counted tragic wisdom as one of African Americans' most valuable spiritual resources. As he describes it, exposure to the physical terrors, psychological traumas, and material deprivations of slavery, recurrent mob violence, and pervasive discrimination led New World Africans and their descendants to develop forms of cultural resistance and resilience, among which he includes a "black sense of the tragic." To be sure, this sensibility was primarily grounded not in any encounter with Greek tragedy but in New World Africans' engagement with American Christianity and their transformation of it into "a kind of 'Good Friday' state of existence in which one is seemingly forever on the cross . . . yet sustained by a hope for a potential and possible triumphant state of affairs."[9] In fact, West has gone so far as completely to dismiss the relevance of Greek tragedy to democratic aspirations: "The Greeks had no notion of tragedy as it applied to ordinary people . . . Tragedy was reserved for the highbrow and upper class."[10] Attentive reading of the texts of Greek tragedy and a familiarity with the large scholarly literature arguing for the central role of Greek tragedy in educating the citizens of Athens' fledgling democracy cautions against any offhanded judgments of Greek tragedy's irrelevance to democratic struggles and achievements. (Also worth considering is Lee Breuer and Bob Telson's artistic marriage of the idioms of Black Pentecostalism and Greek tragedy in *The Gospel at Colonus* [1985], the artistic success of which at least suggests a significant degree of affinity between the two cultural forms of tragic expression based on, among other things, their shared reliance on choral singing.)

To the extent that the moment of connection achieved by Kennedy and his Black audience on a vacant Indianapolis lot the night of April 4 can be attributed to a shared tragic sensibility, that sensibility runs counter to a conventional view of Americans as altogether lacking any serious cultural engagement with the tragic nature of life. Typically, European literati have lamented the American "distaste for tragedy" and connected it to American deficiencies in intellectual or emotional depth and complexity as compared with Europeans.[11] This spirit of complaint has been articulated as well by American literati, including Nathaniel Hawthorne, who once wrote of the United States as, "a country where there was no shadow, no antiquity, no mystery, no picturesque and gloomy wrong, nor anything but a commonplace prosperity, in broad and simple daylight." Of course, a degree of artistic license must be conceded to Hawthorne, whose pronouncement on the *un*tragic nature of the American past occurs in the preface to a romance, *The Marble Faun* (1859). As a Massachusetts native not too many generations removed from the first arrival of English settlers, he was fully aware of the colony's early campaigns of religious persecution and the judicial killings resulting from the Salem "witch" trials (in both of which processes his family forbears took leading roles) as well as the campaigns of slaughter conducted during the so-called King Philip's War.

If the American past has included its share of suffering and brutality, prevailing social and ideological conditions, including the relatively broad diffusion of material prosperity to the descendants of some immigrant groups and the relentless promulgation by mainstream institutions of an ethos of individual achievement, have conspired to give wide credence to the view that, "Americans have always been unequivocally optimistic and bereft of a sense of the tragic."[12] A highly conspicuous product of an upwardly mobile Irish-American clan and a firm believer in the ethos of individualist striving, Kennedy nevertheless did not suffer from a deficit of tragic sensibility. His intensive reading in the literature of tragedy left its imprint on his temperament, arguably helping to foster an emotional resilience that allowed him to expose himself so profoundly to the suffering of others and not be driven by this exposure either to a fatalistic retreat from a robust agenda for change or to a resentment-driven attack on the basic premises of the so-called American dream. In characterizing the contribution of a "Romantic" sensibility to Kennedy's approach as policy maker, Jack Newfield placed emphasis on his unusually pronounced capacity to empathize with the people whose very difficult conditions of life were to be subject to decisions taken by politicians and bureaucrats. "What his romanticism did was provide emotional ballast for his pragmatism, to give it a humanist political thrust. It was what made him different from more detached and conservative friends, like Robert McNamara, Byron White, or Theodore Sorensen. Kennedy identified with people, not data, or institutions, or theories."[13] The contrast Newfield draws between the abstracted Olympian pragmatism of the men of the New Frontier and Kennedy's particularistic and personalistic approach is noteworthy, especially in light of Robert McNamara's later, unexpected public emergence (in several books and the 2004 Errol Morris documentary, *The Fog Of War*) as a foreign policy thinker for whom the notion of tragedy is of no small importance. Let us briefly consider his uses of tragedy and the extent to which they are continuous with Kennedy's.

Appointed by John F. Kennedy to head the Department of Defense and retained by Lyndon Johnson, McNamara presided over, and became the main administrative defender of, the escalation of U.S. military commitments in Vietnam from a few tens of thousands of advisors in 1964 to over a half a million ground troops and a major bombing campaign against the North by the close of 1967. By the time he was moved out of his position as defense secretary in November 1967, the rising rate of U.S. casualties, the effective resistance of North Vietnam against all forms of U.S. military escalation, and growing domestic opposition to the war had made him highly skeptical about the viability of the Johnson Administration's war policy. Since he kept his doubts mainly to himself and continued to act as a vocal advocate of the policy of escalation, McNamara left government service widely and passionately derided by antiwar activists as the callous bureaucratic draftsman of an immoral and catastrophic war policy. Many years after the end of his government service, McNamara returned to the public eye ready to express in public his earlier reservations about the war, analyze the mistakes he made, and draw some lessons from those mistakes.

In such publications as *In Retrospect: The Tragedy and Lessons of Vietnam* (1995) and *Argument Without End: In Search of Answers to the Vietnam Tragedy* (2000), McNamara has made the case that the war was the outcome of mistakes, "an error not of values and intentions but of judgment and capabilities." Offering an account of the processes of Vietnam-era decision-making in which he had had a significant role as Secretary of Defense, McNamara focuses in his 1995 book on his own and his colleagues' mistakes. "We of the Kennedy and Johnson administrations who participated in the decisions on Vietnam acted according to what we thought were the principles and traditions of this nation. . . . Yet we were wrong, terribly wrong."[14] Far from being an antiquarian exercise, McNamara's 1995 *mea culpa* is intended, he goes on to suggest, as a lesson for contemporary and future U.S. citizens and policy makers on how to avoid repeating the costly errors of the past:

> I want Americans to understand why we made the mistakes we did, and to learn from them. I hope to say, "Here is something we can take away from Vietnam that is constructive and applicable to the world of today and tomorrow." That is the only way our nation can ever hope to leave the past behind. The ancient Greek dramatist Aeschylus wrote, "The reward of suffering is experience." Let this be the lasting legacy of Vietnam.[15]

Among the errors or mistakes identified by McNamara as occurring under his watch were the failures of Washington policy makers to inform themselves adequately about the motives and aims of North Vietnam's leaders, to free themselves of an exaggerated fear of what negative consequences might result from the collapse of the U.S.-supported government of South Vietnam, and, finally, to consider fully either the scale of American military commitments needed or the likely costs of such commitments. For example, a January 7, 1964, memorandum to the president arguing against military disengagement from the conflict in South Vietnam, quoted at length by McNamara, demonstrates, "how limited and shallow our analysis and discussion of the alternatives to our existing policy in Vietnam . . . had been." McNamara's memo came at a critical juncture in the development of the Johnson Administration's thinking about Vietnam—"we tilted gradually—almost imperceptibly—toward approving the direct application of U.S. military force." In hindsight, McNamara concludes, "we were at the beginning of a slide down a tragic and slippery slope."[16]

In his later work, *Argument Without End: In Search of Answers to the Vietnam Tragedy*, McNamara seems intent on persuading his North Vietnamese counterparts to join him in acknowledging the role that errors and mistakes on both sides played in causing what he insists were the war's unnecessary suffering and deaths. "I hoped to examine a hypothesis that . . . both Washington and Hanoi had missed opportunities to achieve our geopolitical objectives without the terrible loss of life suffered by each of our countries. . . . Were there such opportunities? If so, why were they missed? What lessons can we draw to avoid such tragedies in the future?"[17]

The book juxtaposes historical analyses of United States and North Vietnamese policy making with transcriptions of direct exchanges between some of the major governmental players that took place during six meetings in Hanoi organized by McNamara from 1995 to 1998 and at a 1998 conference held in Bellagio, Italy. In describing the unconventional organization of this book, McNamara notes that, "The discussions were frank and tough, as befits the first-ever discussion by former enemies of this tragic war. Had this dialogue occurred in real time, rather than in retrospect, I believe the tragedy could have been prevented."[18]

If McNamara is not the first or only U.S. writer on the war in Vietnam to make use of the rhetoric of tragedy,[19] he may be one of the few for whom the term functions as more than a generic description of a painful or burdensome event. One knows that his use of "tragedy" is well-considered and strategic not only from his choices of book titles but also from the frequency with which the rhetoric of tragedy is invoked within each book's pages as well as the substantive role played by a particular notion of tragedy that operates within each of his narratives. To be sure, there are instances in which McNamara's use of "tragedy" or "tragic" accords with the sort of ordinary usage to which newscasters are prone when they report on fatal car accidents or house fires. So, for example, in the course of describing a project of document collection he instigated for the purpose of building an archive to be used by future scholars studying the evolution of U.S. policy toward South and North Vietnam (the so-called Pentagon Papers), McNamara reports that the assistant secretary for international security affairs who had been charged with this task died unexpectedly: "The document collecting started on June 17, 1967,—one month before McNaughton's tragic death in an air accident."[20] Here, use of the cognate is plainly intended simply to refer to an unexpectedly fatal event.

In the majority of references, however, a more complex sense of tragedy is at play for McNamara. Citing Aeschylus's famous formulation, *pathei mathos*, "the reward of suffering is experience,"[21] he appears to advance a notion of tragedy as an experience of suffering that has educative value. There are, in other words, "lessons" to be drawn from one's participation in an unexpectedly fatal or extraordinarily painful event. (The subtitle of his earlier book encapsulates how the notion of education or learning is implied by his use of "tragedy." After all, "The *Catastrophe* and Lessons of Vietnam" or "The *Disaster* and Lessons of Vietnam" do not have the idiomatic punch that "The Tragedy and Lessons of Vietnam" does.)

McNamara's use of "tragedy" also encompasses a sense that the suffering that follows upon a train of decisions and actions was not intended or foreseen by the relevant actors. That is, negative outcomes are a consequence of errors in judgment or mistakes due to ignorance rather than bad will or evil intentions. (One might think here of Oedipus, who, far from intending to kill his father and sleep with his mother took steps to avoid precisely those outcomes.) The overall picture of U.S. policy makers and administrators McNamara's notion of tragedy therefore helps to paint is of men who were well-intentioned, who identified with worthy values, but who nevertheless made very costly mistakes because their information was false or distorted and their judgment was clouded. If any vice can be attributed to them, on this view, it would be laziness (in gathering the relevant data and correctly assessing it) rather than cruelty or arrogance. Thus, even as McNamara's gesture of self-examination, of looking back upon his role in escalating U.S. military involvement, has the appearance of a mea culpa, his resort to a notion of tragedy can be seen as having an exculpatory effect, as relieving him of his just portion of personal responsibility for the needless suffering and death brought about by U.S. policies in Vietnam. Such a conclusion might be easily be reached on a reading of *The Best and the Brightest*, David Halberstam's depiction of the White House policy discussions and bureaucratic maneuvering that resulted in U.S. military escalation in Vietnam.

In Halberstam's book, McNamara appears as the self-assured quantitative analyst, effective policy-debater and can-do bureaucrat; "the mark of him in government, his imprimatur, was his capacity to say that something could be done, understood, mastered, accomplished." The tragic flaw of this McNamara found expression not only in a susceptibility to errors of judgment or in an ignorance of the relevant facts but also in his willful overlooking of contrary facts and his denigrating of critical points of view merely for the sake of winning policy arguments. The elements of McNamara's "overall style" included, "the total belief in what he was doing, the willingness to knock down anything that stood in his way, the relentless quality, so that other men, sometimes wiser, more restrained, would be pushed aside." In his many conspicuous missions to Vietnam, this McNamara "epitomized booming American technological success . . . looking for what he wanted to see . . . never s[eeing] nor smell[ing] nor fe[eling] what was really there, right in front of him." Back at the White House, he would not hesitate to "lie, dissemble . . . in high level meetings" though "always for the good of the cause, always for the right reasons, always to serve the Office of the President."[22]

According to Halberstam's account, McNamara at the end of the 1960s was already, in conversations with friends, trying out the argument about tragic mistakes that he would commit to print decades later (and which, already then, seemed unconvincing to Halberstam).

> When he did (convert to dovishness), he went through a personal crisis. He would confide to friends that if they had only known more about the enemy, more about the society, if there had only been more information, more intelligence about the other side, perhaps it never would have happened, though of course one reason that there was so little knowledge about the enemy and the other side was that no one was as forceful as he was in blocking its entrance into debates.[23]

Not wanting to have information is a different (and more blameworthy) lapse than not having information. Actively trying to stifle inconvenient information is a different (and more blameworthy) vice than lacking the initiative to seek out contrary information. "For all his idealism," Halberstam writes, "he was no better and perhaps in his hubris a little worse than the institution he headed." This allusion to hubris invites the reader to see the evolution of American policy toward Vietnam through the prism of classical Greek tragedy, a perspective Halberstam seemingly endorses in his book's final pages, when he rhetorically asks, "What was it about the men, their attitudes, the country, its institutions and above all the era which had allowed this tragedy to take place?"[24] (Halberstam's resort to the rhetoric of tragedy found at least one detractor in Mary McCarthy who criticizes his "determination to view Vietnam as an American tragedy," which "means that the outcome is ineluctable, foreordained." Lamenting the fatalistically toned grammatical construction of the book—"the dominant Future Past [tense], which persuades the listener that nothing could have been done otherwise, since fate had written its tale in advance,"

McCarthy argues that, "Vietnam is too disagreeably close to us . . . to serve as the source material for tragic art, even in the hands of a gifted dramatic poet" and finds the notion of writing the Vietnam War as an *American* tragedy, as a story about Lyndon Johnson agonizing over tragic policy decisions, "distasteful" given the tremendous suffering and loss of the people of Vietnam.)[25]

As one might expect, it occurred also to Robert Kennedy to see the unfolding of events in Vietnam in terms of tragedy. During his inaugural presidential campaign speech at Kansas State University, and in what one witness characterized as a "confession of error for his role in shaping the early Vietnam policy," Kennedy explicitly evokes the wisdom of ancient Greek tragedy:

> I am willing to bear my share of the responsibility, before history and before my fellow citizens. But past error is no excuse for its own perpetuation. Tragedy is a tool for the living to gain wisdom, not a guide by which to live. Now as ever, we do ourselves best justice when we measure ourselves against ancient tests, as in the *Antigone* of Sophocles: "All men make mistakes, but a good man yields when he knows his course is wrong, and repairs the evil. The only sin is pride."[26]

Vigilance against pride, not concern with miscalculation, is the lesson Kennedy would have tragedy teach about U.S. involvement in Vietnam. (His Oedipus, one might speculate, would be the vigorous and headstrong young hero who does not give way at the fatal crossroads before a man old enough to be his father and who does not hesitate to become consort to a queen old enough to be his mother.)

McNamara, who so insistently and frequently employs the terms, tragedy and tragic, in his narratives and in the exchanges on the war he conducted with his North Vietnamese counterparts, employs a notion of tragedy that limits the causes of wrongdoing to ignorance. This may explain why, in one of the more contentious of those exchanges, with chief war strategist and top commander of North Vietnamese military forces, General Vo Nguyen Giap, "tragedy" is the word on which Giap keys.

> Gen. Vo Nguyen Giap: Excuse me, but we *correctly* understood you—what you were doing in the Tonkin Gulf. You were carrying out sabotage activities to create a pretext that would allow you to take over the war from the Saigon government, which was incompetent.
>
> Robert McNamara: That is totally wrong, General. I assure you: There was no such intent. None. But this is why we need to reexamine each other's misunderstandings—for two reasons. First, we need to identity missed opportunities; and second, we need to draw lessons which will allow us to avoid such tragedies in the future.
>
> Gen. Vo Nguyen Giap: Lessons are important. I agree. However, you are wrong to call the war a "tragedy"—to say that it came from missed opportunities. Maybe it was a tragedy for you, because yours was a war of aggression, in the neocolonialist "style" or fashion, of the day for the Americans. You wanted to replace the

French; you failed; men died; so, yes, it was tragic, because they died for a bad cause. But for us, the war against you was a noble sacrifice. We did not want to fight the U.S. We did not. But you gave us no choice. Our people sacrificed tremendously for our cause of freedom and independence. There were no missed opportunities for us. We did what we had to do . . . to drive you and your puppets out. So I agree that *you* missed opportunities and that *you* need to draw lessons. But us? I think we would do nothing different, under the circumstances.[27]

Objecting to McNamara's attempt to spread or share blame for the suffering of the war in Vietnam, Giap in effect redefines tragedy as an occasion of failure whose burdensome consequences follow from the pursuit of bad or blameworthy ends rather than a painful event caused by inadvertence. In seeming accord with Halberstam's depiction of the character of McNamara's participation in White House policy debates during the period of escalation, McNamara budges neither from his position nor his rhetoric during his encounters with his erstwhile North Vietnamese foes. In fact, the significance he places on "tragedy" is such that, as he recounts several years later in the course of being interviewed by Errol Morris for his documentary, he continued pressing his Vietnamese counterparts to accept the term as the appropriate *Vietnamese* designation for the conflict. So, for example, as he sat down with conference participants to a meal during a break in their formal discussions, he responded to one Vietnamese official's assertions—"You're totally wrong. We were fighting for our independence. You were fighting to enslave us."—as follows:

Do you mean to say it was *not* a tragedy for you, when you lost 3,400,000 Vietnamese killed?! What did you accomplish?! You didn't get anymore than we were willing to give you at the beginning of the war! You could have had the whole damn thing! Independence! Unification![28]

Putting aside the obvious disingenuousness of McNamara's claim about American readiness to make concessions in the lead-up to the war, let us focus on the apparently large importance McNamara conspicuously and consistently places on notions of tragedy in his effort to come to terms with, and elicit worthwhile lessons from, his involvement in the Vietnam conflict. This high level of intellectual and emotional investment invites us to consider the nature of the relationship between McNamara and Robert Kennedy. To what extent, if any, were McNamara's uses of tragedy influenced by the example of Robert Kennedy?

One cannot discount the possibility that Robert Kennedy's deeply personal engagement with tragedy had an influence upon McNamara. As a member of John F. Kennedy's presidential cabinet, McNamara became an admirer of Robert Kennedy in recognition of the latter's crucial role in bringing about a successful conclusion to the Cuban Missile Crisis.[29] McNamara was a regular visitor to the so-called Hickory Hill seminars, informal monthly lectures presented by visiting literati and intellectuals to administration officials and Kennedy associates, at Robert Kennedy's Virginia estate. Throughout his tenure at Defense under President Lyndon Johnson, McNamara remained on friendly terms with Kennedy, dining with him on a regular basis and informally discussing the state of U.S. military and political efforts in South Vietnam. McNamara would have had ample opportunity to become aware both of Kennedy's taste for the literature of tragedy and the Greek spirit and of the importance of this literature as a touchstone for Kennedy's evolving sense of political vocation. McNamara's choices to begin *In Retrospect* with an evocation of Aeschylean wisdom and to conclude it with a "haunting" poem by Rudyard Kipling ("The Palace"), which takes up the theme of transforming defeated human aspirations into the inspiration for renewed human effort, apparently converge with Kennedy's style of expressing a tragic sensibility. At the same time, and as we have already pointed out, McNamara's use of tragedy to assess and distribute responsibility for the infliction of avoidable pain and suffering is significantly different in substance from Kennedy's. Apparently unwilling to concede that ego and character rather than intellect had been at the core of his failures in shaping policy during the Vietnam War, McNamara writes the tragedy of U.S. military intervention in Vietnam as one of intellectual failure. Implicitly evoking the hubris that afflicted Creon, king of Thebes, Kennedy's citation of Sophocles's *Antigone* at Kansas State identifies overweening pride as the basis of the tragedy of U.S. military involvement in Vietnam.[30]

The unusually intense and public engagements with notions of tragedy demonstrated by Kennedy and McNamara reveal how significant the legacy of Greek tragedy can be for how political actors think about agency, solidarity, and political identity. The rhetoric of Kennedy and McNamara exemplify distinctive forms of the politics *of* tragedy and point to several different and, to an extent, contrasting ways in which notions of tragedy can serve to orient political thought. Take, for example, the challenge posed by a divided society (as the United States in the 1960s was to an unusually heightened and publicized degree) in which utilitarian or ethnic or ideological bases for political solidarity are failing or lacking from the very start. At least since Friedrich Nietzsche formulated his famous thesis about the Dionysian significance of the Greek tragic chorus, ancient Greek tragedy (*tragōidía*) has been understood as having fostered, in a significant way, civic solidarity in the ancient polis. To what extent might the modern relics of *tragōidía*—theories of tragedy, Greek tragedies and the other works that now comprise the genre of tragedy, ordinary uses of "tragedy" and related terms—be used to promote political solidarity in the divided societies of our time? Or, to take another example, what "lessons" might these relics of *tragōidía* teach alienated citizens or those aspiring citizens of today's fledgling democracies about exercising responsible forms of political agency? That this question is also worthy of serious consideration is suggested not only by McNamara's tragically inflected efforts at reassessing U.S. involvement in Vietnam but also by the conclusions of many scholars who have studied *tragōidía*'s role in educating a newly empowered democratic citizenry in ancient Athens about the promise and pitfalls of exercising power.

Political solidarity and political agency are just two of several aspects of modern democratic politics on which fresh perspective might be gained through being attentive to the political significance of tragedy. This book delineates the expert and ordinary forms that the politics of tragedy can take, clarifying their sometimes forgotten sources in Athenian experience, and illuminating both their dangers, on the one hand, and their promise to support contemporary democratic citizenship, on the other. As a first step, a preliminary outline of the politics of tragedy is in order.

The Politics of Tragedy in Ordinary Language

Speakers and writers of English have many options at their disposal when it comes to finding the right word to refer to unexpectedly fatal events or instances of large-scale human suffering. So, for example, in the numerous reports of the last voyage of the shuttle Columbia, one could have heard or read of its loss as a "tragedy" or a "disaster," heard or read of the spacecraft's wing as suffering from a "catastrophic" or "disastrous" failure, and heard or read of the event having potentially "disastrous" or "calamitous" effects on the future of the manned space program. In a *New Yorker* article on crisis counseling, "tragedy," "catastrophe," "traumatic event," "tragic event," "horror," and "mass trauma," were among the many words used by the writer to refer to crisis-inducing experiences. Another beneficiary of the English language's wealth of linguistic choices when it comes to making reference to occasions of deep suffering and loss will surely be the emerging field of "disaster studies" or "disasterology," within whose purview (according to a *Chronicle of Higher Education* piece) scholars will study, "calamities," "catastrophic performance failures," "tragedies,"and so on.[31]

The above examples and others one could cite, as well as relevant thesaurus entries, suggest how interchangeable such words as tragedy, disaster, catastrophe, and calamity can be. The degree of interchangeability is not absolute, however. While it would not offend one's ear to switch the relevant terms in the title of a recently published political history, *Cataclysm: The First World War as Political Tragedy*, the same could not be said of the title of a September 2005 article on the effects of Hurricane Katrina: "A Natural Disaster, and a Human Tragedy." "Human disaster" poses no problem in ordinary language use, but natural *tragedy* just does not sound right. (Like the former expression, "natural catastrophe" is also idiomatic. "Natural calamity" and "natural cataclysm" are rare as expressions go but neither one offends the way the linguistic pairing "natural tragedy" would.) Other restrictive idioms include "disaster *relief*" (one would never refer to the movement of emergency supplies to a stricken area as *tragedy* relief), "senseless tragedy" (Have the Columbine or Virginia Tech shootings ever been counted as senseless *disasters* or senseless *calamities*?), and "tragic lessons" (a locution favored, as we have seen, by Robert McNamara in his postwar appraisals of the American experience in Vietnam).

In the examples of linguistic affinity cited above, one term stands out from the others. The pattern appears to be that "tragedy" is less open to being switched out of idiomatic expressions for its near synonyms than any of its near synonyms are. To the extent that "tragedy" is distinctive in this way, it partly has to do with the fact that compared with its near synonyms, this term encompasses two distinct classes of phenomena, including (at the time of the term's original use) a range of theatrical-literary phenomena. In what some dictionaries classify as the term's literal senses, "tragedy" can refer to the distinctive theatrical practice associated with the Festival of Dionysus in ancient Athens (*tragōidíā*) and to many comparable forms of theatrical performance, to the genre whose creation was inspired in significant part by reflection on the nature and significance of *tragōidíā* and its textural relics (e.g., *Oedipus Rex*), or to literary works (say, *Doktor Faustus*) thought to exemplify this genre.[32]

Tragedies in the performative or narrative sense have been vehicles for the presentation of episodes or instances of human suffering and loss, exposure to which presumably affects the capacity of an audience or readership to respond to the difficulties of life. Or so a long tradition of commentary, dating back at least to Plato's writings, would have us believe. Probably in response to a conventional view, notably expressed in the Aeschylean formulation *pathei mathos* and according to which tragic spectatorship was seen as benefiting the polis, Plato, in *Republic*, offered a fierce and searching critique of *tragōidíā* for its purportedly dire effects on the emotional self control of polis citizens. In his *Poetics*, Aristotle opposed his mentor's negative assessment of *tragōidíā* and offered in its stead a notion of tragedy as occasion for a beneficial purging or purification (*katharsis*) of emotions. This disagreement, one could say, inaugurated a longstanding tradition of reflecting on how aspects of plot and characterization or conditions of performance influence the thought and emotion of readers or spectators of tragedy. It is within this tradition of argument that such expressions as "tragic fate," "tragic inevitability," and "tragic irony" (or their foreign language equivalents) first came into use.

Reflection on the nature and political meaning of Greek tragedy influenced the concerns and direction of continental philosophy most notably through the works of Hegel, Nietzsche, and Heidegger, all of whom shared a distinctively German intellectual and literary fascination with the potential significance of Greek tragedy as a resource for revitalizing contemporary notions of German identity and community. By the sixteenth century, "tragedy" (as well as the German "*Tragödie*" and other foreign language equivalents) had taken on what some dictionaries refer to as its figurative sense: an unexpectedly fatal event or an extraordinarily burdensome situation or condition.[33] In a later, corollary development, the adjectival form of the word came also to operate as a substantive—*the* tragic, *Das Tragische*—in philosophical reference to supposedly intractable dimensions of human suffering. Taking on these new linguistic functions, "tragedy" came to be grouped with "disaster," "catastrophe," "calamity," as a near synonym. This development also meant that idiomatic expressions previously developed as part of the functioning of "tragedy" in its original aesthetic contexts (e.g., the tragic flaw of Oedipus, the tragic conflict between Antigone and Creon) came also to be applied in relation to the term's new context of figurative meanings. Thus, one could now speak of conflict between historical actors as "tragic" (the American Civil War, for example) or of the tragic flaws of a political leader (as in the case of the disgraced ex-president Richard Nixon). As one might expect, these idioms, imported from the prior operation of "tragedy" in literary and theatrical contexts, work less well, if at all, when near synonyms that have different etymological trajectories are substituted. One could say that a war was "disastrous" or "catastrophic" and still capture a sense of the high number of fatalities and the large scale of damage that it occasioned but one would lose the rich set of connotations—for example, the notion that an experience of mass suffering has valuable lessons to teach or the sense that such an experience has resulted from a logic or dynamic seemingly beyond human control—that additionally apply with use of the cognate, tragic.

To the extent that idiomatic expressions containing "tragic" or "tragedy" can connote a sense of human agency as being severely constrained, their use has come under justifiable suspicion. At times, ordinary language resorts to the term, tragedy, or to its cognate, in reference to fatal or devastating events can seem inappropriately exculpatory, as when a government spokesperson characterizes a foreseeable or avoidable misuse of state power as "tragic" or as a "tragedy." So, for example, Chairman of the Joint Chiefs General Richard Myers's comment at a Senate Armed Services Committee hearing on abuses at Abu Ghraib that, "the situation is nothing less than tragic," might well have struck some listeners as a self-serving attempt to deflect responsibility away from an administration that had deliberately loosened the restraints on U.S. interrogators' use of coercive techniques (through approval of the so-called Torture Memo), at the same time that it publicly questioned the applicability of the Geneva Conventions to detainees held in U.S. custody.[34] To similar exculpatory effect, a woman who faced sentencing after pleading guilty to drunk driving and vehicular homicide characterized the fatal event as a "tragic accident" in her address to the court.[35] These and other examples of ordinary language use of "tragic" and "tragedy" (say, for the purpose of rallying a group of people on the basis of shared sympathy for a serious loss) manifest one form of the politics of tragedy to be considered in the following chapters.

The notion of *a politics of tragedy in ordinary language* recognizes that insofar as "tragedy" and related terms operate figuratively, in contexts where the suffering at issue is not of characters in a story but of flesh-and-blood people, this use conveys politically significant judgments or appeals, as for example, in cases where the liability of human agents for the occurrence of a burdensome event is under evaluation or, for another example, when a person or group is invited to share a sense of loss. To be sure, many of these uses are offhanded and unreflected and may well pass without second thought or comment. Occasionally, however, especially when the language use itself becomes a subject of contention as in the case of General Giap's sharp retort to McNamara—"You are wrong to call the war a 'tragedy.'"—the political stakes in assessing responsibility for failure and suffering become clear.

The Politics of Tragedy in Theoretical Discourse

Those who deploy the rhetoric of tragedy in more self conscious and theoretically robust ways also often labor under a general suspicion about the political significance and value of their engagements with tragedy. On the view of skeptics, literary critics and academic theorists of tragedy have too often tended to affirm aristocratic notions of tragic heroism, fate, and suffering, thereby elevating tragedy above the struggles and burdens of ordinary folk. Very much in accord with this spirit of skepticism, Terry Eagleton, in *Sweet Violence: The Idea of the Tragic*, deplores how, at least since Hegel, notions of tragedy in scholarly discourse have typically become "reified to a spiritual absolute which presides impassively over a degraded everyday existence."[36] This problem of elitist disregard of certain types of human suffering is related to one of the two poles of a dysfunctional tragic view of life ("the philosophy of nothing-but-tragedy") that Karl Jaspers recounts in a manuscript (*Von der Wahrheit*) that had to remain unpublished for the duration of Nazi rule. (After the postwar publication of the manuscript, the relevant sections on tragedy were republished in a separate German edition and, later, in English translation under the title, *Tragedy Is Not Enough*.)

At one pole of extreme passivity, a readiness to see life in its essence as tragic might lead a person to treat human conflicts and suffering as objects of contemplation offered solely for the aesthetic pleasure of the politically uninvolved spectator. The danger here, to quote Santayana's criticism of Emerson, is that of allowing one's "will and conscience to be hypnotized by the spectacle of a necessary evolution, and lulled into cruelty by the pomp and music of a tragic show."[37] In his criticism of some postwar American intellectuals' "political failure of nerve," C. Wright Mills associated a "tragic sense of life" with a tendency to retreat from political responsibility in favor of "mak[ing] one's goal simply that of understanding."[38] When Kennedy asserted during his address at Kansas State University that, "tragedy is a tool for the living to gain wisdom, not a guide by which to live," he was arguably expressing a similar awareness of how engagement with tragedy might lead one fatalistically to accept the status quo.[39]

At the other pole, of hyperactivity, a taste for tragedy can also find more pernicious political outlets, most notably in a kind of nihilism whereby fixation on the tragic nature of life promotes a delight in suffering and the desire to generate more of it, even in oneself. Here, the example of this pole of tragic dysfunction that Jaspers almost certainly had in mind is Nazism.

> Tragic grandeur is the prop whereby the arrogant nihilist can elevate himself to the pathos of feeling himself a hero. . . . The racial past, the sagas, and Greek tragedy are all invoked. Yet what had then been the reality of faith becomes the now deliberate and dishonest substitute for nothingness. The old beliefs are used as phrases to lend a heroic cast to the very unheroic degeneration of one's own existence. . . . Such perversion of tragic philosophy then sets free the turmoil of dark impulses.

Views of the political value of systematically engaging tragedy, assuming a tragic perspective, or deploying tragic rhetoric remain mixed. As the previously adduced list of philosophers concerned with tragedy suggests, Greek tragedy has long been an attractive subject of intense reflection for German thinkers and writers. Going back at least to the eighteenth-century philhellene art appreciator Johann Joachim Winckelmann's affirmation of the ancient Greeks' singular capacity to represent a calm mastery of dire circumstances (*"edle Einfalt und stille Grösse"*[40]) and extending to East German novelist Christa Wolf's *Kassandra* (1983), her novelistic gloss on Aeschylean tragedy, and beyond, German philosophers and literati have distinguished themselves for the high level of interest and urgency with which they have pondered the nature and meaning of Greek tragedy. In what is perhaps the most famous of these tragic interventions, Nietzsche published his revisionary work on Greek tragedy, *Die Geburt der Tragödie aus dem Geiste der Musik*, that seemed as much, if not more, focused on diagnosing the critical defects of Wilhelmine society and culture than with advancing the state of classical scholarship (and, in the process, effectively ruined his career prospects as an academic philologist).

To the extent that German thinkers and writers made *tragōidía*, the genre of tragedy, and notions of *Das Tragische* central points of reflection about the ills of contemporary society and possible sources of social and political healing, they could be said to have been engaged in a kind of politics of tragedy *in theory*. That is, they systematically sought to theorize the nature of Greek tragedy or the "tragic" for the purpose of deriving worthwhile political and social benefits. For Nietzsche, who watched with concern as the German states morphed into a Prussian-dominated, military-industrial empire, those benefits would have included a form of civic life in which creative individuality could coexist with a vital sense of communal belonging. For Christa Wolf, whose reference point was an authoritarian and corrupt German Democratic Republic of whose capacity to live up to its declared ideals she had become increasingly skeptical, contemporary re-imaginings of Greek tragedy might foster the creation of a community of critical-minded readers whose solidarity would be based not on force or selfish interest but on self knowledge and voluntary commitment to the good of the community.

If German philosophers and literati have been very conspicuous in their engagement as theorists in a politics of tragedy, they have not been alone. Cornel West's efforts to deploy notions of the tragic in support of a progressive program of racial reconciliation and social redistribution in the United States have already been noted. The example of Greek tragedy and notions of tragic catharsis and remembrance played significant roles in the rethinking of both the socialist and liberal traditions of political thought undertaken by Czechoslovak dissident-turned-Czech president Václav Havel as he sought to foster a vital sense of political agency in a populace long demoralized by one-party communist rule. A canny appreciator of the theatrical dimensions of politics as well as an enthusiastic reader of Greek and Shakespearean tragedy, Nelson Mandela drew upon notions of tragedy and tragic rhetoric in his pursuit of national reconciliation in a divided South Africa undergoing a very difficult transition to democracy.

As one might expect (and as later chapters will show), the uses made of tragedy by Nietzsche, Wolf, West, Havel, Mandela, and others vary significantly in terms of how systematic, comprehensive, and premeditated they were or are. Not many of these figures would qualify as political or social theorists in the strict academic sense. However, the uses made of tragedy by any of them are significantly less offhanded and generic than is typically the case in the sort of ordinary uses favored in news reports or in casual conversation. As well, these purveyors of what I will call *the politics of tragedy in theoretical discourse* share a clearer sense of the political significance of their tragedy-inflected utterances. When, for example, on the occasion of his first presidential New Year's "Address to the Nation" in 1990, Havel asserted that the repression and killings engineered by communist regimes in the Soviet Union and Eastern Europe, "must not be forgotten . . . because it is those great sacrifices that form the *tragic* background of today's freedom" (emphasis added), he seeks to do more than simply convey to his audience a sense of the terrible scale of Eastern European peoples' suffering.[41] He is, more significantly, harnessing the rhetoric of tragedy to the purpose of fostering an effective and meaningful sense of political agency in a country where the avenues for autonomous political action had been blocked for over half a century.

The Politics of *Tragōidía*

In variously seeking to promote national reconciliation, strengthen collective solidarity, enhance political agency, foster commitment to the common good, the philosophers, literati, public intellectuals, and democracy activists to be discussed in this book have, whether they realized it or not, pursued a role analogous to (if comparatively much weaker in effect than) the role played by *tragōidía* in ancient Athenian democracy. Scholars fit the flourishing of Greek tragedy into the context of Athens' relatively rapid, far-reaching, and unprecedented transition to democracy that began in 510 BCE with the overthrow of the Peisistratid tyranny (which ruled, with two short interruptions, from 561/560, after its founder, Peisistratus outmaneuvered competing cliques of aristocratic families), took decisive impetus shortly thereafter from the democratic reforms of Cleisthenes (which included reorganization of the tribal bases of Athenian identity and the composition of the city council, as well as an extension to the lower classes of some of the duties and corresponding civic privileges of military service), proceeded with Ephialtes's demotion of the aristocratic Court of Areopagus (462/1) and culminated in Pericles's lowering of the property requirement for the highest political office (458/7) and his institution of paid jury service (around 454). While pressures to democratize must have been present for the entire period, ebbing and flowing according to the events of a given season or year, two compressed periods of institutional consolidation are discernible.

As a result of the first, in which aristocratic networks of leadership and influence were disrupted by the reforms of Cleisthenes, the *demos* attained the political means to defend its interests and curb aristocratic power through open and settled procedures. As a result of the second, spanning the reforms of Ephialtes and Pericles, the political initiative shifted decisively to the *demos* (and, of course, to its chosen aristocratic champions and spokesmen) and remained there until Athens' final defeat at the end of the Peloponnesian War in 404. In the course of these developments, a citizen body, enlarged to include classes of men—shopkeepers, peasants and craftsmen—living close to or at the margins of material survival and with little or no prior experience of political responsibility, had to deal both individually and collectively with pressing issues of resource allocation, internal power sharing, external defense, and foreign relations without benefit of a tradition of rulership, historical precedent, or specialized training.

For an evolving citizen body struggling to mediate fierce struggles over the terms of resource creation and distribution[42] and confronting highly consequential decisions concerning Athens' relations to other city-states and to the Persian empire[43], the need to take broader and longer-term perspectives, to tolerate different points of view and muster arguments with broad appeal, to acknowledge mistakes and learn from setbacks would have been great. The singular culture of public discourse and judgment that arose in Athens partly in response to the needs of an emerging democracy enlisted *tragōidíā* as one of its hallmark institutions. Publicly subsidized performances of *tragōidíā* periodically became the intense, if temporary, focus of polis life with the establishment of the polis festival of Dionysus. Convention holds that the inauguration of the City Dionysia or elaboration of it to include competitive performances of *tragōidíā* occurred around 534 at the instigation of the tyrant Peisistratos.[44]

In the period covering the productions of Aeschylus, Euripides and Sophocles (499–406), *tragōidíā* was no mere entertainment for Athenians. On that point, almost every classical scholar agrees. (As Gilbert Highet's translation of Werner Jaeger's *Paideia* tartly puts it, "the audience, sitting on plain wooden benches about the pounded earth of the round dancing-place, was not already blasé about literature.")[45] Tragic dramas were subsidized by order of the highest polis official, conceived and performed in large part by polis citizens, evaluated by polis representatives chosen by lot and sworn to impartiality on pain of death, and witnessed en masse by polis inhabitants, probably including women, children, and slaves, as the centerpiece of the City Dionysia.

Tragōidíā's enactment of mythic or historical episodes of human striving and suffering, in which actors and chorus engaged each other in speech and lamentation, was of substantial political significance, if the conclusions of a large scholarly literature (as well as contemporaneous observations, including those of Plato and Aristophanes) can be credited. That significance, generally speaking, consisted in *tragōidíā*'s power to work changes both on audience members' awareness of the nature and meaning of human agency and on their emotional response to the pitfalls of human striving. Among the gains in awareness were a more comprehensive apprehension of the frailty of human life (Aeschylus's *The Persians*, for example, inviting consideration of Athens' greatest victory from the perspective of the losers), a better recognition of the risks of action (Sophocles's *Antigone* offering, among other things, a textbook example of the costs entailed by unintended consequences), and a greater appreciation of the autonomous dignity of human action in a world of risk (one might think, in this regard, of *Oedipus at Colonus*, which suggests the kind of authority that might accrue even to a polluted outcast). The drama of human agency, enacted and recollected on stage, mediated through the utterances of a chorus whose members were drawn from the ranks of polis citizens or citizens-to-be, and ritually nested in a program of festal activities that included a civic procession and dithyrambic choral competitions involving hundreds of city singers, stimulated and channeled audience emotions in ways that reinforced audience solidarity and lent a weight of authority to the audience's newfound insights into the dynamics of human action.

If not every scholar of Greek tragedy would sign on to Christian Meier's thesis that, "Attic democracy was *as* dependent on tragedy as upon its councils and assemblies"[46] (emphasis added), few, if any, of them would deny tragedy's political importance. Even if they vehemently disagree about major aspects of the phenomenon, scholars can always find common ground on the question of Greek tragedy's political importance. Take, for example, Friedrich Nietzsche and Gerald Else. Situating the origins of tragedy in orgiastic rites of cultic sacrifice to Dionysus, Nietzsche argued for the central importance of the singing and dancing chorus as the tragic audience's bridge to a vital feeling of redemptive wholeness. According to Nietzsche, the Dionysian experience of *tragōidíā* had a significant impact on Athenian public life, fostering a degree of reflective detachment in citizens that better enabled them to moderate their self-seeking impulses and devote their energies to larger, civic purposes.[47]

Completely rejecting Nietzsche's thesis of the religious origins of tragedy, Else identifies Solon's poetic-political interventions in pursuit of social reconciliation and constitutional balance as a key precursor: "Solon sees himself and the others as actors in a single drama, persons involved equally, each according to his lights, in a reciprocal struggle of aims and desires, hopes and values." He also places rather more emphasis, than Nietzsche, on the importance of the tragic hero: "The hero is the fulcrum of the whole. Without him there would be no tragedy, or none worth having." Widely differing with Nietzsche on several basic issues, Else nevertheless seems of similar mind when it comes to the issue of *tragōidíā*'s political importance. Of particular note to Else, was Greek tragedy's capacity to foster a sort of "double vision" on the part of spectators, who are vividly exposed by the words and song of actors and chorus to consequential differences in, and conflicts over, interest, perception, and aspiration. "But without the chorus there would not be any tragedy either; the hero would be suspended in a vacuum with no sounding board to respond to his passion and no separate standard by which to measure him."[48] Among the kinds of political capacity toward which both Else's notion of "double vision" and Nietzsche's notion of Dionysian contemplation point is the ability to imagine the world from the standpoint of others, even one's political competitors or opponents. Such an ability would be especially important in an environment of political pluralism and contestation. Habits of critical detachment fostered or developed or refined as a result of experiencing *tragōidía* in the theater would have served citizens well as they participated in the sorts of debates and discussions that took place in their assembly meetings, on the council, or in the law courts. Space does not permit a comprehensive survey of the scholarly literature on the politics of *tragōidía*, nor is one required for the purposes of this book. Relevant details from this literature, as well as from the literature of contemporary drama and film criticism, will be forthcoming as needed in the chapters that follow.[49]

The analytical distinctions drawn above between the politics of tragedy in ordinary language, in theoretical discourse, and as embodied in the role of *tragōidía* in ancient Athenian democracy will serve to organize the instances or examples of the politics of tragedy to be considered in the following chapters, which are grouped under three general headings—agency, solidarity, identity—each of which gestures to a major dimension of our experience as political and social beings. The first three chapters take up the theoretical writings and speeches of Václav Havel, the works of Italian neorealist film directors of the early post-World War years, and Cornel West's theoretical articulation of an African-American tragic sensibility, respectively. In all three instances, democratic struggles to challenge repressive regimes—in the first case, a one-party Communist state, in the second, Mussolini's fascist state backed by German troops, and in the third, a U.S. democracy whose capitalist and white supremacist origins gave rise to lasting inequalities of wealth, status, and power—inspired conspicuous episodes of public reflection about the nature and significance of freedom and robust calls for the establishment of meaningful and durable forms of democratic self rule. A fuller understanding of the significance of these episodes of political theoretical reflection and calls for democratic transformation has been lacking to the extent that their tragic dimensions have gone unrecognized or ignored.

Animating Havel's actions as an embattled activist and dissident thinker and, later, as a head of state, has been a basic concern to articulate the premises of, and conditions conducive to, free and meaningful agency in the modern world. Some interpreters of Havel, emphasizing his many references to a metaphysical reality (an order of Being), saw him as reaching outside of political life for a source of standards by which to orient (and place limits on) political agency. For others, his rejection of ideological thinking and questioning of fundamental Western assumptions about the nature of politics placed his thinking in the postmodern camp where the dominant aspiration is to achieve a state of freedom from *all* claims of authority, metaphysical or otherwise. Rather than choose between these neoclassical and postmodern interpretations, I suggest in Chapter 2 a third way of characterizing Havel's project in which central importance is placed on his experience as a playwright and his many references to the theatre and its effects (e.g., catharsis) and to the theatrical dimensions of politics and life. Recognizing Havel as engaged in a politics of tragedy means that his project is not reducible either to an affirmation or rejection of authority but is rather aimed at the achievement of a democratic practice of self reflection and robust agency whereby democratic citizens can submit their freedom of action to an authority beyond (and yet somehow also emanating from) themselves.

As distant as 1940s Italian neorealist film might seem from the concerns of a leading thinker and actor in Czechoslovakia's 1989 Velvet Revolution, basic issues of political and human agency were similarly at stake in the former's emergence as a "movement" of international cinematic importance. The neorealist films of Roberto Rossellini (e.g., *Roma Città Aperta* 1945), Luchino Visconti (e.g., *La Terra Trema* 1948), Vittorio De Sica (e.g., *Ladri di Bicicletta* 1948), and others, have inspired countless cinematic emulators in Italy and across the world and an immense and proliferating scholarly literature. Arguments about how neorealism came to exercise its outsized cinematic influence have gone on for decades, with some critics and scholars emphasizing the films' antifascist politics as the basis of their critical and, to a lesser extent, popular appeal, others pointing to the films' success at wringing existentialist significance from realistic depictions of everyday life, and yet others arguing for the films' aesthetically masterful treatments of the nature of illusion and its interplay with reality. The analysis undertaken in Chapter 3 treats neorealism as a tragic cinema or cinematic form of tragic theatre arising, as *tragōidíā* did, in an era of major political rupture, when democracy replaced dictatorship and novel forms of understanding were developed in response to the theoretical, social, and emotional needs of a newly (if incompletely) liberated citizenry in an environment of democratic aspiration and struggle.

Chapter 4 examines Cornel West's efforts to recognize tragedy's potential to promote democratic agency. For a good part of his career as a public intellectual, West has argued for the relevance of a New World African sense of the tragic. Developed in reaction to the emergency conditions of slavery and Jim Crow and promulgated in distinctive forms of African-American Christian worship, cultural expression and public rhetoric, this sense of the tragic constituted, on West's view, a vital resource for maintaining hope and preserving a sense of political efficacy among an oppressed and ostracized people. West holds out the promise that wider diffusion of the New World African sense of the tragic might inspire citizens in the mainstream as well as on the margins to see the amelioration of the disproportionate suffering to which racial minorities and members of the working class are exposed in the U.S. as an urgent and attainable civic task.

The next two chapters take up examples of the politics of tragedy in which questions of solidarity, of finding common ground among people or groups of people burdened by histories of conflict and division and lacking ethnic, racial, religious, or ideological bases of common identity, take center stage. Among the questions raised by Nelson Mandela's indispensable role in South Africa's transition to democracy was how he could have become a figure of such unifying influence across the country's wide racial, ethnic, and class divides. The attention given in Chapter 5 to the ordinary language uses of "tragedy" and related terms made by Mandela and applied to him by others reveals the working of a politics of tragedy that not only facilitated his personal sense of reconciliation with his captors but also his political efforts as the leader of an emerging post-apartheid South African republic to prevent the outbreak of civil war.

Chapter 6 considers how the surprise attacks against New York and Washington D.C. on 9/11 gave rise to a widespread need to make sense of the large scale and unexpected suffering that resulted. In one discourse of response to this suffering, notions of theodicy were deployed by political and religious leaders for the purpose of fostering feelings of solidarity and consolation. Another discourse, consisting of ordinary language uses and theories of tragedy, went mostly unrecognized. Chapter 6 identifies the contours of a tragic discourse of response to suffering and assesses both its promise and limits as a medium of national consolation and unity in the United States, as compared with theodicy.

The chapters comprising the book's last section on identity investigate a case—Germany—in which national identity became entangled with notions of accessibility to tragedy. Starting with the mid-eighteenth-century publication of Winckelmann's reflections on the nature and significance of Greek art, German literati and philosophers have become known for their distinctively intense engagement with Greek tragedy and notions of the tragic. This tradition of engaging tragedy would come to be seen as highly problematic in the wake of Germany's early twentieth-century history of political and moral catastrophe, a history seen by some to be at least partly consequent upon unhealthy forms of attachment to notions of tragedy. The first chapter (Chapter 7) on identity considers the postwar fate of the politics of tragedy in West German intellectual life, looking particularly at how that politics came to seem contaminated by its association with Nazi ideology. Just as reunification opened up opportunities for rethinking the bases of German identity, it also encouraged attempts at recovering Greek tragedy and notions of the tragic as a means of political theoretical reflection. One such attempt, German playwright Botho Strauss's 1993 polemical essay, "Anschwellender Bockgesang" (Swelling Goatsong), stirred controversy but failed to rehabilitate the politics of tragedy in German intellectual life.

In Chapter 8, consideration is given to an especially conspicuous East German example of tragic engagement, Christa Wolf's mythic retellings, Kassandra (1983) and Medea (1996). How does Wolf square her resort to a German tradition of tragic engagement, in which notions of fate and aesthetic disengagement figure prominently, with an ideology of scientific socialism placing dominant weight on the possibility of progressive social change through rationally directed action? She does so in Kassandra, the argument goes, by enlisting tragedy for the purpose of developing a critical- and community-minded readership that might contribute to the emergence of a new and more authentic form of social democracy. After reunification, the disappearance of a field of conflict between eastern communism and western capitalism seemed to Wolf to eliminate the space in which social democracy might emerge and flourish and led her in Medea to attach herself more conspicuously to a notion of tragedy in which the point was to preserve in memory a model of social democratic culture for possible use in a more propitious, if also distant, future.

Chapter 9 considers *Schultze Gets the Blues* (2004), the first feature film and box office hit by German director Michael Schorr, which takes up the story of a taciturn, rotund, middle-aged bachelor and early-retired mineworker living in an eastern German province, whose life is changed by a chance encounter with the Louisiana folk music, Zydeco. The crucial, if unremarked upon, backdrop of Schultze's life-ending journey to the Louisiana bayou, is the dissolution of the East German nation of which he formerly had been part. The challenge this event poses to former East Germans' sense of self and community serves as the political context for Schultze's impulse to achieve revitalizing contact with a New World African sense of tragedy. A concluding chapter synthesizes the findings of earlier chapters and returns to the case of the 1960s, considering that era's politics of popular mobilization from the point of view of the politics of tragedy.

While the chapters are related by a shared theme (the politics of tragedy) and methodology (close reading of theoretical texts, ordinary language analysis), each can stand more or less on its own. Their cumulative effect should be to evoke an alternative understanding of political theory, one that differs substantially from the Platonic image of the solitary trained expert contemplatively withdrawn from society and subjecting its ideals and practices to the critical scrutiny of reason. The view of political theory implied in the chapters that follow recognizes the significant role of ancient Greek tragedy in the emergence and development of a democratic political culture in which non-specialized citizens could, on both an individual and collective basis, subject their own actions and ideas to critical scrutiny without undermining the solidarity and civic mindedness so crucial to the continued functioning of their democracy.

SECTION I

Tragedy and Political Agency

CHAPTER 2

Václav Havel: The Political Uses of Tragedy in the Aftermath of Communism

Of the many activists who took leading roles in the democratic transformation of Central and Eastern Europe starting in 1989, none attracted as much notice as Czech playwright-turned-head of state Václav Havel. This attention was due in no small part to Havel's charismatic role as "director, playwright, stage-manager, and leading actor in this, his greatest play," the "Velvet Revolution."[1] No less significant to Havel's high profile were his many years as a thoughtful and articulate activist and dissident author of such landmark essays as "The Power of the Powerless," which reflected on the possibilities of democratic self-organization under repressive conditions. To the extent that political and social theorists make it their special task to reflect on the nature, significance, and prospects of freedom, they were likely to find in Havel a highly instructive example of someone who had struggled to define and fulfill the promise of freedom under a wide variety of political conditions. Staking the worth of his consecutive presidencies of the post-Communist Czechoslovakian and Czech Republics on the continued relevance of a perspective he first developed and articulated as a harassed and isolated dissident, that politics ought to have a "spiritual dimension,"[2] Havel was an attractive subject of reflection for the additional reason that he offered the promise of a coherent theory of politics. And because he seemed to base his partisanship for freedom, in the first place, not on an overriding Liberal concern for the protection of individual rights nor on a social democratic attentiveness to the claims of social justice, but rather upon an existential imperative, what he characteristically referred to as a "responsibility" to an "order of Being,"[3] Havel was further bound to draw the attention of political and social theorists for his unconventional way of thinking about politics.

If Havel's implausible political biography and the unconventional terms of his approach to politics invited attempts to engage and classify his thought, the ensuing lack of consensus about its meaning revealed how difficult it was to draw forth a consistent and unambiguous Havelian position on central questions of contemporary theoretical concern, including how citizens can best exercise agency in their political and social relations. Most political and social theorists' answers to that question over the last 40 or so years have come in two general forms. There are those thinkers, whose approaches might fairly be characterized as neoclassical or neohumanist, who identify a fundamental human capacity (e.g., reason) or a universally

valid and accessible framework of meaning (e.g., natural law, progress) as the authoritative means by which humans can orient themselves and exercise their agency to
the fullest extent and in as responsible a way as possible. Other theorists, who might
be assimilated under the label of postmodernism, evince deep skepticism about
claims of authority based on notions of a fundamental human capacity or a universally valid framework of meaning. For them, a fuller appreciation of the nature of
human freedom or agency requires a greater attentiveness to the fluidity of person-
hood and the radical plurality of claims about the meaning of political life or social
relations.

Among the scholarly articles on Havel that seemed to proliferate like mushrooms
in the aftermath of the Velvet Revolution, some cast him as a thinker primarily
engaged in a postmodern project of interrogating claims of authority and exposing
their ground in a suspect tradition of Enlightenment rationalism. Among the elements of Havel's writings inviting interpretations of this sort was his consistent
rejection of ideological thinking and his calls to think independently, to "shed the
burden of traditional political categories and habits and open oneself up fully to the
world of human experience."[4] So, for example, Caroline Bayard likened Havel to Jean
Francois Lyotard, emphasizing their shared determination to "testify" to the "demise"
of the "great emancipatory narratives" that had marked the advent and course of the
modern revolutionary age.[5] For another example, Martin Matuštík framed his assessment of Havel against the backdrop of multiculturalist efforts to resist homogenizing
forms of national identity. In Havel's "existential critique of the motives informing
human identity formation," Matuštík saw an apt complement to Habermas's univer-
salist project of "radical democracy."[6]

Havel's anti-foundationalist impulse was apparent as well to Richard Rorty. In a
discussion of Jan Patočka, philosophical mentor to many members of Havel's generation of dissident activists, Rorty read Havel as rejecting the Platonic view of philosophy as a means of reaching a set of politically authoritative "metaphysical facts" in
favor of the Socratic view of philosophy, outlined by Patočka, that envisions philosophy as a journey of existential questioning.[7] In a later essay, "The End of Leninism,
Havel, and Social Hope," Rorty held up Havel to post1989 leftists as an example of
a political thinker who had found ways to act against injustice without having to
ground his politics in a Hegelian metaphysics of History; "Havel seems prepared
to go all the way in substituting groundless hope for theoretical insight."[8]

For others, Havel's concern both to recognize a fundamental order of meaning
and to reflect on the relevance of that order for the promotion of a certain kind of
civic spiritedness, seemed oriented more toward the classically or humanistically
minded task of defining the purpose of, and appropriate limits to, human freedom.
Havel's ambition to orient politics toward questions of moral and spiritual concern
("to put morality ahead of politics") and to foster a broader and more binding sense
of responsibility ("responsibility to something higher than my family, my country,
my firm, my success") recommended itself to readers of this sort.[9] For example, classical elements of Havel's thought are highlighted by Peter Augustine Lawler who
read Havel as affirming the "dependence of political life on philosophy" against the

modern notion that, "everything is permitted because there is no order to which human beings must submit."[10] Taking a more critical view of Havel's humanism (indeed likening it to religious fundamentalism), Slavoj Žižek deplored Havel's resort to a notion of a divinely created humanity by which the Czech president justified the NATO bombing campaign against former Yugoslavia.[11]

For still other readers, what importantly marked Havel's thinking was its suspension between the poles of postmodern deconstruction of authority and classical affirmation of authority. This suspended quality, whereby Havel's thought remained implicated "in a permanent agon, a never-ending contest between tradition and transformation," reflected, in Jean Bethke Elshtain's view, the independent-mindedness with which Havel tried to understand the contingencies of political life in an age of metaphysical uncertainty. If Havel's resort to philosophical concepts and categories appeared "unnecessarily cumbersome, . . . clumsy and even redundant," it is, in Elshtain's view, due less to any deficiencies in his theorizing than to the paradoxical nature of the spiritual crisis Havel insisted on confronting.[12] In a parallel way, Aviezer Tucker read Havel (in intellectual sympathy with Jan Patočka) as combining, on the one hand, an impulse to reject the Western metaphysical tradition and "bring about Heidegger's existentialist revolution, an authentic relation to Being," and, on the other, an impulse to preserve "the Judeo-Christian moral tradition based on transcendental (divine) absolute laws."[13]

Also noting how Havel often managed to "speak in terms simultaneously postmodern and traditional," Edward Findlay situated Havel's thought in the frame of Patočka's philosophical teaching. That frame effectively bridged the postmodern-classical divide, Findlay argued, because of Patočka's determined effort to recover Socrates's problem-posing method of public philosophical engagement as an antidote to the reifying and solipsizing excesses of the Western metaphysical tradition.[14] Where Patočka was able to maintain a philosophically productive tension in his work, Havel is, by Findlay's lights, less successful. In Findlay's view, the cumbersome ambiguity so characteristic of Havel's work did not reflect, in the first place, a careful mediation of the opposing imperatives of postmodernism and classicism, so much as the adoption of a literary style of theorizing that lacked definitional rigor and consistency. "Unlike the philosophers whom he emulates, however, Havel makes use of metaphysical language without appending to it a rigorous definition or conceptual analysis and the result is a distinct tension between traditional, moral language and postmodern critique." Arguing from the premise that "a generally coherent position can be uncovered in Havel's work only in the light of the philosophy of Jan Patočka and its clear influence," Findlay noted, for example, that Patočka's concept of the "natural" becomes in Havel's usage an "evocative literary symbol," the outlines of which lacked clarity and definition. "Coupled with his use of the concept to defend ecological concerns, it is evident that Havel's appropriation of the term muddies it somewhat as a philosophical concept."[15]

In some respects, the approach outlined by Findlay and Tucker (and anticipated by Rorty) shows great promise in drawing out the implications of Havel's ideas for understanding the kind of guidance or inspiration philosophical reflection can or should promise to proponents of political freedom. It takes as its premise an idea with which few, if any, Havel readers would disagree; that the encounter with Patočka's philosophical teachings was decisive for Havel's thinking about the nature, significance, and possibilities of freedom. So, for example, Havel's critique of ideological thinking for its imposition of a monologically premised world view upon a plurally constituted reality and his affirmation of the individual's capacity to achieve liberating contact with that reality is traced to Patočka's vision of philosophy as an activity that can temper the human will to mastery by inducing a state of existential wonder. "Central to many of his [Havel's] speeches and writings is the Patočka inspired idea that moral responsibility must find its source in an awareness and respect for the enigmatic and mysterious nature of Being."[16]

Havel himself gave ample testimony to the impact that Patočka as writer and teacher of philosopher had upon him. As a young man, he had "hungrily devoured" Patočka's texts in the university library.[17] In the 1960s, Patočka was, according to Havel's report, a regular visitor to the Theatre on the Balustrade, holding "unofficial seminars" with the actors and writers.[18] Recalling the period of arrest he underwent in connection with the founding of Charter 77, Havel poignantly recalled how Patočka used the time they were together in the prisoners' waiting room to engage in philosophical discussion.[19] The fact that Havel chose to fill up most of his weekly four page letter writing allotment in the latter stage of his three-year prison stay by seeking to make sense of his life and its challenges in terms of categories central to Patočka's mode of philosophizing is perhaps the greatest testament of the significance of the Czech philosopher's influence.

If the approach Findlay, Tucker, and others took to discover an underlying coherence in Havel's writings was promising, it was not without its limits. Chief among them was its claim that the sole measure of Havel's coherence as a theorist ought to be a philosophical one, namely, the standards of definitional clarity and consistency set by his philosophical mentor, Patočka. Against that standard, Havel's work inevitably falls short. (Even Havel, admitting that he had "neither the education nor the experience to be a true philosopher," advised his wife and brother to consider his prison letter meditations on existence and responsibility as belonging "more to art or poetry than philosophy.")[20] More to the point, if one accepts Findlay's contention that the theoretical coherence of Havel's political thought can *only* be seen "in light of the philosophy of Jan Patočka's and its clear influence," one is left to wonder what distinctive contribution, if any, has Havel to make to our understanding of the nature and significance of freedom.

The consensus view of those who have studied the influence of Patočka on Havel seems to be that Havel's distinctive contribution lies significantly, if not wholly, in the fact that, as a political activist with experience both inside and outside the halls of power, he has been in a position to demonstrate how the philosophical lessons of Patočka (or Heidegger) can be applied (or misapplied) in politics. Thus, Tucker sees Havel as mainly engaged in a project of developing a "public concept of [Patočka's] life in truth," he faults the Czech president for relying too heavily on a Heideggerian-like "call of conscience to the nation." On this view, Havel's political ineffectiveness as president is primarily due to a misapplication of philosophical concepts, a lack of recognition that the "Heideggerian politics of authenticity appropriate for a persecuted dissident is insufficient when political power and responsibility are assumed."[21]

Even Dean Hammer, who apparently left Patočka and Heidegger completely out of consideration in his analysis of Havel's response to the challenge of founding and maintaining a free republic, inadvertently set Patočkan (or Heideggerian) terms for understanding Havel's notion of freedom. Drawing substantially on *Summer Meditations*, Havel's most politically programmatic book published in English, Hammer argued that Havel's support for a restructured upper house of Parliament, an electoral system incorporating both majority and proportional principles, and a free market economy reflected a larger concern to foster "a new conceptual environment of responsible participation."[22] Understanding this notion of responsibility primarily against the backdrop of Havel's search for "metaphysical grounding," Hammer invites precisely the kind of Patočka-centered analysis of Havel's political ideas that Findlay or Tucker or Petr Lom (1999) have conducted. As they have amply shown, and as Havel has amply demonstrated with his many references to Being, the Czech dissident-turned-president has not shied away from considering political problems in the light of the teachings of Patočka's philosophy (or Heidegger's philosophy as mediated by Patočka).

Rather than accept a consensus view that holds that the basis for Havel's notion of political freedom is to be exclusively found in his understanding of the nature, promise, and limits of philosophical reflection, we will reconsider the relationship in Havel's writings between philosophical reflection and political action in light of the question this relationship so compellingly raises: How is the condition of being free as a philosophical subject involved in solitary reflection related to the condition of being free as a political subject involved in collective action? To the extent that Havel is exclusively read as seeking philosophical solutions to the question of how the thinking "I" becomes the acting "we,"[23] his theorizing about freedom is bound to appear ambiguous, his definitions diffuse, and his argumentation inconsistent as he tests various metaphors (Being, God, nature) for their power to evoke wonder and foster civic spiritedness in his audience. Or his understanding of the nature and requirements of political action will appear compromised by a metaphysical focus on the dynamics of the inner life of individuals and a corresponding neglect of external relationships. To be sure, there is a distinction to be made here between a Patočkan approach to the thinking "I" and a Heideggerian approach. While the latter is held to give way too easily to an inward-turned solipsism, the former is seen (for example, by Tucker) to promote a "we" of philosophic fellowship through its "Platonic-dialogical concept of truth."[24] Notwithstanding this distinction, we will suggest a way of understanding the relationship between the thinking "I" and acting "we" in Havel's thought that does not take as its starting point a philosophically defined project of contemplation associated with Patočka. We will begin rather with a consideration of those instances in which Havel appears to draw significantly, if not primarily, upon his experiences in the theater to evoke the nature and promise of freedom.

Worth noting at the outset is that in addition to being an admirer of Jan Patočka's philosophy and a reader of Heideggerian texts, Havel is a dramatist of long and diverse experience who has had ample opportunity to reflect on what it means to fashion a drama or form a narrative capable of moving an audience. And like so many dramatists before him, Havel has been aided in this sort of reflection by the texts of Greek tragedy and the dramatic genres and theories inspired by them. Examining Havel's various references to tragedy, catharsis, and theater in the pages that follow, this essay will delineate a politics of tragedy in theory that might account for these references and form the basis of an alternative Havelian understanding of the link between reflection and action, theory and politics, the citizen's identity as an "I" and as a "we." In this alternative understanding, the appreciation of what freedom is and promises is more rooted in the spectatorial experience of a dramatic audience than in the contemplative experience of a solitary philosophical subject.

Political Crisis and Greek Tragedy

However unpleasant and stressful, and even dangerous, what we are going through may be, it can also be instructive and a force for good, because it can call forth a catharsis, the intended outcome of ancient Greek tragedy. That means a feeling of profound purification and redemption. A feeling of new-born hope. A feeling of liberation. (1997 Presidential Address of Vàclav Havel to the Czech Parliament and Senate)

By several measures, the news out of the Czech Republic at the end of 1997 was not good. Revelations of the existence of an illegal slush fund of contributions to the Civic Democratic Party deposited in a Swiss bank account led to the resignation of Vàclav Klaus, party leader and prime minister, and his cabinet. Coinciding with the fallout from political scandal at the highest reaches of national government was continuing bad news in other areas of Czech national life—warnings about a banking system overburdened with substandard loans, anemic levels of foreign investment, lagging productivity as compared with Poland and Hungary, racially motivated attacks against foreigners and Roma.[25] Apparently sensing that these difficulties had given rise to a feeling of national malaise, Czech President Vàclav Havel took it upon himself to deliver a kind of "state of the union speech to the Parliament and Senate" on December 9, 1997, in which he wondered, "why so common a democratic event as the fall of one government appears nothing short of a Greek tragedy, and to some extent may even become such a Greek tragedy."[26] This was not the first time that the example of Greek tragedy recommended itself to Havel in his response to an impending political crisis. As one of his biographers reports, at the end of 1990, Havel told an interviewer of the Spanish newspaper, *El Pais*, that, "The time of 'happiness' engendered by the revolution was past . . . and the second act would be one of crisis.

This would be chronic in character and would lead to catastrophe. But finally there would be the catharsis, and after that everything would start to go well."[27]

In his 1997 speech as head of state, Havel offers some clue as to the kind of positive consequences to which political catharsis might lead: feelings of purification, redemption, hope, and liberation. These were the rewards that ancient spectators once enjoyed and which, on Havel's view, might again be enjoyed by his fellow Czech citizens if they come to view their current situation appropriately.

On the face of it, so explicit a reference to Greek tragedy and its cathartic promise in a speech given by a playwright-turned-head-of-state should neither surprise nor perplex us. After all, literary references are to be expected from someone who has made the creation of literature a central activity of his life. If Havel's act of referring to Greek tragedy does not surprise or perplex us, perhaps the significance he claims in that reference should. For, as Havel made clear to the parliamentarians and senators who had gathered to hear his December 9 address, he considered culture to be a vital factor in the development of political and economic life. Indeed, far from viewing culture as "some superstructural 'icing on the cake,'" Havel invited his audience to consider culture, "in the broadest sense of the word," as incorporating those ideals, attitudes, and relationships which influence people's conduct toward one another in economic, social, and political life. More pointedly, Havel suggests to the assembled national legislators that the prospects for increasing the productivity of the Czech Republic's new capitalist order and enhancing the stability of its fledgling democracy will vitally depend on promoting a "culture of human relationships, of human existence, of human enterprise, of public and political life," by which the self-regarding impulses, which have found one-sided expression in the new Czechoslovakia might come to be counterbalanced by a concern for the "general good."[28]

In light of Havel's claim about culture's robust significance in promoting a civic-minded commitment to the public good, we might appreciate his remark about Greek tragedy (which follows closely upon that claim) as something more than a literary flourish, as an attempt at evoking in audience members a sense of the political significance of culture for the future of the Czech Republic by reference to a historically resonant example. For, after all, Aristotle's notion of catharsis has come to stand in the West as the first and most enduring theory of how the reception of art can affect an audience's disposition and capacity to act politically. And classical Athens, as home simultaneously to both the Dionysian festival of tragic drama and institutions of democratic participation like the Assembly and the law courts, has come to serve as a paradigm for many of a civic-minded political life existing in close interdependence with a publicly oriented cultural life. Since the mid-eighteenth century, claims about the political significance of tragic catharsis and affirmations of classical Athens as a paradigm of the interdependence of politics and culture have been repeatedly expressed by German philosophers and men of letters, who have concerned themselves with Greek tragedy and theories of tragedy in response to what they feel to be disabling tensions or divisions or deficits in German (or European) politics, society, and culture.

Among the German philosophers and men of letters whose concern with Greek tragedy was unusually pronounced can be counted Heidegger, for whom Greece, particularly ancient Greek theater, was a privileged site of contact with "Being."[29] Patočka was a student of Heidegger's in 1933 at the very time when Heidegger was turning to Greek tragedy for insights into the nature and philosophical significance of the portentous events of the day.[30] Only a close and extensive reading of Patočka's works (which is outside the scope of this chapter) can reveal the extent to which Heidegger's theoretical engagement with tragedy marked his thinking. And while it may be that a sense of the German tradition's concern with tragedy and the tragic aspects of existence was conveyed to Havel by Patočka, the frequent and varied uses of the Czech equivalents of the term, tragedy, word relatives like "tragic," and coordinate terms like "drama" and "catharsis" to be found in Havel's writings and speeches suggest other relevant influences. If Havel draws upon notions of tragedy to understand the nature and prospects of political freedom, it is not solely due to his encounter with Patočka's philosophy.

In surveying Havel's writings and speeches published in English and Czech, a reader might well be struck by the frequency and occasional prominence of Havel's references to tragedy. (In this regard, someone who has no reading comprehension in Czech is helped by the fact that the English word families associated with terms such as tragedy, drama, and catharsis, share Greek word stems with their Czech language counterparts. For example, the English, tragedy, and the Czech, *tragédie*, can be used interchangeably as can the English, catharsis, and the Czech, *katarze*.) As it turns out, Havel's reference to Greek tragedy in his December 9, 1997, address (which largely echoes his earlier 1990 remarks to a Spanish reporter) is neither casual nor isolated. This evocation of Greek tragedy is one of many related references in his writings that, considered in their entirety, can be seen as expressing a politics of tragedy specifically aimed at promoting political freedom or agency.

In ordinary use, the term, "tragedy," is typically applied to either of two kinds of phenomena: examples or forms of storytelling with sad endings or disastrous, calamitous events. The fact that Havel deploys the Czech equivalents of tragedy and its associated terms according to ordinary usage is, in and of itself, theoretically uninteresting. What raises the prospect of more than ordinary usage and invites further consideration is the frequent and regular way in which Havel's tragic references seem to be occasioned by, or seem to occasion, considerations of the nature, significance, or prospects of freedom. This correlation suggests that Havel relies to an important extent upon tragedy in his project of promoting freedom. Close attention to the emphases and nuances of Havel's tragic references reveal three distinct forms of reliance. First to be discussed is Havel's resort to a notion of tragic catharsis. This notion reserves a political role for theater as a purveyor of alternative images of social organization and promoter of an autonomous sense of community in theater audiences. Next to be considered are Havel's many representations of historical events as tragedies. These examples of tragic remembrance manifest, it will be argued, a wish to preserve a sense of hope in citizens faced with a political environment hostile to autonomous action. Third and last to be considered are Havel's references to, and uses of, tragedy as a means of reconciliation. In these instances, Havel seems intent on counteracting the alienation from public life felt by his fellow citizens as a result of their experience of Communist rule.

In focusing on Havel's uses of, and reliance upon, a tragic framework, my approach differs from the approach taken by John Keane in his biography, *Václav Havel: A Political Tragedy in Six Acts* (1999). Keane applies the tragic label in order to characterize the course of Havel's life in politics (that "sad but inspiring story of an individual whose astonishing life was pushed and pulled, twisted and torn by all the tumultuous political forces of [the twentieth] century."),[31] not in response to Havel's own ordering of his political experience.

In drawing attention to Havel's many references to tragedy, and in organizing these references according to the effects they are intended to have upon people's imaginations and political inclinations, this chapter suggests that Havel reserved significant roles for tragedy in the struggle for freedom. A better understanding of Havel's sense of these roles promises, in turn, to reveal in tragic spectatorship a form of theoretical experience differently and, in some respects, better suited than philosophical wonder to the task of promoting freedom.

Tragic Catharsis

Our survey of the many references to tragedy in Havel's writings takes as its starting point Havel's reflections on his development as a playwright. Havel, after all, was a man of the theatre whose long, intense, and multifaceted experience of theatre life would have occasioned many opportunities to reflect on tragedy and its meaning. From his two-year stint in the army at the end of the 1950s until his eight-year association with the Theatre of the Balustrade came to an end after the Prague Spring of 1968, Havel was deeply involved in all aspects of theatrical production. Co-founder of a regimental theatre company in his days of military service, Havel went on to work for a season as a stagehand at the ABC Theatre, where by his own later report he first came to realize, "that theatre doesn't have to be just a factory for the production of plays . . . it must be something more: a living spiritual and intellectual focus, a place of social self-awareness . . . an area of freedom, an instrument of human liberation."[32] This account of the circumstances of his involvement in theatre, given by Havel in a 1986 interview, is not the first in which he claims a special social and political significance for theatre. Already, in the correspondence he carried on with his wife, Olga, during his longest imprisonment (June 1979–September 1982), Havel had expressed his view that theatre, "of all the artistic disciplines, . . . has the greatest potential to be a social phenomenon in the true sense," because of its capacity to foster a sense of "alliance" or "fellowship" between artists and audience. According to Havel, that distinctive form of community which can come into being between audience and artists during a theatrical performance emerges from their "common participation in a particular adventure of the mind, the imagination and the sense of humor" and a "common experience of truth or flash of insight into the 'life in truth'."[33] Reflecting back in a 1976 interview on the dynamic interaction between his creative impulses as a playwright and the expectations of theatre audiences in the politically promising reform era of 1960s Czechoslovakia, Havel refers to the power of certain kinds of theatre to raise "social self-awareness" and increase the prospects for autonomous social action. "[E]very such act of social self-awareness—that is, every genuine and profound acceptance of a new work, identification with it, and the integration of it into the spiritual reality of the time—immediately and inevitably opens the way for even more radical acts. With each new work, the possibilities of the repressive system were weakened."[34]

Havel's numerous remarks about the theater should be read against the backdrop of his understanding of the logic of Soviet Bloc Communist rule as aiming at the transformation of citizens into willing "agents of the system's general automatism" through the enforcement of dehumanizing levels of "conformity, uniformity, and discipline."[35] In this context, his claims about the theatre's power both to open up alternative ways of imagining life's possibilities and to foster a sense of community[36] relatively independent of the regime's direction and control can be read as indicating the working in his thought of a notion of the political significance of theater as promoter of freedom. The Aristotelian ancestry of this theory is suggested by Havel's reliance on a notion of catharsis to describe the politically relevant effect which theatrical performance is supposed to work on its audience. So, for example, in his remarks about the lessons he drew from his experience at the ABC Theatre, Havel uses the phrase, "electrifying atmosphere," to explain the "magnetic" attraction he and others felt toward the "famous *forbíny*" or dialogues carried on during intermission between artistic director Jan Werich and cabaret actor Miroslav Horníce.

> What was it that radiated from those dialogues? What was it that enthralled everyone time and time again? It was something difficult to describe, perhaps even mysterious. Nevertheless, it was instrinsically theatrical, and it convinced me that theatre made sense. The electrifying atmosphere of an intellectual and emotional understanding between the audience and stage, that special magnetic field that comes into existence around the theatre—these were things I had not known until then, and they fascinated me.[37]

The phrase "*elektrizující divadelní amosféry*" had already served Havel in at two of his letters to Olga. In an even earlier letter, the first in which Havel takes up the theme of theatre and its distinctive promise, he refers to the moment in a performance, when the audience is "suddenly enveloped by a very specific and unrepeatable atmosphere; when a shared experience, mutually understood, evokes the wonderful elation that makes all the sacrifices worthwhile."[38] Interestingly, Havel prefaces this remark about the theatre's power to foster a cathartic feeling of elation by asserting his "interest in public matters, that is, in matters of the polis [*zajímám o věci obecné, tj. o věci polis*]," thereby evoking the political context in which Aristotle originally theorized the nature and significance of tragedy.[39] Also noteworthy in this regard is Havel's description of himself as a, *"zoon politikon,"*[40] or political animal, which is the formulation Aristotle uses in the *Politics* to convey his sense of the central role of political participation in human development. The question of whether Havel ever read Aristotle's *Poetics* or *Politics* is less important than the fact that he chooses to situate his own ideas about the political promise of the theatre in the context of Aristotelian ideas and the example of the Athenian polis. If Aristotle's texts are not the immediate occasion of Havel's references, they are important sources of the tradition from which he is consciously or inadvertently borrowing to frame his thoughts about theater.

Explicit references to *katarze* (catharsis) in Havel's writings and interviews are also not lacking. For example, in response to an interviewer's charge that his plays are pessimistic in outlook and at odds with the activist orientation of his political work, Havel responds that his plays are designed to confront an audience member with hard truths about the grave state of contemporary affairs, not in order to discourage him, but "to propel him, in the most drastic possible way, into the depths of the question he should not, and cannot, avoid asking; to stick his nose into his own misery, into my misery, into our common misery, by way of reminding him that the time has come to do something about it." The best way to appreciate the activist orientation of his work as a playwright, Havel goes on to say, is to see his plays performed in a theatre. For in "that exciting atmosphere of common understanding . . . [e]ven the toughest truth . . . becomes liberating." The result is a kind of "delight (which can only be experienced collectively), because it was finally said, it's out of the bag, the truth has finally been articulated out loud and in public." And in the audience members' collective delight with being so confronted, "there is something that has been a part of theatre from the beginning: catharsis [*katarze*[41]]." This cathartic effect is possible even though, as Havel concedes, his dramas are not tragic in the traditional sense; "there have been times when drama could not get by without great heroes and positive, if tragic characters . . . [but] those times are past."[42] Yet, rather than discard entirely the notion of tragic heroism, Havel would accept the idea that his plays invite a kind of heroism from audience members.

> Jan Grossman once wrote of my plays that their positive hero is the audience. This doesn't just mean that a viewer who is moved by what he has seen may start looking for a real solution . . . . It also means that he becomes this "positive hero" while he's still sitting in the audience, as one who participates and cocreates the catharsis [*katarze*].[43]

One other time during his 1986 interview, when the subject under discussion is Prague Spring, does Havel so explicitly and extensively rely on notions of catharsis and tragedy. Reflecting back on the first tentative steps toward liberalization taken by the Czechoslovak leadership in 1968, Havel recalls, "how powerfully both the Soviets and the Czechoslovak public were affected when our politicians refused to go to that meeting in Dresden [organized by the Soviets] and replied to the letter from Dresden with one of their own." In Havel's judgment, this gesture of defiance had "an absolutely cathartic moral significance [*přímo očistného*[44] *morálního významu*]." Soon thereafter, however, the Czechoslovak leadership went to Moscow and, "behav[ing] like guilty servants," submitted to Soviet demands that they give up their liberalization policies. Speculating about courses of action, short of abject surrender, which were open to the Czechoslovak delegation in Moscow, Havel suggests that they might have tried delaying for time in order "to allow the pathos of the situation [*patovost situace*] to deepen, to wait for the Soviets to make concessions."[45] Havel's use of the term, *patovost*, recalls Aristotle's description in the *Poetics* of the emotional state, pathos, fostered in those who are witness to a tragedy. That there is, for Havel, a kind of tragedy at work in the events of Prague Spring, one can be further persuaded of by the way in which he attempts to wring some positive significance from the Czechoslovak leadership's surrender to Soviet intimidation.

[T]he sad and perhaps even tragic thing [*přímo tragické*[46]] is that, from society's point of view, it was extremely fortunate that our leadership was so clumsily straitjacketed and taken off to Moscow. [T]his had a lot to do with stimulating the popular, nonviolent resistance to the occupation, and, [it temporarily eliminated] the main obstacle to a genuinely authentic manifestation of the social will.[47]

Among the events of 1968 that Havel endows with tragic significance is, first, the Czechoslovak political leadership's act of defiance and, second, that same leadership's act of submission. Havel's logic in this tragic rendering of historical events can perhaps best be understood with reference to his theory of catharsis. As Havel understands it, catharsis is the response of collective delight evoked from audience members who have, by means of their witnessing a performance, been confronted with hard truths. The cathartic significance of the Czechoslovak political leadership's initial act of defiance can be seen, then, to lie in its having brought home to the Czechoslovak public a hard or difficult truth, perhaps the truth of the extent of Soviet domination of Czechoslovak life. In this regard, one might even say that the Czechoslovak leaders were enacting, at least initially, a "heroic" role. However, as we have seen, if there is a hero in Havel's dramaturgy, it is the audience member who "co-creates" the catharsis and feels impelled to act by his or her new insight and shared feeling of delight. By this logic, it would seem to follow that in the historical tragedy Havel tells about the events of 1968, the true heroes are the Czechoslovak citizens who, in the aftermath of their leaders' unheroic submission, acted spontaneously and nonviolently to exercise their freedom. On this view, more than the ordinary significance should be read into Havel's characterization of the period of Soviet-led occupation and Czechoslovak resistance as "dramatic [*dramatický*],"[48] as the "final act . . . of a long drama originally played out . . . in the theatre of the spirit."[49]

Tragic Remembrance

To the extent that a theory of tragedy is suggested in Havel's representation of events of 1968 in Czechoslovakia, a comparison can be made with Hannah Arendt's casting of historical events as tragedies. A political theorist noted for her tendency to incorporate literary themes, characters, and plot conventions, into her investigations of the nature and meaning of politics, Arendt often categorized historical events as tragedies. Drawing on the tragic premise that human aspirations retain a significance even if they suffer utter defeat, Arendt's apparent aim in these instances was to uncover, highlight, and preserve in memory past attempts by citizens and aspiring citizens to be free. So, for example, in her 1958 essay, "Totalitarian Imperialism," Arendt describes the 1956 revolutionary outbreak in Hungary as a "true event whose stature will not depend upon victory or defeat" because "its greatness is secure in the tragedy it enacted." Events in revolutionary Hungary unfolded as a "stark and sometimes sublime tragedy" not only because Hungarian citizens' aspirations for freedom were defeated but also because this defeat might still serve to "illuminate" something Arendt considered worthy of notice and remembrance, a basic human aspiration to exercise freedom of thought and action.[50] What distinguishes Arendt's use of the term, tragedy, in this and other instances from other obervers' more ordinary uses to describe events that end badly,[51] is the role which she reserves for tragedy in the promotion of political freedom.[52] Arendt's use of the term, tragedy, is consistent with her longheld idea that the defeat of human aspirations to political freedom, if it is made an appropriate object of historical or poetic remembrance, may yet inspire future attempts to be free.

It is an Arendt-like, if not Arendtian[53], sense of both the urgency and high political significance of remembrance which seems to inform Havel's tragic rendering of the events of 1968 when he asserts that, "[t]hat week in August is a historical experience that cannot be wiped out of the awareness of our nations." Similarly, the founding of the embattled Czechoslovak human rights organization, Charter 77, is, for Havel, "a phenomenon which—no matter how the Charter turned out—would be impossible to wipe out as a national memory. It would remain in that memory as a challenge that, at any time and in any new situation, could be responded to and drawn on."[54] (138)

Passages in which Havel expresses his sense of the lasting significance of acts of freedom, even those which meet with apparent defeat, in explicitly tragic terms are also not lacking. So, for example, Havel resorts to Marx's formulation that, "events in history repeat themselves, first as tragedy, and then as farce," to evoke what he takes to be the gross discrepancy in outcome and significance between the reformist impulse of the late 1960s Czechoslovak leadership and the official reform policy of the Czechoslovak establishment twenty years later.[55] In a 1986 reference to criticisms which the Czech expatriate writer Milan Kundera had lodged against Czechoslovak dissidents for the discrepancy between what they achieved politically by their actions and what they were made to suffer by the regime for their actions, Havel insisted that efforts undertaken on behalf of human dignity and individual rights, even those with no foreseeable chance of success and a high probability of provoking severe countermeasures, are not "tragically empty of meaning [*tragicky zbaveni jakychkoli smysluplnějších*]." In his polemic with Kundera, Havel's concern is to defend the meaningfulness of human action (and dissident activism, in particular) in the face of an "(a priori) skepticism regarding civic actions that have no immediate hope of being effective."[56] Such skepticism, on Havel's view, tends to promote a fatalistic acceptance of the political status quo (what he calls "degenerate realism" in another context)[57] and a deterministic view of history in which individual deeds count for nothing.[58]

To be sure, Havel does not always choose to express a sense of the significance of remembrance in tragic terms. Other instances can be cited in which the controlling influence is almost certainly that of Patočka's philosophical teaching. So, for example, while living under a four-and-a-half year prison sentence, Havel insisted to his wife, Olga, that, "faith in meaning transcends all relative utility, and is therefore independent of how things turn out: everything—even what turns out badly—has its own admittedly obscure meaning." This affirmation of faith follows a somewhat cryptic mention of "the eternal, absolute 'memory of Being.'"[59] In a later letter to Olga, Havel comes back to the idea of remembrance, choosing to view it through a Patočkan prism.

> Several times in my letters, I've mentioned my belief that the assumption of something stable to which everything fleeting relates in one way or another, of a kind of "absolute horizon" against which everything ephemeral transpires, is very deeply built into the way we look at things and how we behave. If not consciously, then at least subconsciously, we always assume—figuratively speaking—the exist-ence of a kind of tablet on which everything is drawn or written down, and we reject the notion . . . that everything is condemned to vanish without a trace.[60]

The approach to remembrance which Havel outlines in several of his letters to Olga (and which he reiterates at the start of *Summer Meditations*)[61] differs from the approach previously identified under the rubric of tragedy in at least one noteworthy respect. Havel frames *tragic* remembrance in explicitly political and collective terms; remembrance of acts of freedom in the Czechoslovak past such as the resist-ance to the Warsaw Pact invasion in August 1968 or the foundation of the human rights organization, Charter 77, depends on "the awareness of our nations" or "national memory." By contrast, the "memory of Being" is dependent on a meta-physical awareness or intuition, "a conscious or subconscious certainty," which indi-viduals presumably share.[62] To the extent that Havel seeks to ground the guarantee of remembrance promised by "the memory of Being" in a shared intuition of a meta-physical truth, he opens himself up to the charge of Platonic reification, of seeking to impose ground rules on political conduct by resort to a transcendental standard. By contrast, Havel's evocation of the guarantee of remembrance promised by tragedy is not open to this charge; here memory is historical, not metaphysical, and its seat is in collective experience not individual intuition.

Tragic Reconciliation

Given Havel's commitment to live his life on terms that marked him and his fellow dissidents out as a threat to the "post-totalitarian" order of Communist Czechoslovakia, his determination to refute what he takes to be Milan Kundera's negative judgment of dissident activism is understandable. Understandable as well, in this regard, is his choice to formulate that refutation from a tragic point of view which invests the deeds of even the most overmatched of historical actors with some degree of hope-inspiring significance. Although, in his polemic with Kundera, Havel insists on the promise of a tragic perspective to sustain hope with reference to the challenges posed to freedom in post-1968 Communist Czechoslovakia, in other instances (notably in his 1985 address, "Anatomy of a Reticence"), he situates his tragic view of human action in a larger geographical and temporal context, emphasizing Central Europe as a centuries-long site of burdensome, if not tragic, experiences. So, for example, in a 1990 speech, Havel characterizes the region as, "the traditional crossroads of all European conflicts" and "a place that saw the origins of the most varied of European catastrophes." In such a place, Havel goes on to suggest, "fear and danger are the very dimensions of human experience that must be felt and analyzed most intensely."[63]

In Havel's contention that fear must be *felt* as well as analyzed, one can hear a partial echo of the Aristotelian definition of tragedy as, "a representation of an action ... [which] by means of pity and fear bring[s] about the purgation of such emotions."[64] Such an echo would be consistent with Havel's sense that Central European literature of the nineteenth and twentieth centuries was richly endowed with "tragic authors" like Franz Kafka who had undertaken to confront the special burdens of their shared history in a tragic mode. Of the legacy of these writers, Havel is particularly struck by what is for him its characteristic fusion of comic and tragic elements.

> [I]n our Central European context what is most earnest has a way of blending uneasily with what is most comic. It seems that it is precisely the dimension of distance, of rising above oneself and making light of oneself, which lends to our concerns and actions precisely the right amount of shattering seriousness.[65]

What endows the tragi-comic literary creations of Kafka, the "Czech [Jaroslav] Hasek," and the "Austrian [Robert] Musil" with a larger, existential significance, in Havel's view, is their use of irony and black humor to deflate any pretensions the reader might have of fully mastering his or her fate. In its promise to deflate human pretensions, the literary tradition of which these authors are a part, stands for Havel, as an urgently needed counterpoise to the claims of utopian visionaries who would single-mindedly and uncompromisingly transform social reality according to their ideal blueprint. "[T]ragically oppressed by the terror of nothing and fear of their own being," these would-be agents of utopian transformation, "need to gain inner peace by imposing order . . . upon a restless world . . . [thereby to] rid themselves of their furies once and for all." At the root of the problematic utopianism, which Havel here makes his target, is an incapacity to become reconciled to life's existential burdens and a susceptibility to the "illusion that the demanding, unending, and unpredictable dialogue with conscience or with God can be replaced by the clarity of a pamphlet [which] can liberate [human beings] from the weight of personal responsibility and timeless sorrow." Among the "extreme examples of this mental short circuit, some quite sad, some rather tragic, and some nothing short of monstrous," Havel lists "Marat, Robespierre, Lenin, Baader, Pol Pot."[66]

The notion of tragic art as providing an occasion for becoming reconciled to existential burdens constitutes a third distinctive aspect of Havel's tragic thought. Just as with his other conceptualizations of tragedy, as community-forming theatrical performance and as hope-inspiring memorial of failed aspirations, Havel's notion of tragedy as reconciliatory acceptance of existential burdens is meant to serve the cause of freedom. It does so, in Havel's account, by fostering an acceptance of those burdens which are imposed by "life's outrageous chaos and mysterious fecundity"[67] and which cannot be abolished without doing serious injury to human plurality and autonomy.

Affirming the reconciliatory promise of a Central European tragic sensibility against a backdrop of utopian transgressions against freedom, Havel takes care also to concede a positive role in the promotion of freedom to the utopian imagination. After all, "visions and dreams of a better world . . . [and] the transcendence of the 'given' which they represent" have their proper role in inspiring human beings to act in order to change the world (i.e., to exercise their freedom).[68] What Havel seems to be after with his endorsement of tragic reconciliation in this instance is a kind of acceptance of the "givens" of life which does not inappropriately constrain the impulse to act and transcend these "givens." A useful example of how tragedy might work to reconcile us in a way that steers clear of the inappropriate extremes of utopian hyper-activism and resignatory inactivism is provided by Havel in his 1988 appreciation of the life of Frantisek Kriegel, a medical doctor and reform-minded Communist, who was the only member of the Czechoslovak leadership not to sign off on the Soviet rollback of Prague Spring. Expelled from the Party and ostracized as a result of his lone dissent, Kriegel nevertheless remained a committed socialist and continued to promote reform until his death in 1979 while subject to round-the-clock police surveillance.

Initiating his reflections on the meaning of Kriegel's life' with the question, "Wasn't this man actually a tragic figure, one of the great tragic figures of our recent history?", Havel clearly indicates his sense that Kriegel's story is best told as a tragedy. It is a tragedy, one learns, because of the way in which Kriegel chose to live his life, accepting the burdens of an existential conflict which most of his fellow citizens chose to avoid. As Havel describes it, this conflict was grounded in Kriegel being simultaneously committed to an ethic of personal care and to an ethic of political commitment. So, on the one hand, Kriegel "loved people as individuals and served them all his days." So, on the other hand, "he could not confront human suffering solely as a good neighbor and doctor, but . . . had also to try to understand the social context of that suffering and discover a social way to eliminate it." Communist ideology became Kriegel's chosen means for "understand[ing this] social context."[69]

For Havel, the experience of living under Communism had taught the difficulty of leading a life equally subject to compassion for concrete individuals and commitment to the Party as guardian of their collective well-being. To act consistently on the basis of compassion for individual people in their everyday lives usually required one to sacrifice one's commitment to the Party as instrument of their class interests. Conversely, to remain committed to the tenets of Party ideology, usually required one to harden oneself against the sufferings of individuals in their everyday existence and accept Lenin's alleged contention that in politics one must break some eggs in order to make an omelet.

Rather than respond to the burden of his conflicting impulses by compromising either his ethos of personal care or his political commitment to the Party as vehicle of social change, Kriegel as much as possible sought to honor both. As a result, "all the compromises he had to make at one time or another . . . were always intrinsically authentic, sincere, and honest . . . [and] did not emanate from insidious self interest." For Havel, it was Kreigel's uncomplaining insistence on living as much as possible with the "discrepancy between his [political] convictions and his natural humanity" that lent his life its tragic dimension.[70]

As framed by Havel, the drama of Kriegel's life recalls *Antigone*, another drama in which, as Hegel, one of the foremost contributors to the German tradition of tragic engagement, taught, the central conflict lies in the opposition between an ethic of personal care ("the family as the natural ground of moral relations") and an ethic of political duty ("ethical life in its social universality"). Hegel, it will be remembered, reinterpreted the basic content of Greek tragedy as consisting of a conflict between characters whose words and deeds embody different and opposed ethical claims. In the course of the enactment of a tragedy, what had initially appeared as irreconcilable and contradictory ethical claims come to be revealed through tragedy's "vision of eternal justice" as "fundamentally and essentially concordant" aspects of a more objective reality. It was this revelation, according to Hegel, which constituted the basic ground for Greek tragedy's characteristic effect: reconciliation.[71]

Unlike Hegel, Havel envisions a kind of reconciliation promotive of a civic-minded spirit of independent initiative taking rather than to a resigned acceptance of the "cunning of reason."[72] Specifically, Havel aims at a reconciliatory effect that might lead Czechoslovak citizens, especially younger ones, to take seriously political life, which, on Havel's view, had degenerated by 1988 into a struggle for special privileges by self-interested career bureaucrats, "who are driven at breakneck speed through the traffic in their limousines, or are occasionally seen on TV reading tedious platitudes that have scarcely any bearing on real life." It is against the backdrop of this alienating spectacle of political decline and corruption that Havel places his hopes in the promise of the story of Frantisek Kreigel's conscientious and tragically conflicted pursuit of the common good to foster reconciliation, "help[ing] young people to realize that even in today's world it is possible to work for something meaningful so long as they do not fear obstacles."[73]

Tragedy after the Revolution

From our perspective over two decades after the revolutionary events of 1989, Havel's attempt in 1988 to impress his fellow citizens with a sense of the possible dignity of political affairs (to "bring home to them that politics and politicians are not necessarily objects of mockery, but can also be objects of respect")[74] by casting Kreigel's life as a tragedy seems remarkable for its timeliness. Within a year of the circulation of this story and entirely in the spirit of its tragically mediated call for the renewal of political engagement, many of Havel's fellow citizens had taken public matters back into their own hands. Back in those heady days of revolution and transition to multiparty democracy with its attendant freedoms, one might have expected Havel to discard his tragic perspective on public affairs. After all, happy endings are usually the stuff of which comedy, not tragedy, is made.

And yet, as even a quick survey of Havel's post-1989 writings will confirm, the frequency of tragic references has not diminished. Only the political context in which these references are supposed to work their various effects has significantly changed. Whereas in the former context of post-totalitarian repression, Havel evoked the power of tragic catharsis to foster pluralist ways of imagining the world and sharing a sense of community, in the post-revolutionary era of collapsed political authority, Havel seems concerned to evoke the theater's capacity to promote order as much as its capacity to foster plurality. If one of the recurrent themes of his presidential addresses has been that the "old world has collapsed . . . [and that] no has yet created a new one,"[75] one of the resources Havel repeatedly taps for inspiring a new sense of democratic authority is theater. So, for example, in a short message directed at theatergoing people across the world and released on March 27, 1994, International Theater Day, Havel prefaces his brief remarks about the significance of theater as "one of the important islands of human authenticity," with a reference to an international environment in which globalizing norms and practices provoke, and "collaps[ing Cold War and colonial] orders" permit, the emergence of new and potentially threatening forms of ethnic, religious, racial, and cultural assertiveness. For Havel, a fundamental challenge raised by this transitional, "especially dramatic" environment consists in the discovery of a "new, genuinely just order." In this short address, Havel does not indicate how theater might contribute to the discovery of new forms of order beyond broadly referring to the theater's power to "transcend" existence by "giv[ing] an account of the world and of itself."[76]

Havel apparently saved a fuller consideration of the relationship of theater to the contemporary problem of order for a later (October 4, 1996) address given at the Academy of Performing Arts in Prague. In these more extensive remarks, which seem aimed as much at his fellow politicians as at the audience of performance art students and instructors before whom he was speaking, Havel argues that among the many theatrical dimensions of politics, there is one which politicians unjustly neglect. The dimension Havel has in mind is theater's role in giving expression to human beings' fundamental intuition that the "world was more than just a terrain through which they moved and found nourishment, but was also governed by a mysterious order." So, for example, Havel connects the human sense of dramatic order to the various ways by which existence has come to be understood as having a spatial and temporal order: "Aristotle once wrote that every drama had a beginning, a middle, and an end, with antecedent following precedent. This is a precise expression of what I mean when I say that theater is a particular attempt to comprehend the logic of space and time, and thus the logic of Being itself."

Through its distinctive mode of ordering human experience, theater can, on this view, improve the capacity of people to recognize "whether political actions have a direction, a structure, a logic in time and space, a gradation, and a suggestiveness, or whether they lack all of these qualities and are merely a haphazard response to circumstances."[77]

While evocative, Havel's use of the notion of dramatic structure to intimate a fundamental order of existence is marked by a characteristic diffuseness and lack of specificity. However theoretically unsatisfying this discussion appears to be, it nevertheless provides an occasion for noting an instance in which Havel considers the post-1989 lack of order in terms of its pernicious effect on politics. The "haphazard" nature of political conduct which Havel implicitly deplores in this address and for which he sees the adoption of a theatrical perspective as a partial corrective is, as he makes clear on other occasions, the result of an approach to politics which favors the pursuit of short-term advantage narrowly conceived over what is advantageous in a broader sense and over the longer term. In Havel's 1997 speech before the Czech Parliament and Senate, which drew our attention earlier for its explicit appeal to Czech citizens to consider recent demoralizing setbacks from the perspective of Greek tragedy, Havel provides a framework by which we may better understand his earlier criticism of "haphazard" forms of political conduct. The problem, insofar as it afflicts the Czech polity, is traced by Havel to the republic's narrow reliance on the profit motive as a basis for founding a new democracy. "Unqualified liberalism," as Havel calls it in his address, has in important respects failed as a principle of democratic foundation because it too easily dismissed the importance of culture and its role in fostering a capacity in democratic citizens to think beyond the requirements of a narrowly conceived self interest.

> Morality, decency, humility before the order of nature, solidarity, concern for future generations, respect for the law, the culture of interpersonal relationships—all these and many similar things were trivialized as "superstructure," as icing on the cake, until at last we realized that there was nothing left to put the icing on: the forces of economic production themselves had been undermined.[78]

One of the lessons Havel would have his fellow citizens draw from their recent political and economic setbacks is that a democracy, especially a newly founded one, cannot function well if the self-interested dispositions of its citizens are not mediated by a concern for the common good. In light of that lesson, Havel's continued use of a tragic framework makes sense. In the post-1989 Czech political order, tragedy, in its role as facilitator of catharsis, promises to promote a more balanced exercise of freedom in the new liberal individualist order of the Czech Republic by renewing a sense among Czech citizens and politicians of larger and more long-term commitments; this sense might limit the anti-social excesses of behavior to which narrowly self-interested individuals may be driven. Here, in this new setting of democratic foundation, the sought after effect of tragic catharsis is more: one of conforming citizen behavior in a disfunctional (Liberal) environment of plurality than of pluralizing citizen behavior in a disfunctional (Communist) environment of conformity.[79]

Tragedy's role in fostering a sense of larger commitments is not confined by Havel to relations between citizens of the Czech Republic. He would also have tragedy work its community-forming effects across national borders. So, for example, Havel resorts to tragic imagery in his 1993 *Foreign Affairs* article, "The Co-responsibility of the West," criticizing Western politicians for their failure adequately to promote democratic values and practices in post-communist countries. "The pragmatism of politicians who want to win the next election, for whom the higher authority is therefore the will and the mood of a rather spoiled consumer society, makes it impossible for those people to be aware of the moral, metaphysical, and often tragic dimensions of their own program." Havel goes on to implore the West not to "look on [the post-revolutionary political processes of post-communist European countries] as though it were . . . [an] audience on the edge of their seats at a horror movie. It should perceive these processes . . . as something that intrinsically concerns it, . . . that demands its own active involvement."[80]

To the extent that one accepts the thesis that Havel thinks of tragedy in terms of its political uses, one might see in the image of horror movie spectatorship a negative foil to tragic spectatorship. While the former experience leaves its audience enervated and atomized, the latter experience is expected to leave its audience energized and unified, and, therefore, more willing and able to act in concert.

If Havel is led to formulate differently the promise of tragedy in its role as facilitator of catharsis in response to changes he perceives in the kind of challenges which post-Communist conditions pose to freedom, then we might also expect differences in the way he formulates the promise of tragedy in its other roles as guarantor of remembrance and medium of reconciliation. In a pre revolutionary context in which Communist authorities were intent not only to repress all instances of political initiative-taking but also to strip these instances of any power to survive in narrative, tragedy stood, for Havel, as a highly resonant token of the power of remembrance to preserve a sense in citizens that freedom was worth striving for even in the most unpromising of circumstances. With the collapse of Communism and the lifting of the heavy hand of one-party dictatorship, one might have expected Havel to dispense with tragedy in its role as a mode of remembrance. After all, what need is there to remember freedom, if the obstacles to it have been removed? Interestingly, from the very start of his first presidency in Czechoslovakia's new democratic era, Havel reveals a sense for the continuing, if slightly altered, usefulness of tragic remembrance in politics. Consider, for example, his remarks on the occasion of his first presidential New Year's address to the Czechoslovak nations (cited in Chapter 1) in which he urged his listeners not to forget, "the rivers of blood that flowed in Hungary, Poland, Germany, and most recently in such a horrific manner in Romania, as well as the sea of blood shed by the nations . . . because it is those great sacrifices that form the tragic background of today's freedom."[81]

Clues as to the possible motives for Havel's dramatic invocation at the inauguration of Czechoslovakia's new era of democracy of the "tragic background" of freedom are not lacking in the text. Havel begins the address by noting various burdensome aspects of the legacy inherited by the new order from the old. Foremost among them is what he calls, "a contaminated moral environment," the main effect of which is that Czechoslovak citizens "learned not to believe in anything, to ignore each other, to care only for [them]selves." Having experienced a moral education that made the atomized pursuit of narrow self interest the norm, Czechoslovak citizens will be strongly tempted to abdicate their responsibility to meet urgent challenges of the new era. Among those challenges to which Havel calls his fellow citizens is active participation in politics; "Let us make no mistake: the best government in the world, the best parliament and the best president in the world cannot achieve much on their own . . . . Freedom and democracy require participation and therefore responsible action from us all." Immediately after this call for citizen activism in politics, Havel, in a fitting if also possibly undeliberate echo of Aristotle's claim about the purgative effects of tragedy, formulates what he takes to be the reward awaiting his fellow countrymen and women if they choose to act responsibly. "If we realize this, then all the horrors the new Czechoslovak democracy has inherited will cease to appear so terrible. If we realize this, hope will return to our hearts."[82]

It is following upon Havel's expression of concern that Czechoslovak citizens become actively involved in the political life of their new democracy that he reminds them of the "tragic background" of their newly found freedom. In this reminder, Havel signals that tragedy as a mode of remembrance continues to have a role in promoting freedom. If the obstacle to freedom had formerly been a coercive apparatus of mass political mobilization and control whose ultimate effect was to foster a widespread sense of alienated withdrawal from concern with public affairs, the new obstacle appears to be the survival of that condition of alienation even after the coercive apparatus has been dismantled. Appropriately, then, Havel's presidential reminders of past efforts to exercise freedom seem aimed not at consoling an embattled citizenry with the promise that its defeats will be remembered so much as at spurring a newly liberated citizenry to "act independently, freely, reasonably" and reject its "indifference to the public good."[83]

If worry about the threat posed to freedom in the new democratic order by citizen indifference to the public good leads Havel to continue an earlier reliance on the beneficial effects of tragic catharsis and tragic remembrance, one might expect that tragic reconciliation would be seen by him as no less deserving of continued use. Originally, it had been in response to the alienating spectacle of bureaucratic career-ism under Communist Party auspices that Havel had chosen to exploit the reconcili-atory power of tragedy to muster in young Czechoslovakians a sense of the possible dignity and worth of political life. Perhaps in telling the story of Frantisek Kriegel's struggle in 1988, Havel already anticipated the need for reconciling citizens to the disappointments they would inevitably come to feel after the fall of Communism. A new democratic order might lessen the citizen's burden of having to live according to the conflicting requirements of an ethic of personal care and an ethic of political commitment but it could not eliminate that burden.[84] "The tragic paradoxes that I sense in the personality, achievement, and fate of Frantisek Kriegel are not exclusive to him, nor even to communists. They epitomize or even symbolize much deeper paradoxes, possibly even the fundamental paradoxes of modern times."[85]

Conclusion

In collecting references to tragedy scattered throughout Havel's writings and speeches, suggesting their affiliation, and lending them a strategic significance, I have taken an oblique approach to making sense of Havel's political thought. In general, taking such an approach runs the risk of mistaking what is peripheral for what is central, of missing what is distinctive and profound for what is pedestrian and superficial. In the case of a political thinker such as Havel, whose approach to understanding the nature and significance of freedom is highly eclectic and allusive, the risks seem all the greater.

One reason for running those risks is the fact that Havel's multiple and diverse references to tragedy reflect a more developed sense of the political uses of tragedy than is implied by the casual, even banal, references to tragedy sometimes to be found in ordinary use. Taken together, these references constitute a politics of tragedy. To be sure, the references to tragedy in Havel's writings and speeches are not always consistent with his partisanship for freedom and occasionally even work against it.[86] Nor are these tragic references as consciously and systematically worked out by Havel as his references to an order or mystery of Being. (This pattern holds as well in his latest book, *To the Castle and Back* [2007], where references to tragedy, theater, and drama—e.g., the "tragic case" of Gorbachev, the Czechoslovakian revolution as "a drama in several acts"—are diffuse and theoretically undeveloped compared with references to the preeminent importance of "the structure of Being.")[87] Attention to the diverse uses to which Havel puts tragedy is nevertheless worthwhile because it reveals an alternative approach to what many of his academic readers believe to be the larger issue to which his political thought seems most urgently addressed: How to promote the activity of thinking in ways that incline citizens to seek the rewards of freedom and exercise agency meaningfully and with an eye to the common good? To the extent that illumination of this issue is sought exclusively on the conceptual grounds of Jan Patočka's existentialist teachings and their influence on Havel's thought, the interpretive task mainly becomes one of determining the nature and promise of philosophical contemplation. While there is certainly something to be said for adopting this approach, it does have its limits. Chief among them is its tendency to give rise to one-sided formulations of the nature and significance of political freedom.

In making philosophy one's main or exclusive point of departure, the question of how to be free politically (of necessity a question that cannot be answered with exclusive reference to the perspective, interest, need, or experience of one person) arises only as a corollary to the question of how to be free as a subject involved in philosophical contemplation, an activity for which solitude is an important prerequisite. Achieving a kind of contemplative contact with existence in which a wonder-inducing intimation of the extent of its infinitude is gained, the philosophical subject is liberated for a time from the worldly press of personal ambition or desire. Returning to the company of others, the subject can seek to convey to them a sense of the fundamental interrelatedness of all things, if not inspire them to engage in the activity of philosophical contemplation themselves. What ought to result (on this view) is a community of people better able to mediate personal interest and public good in both their thinking and their actions. The experience on which this political outcome of well-adjusted citizenship hinges is a state of contemplative contact with existence (Being) that can only be undergone in solitude. And if not everyone chooses or is able to achieve this state, then those who have must be counted on to convey its politically relevant lessons in a rhetorically convincing manner.

Seeing the challenge of achieving political freedom from a philosophical standpoint is what Havel mostly seems to be doing when he evokes the order or mystery of Being. When he evokes tragedy, he assumes a different sort of standpoint on the nature and significance of political freedom, the standpoint of the tragic spectator. The tragic spectator watches in company, not in solitude. What tragic spectators watch is not the infinitude of existence but the dramas of human existence, in which they are also implicated as actors, and about which they can gather and share their impressions. One might expect the resulting discourse to encompass a larger, more diverse set of interlocutors than even the sort of dialogical model of philosophical encounter Patočka is thought to have promoted.

Rather than depend on intuitive appeals to a relatively abstract notion of an "order of Being" and risk lapsing into a stance of classicist reification, at one extreme, or a stance of postmodern solipsism, at the other, tragic spectatorship relies on more available and accessible objects of contemplation. At the very least, adopting a tragic perspective on the performance of a play at the Theater of the Balustrade or on the events of Prague Spring or on the difficult life of Dr. Kriegel promises insights into the premises of, and conditions conducive to, free and meaningful agency in political life that are less accessible through metaphysical theories of politics. Of the insights made available by Havel's politics of tragedy in theory, at least three are worthy of being singled out: that the basis of community extends beyond the fulfillment of individuals' material self interests to shared forms of aesthetic response; that the risks of individual political agency are worth taking in part because perishable human deeds can survive in memory; and that active involvement in politics is worthwhile even if the nature of political commitments are necessarily in some degree of tension with the demands of private conscience.

CHAPTER 3

Italian Neorealism: Tragic Cinema in the Aftermath of Fascism

Following up an analysis of the political thought of Václav Havel with a consideration of a renowned movement of 1940s Italian cinema might well seem, on first consideration, a bit of a stretch. After all, what basis is there to consider the political writings of a Czech playwright and activist responding to the challenges of Communist repression and democratic transition in the last quarter of the twentieth century together with a mid-century Italian film movement whose heyday came shortly after the defeat of Italian fascism in a postwar environment of military occupation, economic deprivation, and democratic aspiration?

A second look at the two cases does reveal political parallels worth noting. Both Havel and the directors, critics, and audiences of neorealist films spent a good part of their lives in countries ruled by repressive, mass mobilizing, one-party states. Additionally, both Havel's works and speeches and neorealist films came to be strongly associated with popular aspirations for democratic freedom in countries undergoing, and eras marked by, transition from authoritarian to democratic systems of government.

One might even infer a neorealist influence upon Havel, who had the opportunity as a man-about-town during his student days in mid-1950s Prague to view (if not the Italian originals) neorealist-inspired works of Czechoslovak cinema.[1] We know from studies of early postwar Czechoslovak cinema that aspiring Czechoslovak directors and screenwriters were exposed to neorealist films in classroom screenings and to the teachings of major figures of the movement, including Cesare Zavattini (screenwriter of *Bicycle Thieves*) and Giuseppe de Santis (director of *Bitter Rice*), who visited Prague's film school numerous times. By 1959, the influence of neorealism on the work of Czechoslovak filmmakers was so obvious that the hard-line Czechoslovak minister of culture used the occasion of the First Film Festival of Czechoslovak Films to decry the influence of the Italian neorealist formula in the more liberated film culture that had emerged in the wake of Soviet revelations of Stalin's excesses in 1956. One Czech film scholar suggests that parallel environments of political opening or liberation facilitated the rise of both Italian neorealism in the mid-to-late 1940s and the neorealist-inspired Czech New Wave ten years later: "Italian postwar experience reverberates in [post-1956] Czechoslovakia."[2]

The parallels between the political environments of Havel's period of political activism and Italian neorealist production and possible lines of Italian neorealist influence upon Havel via Czechoslovak cinema, in and of themselves, form a slender basis for considering Havel and Italian neorealist directors together. More decisive as a basis of comparison, from our perspective, is a common dynamic at play in both cases: the politics of tragedy. Just as Havel's reflections about the nature and meaning of being free in politics can be understood as constituting an exercise in, and expression of, the politics of tragedy, so (it will be argued in this chapter) the films that have come to define that short period of neorealist creativity and critical and (to a lesser degree) popular acceptance in Italian cinema can also profitably be seen as manifesting the working of a politics of tragedy. And, as was later to be the case with Havel, neorealist engagement in a politics of tragedy occurs in tandem with, and partly in response to, heightened concerns about issues of democratic agency and freedom. So, for example, such questions as, What is the nature and significance of freedom? What possibilities for exercising freedom exist in a system of dictatorship and repression? What obstacles to freedom remain even after a system of dictatorship and repression has been overthrown? were central (if, at times, indirectly addressed) concerns in such films as Roberto Rossellini's *Open City* (1945) and *Paisan* (1946), Luchino Visconti's *The Earth Trembles* (1948), and Vittoria De Sica's *Bicycle Thieves* (1948).

Building as it does on venerable notions of tragic catharsis, remembrance, and reconciliation, Havel's politics of tragedy is conducted primarily (if also in a rather *ad hoc* manner) as a theoretical discourse. The case for neorealist films as purveyors of a politics of tragedy will be based more on the evidence of both ordinary language characterizations of neorealism as a "tragic" cinema and of parallels to be drawn between select Italian films of the 1940s and *tragōidía*. Examining the Czech and Italian cases in succession will therefore allow consideration of the full complement of manifestations of the politics of tragedy—in theoretical discourse, in ordinary language use, and in its original Athenian form—as well as providing insights into how each of these manifestations bears on issues of agency and freedom.

* * *

A time is coming, very soon I think, when we will go [to the cinema] to see what a man does in his most ordinary daily activities with the same interest the Greeks had in going to their dramas. (Cesare Zavattini, *La Fiera Letteraria* 1951)[3]

Few national cinemas can claim the breadth and depth of international influence once claimed by the Italian cinema. This oversized influence was largely based on the legacy of the neorealist period of film production, which has conventionally been dated from the end (or near end) of fascist rule until the mid-1950s. Rosellini's *Open City* and his follow-up, *Paisan*, and De Sica's *Bicycle Thieves* elicited strongly positive notice from national and international critics and generated robust box office receipts in Italy and abroad. While less successful at the box office and more contested by critics, other neorealist films, including Visconti's *The Earth Trembles*, gained loyal followings and came eventually to be elevated to canonical status in world cinema. Federico Fellini and Michelangelo Antonioni worked as scriptwriters on many neorealist films and their later careers as internationally celebrated filmmakers bore the imprint of earlier collaborations with Rossellini and others. A later generation of gifted Italian directors, which included Pier Paolo Pasolini, Ermanno Olmi, and Elio Petri, took direct inspiration from the neorealist legacy. Neorealist films also inspired and influenced filmmakers outside of Italy, winning the Italian cinema a reputation for aesthetic power and political relevance among the *Cahiers du Cinéma* critics (and soon to be directors of the French New Wave) in Paris, Satyajit Ray in India, and film directors in Japan, Spain, Eastern Europe, and Latin America.[4]

What was at the basis of the postwar emergence of "neorealist film" as a touchstone both of intense debate and discussion among film critics and scholars and of lasting inspiration for filmmakers in Italy and abroad? In film criticism and scholarship, the elements that have often been cited as distinctive of neorealist film have been a commitment to depict everyday life and ordinary people through resort to techniques characteristic of documentary film (e.g., natural sets and lighting, loosely scripted scenes, and the use of nonprofessional actors in major roles) and a preference for addressing the burdensome conditions of wartime and early postwar Italy (e.g., the violence of war, the oppression of fascist rule and German military occupation, postwar scarcity and mass unemployment). To be sure, the films considered under the rubric of neorealism do not fit any simple formula. To take one of the earliest examples, the two main characters of *Open City*, a film about the pursuit of underground resistance leaders and the brutalities of the German occupation of Rome, are played by professional actors (Aldo Fabrizi and Anna Magnani). Another neorealist classic, *Bicycle Thief*, which depicts the travails of a man from the poverty-stricken Roman suburbs who desperately and unsuccessfully searches, with his son, for the stolen bicycle he needs to recover in order to keep his newly acquired job, was tightly scripted by Cesare Zavattini.

Further complicating the challenge of defining neorealism is the fact that from the very start of its career in the spring of 1948 as a term describing the new Italian cinema,[5] it has given rise to different and, to an extent, mutually exclusive schools of interpretation. Rossellini biographer Tag Gallagher makes much of the difference between the historicist approach of the Italians and the philosophically minded approach of the French critics.

> [For] the Italians . . . film had an ideological, social purpose: to provide a model, an explanation, a sermon. Movies are theater. The French talked about *reality*: film is an imprint, a witness . . . Movies are experiences. Italians sought an ideology, a mindset toward history, solutions to practical problems. . . . Whereas what the French sought was sensation.[6]

National styles of film interpretation posited by Gallagher correspond roughly to the distinctions Mira Liehm, in *Passion and Defiance*, her history of Italian film, draws between the sociohistorical and the humanist approaches to neorealism. As she puts it, the sociohistorical critics tended to see "neorealism as an exclusive expression of the war and antifascist resistance, with an emphasis laid on social concern."[7] Thus, Umberto Barbaro, writing for the Italian Communist daily, *l'Unità*, on August 24, 1955, warned that, "we can never fully understand the neorealism of the Italian cinema unless we take ourselves back to the spirit and history of antifascism."[8] That spirit of unified purpose, shared sacrifice, and democratic aspiration, of which neorealism purportedly came to be the cinematic expression, was fostered among antifascists of all political stripes in the course of their very costly partisan struggle against German troops and fascist militias in northern Italy from late 1943 until mid-1945. The problem with a view focused on this partisan struggle, according to Liehm, was that its mostly left wing proponents, "attempted to tie down all subsequent developments to this original impulse," with the result that neorealism came to be too narrowly identified with an ideological concern for the suffering and exploitation of working people.[9]

Making the French film critic André Bazin the standard bearer of humanist interpretations of neorealism, Liehm writes of him that, "cinema's way of explaining reality" was what counted, "not what was explained."[10] Bazin considered neorealist representations of ordinary people's suffering and alienation more from a phenomenological standpoint—"the world *is* simply, before it is something to be condemned"[11]—rather than from a standpoint privileging issues of social justice or a leftist politics of mobilization. So, for example, in a discussion of De Sica's neorealist oeuvre, he argues that, "a society which does not take every opportunity to smother happiness is already better than one which sows hate, but the most perfect still would not create love [that sentiment which is most characteristically expressed by the neorealist aesthetic, in Bazin's view], for love remains a private matter between man and man."[12]

To Liehm's two categories, a third can be added under the rubric of aestheticism. Aestheticist approaches to neorealist films tend to emphasize directors' responsiveness to, "the demands of film art," rather than their identification with a political stance or their concern with existential issues. For Peter Bondanella, who might fairly be categorized under this aestheticist designation,

> Italian . . . directors were concerned not only with social realism in their works. On the contrary, they were seeking a new . . . cinematographic language which would enable them to deal poetically with the pressing problems of their times.[13]

Visual realism is here not an alternative to creative artifice, but merely another, highly sophisticated and nuanced form of it.[14]

If the slew of recently published books on postwar Italian cinema written from a Lacanian psycho-cultural perspective is any indication, neorealism continues to inspire diverse schools of interpretation a half century after its heyday.[15] This chapter offers a new context for understanding the wide circulation, significant public role, and lasting influence of neorealist films. Highlighting the importance of a wartime environment of authoritarian collapse and democratic aspiration in the wake of which "neorealism," as a label for particular films, as a point of theoretical dispute and historical reference, and as a creative inspiration for future filmmaking, came to take on relatively large cultural significance, this chapter treats neorealism as a tragic cinema or cinematic form of tragic theater arising, as Greek tragedy did, in an era of major political rupture, when democracy replaced dictatorship and novel challenges were posed to a newly empowered citizenry. Classical scholars have made much of the fact that Greek tragedy (*tragōidíā*) and Athenian democracy developed at the same time. They have speculated that *tragōidíā* supported democracy by fostering citizens' capacities to reflect on the challenges of exercising power without benefit of specialized knowledge, to make considered judgments about important issues in the absence of precedents, and to maintain a viable and vital sense of civic solidarity in the face of the inevitable strains and tensions between classes, factions, and individuals.

As was the case with their ancient Greek predecessor, modern democracies have, by and large, emerged out of periods of struggle against monarchical or oligarchical regimes, in which restrictions on who could share power were usually and to a large degree legitimated by tradition and custom. Under such conditions, establishing a democracy meant breaking with a non-democratic past and facing serious deficits of political experience and authority. Newly empowered citizens of a democracy have additionally faced the challenges of generating viable forms of identity and solidarity. *Tragōidíā* helped Athenian democrats make up those deficits and meet those challenges. This chapter analyzes the uses of tragic rhetoric by film critics and historians of neorealism, draws parallels between key aspects of *tragōidíā* (myth, chorus, theater) and elements of neorealist films, and highlights strategic invocations of Greek tragedy by major figures of the "movement" in order to suggest how similar deficits and challenges existing in wartime and postwar Italy might have conditioned the conception and reception of neorealist films.

To say that neorealism was a *tragic* cinema is not to argue for the primary importance of narrative conventions in analyzing neorealist films. To characterize neorealism in terms of the genre of tragedy is to risk oversimplifying the phenomenon. This risk holds for the films considered under the rubric of neorealism, whose adherence to the conventions of tragedy is by no means uncontested. So, for example, Frank Tomasulo has argued that *Bicycle Thieves*, despite its tragic aspirations, "fail[s] to think beyond the level of the family melodrama."[16] Critics have also noted the hybrid, tragicomic features of Rossellini's *Open City*, in which elements of comedic slapstick (e.g., the routine in which the parish priest knocks an old man unconscious with a frying pan) jarringly give way to tragedy.[17] This point holds as well for tragedy as a genre category, which, since the time of its first recorded emergence as a subject of reflection in the works of Plato and Aristotle, has generated countless and, at times, conflicting attempts at definition.[18]

Attempting to characterize neorealism in terms of the genre of tragedy carries the additional risk of needlessly becoming entangled in disputes over neorealism's "realism." On one side, there was the general view that held a film to be neorealist to the extent that its creators eschewed aesthetic conventions and instead strove to apprehend the social world, and particularly the world of the economically vulnerable, in as unmediated a way as possible. As Cesare Zavattini, screenwriter for *Bicycle Thieves* and *Umberto D* (1951) and one of the foremost proponents of this perspective put it, the point of neorealist film was "to extract ourselves from abstractions" and demonstrate "an unlimited confidence in things, events, and in men."[19] Taking the other side are those who have found claims about neorealism's lack of narrative and technical artifice utterly unconvincing in the face of such obvious counterexamples as *Open City*, whose plot is shaped to a large extent by the conventions of melodrama, or *Bicycle Thieves*, with its technically sophisticated construction (e.g., "ten major dissolves," "250 moving shots").[20] Highly skeptical of claims about the non-mediated nature of neorealist film, as well as of the distorting influence of leftist ideology, Bondanella has argued that the great achievement of neorealist films, and the reason for their wide and lasting influence, had less to do with their mobilizing power as documentaries of social struggle as with their display of artistically compelling reflections on the nature of reality and illusion.[21]

While conceding the validity of Bondanella's point about the importance of the aesthetic dimension ("the demands of film art")[22] in understanding the achievements of neorealist film directors, our argument aspires to clear a theoretical space for appreciating, in a new way, the importance of the political dimension of neorealism. For this reason, Zavattini, who is so dead set against the use of traditional narrative conventions (including, as it turns out, the conventions of tragedy) in neorealist film, will serve (in a later section of this chapter) as an interesting test case for the plausibility of the argument to be offered here, which relies centrally on a non-genre understanding of tragedy. Evoking neorealism as a *tragic* cinema acknowledges the rhetoric of tragedy as a typical (if also contested) means of assigning significance to neorealism and points to the historical practice, *tragōidíā*, from which that rhetoric ultimately derives. In turn, consideration of the political functions of *tragōidíā* in the full emergence and development of Athens' democracy in the fifth century BCE invites reflection on how Italy's environment of wartime and early postwar struggle for democratic self rule led some important makers and interpreters of neorealist films to envision the nature and significance of their cinema in relation to Greek tragedy. If *tragōidíā* did not exercise as direct an influence on neorealist filmmakers, critics and audiences as more historically proximate performance traditions (say, the Italian tradition of the *commedia dell'arte*[23]), traces of its ancient role in democratic development, indirectly preserved in the elevation of tragedy to genre status in Western literature as well as in the generic uses of "tragedy" in ordinary language, nevertheless helped promote (however inadvertently) the positive reception of Italian neorealism.

An approach that emphasizes political context generally aligns with the sociohistorical interpretation of neorealism as Liehm describes it. However, in contrast to traditional leftwing approaches that tried to fit neorealism into a narrative of antifascist struggle, a *tragōidíā*-centered sociohistorical approach focuses on the generic demands raised by the experience of democratic political foundation. That focus distinguishes this approach as well from John Hay's argument about the significance of Italian cinema for the formation of a national-popular culture under fascism.

Casting "popular Italian films as social rituals enabl[ing] their audiences to renegotiate or clarify their changing cultural, material, and political environments, to discover meaning in a world where the traditional authority of Church and State had significantly eroded," Hay emphasizes modernization as the key context for understanding the cultural-political significance of Italian films in the 1920s and 1930s.[24] Accepting Hay's contention that "national cinemas have come to be particularly important stages for modernization" and appreciating the rich implications of his sociohistorical approach to fascist era film for understanding neorealist film,[25] we nevertheless limit our consideration of the relevant sociohistorical context of neorealism's emergence and reception to the environment of authoritarian collapse and democratic transformation that existed in Italy from the mid- to the late 1940s. Modernization processes tend to undermine traditional notions of authority and identity and foster a sense of disorientation and stress in people who can no longer take the routine functioning of social and political affairs for granted. If, in general, democratizing environments tend to be associated with modernization and are often counted as products of that process, they generate additional challenges for people. In particular, in periods of democratization, the process of generating new and viable senses of authority and identity is more bottom-up than top-down. When, in the last year or so of fascist rule, film directors and critics began to call for a new cinema that might finally reveal the harsh realities of Italian life, the belief was that only through such an unsparing exercise in self exposure might the Italian people be persuaded to commit themselves to taking an active role in the political regeneration of the country. To the extent that the cinema under fascism considered by Hay contributed to the modernization of Italian society, its goal was the formation of a passive, not active, citizenry.

If, in placing major emphasis on the role of democratic impulses of liberation and renewal in the emergence of neorealism, the analysis to be undertaken here is sociohistorical in approach, it remains more attuned than other sociohistorical accounts of neorealism to wider dimensions of neorealist films' appeal, including those existential and aesthetic dimensions emphasized in other schools of interpretation. This is so because of the use of *tragōidíā* as the relevant basis of comparison. For, in addition to their original contributions to the development of the theoretical capacities of democratic citizens in ancient Athens, Greek tragedies would survive as canonical texts and eventually become touchstones of aesthetic achievement and existential reflection in western culture.

In her thought-provoking study of the relationship between political innovation and theater, Karen Hermassi rhetorically asks, "Is it only coincidence that just as each decisive political foundation made its historical appearance, it has been accompanied by a brief flourishing of remarkable drama?"[26] It isn't a coincidence, Hermassi argues, because the act of breaking with the political past and bringing forth forms of government in which a new, enlarged citizen body takes on (or is meant to take on) the burdens and privileges of rule poses political theoretical challenges to which the experience of drama has historically provided some compelling and exemplary responses. In the environment of democratic aspiration and anticipated change in wartime and early postwar Italy, the most resonant and exemplary responses to the urgent challenges of establishing new forms of democratic authority and identity were forthcoming not on the Italian stage but on its film screens.

Ordinary Language Uses of Tragedy

Preliminary hints of a plausible link between neorealism and *tragōidíā* are hidden in plain sight, namely in the generic uses of the rhetoric of tragedy by critics and historians of neorealism. *Tragōidíā* has left many traces in modern linguistic usage. Besides referring to that distinctive theatrical practice associated with the Festival of Dionysus of ancient Athens, the English term, "tragedy," has become available for reference to forms of theatrical performance thought to resemble *tragōidíā* in significant ways, to particular works of literature (say, *Richard III* or *Death of a Salesman*) or the genre of which they are considered examples, and, finally, (in what some dictionaries refer to as the figurative meaning) to unexpectedly fatal events or extremely burdensome situations or conditions. One can happen upon "tragedy," its adjectival form, tragic, and such related terms as drama, theater, and catharsis in a wide variety of linguistic contexts, from academic treatises to daily news reports, from the specialized discourses of scholars to the ordinary conversation of non-specialists.

Among those who have availed themselves of the use of "tragedy" and related terms are many of the film critics and scholars who have written about neorealism. So, for example, in a survey of English newspaper and magazine reviews of *Paisan* one finds the critic of the *News Chronicle* referring to the film as "humorous and tragic. . . . A splendidly positive film of our tragic times." Another critic noted that each of the film's episodes save one is "permeated with a sense of tragic irony." The survey's author describes the last episode as one focused on "the scattered and tragic resistance to the Germans."[27]

Similar patterns of usage are to be found in histories of neorealism published in English or Italian. Film critic and director Luigi Chiarini's account of the historical context in which neorealist films first appeared is rife with the vocabulary of tragedy in its description of the conditions of the times: "the tragic events of the war," a world that "had tragically collapsed," "the tragedy of war and occupation," "tragic fraternal strife." Rossellini's *Paisan*, in particular, invites Chiarini's use of this vocabulary as when he writes, in reference to that film, that, "the whole of Italy is reflected in its tragedy, its sorrows, its qualities and defects, its religion and its heroism."[28]

In her history of Italian film, Mira Liehm situates the emergence of neorealist films in an Italy variously described as that "tragic country with the smiling face" and a "tragic country, hungry and desperate, occupied by foreign soldiers." She approvingly quotes Brunello Rondi's claim that "the new Italian cinema is imbued with a tragic sense of human coexistence." Most striking is her decision to conclude her book with a passage in which the future promise of Italian postwar film is summed up explicitly in terms of the access its best directors and films might give to the tragic dimensions of human existence: "That [Italian] cinema, having achieved so much that warrants preservation on the shelf of history along with the other arts, can now begin to contemplate some of the grand human themes, starting with Unamuno's 'tragic sense of life'."[29]

Millicent Marcus, in her book, *Italian Film in the Light of Neorealism*, also makes copious use of the vocabulary of tragedy. She refers to the "tragic mode" and shift from "domestic comedy to public tragedy" of *Open City*; to the "tragic identity and background" of the protagonist of *Bicycle Thieves* as well as the "tragic necessity" of his fall; to the "tragic end" of Silvana in Giuseppe De Santis's *Riso Amaro/Bitter Rice* (1949); and to the atmosphere of "gaiety that lies beyond tragedy" evoked in the final scene of *Umberto D* and characteristic of that film's "tragic vision."[30]

Likewise, one can hardly turn a page of the chapter, "The Masters of Neorealism: Rosssellini, De Sica, and Visconti," in Bondanella's standard history of postwar Italian film, without coming upon "tragedy" or a related term. Rossellini's *Open City* conveys the "tragedy of Italian experiences during the German occupation," "the tragedy of warfare," and "the most tragic of human experiences." De Sica's *Sciuscià/ Shoeshine* (1946) variously dramatizes the "tragedy of childish innocence corrupted by the adult world," "the tragic impact of the adult world on youthful friendship," or "Pasquale's tragedy." Visconti's *The Earth Trembles* is an "archetypal drama," employing the device of a "tragic reversal," and leading to a "pessimistic conclusion . . . closer to Greek tragedy than to the revolutionary conclusion of the projected Marxist trilogy."[31] And this is merely a small sample of a much larger pattern of references in Bondanella's chapter.

The uses of "tragedy" and "tragic" highlighted above are of two general types. On the one hand, such references are deployed in the service of historical description. In particular, the language of tragedy is used to describe the extreme difficulties of life in Italy under conditions of foreign occupation, partisan warfare, and wartime and postwar scarcity. On the other hand, the vocabulary of tragedy is deployed in the service of aesthetic analysis. So, for example, film scholars resort to aesthetic concepts, including, "tragic necessity," "tragic reversal," and "tragic irony," which are ultimately derived from a Western tradition of critical engagement with such texts as the tragedies of Aeschylus, Sophocles, and Euripides, and Aristotle's *Poetics*, to make sense of neorealist characters and plots.

In all of the cases noted above, tragedy is partnered with neorealism without a second thought. Neorealist films are seen unproblematically as having a tragic dimension whether this dimension is aesthetic (their plots and characters aligning with long-standing notions of literary convention), historical (their emergence under the crisis conditions of mid-to-late 1940s Italy seeming apropos), or both. In and of itself, the fact of these resorts to the vocabulary of tragedy in the literature of neorealism seems unremarkable. Conditions in Italy during occupation and wartime were terrible, after all, and it should come as no surprise that film scholars would reach for the most available and appropriate terms to convey this historical fact. Likewise, it should surprise no one that neorealist works, so focused on the theme of suffering and so populated with hard-luck characters, would invite use of the aesthetic vocabulary of tragedy.

Notwithstanding the many good reasons to overlook these word choices, it may be worth noting that the historical and aesthetic vocabularies of tragedy are linguistically traceable back to ancient Greek tragedy or *tragōidía*. This genealogy raises the possibility that the word choices of Chiarini, Marcus, Bondanella and others are not as casual or diffuse as they first appear and that their presence signals a recognition (however unreflected or inadvertent) of the larger cultural and political parallels between neorealism and *tragōidía*.

Parallels between Tragōidía and Neorealist Films

Athens emerged as a democracy in the fifty or so years after the overthrow of the Peisistratid tyranny (around 510 BCE), beginning with Cleisthenes's reforms at the end of the sixth century and culminating with the institutional changes led by Ephialtes and Pericles in the middle part of the fifth century. Running parallel with Athens' transition to democracy, *tragōidía* evolved to become a hallmark of the city-state's distinctive culture of public discourse and judgment. Convention holds that the inauguration of the City Dionysia or elaboration of it to include competitive performances of *tragōidía* occurred around 534 at the instigation of the tyrant Peisistratos. Peisistratus was a savvy ruler, who cultivated the support of the *demos* (and undercut the influence of his fellow aristocrats and rivals) by reportedly establishing a loan fund for peasants and a circuit court to which they might have legal recourse. His reputed founding of the City Dionysia, as well as his reorganization of the Panathenea (where epic poetry was competitively recited before a public audience), were very much in line with his strategy of cultivating popular support, although the basis of the appeal of these festivals was not the promise of either material support or legal protection but the reward of being engaged collectively as spectators and auditors in divinely sanctioned performance events of no small interest. As Werner Jaeger writes in reference to the effect of the cultural policy of the Peisistratids, "public interest in religion and the arts was of course not a new thing, but it was suddenly increased to a vast extent when they were systematically cultivated by a rich and powerful ruler."[32] When Peisistratid rule was ended (and after a return to rule by aristocratic clique was averted), management of the festivals came into the hands of officials accountable to a reestablished and newly democratized citizen body.

From *tragōidía*'s evolution in ancient Athens from a performance activity enjoying the patronage of a tyrant to a profoundly influential civic practice under Athens' democracy and, eventually, a source of standards for Western drama and literature, one can generalize a pattern to which the course of Italian cinema from the period of fascism to the founding of the Italian Republic adhered. As Mary Ann Frese Witt notes, cinema was only one component of a larger complex of activities in which the fascist predilection for public spectacle, "a kind of everyday theatricality, with mass gatherings in the piazza, the stadium, and the amphitheater, parades, costumes, the loudspeaker, the chant—all the trappings of mass performance," found expression.[33] Artistic pride of place in this mass performance program of fascist rule was given to the theater, which Mussolini reportedly valued more highly (for its spiritual, as distinguished from its propaganda, effects) than cinema. Reenactments of ancient drama, particularly Greek tragedies, were staged in

> outdoor spaces such as the Greek and Roman ruins at Paestum, Fiesole, and Syracuse as well as in Rome itself, serv[ing] not only to reinforce the link the regime wished to promote between classical glory and fascist present but also to inspire an emotional and "religious" binding of the masses analogous to the exaltation produced in the political festivals.[34]

Notwithstanding elite prejudices in favor of theater, the cinematic experience was, Hay suggests, the performance medium of greater social impact under fascism because it was more socially inclusive, more widely available, and more centrally engaged with issues of identity and community urgently raised by Italy's experience of rapid modernization.

> [C]inema did offer its audiences something which neither theater nor radio could offer: bigger-than-life images whose mere presence suggested transcendence and inspired awe while at the same time entertaining. Cinema in Italy shared both outdoor theater's sense of grandeur and limitlessness and the cabaret's sense of relaxed intimacy and seriousness. As a kind of hybrid mode of performance, it seemed more adapted to reaching broader social strata while . . . entertaining by addressing the conflicts and tensions between high and low social/cultural experience.[35]

Of course, even allowing for its social and cultural significance under fascism (and its role as proving ground for the talents of many of the directors, screenwriters, and film critics who would later go on to create the legacy of neorealism), the Italian cinema only became a cinema of world significance in the period after fascism's fall during a time when agitation for a popular and participatory democratic republic was at its height. That agitation found its deep sources in the longstanding grievances of working people in Italy's countryside and urban centers.

The culminating achievements of the Risorgimento period (1827–1871)—expulsion of foreign rulers and unification of the Italian states—did little to change the low status and marginal living conditions of Italy's peasantry, especially in the south where the survival of a quasi-feudal social hierarchy and the imposition by northern elites of free trade agricultural policies combined to impoverish peasants further.[36]

In the meantime, peasants of both the north and the south and members of a fledg-ling industrial labor force in the northern cities were kept out of political life as much as possible by an Italian bourgeoisie which, lacking the numerical weight, social prestige, and self confidence of middle classes in Great Britain and France, adopted an exclusionary political strategy in the post-Risorgimento years. During those rare instances when peasants' frustration with burdensome social conditions found collective, public (and sometimes violent) expression, the changes for which they called—debt relief, reform of agrarian contracts, security of tenure, and land redis-tribution—would have been well understood by their ancient counterparts living in the rural districts of ancient Athens, whose dogged pursuit of more just conditions of work and life marked the rise and development of their democracy.

Exploiting the ongoing social and political tensions caused by the frustration of the laboring classes and by the fears aroused in the middle and upper classes by workers' autonomous political and social mobilization in the wake of World War One, Mussolini established his fascist dictatorship in 1922. Unlike its parliamentary predecessor, the fascist regime championed the political mobilization of the masses but on terms it strictly controlled through a mixture of coercion, patronage, and propaganda. Despite the populist pretenses of Mussolini's regime, the disconnect between Italy's ruling elites and the masses of ordinary working people, famously analyzed by Antonio Gramsci in terms of the Italian bourgeoisie's failure to establish hegemony, continued. The regime's failure to fulfill its promises of improved living standards and its conscription of the masses for military service in poorly justified and incompetently led wars of conquest further alienated the populace.

After the successful Allied invasion of Sicily and the commencement of bombing attacks on Rome in July 1943 led to a palace coup against Mussolini by the king and the Italian military high command, events seemingly tended toward the reestablish-ment of rule by pre-fascist elites at the continued cost of the subordination of the laboring classes. (In the wake of the announcement of Mussolini's fall, popular dem-onstrations against fascist rule and the continuation of the alliance with Germany were bloodily repressed in several cities.)[37] However, the king's indecisive leadership and Allied mistrust combined to delay Italy's switch of sides (the Forty-Five Days) until German military forces could consolidate their hold on the central and north-ern sections of the Italian peninsula. As a result, the Italian populace in those areas suffered terribly as Allied troops slowly advanced against well-entrenched German defenders while partisan actions behind German lines were brutally put down with help from Italian fascist militias. The liberation of Italy through a combination of Allied military advances and, in the last phase, large-scale partisan operations, was not completed until May 1945.

In the course of an almost two year long liberation struggle in the north, many partisans came to consider their desperate fight to be the prelude to establishing a democratic order in postwar Italy. Differences between various factions (Communist, Socialist, liberal, Catholic) over what precise form that order ought to take did not lead to disabling divisions within the partisan movement mainly because of the decision by the leadership of the largest and best organized partisan grouping, the Communists, to support a broad-based antifascist front, and forego an organized attempt to transform Italian society through revolutionary means.[38] Aspirations for a more just and participatory democratic order were evident as well in the Allied-occupied south among a long-suffering peasantry whose desperate living conditions led many to demonstrate, occupy farmlands, and, in some few places, found village republics.[39] It was in this atmosphere of democratic expectation and grassroots struggle and activism that *Open City, Paisan, The Earth Trembles*, and *Shoeshine* were scripted and shot. In the face of this coincidence, the temptation, especially on the Left, has been to see neorealism as an extension of the antifascist struggle.

Mindful of *tragōidía*'s precedent-setting role in ancient Athens, we see the creation and evaluation of these films as also having been conditioned by the challenges of generating viable senses of democratic authority and identity. Having thus far offered only indirect evidence of a parallel between neorealist films and *tragōidía*—consideration of the generic uses of the rhetoric of tragedy by critics and historians of neorealism, similarities drawn between environments of democratic struggle in fifth-century Athens and early twentieth-century Italy—we now proceed to more direct evidence: structural resemblances between key aspects of *tragōidía* (myth, chorus, theater) and characteristic elements of neorealist films as well as strategic invocations of Greek tragedy by some major figures of neorealism.

Neorealist Icons and Tragedy

The ways in which *tragōidía* is thought to have contributed to the political education and capacity of an emerging democratic polity are several. We limit ourselves to consideration of three aspects of *tragōidía* often highlighted as having a special significance for the formation of new and vital forms of democratic authority and identity: the reconfiguration of myth, the employment of choral singing and dancing, and the establishment of the theater as preeminent site for collective spectatorship.

The mythic world of epic heroes, with its emphases on status, custom, and lineage, had figured centrally in the mental infrastructure of the old aristocratic order. Insofar as proponents of popular inclusion practiced more rationalistic and legal modes of thinking in their struggle against that old order, they confronted myth as something alien and other. At the same time, the old world of myth was, in important ways, the source out of which their modes of rational discourse and legality originally developed. A mythic world of epic heroes that could not wholly be discarded came to be enlisted as the material through which newer modes of rationalist, legalistic thinking were introduced and tested against older religious conceptions of propriety and justice.[40] In the process, a portion of the authority of ancient myth could be won over for the emerging order of rational and legal discourse and the new citizen body could come to feel that the more inclusive and reflective form of political agency they collectively exercised had the blessing of the gods. (In the case of *Open City*, among other neorealist films, Italy's iconographic legacy of Catholic belief served as one potent mythic source for endowing acts of human agency with a new sense of dignity, a point that will be expanded upon below.) Personifying the creative appropriation of older mythic materials for newer civic purposes was the figure of the tragic hero who, by turns, is the arrogant and hubristic hero of epic poetry *and* the sort of political statesman called for by a newly emerging democracy, a self-reflective leader more able to take fellow citizens' views and positions into account.[41]

In addition to its reconfiguration and revaluation of epic myth, ancient tragedy offered theatergoers the spectacle of a singing and dancing chorus. The central importance of choral performance for the civic culture of fifth century Athens is evoked by Plato's formulation in the *Laws* of the standard view of education, *achoreutos apaideutos* (no chorus, no education).[42] Composed, according to tradition, of 12 to 15 citizens or citizens-to-be who were given leave from other civic responsibilities for intensive rehearsals conducted regularly over the course of months, each tragic chorus constituted a microcosm of the polis community. The sense of audience identification with the choral presence on the tragic stage (*orchestra*) during the three-a-day, three day period of dramatic performances was probably amplified by the fact that the Dionysian festival was also an important occasion for Athenian men and boys to sing and dance competitively in dithyrambic choruses enrolling (in total) a thousand or so individuals and representing the tribes of the democratic polis.[43] Among other presumed functions, the chorus served to express the community's folk wisdom about the rewards and pitfalls of agency ("the inherited, gnomic wisdom of social memory and of oral tradition,"[44]), its skepticism toward, or deference to, the mentality of heroic self-assertion, and its solidarity in the face of ongoing social tensions and conflicts. For polis citizens learning to master the tricky challenge of being subject to an authority, they were also always in the process of constructing, the tragic chorus was an institution of no small importance:

> The chorus requires the audience to engage in a constant renegotiation of where the authoritative voice lies. It sets in play an authoritative collective voice, but surrounds it with other dissenting voices. The chorus both allows a wider picture of the action to develop and also remains one of the views expressed. (Goldhill)[45]

Suggestive, in this regard, is the importance given to the choral nature of Italian films in the 1940s. Reflecting, in 1953, on the earlier part of his career, Rossellini identified "*coralitá*" as one of the noteworthy elements of continuity in his filmmaking style of the previous decade.

> I have no formulas or preconceptions, but if I were to look back on my films, undoubtedly I would come across elements which are in themselves constant, and which are repeated not systematically but naturally, especially the aspects of the chorus. Realistic film is in itself a chorale. The sailors of *La nave bianca* are as important as the refugees at the end of *L'Uomo della croce*, as the population of

Roma città aperta, the partisans of *Paisà* and the monks of *Francesco, giullare di Dio*.[46]

Rossellini's attentiveness to the choral nature of his films may owe something to the Christian Democratic film reviewer Carlo Trabuco, who is credited with first using the notion of *"coralitá"* in reference to *Open City*,[47] or it may derive earlier from the notion's currency among fascist-era film reviewers, who related it to the regime's affirmation of the virtues of collectivism over individualism.[48] As we shall discuss below, the meaning of the chorus will become more multiform in neorealist films, not so much one-sidedly favoring one pole of experience (collectivism) as appreciating and mediating the respective demands of community and individuality in ways that were more responsive to the sorts of challenges raised by democratization and more analogous to the functions of the tragic chorus in ancient Athens' democracy.

Tragic heroes and chorus came together as performers in the theater, a site of collective spectatorship (*theatron*, from the verb, *theāsthai*, to watch, look at)[49] in which all groups of the Athenian polis, even the ones of lowest status, could gather. Cut into cliffs or hills and utilizing wooden or stone benches, theaters were not characteristic of all Greek city-states; they seem to have been "a monument of the large democratic or oligarchic polis in regions in which dramatic performances were an integrated part of the political and religious culture."[50] The civic importance of theater attendance in democratic Athens can be gauged by the fact that, from the time of Pericles, the two *obol*-per-day seating charge for Athenian citizens was paid out of the city treasury.[51] A parallel can here be drawn with the efforts undertaken by the OND (Opera Nazionale Dopolavoro), the Italian state institution dedicated to promoting leisure time activities under fascism. In addition to its several hundred fixed theaters, it managed 42 mobile cinemas that (in 1937) reportedly reached 9,900,000 spectators in 26,641 showings.[52] After the war, Italians remained enthusiastic moviegoers compared to the inhabitants of higher population countries like France and West Germany, attending the cinema in numbers that grew rapidly from 1946 to 1955 (peaking in the latter year at 819.4 million) and held steady at around 740 million through the beginning of the 1960s (outpacing even the British by 1959).[53]

In providing a space for the enactment of mythic lives and deeds that were also somehow contemporary, the theater allowed spectators to practice modes of thought by which they might achieve reflective distance on the routines and arrangements of their own lives and confront the antinomies and tensions of the new democratic order on terrain less fraught with political urgency than the courts, executive council, or city assembly.[54] Put another way, it was on the ascending rows of theater benches that audience members could (through exposure to *tragōidía*) find both acknowledgement of the burden of decision felt by self-consciously historical beings and temporary reprieve from those burdens in the experience of mythic timelessness. As Hermassi, referring specifically to Aeschylean drama, remarks, "tragedy would underscore decision and risk by closing in on historical events and persons," while at the same time preserving a "mythical sense of time," the essential qualities of which were permanence, circularity, and eternity. Tragedy could thereby endow human deeds, the most perishable and fragile of things, with the sort of gravity and dignity on which Athenian citizens' emerging sense of the rationality and autonomy of politics partly depended.[55]

With this excursus into the political significance of ancient Greek tragedy, we have seemingly strayed far from the concerns of neorealist film critics and scholars, even given their tendency to adopt the language of tragedy. Why not rest on the notion that "tragedy" or "tragic" is meant by these critics and scholars to refer to nothing more than sad times or hard-luck characters? The possibility that parallels between the political contexts of Greek tragedy and Italian neorealism underlay such usage is perhaps better seen in those cases of film criticism and commentary where resort to the vocabulary of tragedy is ambiguous or ambivalent. In such cases, one finds notable critics, screenwriters, and directors of neorealist films drawing distinctions between the different senses of "tragedy" and singling out one sense, in particular, for its affinity with neorealist films: ancient Greek tragedy. Take the case of Bazin, a French intellectual deeply influenced by the early twentieth-century currents of Catholic personalism and phenomenology and, according to Liehm, one of the foremost promoters of the "humanist" school of interpretation of neorealism.[56]

Bazin typically presents tragedy as something that neorealism decidedly isn't. So, for example, he affirms as the primary aspect of neorealist films their nature as "unreconstituted reportage," and follows up with the statement that, "the action could not unfold in just any social context, historically neutral, partly abstract like the setting of tragedy."[57] Similarly, in his analysis of *Bicycle Thieves*, Bazin takes care to distance the film from conventional genres of tragedy. "The film shows no extraordinary events such as those which befall the fated workers in Gabin films. There are no crimes of passion, none of those grandiose coincidences common in detective stories which simply transfer to a realm of proletarian exoticism the great tragic debates once reserved for the dwellers on Olympus." "One must," he continues, "take care not to confuse it [*Bicycle Thieves*] with realist tragedy."[58]

Bazin's move to distance neorealism from conventional aesthetic notions of tragedy makes sense in light of his position that "neorealism is more an ontological position than an aesthetic one," which follows from a conceptualization of neorealism as a kind of phenomenological cinema in which the point is to give equal weight to people, things, to phenomena, in general.[59] (So, for example, *Umberto D.* is constituted by a, "succession of concrete instants of life no one of which can be said to be more important than another, for their ontological equality destroys drama at its very basis.")[60] Only in adhering to this egalitarian aesthetic, on this view, could one foster a redemptive intimation of the fullness of existence, the wonder that things exist at all. Under such a conception of neorealism, notions of dramatic arc, of plot development, of tragic heroes, of anything that might imply a rank order of phenomena would be problematic, to say the least.

And yet, Bazin (at least so far as his 1949 review of *Bicycle Thieves* goes) is either unwilling or unable totally to give up on the possibility of affinities between tragedy and neorealism. Thus, he writes of the film, that it is "solidly structured in the mold of a tragedy." This is best seen from the point of view of the workman's son, who is "the intimate witness of the tragedy, its private chorus." Bazin continues: "It is the admiration the child feels for his father and the father's awareness of it which gives its tragic stature to the ending."[61]

A similar ambivalence about tragedy is detectable in leftist screenwriter and De Sica-collaborator Cesare Zavattini's reflections about neorealism. Conceptualizing neorealism as a form of realism in the service of a humanitarian socialism ("This powerful desire of the cinema to see and analyse, this hunger for reality, for truth, is a kind of concrete homage to other people, that is, to all who exist"), Zavattini rejects the tendency of traditional cinema to "insert a story into reality." Committed to the notion that contact with the reality of the everyday lives of people will evoke in neo-realist film audiences a more powerful and lasting sense of "the responsibility and dignity of every human being," he deplores the "interference of imagination," by which he apparently means the influence of literary conventions on cinematic representations of reality. Although tragedy is nowhere mentioned by name in this regard, it is implicitly presented as the main obstacle of his vision of neorealism as a "non-abstract and concrete study of man."[62]

> The most important characteristic of neorealism, i.e., its essential innovation, is, for me, the discovery that this need to use a story was just an unconscious means of masking human defeat in the face of reality; imagination, in its own manner of functioning, merely superimposes death schemes onto living events and situations.[63]

Zavattini's notion of story telling as a means for inappropriately aestheticizing human suffering parallels the sorts of criticisms left-wing critics (such as, for a recent example, Terry Eagleton's critical remarks about the "inhumane humanism" and "spiritual aristocraticism" of some interpreters of tragedy)[64] have long lodged against writers and theorists of tragedy for purportedly ignoring the institutional bases of human suffering in favor of a fatalistic acceptance of the human condition as incapable of significant improvement. What these critics describe in terms of tragic fatalism or a "political failure of nerve,"[65] Zavattini refers to as "a profound and unconscious lack of confidence in confronting reality."[66] As a corollary to their rejection of tragedy's propensity to foster fatalism, leftwing critics deplore the elitist assumption of tragic literati and theorists that only the lives and sufferings of extraordinary (i.e., aristocratic) characters merit attention. Consistent with this negative view, Zavattini declares:

> I am against exceptional persons, heroes. I have always felt an instinctive hatred towards them. I feel offended by their presence, excluded from their world as millions of others like me. We are all characters. Heroes create inferiority complexes throughout an audience. The time has come to tell each member of the audience

that he is the true protagonist of life. The result would be a constant emphasis on the responsibility and dignity of every human being. This is exactly the ambition of neo-realism: to strengthen everyone, and to give everyone a proper awareness of a human being.[67]

Notwithstanding Zavattini's rejection of the purportedly pernicious effects of those literary conventions so closely associated with great works of tragedy (say, *Oedipus Tyrannis* or *King Lear*) and the genre of which they are touchstones, he apparently does not want entirely to give up on tragedy. The remark (reproduced in translation after the introductory paragraphs of this chapter) appears in his description of a film project, *Mia Italia*, in which he planned to apply his neorealist vision to the various social environments of Italy and allow people to speak for themselves and reveal their conditions of life on their own terms. In attempting to capture what it would mean to fulfill the progressive mission of his projected film, Zavattini interestingly has recourse to tragedy: "*Verrà il momento, credo, molto presto, in cui andremo a vedere cosa fa un uomo nelle sue più minute azioni quotidiane, con lo stesso interesse che una volta ponevano nell'andare a vedere i drammi greci.*"[68] However, the form of tragedy he has in mind is not tragedy as genre or historical condition but *tragōidíā*, the performance institution of ancient Athens. From this original form of tragedy, Zavattini appropriates the image of ancient theatergoers drawn to performances of *tragōidíā* as a benchmark for the kind of interest neorealist films should elicit from their modern Italian audience.

In this regard, might Bazin also be seen as evoking not just any sort of tragedy but *tragōidíā* in his likening of the son in *Bicycle Thief* to a "private chorus"? Just as with the citizen chorus of old, on such a view, the boy would also provide a critical minded but sympathetic witness to the strivings and sufferings of the tragic hero, in this case, the father searching for his stolen bicycle. Like the heroes of *tragōidíā* as analyzed by Vernant, the father in *Bicycle Thief* is a hybrid figure, a man embodying, on the one hand, traditional hierarchy and authority in the form of a "conventional patriarch" or "newly reinstated paterfamilias" and, on the other, democratic equality and solidarity in the form of a defeated and, in the end, humiliated father to whom the son will "offer . . . an entirely new relationship" based on a recognition of the limits of individual agency.[69] Accordingly, the body language and relative positioning of the father and son oscillate throughout the film, with some sequences emphasizing separation and hierarchy (usually during moments when the father feels especially weighed upon by the urgency of retrieving his bike and stalks off heedless of his son's difficulties in keeping up) and others emphasizing solidarity and equality (as when father and son fraternally sit down together to a meal).

Consistent with this reading of the father as a tragic hero in the ancient mold, Bazin unintentionally casts the son in the image of the singing and dancing chorus of *tragōidíā*. In describing the son's role in the film as a "dramatic reserve, which, as the occasion arises, serves as a counterpoint, as an accompaniment, or moves on the contrary into the foreground of the melodic structure," Bazin metaphorically endows him with a musical dimension. And Bazin follows up this evocative image of the son as singing chorus with a reference to the significance of the boy actor's performance as choric dancer:

> [The child's] function in the story is . . . clearly observable in the orchestration of the steps of the child and of the grownup. Before choosing this particular child, De Sica did not ask him to perform, just to walk. He wanted to play off the striding gait of the man against the short trotting steps of the child, the harmony of this discord being for him of capital importance for the understanding of the film as a whole . . . . Whether the child is ahead, behind, alongside—or when, sulking after having had his ears boxed, he is dawdling behind in a gesture of revenge—what he is doing is never without meaning.[70]

Neorealist cinema became known for its conspicuous use of child characters, including Pina's son and Romoletto's band in *Open City*, Giuseppe and Pasquale in *Shoeshine*, and· Edmund in *Germania Anno Zero*/Germany Year Zero (1947). According to one film critic, such characters, usually played by amateurs, "lent the perfect semidocumentary presence to the neorealist aesthetic, walking through blighted war ruins with haunted, saucer eyes, taking it all in."[71] Bazin's suggestive remarks about the choral nature of the son in *Bicycle Thieves* raise the possibility that the large presence of children in neorealist cinema is an effect of their fulfilling the role of the tragic chorus, inviting a sense of identification from an audience of prospective democratic citizens who are both products, and (presumably) the new masters, of institutions and traditions inherited from an undemocratic past.

For a more obvious example of *coralità*, one need only consider the final shot of *Open City*, in which the parish boys, stricken by their witness of Don Pietro's execution, make their way back, "with heads lowered and hand-in-hand," along Via Nomentana. In arguing for the iconic importance of this scene for later Italian filmmakers, Gian Piero Brunetta explicitly characterizes this mournful file of boys as a chorus—"All the succeeding visual avenues of Italian film take as their material and ideal starting point this long field across which a small chorus of silent figures walk toward Rome on a bright summer morning of 1944."—and evokes their role as figures of identification for the audience. "In this final scene, after having created [in the shot of Don Pietro's execution] a perfect congruence between the gaze of the boys and that of the spectators, Rossellini places in one prospect, along the same visual access, the spectators, the protagonists of the action, and the urban space."[72]

This account collects all of the components of ancient tragic drama: chorus, protagonists, spectators, the hillside prospect (which places the film viewer, so to speak, on the ascending rows of an ancient theater), and the urban space (which occupies what would, in the Athenian Theater of Dionysus, be the *orchestra* or stage). There are, of course, many examples of choral gatherings in *Open City* (e.g., the column of German troops on the march in the film's opening scene, the crowd of women rioters at the bakery, the residents gathered in the courtyard and on the sidewalk during the

German military's search of their apartments for partisans), but the example of *coralitá* with which the film ends and the one that most powerfully invites feelings of identification is the one that most richly evokes the topography and component parts of *tragōidíā*. Needless to say, to the extent that this boy's "chorus" did invite postwar Italian audiences' sense of identification, the intended effect was not to foster a sense of individual subordination to the mass-mobilizing purposes of a fascist state, but rather to evoke both a feeling of collective solidarity in the face of wartime suffering and newfound hope in the possibility of a cooperative effort (in particular, between Catholics and communists in a Popular Front alliance that might outlast the war and shape a postwar democracy) to forge a better future.

Rossellini's compelling presentation of ordinary Romans as the chorus or collective protagonists of his film stands as a notable fulfillment of that vaunted neorealist ability to shoot crowd scenes. We suggest that the "*coralitá*" of neorealist films, their narrative and visual nesting of individual stories in a context of collective judgment and agency, as well as their enlistment of ordinary people in a performance event, harkens back to the prominent role of the citizen chorus in ancient Greek tragedy. And just as the chorus of *tragōidíā* provided an opportunity for ancient spectators to identify with each other as agents in a collective political enterprise and feel that enterprise to be sponsored by a higher authority, so might the choral nature of neorealist films be seen as similarly fostering a sense of democratic identity and authority in aspiring citizens of modern Italy.

While the significance of *tragōidíā* to neorealism can be imputed only indirectly in the case of *Open City*, the linkage is much more explicit in Rossellini's commentary on his decision to make *Stromboli* (1949).

> For some time I matured the idea of treating, after the war dramas, this postwar tragedy. . . . If the protagonist was a borderline case, so was the island. So I first reduced the series of events my character was going to live through to their barest structure, and focused the tragedy on her and her torment. Then, for counterpoint, I needed nature, awesomely hostile, and people, totally uncomprehending and unsympathetic. *Stromboli* provided me with both, perfectly. In other words, the structures of ancient tragedy were the only ones I thought adequate to give life to this struggle between Creator and creature.[73]

Rossellini published this explanation of his artistic choices in defensive reaction to the almost universally hostile reception afforded his film by critics and its poor performance at the box office. In addition to its occasioning scandal-mongering about his romantic relationship with the female lead, Ingrid Bergman, *Stromboli* had to sustain attacks from many critics who saw it as yet another sign of Rossellini's deviation from an earlier neorealist commitment. In his response to the various forms of uproar, Rossellini takes artistic refuge, so to speak, in the inspiration provided by *tragōidíā*. Judging from his later claim about the choral nature of realist film, this association of neorealism with ancient Greek tragedy was an important and lasting one for him. And judging from the critical and scholarly responses, his film work, particularly those neorealist monuments to the Italian Resistance, *Open City* and *Paisan*, did their part in suggesting the link between neorealism and *tragōidía* to others. Giuseppe Ferrara's retrospective look at the former film is characteristic:

> Neorealism, in short, gives birth to a language of struggle which grasps not only momentous historical connections but simultaneously the minutes lived by men within the historical perspective. The elements in the death of Pina; her running briefly behind the German trucks as they take her husband away, her shout of rebellion immediately followed by a charge of machine-gun fire, her body on the bloody pavement, explain in precise detail both an individual and a collective tragedy; not only does it represent the tragedy of the entire Italian people, but it constitutes, in the history of cinema and human culture, one of the first expressions of *historical man* through the language of conflict.[74]

What would, in the absence of a consciousness of the significance of *tragōidía* for the rise and maintenance of Athenian democracy, have seemed to be casual uses of the language of tragedy appear instead as historically apt evocations of the parallel ways by which neorealism and *tragōidía* promoted democratic change. If, in his claim about neorealism's singular capacity to create a "language of conflict" in which the events of ordinary experience become endowed with an historical significance, Ferrara did not specifically have in mind *tragōidía*'s ability to endow autonomous human actions with myth-like gravity, his word choices inadvertently attest to that earlier precedent. One is still left to wonder, though, how it is that scenes from the film achieve that singular effect of conveying the unique and irreducible particularity of a given act or deed while at the same time allowing that act or deed to reveal or sponsor a wider symbolic and universal meaning. To put the question in the terms to which scholars of ancient Greek tragedy have accustomed us, how does *Open City* successfully marry myth and history? P. Adams Sitney's iconographic method of analyzing Italian film offers the means for a plausible answer.

Sitney's study, *Vital Crises in Italian Cinema: Iconography, Stylistic, Politics* (1995), is premised on a claim about the pervasive presence and singular importance of iconographic images in Italian cinema: "iconographic representation so permeates Italian life that it is not surprising to find it central to the native cinema."[75] Of particular significance, in this regard, is the rich legacy of Catholic images and notions made available by Italy's traditions of painting, architecture, and literature. According to Sitney, postwar Italian film directors, notably including Rossellini, De Sica, and Pasolini, appropriated aspects of this legacy partly in an effort to criticize the Church's political role in Italian society. So, for example, drawing heavily on Meyer Schapiro's 1946 review of *Open City*, Sitney notes the various allusions to, and creative appropriations of, Catholic icons. Manfredi, the Communist partisan, becomes a present-day version of the Christian proselytizer Paul when he undergoes "conversion" by taking on the false identity of Giovanni Episcopo (whose surname is the Italian word for the ecclesiastical title of bishop). After Manfredi's death in a Gestapo torture room, Pietro, the partisan-priest, is shot while tied to a chair with his back to a firing squad, thereby recalling the inverted crucifixion of his apostolic namesake. Sitney also notes how the film unconventionally reenacts each of the seven sacraments in profane contexts that underline their meaning as spontaneous gestures of human solidarity and agency rather than as ritualistic expressions of the Church's institutional authority. So, for example, "the plot turns around the 'baptism' of a newspaper, *L'Unità*, the underground organ of the Communist Resistance; [the boy] Marcello tells Don Pietro that he repeatedly misses school because 'the way things are' makes catechism a waste of time; instead he prepares for his 'confirmation' by imitating the fighters in Romoletto's gang."[76]

Accepting Sitney's analysis of Rossellini's appropriations and subversions of Catholic icons, one might draw a parallel between neorealist uses of Catholic iconography and *tragōidía*'s ambiguous use of myth as depicted by Vernant. *Tragōidía* both contested myth's timeless sense of authority and enlisted it in the service of more historically grounded and rationalistic modes of democratic reflection. Analogously, in *Open City*, even as the Catholic sacraments are subverted, indirect homage is paid to their continued power as icons in the Italian mentality. As time-tested symbols of divine presence, they help to endow fleeting and seemingly fruitless human actions and gestures with redemptive symbolic weight. If the Church-consecrated marriage of Pina and Francesco is forever foreclosed by her brutal murder at the hands of the German occupiers, the "marriage" of Communist and Christian movements of resistance is sanctified by the sacrifice of their respective martyrs, Manfredi and Pietro.[77]

> [The partisan struggle was] the moment of the great rupture with the past, of a break which opened the way to the active participation of the popular masses in the further political and social development of the country; it was a revolutionary democratic impulse of an unmistakable and lasting character.[78]

As it turned out, wartime aspirations for a participatory and egalitarian Italian democracy would be mostly defeated. The Christian Democratic Party, formed by conservatives with the active support of the business class and the Catholic Church, outmaneuvered the leftwing parties in the national unity government in the early years of the postwar period. Progressive programs of reform in land ownership and labor relations and attempts to purge the upper levels of state administration of holdovers from the Fascist period were blocked, delayed, or watered down. Election rallies, political protests, land occupations, and other manifestations of working-class, political, and social mobilization were often suppressed by local police and military units, sometimes using deadly force.[79] Throughout most of this period of conservative retrenchment, the Communists remained within a national unity government led by Christian Democratic prime ministers, a cause for no small frustration on the part of many left-wing voters. In what was perhaps its only major victory, the forces of the Left did push through a major constitutional change: the transformation of Italy from a constitutional monarchy into a republic by national referendum on June 2, 1946. Considered against the backdrop of *tragōidía*'s association with ancient Athens' development of democratic political institutions and culture, the coincidence of this point of constitutional transformation in modern Italian history with the critical and popular success of *Open City* (first in box office in Italy for the 1945–1946 season) is suggestive.

In the 1948 elections, the Christian Democrats won an absolute majority and, by the end of 1949, the Italian Parliament passed the "Andreotti Law," certain provisions of which—government authority both to ban public screenings of films determined to be not in "the best interests of Italy" and to prevent their foreign export—were deliberately aimed at choking off the production and distribution of neorealist films.[80] In light of the fact that neorealist films never constituted a major portion of Italian film production (less than a third of the 822 films produced between 1945 and 1953 and perhaps as little as four percent)[81] and they did not (with some few exceptions) perform well at the box office, the alacrity with which the Christian Democratic government acted against them is noteworthy. Concerns about neorealist cinema's supposedly negative effect on Italy's image in foreign countries and the association of neorealism with Communist sentiments surely had much to do with the drafting and passage of the legislation. Might another factor have been a recognition, however dim, of neorealism's *tragōidía*-like function as educator of citizens for participatory democracy?

In evoking Greek tragedy as a model for understanding the nature or significance of neorealist films, Bazin, Zavattini, and Rossellini invite us to think about neorealism's status in early postwar Italy in relation to the political theoretical challenges raised by the collapse of the old fascist order and the struggle for a new, democratic order. Generic uses of "tragedy" by critics and historians of neorealist cinema suggest that an important basis of neorealism's lasting attraction was its association with literary conventions of genre and commonsense notions of human suffering. After the defeat of fascism and Nazism, and before Cold War tensions led Western political elites to dismiss and, at times, demonize participatory models of democracy, film critics and audiences in Italy and in foreign lands may have also been recalled, if only distantly, to a memory of the West's earliest, successful campaign for participatory democracy through their encounter with a modern, cinematic analog to the most ancient form of democratic art.[82]

CHAPTER 4

Cornel West: Tragedy and the Fulfillment of American Democracy

In recognizing different dimensions of the politics of tragedy at work in the political thought of a dissident playwright and later president of a post-Communist Czech Republic and in the creation and reception of key neorealist films of the early, post-fascist years of the Italian republic, we have raised some important questions about democratic agency. Under the conforming pressures of a one-party state and in the absence of structures enabling autonomous political action, how are citizens' appreciation for the requirements of collective democratic agency and their taste for autonomous civic engagement to be fostered? And in the event that a repressive regime collapses and opportunities for autonomous political agency arise, how are citizens who have never exercised political freedom going to muster the political judgment and the virtuosity of action necessary to achieve a viable and lasting democracy? Havel's political writings and speeches suggest the manifold importance of theater both as a space in which alternative forms of collective identity and alternative modes of collective agency can be imagined and as a rich source of metaphors (tragedy, drama, catharsis) by which instances of political freedom can be remembered and appropriately prized. The critical reception of neorealist films and the parallels that can be drawn between those films and Greek tragedy suggest how tragedy can be a resource for generating a form of self-authorizing democratic agency in polities accustomed to rule from above and lacking traditional sources of democratic authority.

In the example of the politics of tragedy to be considered in this chapter, democratic agency remains a foremost concern. However, in this case the political context is not a repressive one-party state of the Right or the Left but a multi-party democracy in which majority rule co-existed with slavery and, later, a system of political disenfranchisement, social discrimination, and economic exploitation of an African-descended minority. In addition to facing the challenge of mustering critical energy against an ostensible democracy, the politics of tragedy on offer in the writings of African-American public intellectual and democratic theorist Cornel West also operates in a culture famously lacking a sense of the tragic. Americans' purported deficit when it comes to appreciating the tragic aspects of life is evoked time and again by European observers who connect this deficit to what they take to be Americans' proclivity to act intemperately or hubristically. Take, for example, the episode of contentious disagreement in early 2003 between the George W. Bush administration and

the leaders of France and Germany and European publics over the question of invad-
ing Iraq, which provided an occasion for some European intellectuals to evoke the
longheld idea, that Americans lack a sense of the tragic. In an historical survey of
European intellectuals' hostile views of Americans and their culture, Simon Schama
noted the Romantics' negative reaction to the "distaste for tragedy" in American life.[1]
In a review of books on U.S. post-Cold War status as lone military superpower, Tony
Judt suggested that, "what is missing in recent American commentary is . . . a sense
of the tragic."[2] Terry Eagleton, author of a book on the contemporary relevance of
notions of tragedy, implicitly held American culture to account for its deficient
appreciation of tragedy when he referred to a " 'dogmatic American voluntarism' for
which the world is 'perpetually open'."[3] Lacking a tragic sensibility through which to
appreciate fully the larger contexts and meaning of either their individual or collective actions and purpose, Americans appear in these commentaries (at best) as
naïvely believing that their moral rectitude gives them title to preeminent power and
influence or (at worst) as cynically deploying a moralistic vocabulary to mask the
untrammeled pursuit of a narrowly conceived individual or national interest. What
seems ultimately to be of concern in these criticisms is American power and the
consequences that follow when a sense of appropriate limits is completely lacking in
its use.

The notion that tragedy teaches a sense of limits and its corollary, the view that
tragic wisdom consists of knowing the true extent of one's powers, form part of a
long and venerable tradition of thinking about tragedy. They are memorably encap-
sulated in the ancient Greek adage, nothing to excess, and they form the backdrop,
to take one notable example in American scholarship, of Martha Nussbaum's *The
Fragility of Goodness* (1986). Relying on the dramas of Aeschylus, Sophocles, and
Euripides, Nussbaum's book criticizes the hold that Kantian-inspired notions of
a consistent, coherent, and autonomous ethical self have upon contemporary moral
theory.[4]

If knowing and accepting limits is a familiar lesson to those who think about
tragedy and one that is often dispensed to counteract political hubris, it is not the
only possible lesson. Generally speaking, the relation of tragedy to action is two-
sided. On the one hand, possession of a sense of the tragic can have the effect of
reducing the chances of hubristic or intemperate exercises of human agency. In this
case, tragedy becomes a remedy for defective agency. On the other hand, possession
of a sense of the tragic can have the effect of encouraging appropriate or necessary
exercises of agency that might not otherwise happen. Appreciation of this latter
aspect of the relation of tragedy to agency is relatively meager in the tradition of theorizing tragedy. One exception to this lack of appreciation can be found in Nietzsche's,
The Birth of Tragedy, where a link is drawn between the ancient Greeks' tragic sensibility and their capacity to act: "It is the people of the tragic mysteries that fight
the battles against the Persians. . . . Who would have supposed that precisely this
people . . . should still have been capable of such a uniformly vigorous effusion of the
simplest political feeling, the most natural patriotic instincts, and original manly

desire to fight?"[5] Here, tragedy is seen as a promoter of agency or, one might say, as a remedy for passivity or deficient agency.

It is this latter understanding of tragedy as a promoter of agency that Cornel West, among the rare American proponents of a tragic sensibility, seems mostly to have in mind in his many references to, and considerations of, tragedy. Like the European critics referred to above and unusually for a contemporary American intellectual, West focuses a major part of his criticism of American culture on its purported lack of engagement with tragedy. However, somewhat against the grain of most European critiques, West values the tragic sensibility mostly for its promise to spur action rather than limit or restrain it. In particular, West aims to empower U.S. citizens, encouraging them to exercise forms of agency conducive to the well functioning of a more participatory and inclusive democracy. In this latter respect, West conducts a politics of tragedy that converges with the Havelian and neorealist forms of the politics of tragedy we have examined in the previous two chapters. In these latter two cases, eras of broad democratic aspiration for participatory forms of self rule—in Czechoslovakia, the reform era initiated by the Soviet Union's 1956 reassessment of Stalin's rule to the Prague Spring of 1968, in Italy, the 1943–1945 partisan uprising against fascism, Nazi occupation, and the old order that culminated with the 1946 referendum establishing republican government—were eventually defeated but not before fostering modes of political theory whose role and aims converged with the role and aim of *tragōidía* in ancient Athens. West's resort to tragedy occurs in a similar context of democratic aspiration and defeat, starting with the expansion and intensification of democratic participation during the Civil Rights era and extending through the 1970s-era feminist activism until the backlash years of the Reagan-Bush presidencies.

References to the "tragic" and to "tragedy" are spread throughout West's writings, suggesting that notions of tragedy are, and have long been, significant in his thinking about the nature of theory and its relation to politics. Take, for example, West's project of extending and reorienting the American pragmatist tradition. In an essay he developed from a book project on the pragmatist thinker Josiah Royce, he argued that pragmatism, "has not come to terms with a sense of the tragic and hence we need a revisionist understanding of this tradition, even as we build upon the best of it."[6] His most systematic attempt at revising pragmatism, *The American Evasion of Philosophy* (1989), resulted, West writes, from his "vow to write a book on pragmatism that injected a sense of the tragic."[7]

West's critique of pragmatism culminates in his affirmation of "prophetic pragmatism," a mode of thinking and acting based on a synthesis of pragmatist, Marxist, and Black Christian insights that West often explicitly links to tragedy. Prophetic pragmatism "calls for utopian energies and tragic actions." Its "praxis . . . is tragic action with revolutionary intent usually reformist consequences, and always visionary outlook." Presented as one of the foremost "contribut(ors) . . . to the political project of prophetic pragmatism," Martin Luther King, Jr. is seen by West as having "come out of a black tradition with a profound sense of the tragic."[8]

Sometimes, West's preoccupation with the tragic includes consideration of the comic aspects of social and political existence. So, for example, in response to a recent interviewer's question, West suggested that what the "'black experience' [has] to offer American philosophy" is "a profound sense of the tragic and the comic rooted in heroic efforts to preserve human dignity on the night side, the underside of modernity."[9] This pairing of tragedy and comedy in West's thought is often expressed under the rubric of the "tragicomic." Take, for example, the character of West's response to the interpretations and critiques of his work collected in *Cornel West: A Critical Reader* (2001); in the book's concluding essay, West stakes the value of his "voice and vision . . . on the insightfulness and truthfulness of the rich traditions of tragicomic darkness and world-transforming compassion linked to radical democratic practices and struggles."[10] Styling himself a Chekhovian Christian, West insists on the importance of maintaining a particular Christian perspective on the world, one that foregrounds "the tragic and majestic among everyday people and ordinary folk."[11] The frequency of West's references to tragicomic or tragic aspects of social, political and cultural existence in his "Afterword" is especially noteworthy given that only two of the nineteen contributors give any serious attention to West's engagement with tragedy, one of whom implicitly criticizes West for not adequately working out the meaning and significance of this notion.[12] In light of this pattern of personal interest in, and theoretical commitment to, notions of the tragic, it should come as no surprise that in his first semester back at Princeton University after West's highly publicized departure from Harvard in 2002, he chose to teach a freshman seminar titled, "The Tragic, the Comic and the Political."[13] Reportedly, West was at work on a book of the same title after his arrival at Princeton.[14]

The character and duration of West's engagement with notions of tragedy invite several questions. For what does the tragic stand in West's thought? To which theoretical and political purposes does he put his many references to the tragic? What does West's theoretical engagement with the tragic teach us about the facilitating conditions, aims, and significance of democratic agency?

It may be useful at the outset to note some general patterns of West's theorization of the political significance of the tragic. West values the tragic primarily as a means for enhancing human beings' ability to exercise their agency and, ultimately, to live more meaningful lives less burdened by social misery and oppression. As the previously listed examples of his usage suggest, West prefers to characterize the tragic as a kind of sensibility, a "*sense* of the tragic" that can be gained from exposure to very difficult or burdensome (tragic) events, situations, or circumstances. West's choice to highlight this sensibility is motivated by his wish to respond effectively and appropriately to two sorts of human suffering: existential anxiety or dread and social misery and oppression. West leaves no doubt that he sees the reduction of the latter sort of suffering as a central aim of his intellectual mission. So, for example, he attests to an "obsession with modernity and evil, with forms of unjustified suffering and unnecessary social misery in modern times."[15] And, in one interview, he characterizes the "vocation of the intellectual" as "let[ting] suffering speak, let[ting] victims be visible and let[ting] social misery be put on the agenda of those with power."[16]

It is not always entirely clear when West invokes the tragic sense what specific form of agency he has in mind. In a general sense, political agency broadly understood is what seems mostly at stake for him. Possible contexts for political agency include "communities, groups, organizations, institutions, subcultures and networks."[17] Presumably, these contexts could support participation in social movements, community support and outreach programs, litigation, as well as electoral politics. The ways in which the tragic sensibility is supposed to inspire and enable agency are multiple and it will be the main purpose of this chapter to outline these multiple ways. In the case of demoralized and distressed people (in the American context, members of the so-called Black underclass as well as African Americans of the middle class), tragedy is seen by West as a means of fostering the kind of hopefulness that might alleviate despair, forestall self-destructive action, and generate feelings of individual and collective political efficacy. Tragedy also functions, in West's framework, as a means of heightening the appreciation of left intellectuals for the existential dimensions of political and social agency. Understanding better how questions of meaning interact with issues of material redistribution, left intellectuals will better understand forms of agency not fully comprehensible from a purely materialist standpoint. A third function of tragedy suggested by West and considered in this chapter will be tragedy's power to foster a sense of community across class and racial lines through its capacity to convey a sense of marginal people's sufferings to people of (middle class) privilege. The idea here is that tragedy's community-fostering effect can help form the political basis for successfully pursuing a program of progressive political and social reform. In all three contexts (African-American middle- and underclass demoralization, left intellectual narrowness, and middle class indifference), the promotion of a sense of the tragic is intended by West to foster forms of agency compatible with his vision of a progressive democracy in which activist citizens are more sympathetically aware of, and politically responsive to, the burdens of social misery and oppression that selectively afflict their fellow citizens, if not also themselves.

To the extent that a concern with suffering lies at the center of West's self-conception as an intellectual, his preoccupation with notions of the tragic should come as no surprise. After all, literary and performative tragedies as well as theories of the tragic nature of the human condition or of particular events or situations in human affairs invite serious attention to, and systematic reflection on, the nature and meaning of human suffering. Attending to, and reflecting on, the nature and meaning of human suffering through watching or reading tragedies or by contemplating the tragic nature of existence, we expect to feel better able to cope with suffering and empowered to act in ways that may lessen it.

Fashioning a tragic-centered discourse in order to respond to human suffering is not without its pitfalls, however. At one extreme, evocation of the tragic nature of life can lend itself to fatalistic acceptance of a status quo that seems impervious to ameliorative action. At the other extreme, the resort to tragedy can become a means by which individuals or groups seek to escape moral responsibility for acting inappropriately and inflicting avoidable harm on others. Consider, for example, the evolving response of Prime Minister Ariel Sharon (as reported on National Public Radio) to a July 22, 2002, Israeli missile attack on an apartment complex in Gaza which killed the military leader of Hamas and 14 Palestinian civilians, including 11 children.[18] Initially referring to the operation as a "great success," Sharon's spokesperson came eventually to characterize the event as a "terrible tragedy" in an attempt to deflect growing international and American condemnation.

West is aware of the pitfalls of tragic resignation and tragic irresponsibility. One way that he acknowledges their dangers is by giving due notice to C. Wright Mills's rejection of the "'tragic view of life'" as a "political blind alley, as sociologically unreal, and as morally irresponsible." In *The American Evasion of Philosophy*, Mills's work stands as a serious challenge to West's project of incorporating a sense of the tragic into American pragmatism. Of all the figures West considers in that book, Mills is the one who most explicitly and comprehensively addresses the dangers of adopting a tragic point of view. According to Mills, the tragic view lends itself to a kind of "romanticism" which dissipates the impulse to engage in social or political critique by promoting a false sense of community. It is, "a way of saying to oneself: 'We're all in this together, the butcher and the general. . . . ' But 'we' are *not* at all in this together—so far as such decisions as are made [and] so far as bearing the consequences of these decisions are concerned."[19] Mills rejects the "tragic view" for its uses by intellectuals to justify their stance of political resignation, on the one hand, and by corporate and governmental elites to excuse their irresponsible action, on the other.

In a world of big organizations, the lines between powerful decisions and grassroots democratic controls becomes blurred. And tenuous, and seemingly irresponsible actions by individuals at the top are encouraged. . . . The sense of tragedy in the intellectual who watches this scene is a personal reaction to the politics and economics of irresponsibility. Never before have so few men made such fateful decisions for so many people who themselves are so helpless.[20]

West acknowledges that Mills has good reasons to be critical of tragedy; "Mills must hold at arms length the pervasive 'tragic-sense-of-life' perspectives that either foreclose social action or limit it to piecemeal social engineering."[21] Like Mills, he recognizes that an intellectual taste for tragedy or tragic motifs can easily coexist with a mood of political resignation. Such a recognition underpins, for example, West's reaction to Martin Heidegger's tragically mediated response to modernity's crisis of meaning. Explicitly rejecting Heidegger's sense of the tragic for its promotion of a fatalistic view of history that highlights "fate, heritage and destiny," he finds that Heidegger's work inappropriately "dramatizes the past and present as if it were a Greek tragedy with no tools of social analysis to relate cultural work to institutions and structures or antecedent forms and styles."[22] Also like Mills, West recognizes that particular social and political contexts can elicit popular attitudes akin to tragic resignation. So, for example, in a 1994 *Newsweek* editorial summing up the legacy of the 1980s, West criticizes the Reagan-Bush-era assault on the legitimacy of the welfare state for its effect on "confused citizens [who] now oscillate between tragic resignation and vigorous attempts to hold at bay their feelings of impotence and powerlessness."[23]

Aware of the danger of tragic resignation, West nevertheless insists that "the 'tragic' is a polyvalent notion,"[24] that alternative forms of tragic thinking, more supportive of activist, critical-minded, and collective democratic political participation, are available for use by cultural and social critics.

> Tragedy is not a monolithic notion with universal meaning and homogenous usage. Rather it is deployed in different ways by various people in specific circumstances so that it provides varying results. A tragic sense of life is indeed a defensible response to the battered hopes and dreams, the heart-tearing atrocities and brutalities of this century. But this response in no way *necessarily* entails privatistic quietism, cold war accomodationism, academic professionalism, or individual martyrdom.[25]

Consonant with his view that progressive and activist modes of tragic engagement are available, West insists that, "the notion of the 'tragic' is bound to the idea of human agency" and that, therefore, "tragedy can be an impetus rather than an impediment to oppositional activity."[26] These themes were already anticipated in West's first book, *Prophesy Deliverance!* (1982), in which he affirms an Afro-American Christian perspective that contrasts "those who remain objects of history, victims manipulated by evil forces" ("the pitiful") and those who "become subjects of history" ("the tragic").[27]

The general outlines of West's framework for thinking about the problem of human suffering are clear. He sets as the central task of the intellectual the lessening of human suffering. Seeing the promotion of democratic forms of agency as instrumental to that task, he endorses a tragic mode of thinking as an effective means. What has yet to be systematically considered is how West envisions the "tragic" to function. How does having a tragic sense enhance one's capacity to be a responsible agent of history rather than its victim?

West conceptualizes the relationship between tragedy and agency in different ways. The differences depend on the context in which the exercise of agency is, in his judgment, either lacking or defective. Three general contexts of deficient or defective agency seem most relevant to West's resorts to tragedy: mainstream American indifference to the costs of racism and socioeconomic inequality, left intellectuals' neglect of the existential bases of social and political mobilization, and African-American middle class and underclass retreats to privatized modes of despair. In partial response to American indifference to racism and socioeconomic inequality, West attempts to incorporate a sense of the tragic into American pragmatism. In response to leftist intellectual neglect of existential suffering, West attempts to incorporate a sense of the tragic into Marxism. In partial response to African-American despair, West attempts to show how a sense of the tragic, developed within the tradition of African-American Christianity and extended by African-American artists, remains available to endow life with meaning.

African-American Christianity and Tragedy

For many theorists of tragedy or a tragic sense of life, Greek tragedy constitutes an important, if not indispensable, point of intellectual and spiritual access to the subject. In reflecting on the tragic dimensions of human agency, these theorists might refer to characters and scenes from Greek tragedies, cite Sophoclean or Aeschylean or Euripidean verse, or survey theories of the origins and social-political significance of tragedy in the ancient Greek city-states.

To all appearances, Greek tragedy is not a significant point of reference for West's reflections on the tragic. In the few references he makes to Greek tragedy, he is dismissive of it. At times, the problem for West lies with the restriction of Greek tragedy to a subject matter—the deeds and sufferings of aristocrats and heroes—of spiritual relevance only to the upper class. "The Greek had no notion of tragedy as it applied to ordinary people. . . . Tragedy was reserved for the highbrow and upperclass. Only comedy was applicable to ordinary people."[28] Other times, Greek tragedy is problematic because it assumes a cultural coherence in its audience that no longer exists. "[T]he context of Greek tragedy—in which the action of ruling families generates pity and fear in the audience—is a society that shares a collective experience of common metaphysical and social meanings. The context of modern tragedy . . . is a fragmented society with collapsing metaphysical meanings."[29] At still other times, Greek tragedy is "unacceptable" because it fosters an inappropriate mood of aesthetic withdrawal from public affairs; "its mode of closure elevates Fate and its positive form of knowledge remains contemplative."[30] The gist of West's criticisms of Greek tragedy is that it is irrelevant to the struggles and sufferings of ordinary people and does not promise the sort of insights that either motivate or enable people to lessen those sufferings.

West's scattered dismissals of Greek tragedy are not altogether fair. Arguments can be and have been made for the relevance of Greek tragedy to contemporary models of participatory democracy.[31] (Some of those arguments may even have a hearing in West's freshman seminar, "The Tragic, the Comic, and the Political," which includes *Antigone* on its syllabus.)[32] For the purposes of this paper, the plausibility of West's critique is less the issue than the fact that Greek tragedy does not inspire or guide West's attempt to foster human agency through engaging the tragic. Instead, intellectual and spiritual access to the tragic is gained by him through African-American Christianity. "[T]he church taught me the lesson of the cross. The only way to hope, to faith, to love is through the blood. The cross is the symbol of the impossible possibility . . . of holding on to faith, hope, and love in the kind of world in which we live, the kind of world in which blood is in fact always flowing."[33]

The lesson of the cross, particularly the consequences of this lesson for linking tragedy and agency in the American context, takes on a special significance in relation to what West refers to as the "African encounter with the absurd in the United States: an existential situation in which no reasons suffice to make any kind of sense or give any type of meaning to the personal circumstances and collective condition of Afro-Americans."[34] As West recounts it, enslaved Africans and their descendants in British North America faced horrendous living conditions with little or no cultural resources to make sense of their suffering. "During the colonial stage of American culture, Africans were worse than slaves; they were also denuded proto-Americans in search of identity, systematically stripped of their African heritage and effectively and intentionally excluded from American culture and its roots in European modernity."[35] Suffering that cannot be made sense of (suffering that is, in West's word, absurd) fosters despair and hopelessness, states of mind and spirit that are conducive to deficient (e.g., fatalistic resignation) or defective (e.g., suicide) forms of agency. African Americans as a people managed to save themselves from a too debilitating exposure to despair and hopelessness by, "creatively appropriat[ing] a Christian world view . . . and thereby transform[ing] a prevailing absurd situation into a persistent and present *tragic* one, a kind of 'Good Friday' state of existence in which one is seemingly forever on the cross . . . yet sustained by a hope against hope for a potential and possible triumphant state of affairs."[36]

The affinity felt by an oppressed people for a religion that "looks at the world from the perspective of those below" is something entirely to be expected. As West notes, African slaves and their American descendants could, "find historical purpose in the exodus out of slavery and personal meaning in the bold identification of Jesus Christ with the lowly and downtrodden." Additional grounds for African American appropriation of Christianity were to be found in the emphases the Methodist and Baptist churches placed on, "individual experience, equality before God, and institutional autonomy."[37]

Where West strays from conventional accounts of the African appropriation of Protestant Christianity in North America is in his insistence on considering that process under the rubric of the tragic. Sometimes, the tragic perspective is something Africans bring to Christianity; "the black sense of the tragic is very much at the center of black Christianity."[38] Other times, the stress is more on the tragic resources made available by Christianity to Black Americans; "Black Christian eschatology is anchored in the tragic realism of the Old Testament wisdom literature and the proclamation of a coming kingdom."[39] Whatever the direction of influence, what remains most noteworthy in West's account is the centrality of a notion of the tragic in his conception of African-American Christianity. "This creative appropriation, with African styles and forms within a new faith context, made new sense of the circumstances and gave new meaning to the lives of Afro-Americans by promoting a world view in which the problem of evil—the utterly tragic character of life and history—sits at its center."[40]

While Christian themes of redemptive struggle and suffering can be considered under the label of the "tragic," not every theorist of tragedy would hold the promise of Christianity mainly to reside in a sense of the tragic. In fact, many have argued that belief in Christian redemption is incompatible with notions of tragedy. So, for example, Karl Jaspers holds that, "Christian salvation opposes tragic knowledge. The chance of being saved destroys the tragic sense of being trapped without chance of escape."[41] (Of course, arguments for the compatibility of the Christian master narrative with notions of tragedy are also not lacking.)[42]

Even if Christian belief can be characterized in such a way as to be made compatible with notions of the tragic, such notions are not necessary to make the historical point that Protestant Christianity fulfilled African Americans' urgent need to endow an extreme ("absurd") situation with meaning. Why, then, West's insistence on highlighting a "sense of the tragic" in African-American Christianity? It has partly to do with the scope of West's engagement with the Christian tradition, which is not limited merely to offering an historical account of the phenomenon. At issue in his engagement are larger political and existential concerns, ones which find particular expression in a wish to promote forms of agency conducive to African American survival and flourishing. After all, Christian otherworldiness, with its promise of heavenly compensation for earthly suffering, can promote an orientation of fatalistic resignation, of accepting the status quo, no matter how unjust. It is precisely in opposition to such an orientation ("an escapist pie-in-the-sky religion") that West seems intent on identifying an African-American Christian tradition that is activist in spirit and deed. The kind of orientation in this tradition of Christian thought and practice that he highlights is therefore not merely one of "waiting . . . for the Lord to intervene and the Kingdom of God to come." It is one of "aggressive waiting." West is careful to add the qualification that, "this 'waiting' is not of the quietistic sort, but rather encourages action while tempering one's exorbitant expectations."[43]

Whether the African-American Christian orientation is characterized as one of "aggressive waiting" or "revolutionary patience" (another label favored by West), the emphasis seems to be on approaching the social world in such a way that avoids the extremes of passivity and activity. Those extremes are, on the one hand, the kind of visionary religiosity that forecloses political activism ("an escapist pie-in-the-sky religion"), and on the other, a political activism that instrumentalizes religious vision ("a sophisticated political ideology in religious veil"). What West seems to be after is a middle approach between these extremes, one that mediates between their competing demands. In conceptualizing an African-American Christian orientation that achieves an appropriate mediation of vision and action, West interpolates an awareness of the tragic; prophetic African-American Christianity "contains elements of both (religion and political ideology), plus an enduring emphasis on the deeply tragic quality of everyday life of a culturally degraded, politically oppressed, and racially coerced labor force and unique individuals who face the ultimate facts of human existence: death, disease, disappointment, dread, and despair."

The emphasis of African-American Christianity on the tragic dimensions of life "imbues Afro-American thinking with [among other things] the sobriety of tragedy," by which term I take West to be referring to the "tempering" effect which a tragic sense presumably has on "exorbitant expectations."[44] West's linking of tragedy to sobriety is consistent with his concern about fostering democratic agency. If one acts without a discipline founded on a realistic understanding of the structural constraints present at a given historical moment, one's efforts to bring about change are less likely to succeed. The effect of repeated failures of this sort is likely to be discouragement, demoralization, and, ultimately, a lapse into passivity.

A role for tragedy in opening up African-Americans' appreciation for the possibilities of liberating action is further asserted in the contrast West draws in "Subversive Joy and Revolutionary Patience in Black Christianity" between the black Christian conception of the tragic and Greek and modern notions. Acknowledging that Greek and modern notions differ significantly from each other (e.g., while the former assumes a moral order and the meaningfulness of suffering, the latter calls the very possibilities of moral order and meaningful suffering fundamentally into question), West nevertheless emphasizes an effect they share that sets them apart from the notion he identifies with the Afro-American Christian tradition. Greek and modern notions of the tragic offer contemplative rewards only (the pleasure gained in contemplating fate and accepting it as, in Greek tragedy, or debunking it, as in modern)[45] and do not inspire or facilitate ordinary people's engagement in "purposeful struggle, especially communal and collective struggle."[46] By contrast, the black Christian conception of the tragic is held by him to be more conducive to purposeful and collective forms of agency.

> The tragic sense of life in black Christian eschatology views suffering as a stepping-stone to liberation. Yet liberation does not eradicate the suffering in itself. Therefore suffering is understood only as a reality to resist, an actuality to oppose. It can neither be submitted to in order to gain contemplative knowledge nor reified into an object of ironic attention. Rather it is a concrete state of affairs that produces discernible hurt and pain, hence requiring action of some sort. Black Christian eschatology focuses on the praxis of suffering, not a distancing from it.[47]

A link between a tragic sense of life and the propensity to engage in action or praxis is clearly made, although the workings of that link are not detailed. How the tragic sense of black Christianity promotes action seems to have something to do with the kind of access to hurt and pain which that sense affords. The claim is that hurt and pain is made more "concrete," more "discernible," less an object of reflective distancing, when seen through the tragic prism of black Christianity. Presumably, this means that one is given greater access to the particular reality of human suffering; it is this exposure to reality that, in turn, impels ("requir[es]") one to engage in action.[48]

In what is almost certainly a later addendum to the original version of "Subversive Joy and Revolutionary Patience," West concludes his argument by rather abruptly subsuming the tragic sense under the notion of the "tragicomic character of black life." On the one hand and in its "comic" aspect, the tragicomic "is utopian and breeds a defiant dissatisfaction with the present and encourages action." On the other hand and in its "tragic" aspect, the tragicomic "tempers exorbitant expectations."[49] Whether the operative notion is labeled as "tragic" or "tragicomic," the view of the end is the same; a mode of African-American thought and practice that navigates between the extremes of unmotivated passivity (deficient agency) and unreflective activity (defective agency).

For an idea of the challenges facing the African-American community, which the tragic sense, on West's view, is supposed partly to meet, one has only to consider his analyses of the crises of members of the black middle class and underclass in the United States. Members of the black middle class are prone to a state of political passivity because the term on which American society grants them economic success is a psychologically demoralizing and politically demobilizing repression of their sense of self. "They must not be too frank and outspoken and must never fail to flatter and be pleasant in order to lessen white unease and discomfort."[50] Assimilation, the quintessential middle class goal, therefore poses special challenges to African Americans. The achievement of middle class status tends to make them "highly anxiety-ridden, insecure, willing to be co-opted and incorporated into the powers that be."[51] Collectively speaking, this orientation undermines the basis for political solidarity and the possibility of group action for the purpose of transforming American society. Individually speaking, "this suppression of black rage . . . backfires in the end. It reinforces a black obsession with the psychic scars, ontological wounds and existential bruises that tend to reduce the tragic to the pathetic. Instead of exercising agency or engaging in action against the odds, one may wallow in self-pity, acknowledging the sheer absurdity of it all."[52] West's allusion to "tragic" and "pathetic" states is no mere rhetorical flourish; here, as elsewhere in his writings, the loss of the tragic correlates with reduced possibilities of human agency.

If a particular set of responses by middle class African Americans to the conditions of assimilation in American society can stand for the extreme of passivity or deficient agency, a different set of responses by members of the African-American underclass can stand for the opposite extreme of unreflective activity or defective agency. In a 1987 interview, West laments the varieties of self-destructive behaviors afflicting the black underclass: "pervasive drug addiction, pervasive alcoholism, pervasive homicide, and an exponential rise in suicide." For West, these behaviors, which include examples of unreflective action or defective agency (murder and suicide) as well as "overwhelming passivity" or deficient agency (drug addiction and alcoholism), constitute a syndrome of "walking nihilism."[53] (In another context, he calls these behaviors, "tragic forms of expression."[54])

In highlighting the forms of deficient or defective agency that afflict members of the African-American middle class and underclass in the 1980s, West opens himself up to the charge of blaming the victim.[55] It is a charge he has vehemently denied, insisting in one interview that his focus on the problem of nihilism among inner-city African Americans, "in no way excuses the structural and institutional forces that are at work: . . . unemployment . . . the failed educational system . . . consumer culture. . . . [and] the larger racist legacy."[56] For our purposes, the question of causality in West's analysis of community breakdown is not the issue. The issue is the viability of tragedy as a resource for responding to breakdown. The suggestion here is not that West prescribes a sense of the tragic as conveyed by African-American church practice as a cure for inner city ills. The point, rather, is that West attributes a significant role in the flourishing of individuals and communities to cultural influences and one cultural resource available to African Americans in crisis is a tragic sensibility that has a track record of fostering effective modes of individual and collective agency. In this particular instance, the "poten(cy)" of which West is speaking is the power of the African-American church experience to keep individuals from lapsing into a state of fatalism so extreme that addiction or suicide is the result. Here, the relevant form of agency is individual adjustment to extremely burdensome conditions of life. Needless to say, the African-American church experience has demonstrated more political and collective forms of potency, especially during the 1950s and 1960s civil rights movement.

Marxism and Tragedy

This (prophetic pragmatist) sense of the tragic highlights the irreducible predicament of unique individuals who undergo dread, despair, disillusionment, disease and death and the institutional forms of oppression that dehumanize people. Tragic thought is not confined solely to the plight of the individual; it also applies to social experiences of resistance, revolution, and societal reconstruction.[57]

As West makes clear in presenting himself as a proponent of prophetic African-American Christianity, the problem of human suffering constitutes the main impetus of his intellectual praxis and a sense of the tragic constitutes one of his chosen means of response to this problem. Of course, the problem of human suffering can be addressed under rubrics other than the "tragic." So, for example, notions of social justice animate Marxist critiques of the sorts of suffering attributed to capitalist exploitation. By contrast, notions of tragedy have found little, if any, purchase in mainstream Marxist thought. The attitude many Marxists take toward tragedy is generally of the type exemplified by the view of C. Wright Mills (discussed above); tragic views of life are illegitimate and pernicious because they promote fatalism in people whose interests are ignored or abused by status quo political and social powers.[58]

West counts himself a socialist and therefore accepts Marxist critiques of capitalism and endorses social democratic calls for social justice. Unusually for a socialist, however, he believes Marxist thought to be incompletely responsive to the challenge of recognizing and addressing the full extent of human suffering. In particular, he sees a Marxist blind spot when it comes to forms of existential suffering, that is, suffering that results from the consciousness of vulnerability and mortality that individuals feel subjectively. "The structure of identity and subjectivity is important and has often been overlooked by the Marxist tradition."[59] Promotion of a sense of the tragic and Marxist-inspired critique of modern forms of social injustice therefore become twin imperatives of West's intellectual praxis.

In the task of fashioning a comprehensive theoretical response to both the existential and social forms of human suffering, West found an early guide in the Marxist theorist of culture and literature, Georg Lukács, for whom, "the quest for (individual) meaning and the quest for (social and political) freedom are inseparable." Attesting to the claims on his own intellectual praxis of both a "Kierkegaardian" preoccupation "with the meaning of life and the absurdity of the human condition" and a Marxist-mediated "struggle against injustice and institutional and personal forms of evil," West sees "some parallel between [his] own pilgrimage and that of Lukács." Ackowledging the influence of Lukács's *History of Class Consciousness* (1923) on his own early thinking, he notes that Lukács began his intellectual career focused on such subjects as "existential angst, . . . Dostoyevsky, . . . the meaning of life, . . . spiritual sterility."[60] This was the period during which Lukács published *Soul and Forms*; an entire chapter of the work is dedicated to developing a notion of the tragic. With his later turn to politics in the form of Communist Party membership, Lukács added a commitment to political and social freedom to his earlier engagement with questions of existential meaning. Lukács's eventual adoption of "teleological Hegelian Marxism" and his "retrograde Stalinist politics" suggest that his attempt at integrating the search for meaning and the quest for political and social freedom was ultimately unsuccessful. West implicitly faults Lukács for accepting the premature closure on the quest for meaning afforded by Hegel's notion of the "cunning or Reason" as well as for failing to acknowledge the leap backward in the quest for freedom effected under Stalinism.

If Lukács remains, for West, only a partly effective guide in the quest to integrate or balance existential and socialist imperatives of meaning and justice, respectively, Raymond Williams stands as a much more successful pathfinder. Like Lukács, Williams found tragedy a subject on which it was worthwhile to reflect and write; in Williams's case, the result was a book- (not chapter-) length treatment. More importantly for West, the lessons of tragedy seem to have shaped Williams's praxis as a Marxist thinker in ways that they presumably did not in the case of Lukács. West sees the work of Williams, particularly the "masterful yet overlooked book *Modern Tragedy* (1966)," as offering a "tragic revolutionary perspective" consistent with the "praxis of prophetic pragmatism [which] is tragic action and revolutionary intent."[61]

The formulation, tragic revolutionary perspective, is one that might easily be applied to readings of the revolutionary tradition in which the emphasis is placed on the failure of revolutions to fulfill popular aspirations for a more just distribution of social resources or a more responsible and responsive government. So, for example, "revolution as tragedy" is the formulation John Farrell uses to characterize the responses of nineteenth-century English writers and intellectuals to the history of revolutionary action.

> Revolution does not work cautiously. If revolutions have shared any one trait in common, it has been a commitment to totality. The victims of the dramatic dialectical dance are trapped because they try to follow revolution in some of its developments but not in its totality. Their measured sympathy is always at odds with revolution's fury against fine distinctions. As a result, the feeling they know most intimately is the feeling of cultural estrangement. Many writers who faced this situation tried to identify its terrible burdens by invoking the tragic vision.[62]

In this case and others like it, "tragic" becomes a watchword for failure and tragic action is seen as action doomed to fail. The implicit lesson to be drawn from such a perspective is to forego acting with revolutionary intent, to accept the limits on agency imposed by the social and political status quo. From what we have learned of the role of the tragic in West's reading of African-American Christianity, we expect him to view the relationship of tragedy to revolutionary agency very differently. He seeks to foster revolutionary agency, not diminish it, and promotion of a sense of the tragic is one of his means of doing so. (In this regard, an interesting comparison can be drawn between West and Hannah Arendt, who, from her own very different starting point, also saw tragedy as a means of fostering revolutionary agency.)[63]

How revolutions, even failed ones, can promote revolutionary social democratic agency, we learn from West's extensive quotation of a passage from Williams's book, *Modern Tragedy* (1966), in which the "tragic action, in its deepest sense," is seen not as "the confirmation of disorder," but, rather, as a token of the possibility of "experience[ing], comprehen[ding], and resol[ving]" the disorder of a society in crisis. In this context, accepting that action is tragic means both acknowledging "the evil and the suffering" to which an unjust social order can give rise and not permitting that evil and suffering to discourage acts of purposeful and collective struggle and resistance. In allowing us to be receptive to the particular and concrete suffering of others ("to recognize this suffering in a close and immediate experience"), the tragic fosters the kind of solidarity with others that facilitates collective action. "(W) hat we learn in suffering," according to Williams, is not tragic resignation, but "revolution because we acknowledge others as men and any such acknowledgement is the beginning of struggle."[64] This notion that suffering might teach lessons of value to those who struggle for more just and meaningful lives may be what West has in mind when he states that Williams, "understood on a deep level that revolutionary activity was a matter as much of feelings as facts, of imagination as organization, of agency as analysis."[65]

For Williams, the tragic is a way of organizing our perceptions of disorder and suffering, of seeing their larger structural causes and contexts as well as their particular effects on the lives of individuals and communities, in such a way that revolutionary agency is not discouraged in the face of overwhelming odds or painful failures. His understanding of the tragic as a category applicable to the suffering caused by social structures and his understanding of the potential of tragedy to promote robust, progressive forms of human agency constitute some of the bases of West's appreciation for his work. Another basis is William's ability to bring to light forms of resistance and struggle carried out by the dispossessed and downtrodden in even the most apparently unpromising of political times.

Williams recognized the vital role played by community and tradition in generating resistance, struggle, and other forms of individual and collective agency.[66] In an appreciation of Williams's legacy, West singles out his book on tragedy as well as his six novels as markers of "his refusal to sidestep the *existential* issues of what it means to be a left intellectual and activist—issues like death, despair, disillusionment and disempowerment in the face of defeats and setbacks."[67] Williams's recognition of the role of community and tradition in generating individual and collective agency and his attentiveness to existential issues are not unrelated, if we see West's appreciation of Williams in the context of West's larger critique of Marxist thought.

For West, mainstream Marxist thought has traditionally been inattentive to existential issues and this inattention has prevented Marxists (with a few important exceptions) from adequately understanding the role of community-wide, tradition-borne "structures of meaning"[68] in forming or conditioning social and political ideas and practices. So, for example, an analysis singling out modes of production goes only so far in explaining the origins, nature, and longevity of racist discourses and practices in the West. For a more complete picture of how modes of racist agency have evolved and developed, consideration must be given to the "predominant ways in which Western peoples have come to terms with their fears of 'extinction with insignificance,' of existential alienation, isolation and separation in the face of the inevitable end of which they are conscious."[69] Such a consideration might reveal that the characterization of "black people as . . . Other and Alien" has something to do with the ways in which the need for existential reassurance in Western civilization becomes articulated in modern ideologies of racial difference. "The deep human desire for existential belonging and for self esteem . . . the need for and consumption of *existential capital*—results in a profound, even gut-level, commitment to some of the illusions of the present epoch."[70]

As formulated by West, Williams's legacy, more than the legacy of any other culture-sensitive Marxist, demonstrates how attention to notions and uses of the tragic can provide a way both to take seriously people's existential strivings to live decent and meaningful lives and to understand more fully how these strivings find expression in forms of agency that are humane or pernicious, functional or defective. Is the process of understanding better the nature of social and political agency through tragedy a form of agency itself? If it isn't, it is, West suggests, at the very least a precondition for exercising agency in a responsible and appropriate way. "Williams speaks to us today primarily because he best exemplifies what it means for a contemporary intellectual leftist to carve out and sustain, with quiet strength and relentless reflection, a sense of prophetic vocation in a period of pervasive demoralization and marginalization of progressive thinkers and activists."[71]

American Pragmatism and Tragedy

> *The tragic view—of Unamuno or Melville or Faulkner or Morrison or Coltrane—is a much more morally mature view of what it is to be human. The triumphant view of good over evil, which is Manichaean, is sophomoric, childish. It has been dominant in America because our civilization is so spoiled.*[72]

As with African-American prophetic Christianity and Marxism, American pragmatism constitutes a major intellectual source for West's thought. Mirroring his engagement with these other sources, West's engagement with pragmatism is significantly conditioned by a notion of the indispensability of a tragic sensibility for fostering participatory and inclusive modes of democratic agency. While references to tragedy or a tragic sense are relatively limited in his major work on African-American prophetic Christianity (restricted, for the most part, to a couple of pages of text and a long footnote in *Prophesy Deliverance!*) and are mostly oblique in his consideration of Marxist theory (except when the focus is on Raymond Williams), a notion of the tragic and an argument about its absence explicitly frame West's most important work on pragmatist thought, *The American Evasion of Philosophy: A Genealogy of Pragmatism* (1989).

In *American Evasion*, assessments of American pragmatist thinkers importantly hinge on whether and to what extent they can be seen by West to have mediated their cultural and social analyses through a tragic sensibility. By this measure, Emerson, the great precursor of American pragmatists, and pioneering pragmatist thinkers, Charles Sanders Peirce, William James, and John Dewey fall short. The intellectual legacy of Emerson and the founding generation remains incomplete until major twentieth-century developments in world politics—the rise of fascism and Stalinism, Third World de-colonization, the emergence of the United States as global superpower—call forth appropriately tragic modes of theoretical response in a new generation of pragmatists. "A deep sense of tragedy and irony creeps into American pragmatism, a sense alien to Emerson, Peirce, James, and Dewey. American pragmatism, like America itself, reaches maturity."[73]

While major aspects of West's book—for example, the claim that American pragmatist thought was significantly enabled by the life and work of Emerson or the choice of whom to place in the roster of pragmatism—have been contested,[74] the only aspect to be taken up here is West's claim that the American pragmatist tradition suffers from a major deficit, which consists of American pragmatist thinkers' failure to incorporate a tragic sensibility in their intellectual praxis and thereby adequately to "keep track of social misery."[75]

The problem starts with Emerson, whose robust faith in human powers, provocative questioning of accepted verities, and affirmation of the dignity of individual human personality crystallized into an "optimistic theodicy" that provided neither the analytical resources nor the motivational rhetoric to respond adequately to forms of human suffering which resulted from oppressive social structures. Aware of the serious limits placed by economic and racial inequalities on "human will and personality," Emerson nevertheless, "did not move toward a tragic vision. Rather he deepened his mysticism, increased his faith in the nature of things, and adjusted himself (though never fully) to the expanding world dominance of the 'imperial Saxon race.'" Emerson's optimistic theodicy, "made it difficult for him and for subsequent pragmatists to maintain a delicate balance between excessive optimism and exorbitant pessimism regarding human capacities."[76]

According to West's account, several promising starts toward formulating a pragmatic theory of the tragic were made in the mid-twentieth century against the backdrop of economic depression, world wars, and superpower rivalry. These traumatic events accelerated trends in the U.S. economy (corporate industrialism) and government (bureaucratic regulation) that placed increasing pressure on the Emersonian ethos of self-making. "Pervasive in (the) writings of (mid-century intellectuals Sidney Hook, Lionel Trilling, Reinhold Niebuhr, C. Wright Mills, and W. E. B. Du Bois) are a sense of the tragic, a need for irony, a recognition of limits, and constraints and a stress on paradox, ambiguity, and difficulty." Ultimately, however, none of these intellectuals fulfill their initial tragic promise. As noted earlier, Mills rejects political or social notions of tragedy as convenient excuses for intellectuals to abdicate their role as political and social critics. Though Trilling, "wanted to guide the (intellectual class) away from the simplicities of the left and infuse cold war and corporate liberalism with a sense of the tragic," he eventually "concluded that even the most attractive tragic vision can have neither redemptive nor ameliorative consequences acceptable to his kind of liberalism. [T]he very assertion of the will, even engendered by a tragic vision, could not but be utopian, antinomian, or anarchic in modern times."[77]

Hook, who explicitly set himself the task of theorizing the tragic dimensions of political and social life, does, "maintain the desirable balance between excessive optimism and exorbitant pessimism," but only in his early work. In the end, his tragic view comes to justify an unqualified defense of U.S. corporate liberalism against the greater evil of Soviet Communism, leading him to lose track of the social misery generated by capitalism and racism at home. Similarly, Niebuhr, who "held the most complex view of the 'tragic' in the progressive tradition," eventually adopted a cold war liberalism that reflected a, "growing complacency toward injustice at home."[78]

The case of Du Bois, as presented by West, raises an interesting question. Given the fact that Du Bois is the only African American considered by West in his study of American pragmatists and the only one who spent a significant time living in the Jim Crow South, does his experience of racial difference and oppression lead him to configure the tragic in a way that meets West's standard? As it turns out, even as Du Bois shows himself to be much more sensitive than his fellow mid-century intellectuals to the suffering of African Americans in a white supremacist and corporate capitalist social system, he falls short of West's standard. As we'll see, the problem lies in the limited degree of access to African-American suffering that Du Bois allowed himself. A sign of that limitation is a sense of the tragic that lacks adequate depth because it holds the particularity and concreteness of pain and suffering too much at bay.

In placing race at the center of his analysis of the nature and extent of injustice and misery in the United States, Du Bois sets himself apart, in West's survey, from pragmatist thinkers who demonstrated neither the will nor the capacity to confront one of the great, "usually overlooked costs concealed by American prosperity." Du Bois's achievement in this regard highlights the sad fact that, "although none of the pragmatists were fervent racists themselves . . . not one viewed racism as contributing greatly to the impediments for both individuality and democracy." Although not subject to the kind of "blindnesses and silences in American pragmatist reflections on individuality and democracy" when it came to the issue of race, Du Bois's understanding of, and access to, the suffering of African Americans was nevertheless limited by a defect he shared with his fellow mid-century intellectuals: a middle class intellectual paternalism. "All five figures . . . display varying degrees of suspicion of working- and lower-class people with limited education."[79] The basis of this suspicion is a view prevalent among those who achieve intellectual mastery, vocational aptitude, and social status through higher education; that social criticism is the exclusive purview of an educated middle class elite. To the extent that Du Bois shared this attitude of educated middle class paternalism, he was unable "to immerse himself in black everyday life [which] precluded his access to the distinctive black tragicomic sense and black encounter with the absurd. He certainly saw, analyzed and empathized with black sadness, sorrow, and suffering. But he didn't feel it in his bones deeply enough."[80]

For West, Du Bois's tendency to remain overly detached from the "tragedy of life and the absurdity of existence" was notably exemplified in his response to the death of his eighteen-month-old son from diphtheria. "What is most revealing in this most poignant of moments is Du Bois's refusal to linger with the sheer tragedy of his son's death (a natural, not a social, evil)—without casting his son as an emblem of the race or a symbol of black deliverance to come."[81] Here, ideological generalization becomes an inappropriate, if understandable, means for holding off, to an extent, the suffering and pain of an intensely particular and concrete loss. In the case of the other mid-century intellectuals, this process of distancing oneself from the pain and suffering of members of the working- and lower classes by means of middle class stereotyping of the "masses" as ignorant and potentially unruly (if also pitiable) was made even easier by lack of experience with the life conditions of working- and lower-class African Americans.

Feeling the sadness, sorrow, and suffering of people at the bottom or on the margins of American society is what the tragic sense promises to American pragmatist thinkers. This promise is held out by West also to members of the American middle class, whose "Teflon existence, [of] hav[ing] no sense of the ragged structures of necessity, not being able to eat, not having shelter, not having health care," has been shared, if not also indirectly endorsed, by most pragmatist thinkers.[82] West's notion of prophetic pragmatism is premised on bringing that sadness, sorrow, and suffering more effectively to bear on the pragmatist project of theorizing and promoting the conditions necessary for the flourishing of individuality and democracy. Given the degree of illegitimate suffering permitted by the present beneficiaries of the U.S. social order, a tragically infused pragmatism is bound to be a pragmatism of activism, of struggle, and of opposition to the status quo. "Human struggle sits at the center of prophetic pragmatism. . . . It calls for utopian energies and tragic actions, energies and actions that yield permanent and perennial revolutionary, rebellious, and reformist strategies that oppose the status quos of our day."[83] In this project, the role of the tragic is not only to awaken the privileged to the suffering of the marginalized but also to provide a means for imagining the pain of others more concretely. In facilitating access to universally experienced existential forms of human suffering, tragedy makes it more possible for the privileged to share a sense of suffering with the deprived. If West is to be believed, such access to the suffering of the marginalized can form an important basis on which to build the sort of "principled transracial and inter-racial coalition and alliance" necessary to "change . . . the situation of poor people and especially poor people of color."[84]

This chapter has systematically considered Cornel West's endorsements of, and engagements with, notions of tragedy, analyzing, in particular, his claim that a tragic sensibility can foster participatory and inclusive forms of individual and collective agency. Readers of West's work who have previously taken up these questions have mostly concluded that his use of the tragic is highly questionable. For example, in a review of *The American Evasion of Philosophy* (1989), Lorenzo Simpson argues that, "the conception of evil and of the tragic that West commends to us . . . may well enervate the struggle for more democratic arrangements unless it is mediated by what West himself admits to being an unconvincing religious appeal."[85] Another reviewer of the book, Elizabeth Spelman, suggests that the notion of the tragic as applied by West to African American experiences of slavery and segregation can be taken too easily to absolve racist perpetrators of moral responsibility for their acts. "Thinking of North American racism as 'tragic' tends to suggest a picture of white America as basically good and well-intentioned."[86] While the former critic is concerned that tragedy will give way to a politically disabling resignation (or deficient agency, one might say), the latter resists the reconciliatory promise that appeals to tragedy invoke because these appeals may give license to forms of defective agency. To the extent that these criticisms are restricted to consideration of West's *American Evasion*, they can only give a partial picture of the complexity of West's engagement with the tragic. That engagement is complex, I have argued, partly because West invokes the tragic in various theoretical contexts—American pragmatism, African-American Christianity, Marxist thought—in order to respond to different situations in which the exercise of political agency is, in his judgment, either lacking or defective.

Three general situations of deficient or defective agency seem most relevant to West's resort to tragedy: African-American middle class and underclass retreats to privatized modes of despair, left intellectuals' neglect of the existential bases of social and political mobilization, and mainstream Americans' indifference to the costs of racism and socioeconomic inequality. In partial response to African-American despair, West attempts to show how a sense of the tragic, developed within the tradition of African-American Christianity, remains available to endow life with meaning and to generate a sense of personal and collective efficacy. In response to leftist intellectual neglect of existential suffering, West attempts to incorporate a sense of the tragic into Marxism. In partial response to American indifference to racism and socioeconomic inequality, West attempts to incorporate a sense of the tragic into American pragmatism and suggest a resource for fostering political solidarity across racial lines.

Recognition of the tripartite pattern of West's many endorsements of a tragic sensibility reveals a significant dynamic within West's theoretical project that is left relatively undeveloped by him and unnoticed by those of his readers who have considered the tragic dimensions of his thought. Premised on a distinction between existential and social forms of suffering, West's promotion of a tragic sense is primarily aimed at reduction of the latter sort of suffering. Close consideration of West's argument about the tragic deficiency of Marxist thought, in particular, reveals the working of a notion of the importance of managing existential suffering for the purpose of individually mustering and collectively aggregating the political will to reduce levels of social misery and oppression.

Existential burdens—what West variously refers to as "the dark shadows of death, dread and despair," "depths of despair, layers of dread, encounters with the sheer absurdity of the human condition"[87]—afflict human beings universally, though variably. By contrast, the burdens of social oppression and misery appear much more unevenly distributed. (West alludes to this uneven distribution when he says that he is "fundmantally [concerned] with wrestling with the problem of evil in modernity, especially as it relates to people of African descent in particular. And all human beings catch hell in general, but it has very much to do with the dark side, the underside of the human predicament.")[88]

It is on the opening up of access to universally experienced existential forms of suffering that West seems mostly to stake the tragic sensibility's promise of solidarity. If the privileged will not or can not feel the social misery and oppression of their fellow citizens, they might at least feel some sense of existential dread and this dread can form the basis of a shared sense of suffering with the deprived. This reliance on the bridging potential of existential suffering makes particular sense in a national context in which notions of social justice have apparently had relatively little purchase on the consciousness of the socially privileged. This is especially so in the United States because notions of racial difference and forms of racial division have fundamentally structured relations between upper and lower classes and among groups within the same class.

Fostering solidarity between people who are divided by class structure and/or racial identification is only one aspect of the promise West attributes to the tragic.

After all, as a self-identified pragmatist, West commits himself to a vision of democratic solidarity *and* individuality. Just as the awakening of feelings of solidarity is important for social progress, on this view, so also is the promotion of individuality. Effective democratic movements require individual members who are capable of supporting each other and a movement's goals without lapsing into a state of demoralization and fatalistic retreat into private life when the chips are down or sliding into a state of uncritical deference and self-congratulatory smugness when success seems near at hand. So, for example, in his analysis of African-American prophetic Christianity, West emphasizes the importance of steering a middle course between the extremes of uncritical action and uncommitted passivity. Considered against the backdrop of his discussion of Marxism's "tragic" neglect of the importance of "existential capital," West's portrayal of the tragic sensibility as an effective guide for navigating this middle course makes sense. In African-American Christianity's activation and channeling of that existential dread or anxiety human beings feel as they contemplate the fundamental fragility (and inevitable end) of individual life, West sees one important means by which African-American individualities have been fostered and maintained, husbanded for collective deployment during those rare moments in American history when political and social transformation is possible through group action.

Taken in isolation, West's affirmation of the tragic aspects of African-American church thought and practice or his emphasis on the absence of the tragic in American pragmatism may well seem theoretically anemic. A survey of West's many references to the tragic that does not adequately differentiate between them, leaves the impression that West is concerned more with exhorting his listeners or readers to act politically through invocation of emotionally loaded terms ("tragic," "tragedy") than with persuading his listeners or readers of the political significance of a tragic sensibility through explication of that sensibility's underlying psychological or political dynamic. As it is, the level of explication of this dynamic in West's work is inadequate. So, for example, West's off-handed characterization of the death of Du Bois's 18-month-old son from diphtheria as a "natural, not a social, evil"[89] invites questions about how to draw the line between existential and social forms of suffering. There is, in addition, West's occasional tendency to offer assessments of the nature and worth of a work, a genre of works, or a tradition of thought that are sweeping (as, for example, when he dismisses Greek tragedy *in toto* as irrelevant to democratic political thought) or unsupported (as, for example, when he implicitly ranks the worth of the tragic vision of Chekhov and Kafka above that of Du Bois without specifying his ranking criteria).[90]

While serious, the weaknesses listed above are by no means disabling. And, to be fair, West has conceded that his tragic approach is undertheorized.[91] It nevertheless bears noting that West's resorts to tragedy and "the tragic" are more deliberate and systematic than the scattered and mostly offhanded references to tragedy, catharsis, and Greek drama to be found in Havel's speeches, letters, and political writings, not to mention the directors, critics, and historians of Italian neorealist film.

Notwithstanding these differences, West's enlistment of tragedy for democratic purposes shares a fundamental aspect with both Czech and Italian participants in the politics of tragedy. Far from being an excuse for fatalistic withdrawal from public life, their resorts to tragedy serve the purpose of encouraging broad democratic agency. It was precisely in this activist spirit of tragedy that West, contemplating in 1991 the painful disjunction between the democratic gains manifested in the grassroots activism of the 1950s and 1960s, on the one hand, and the political retrenchment of the Reagan years when government was maligned as the problem and the egalitarian ethos of previous decades was denigrated in favor of "up-by-the-bootstraps" individualism, on the other, saw tragedy as a vital resource. "A sense of the tragic is an attempt to keep alive some sense of possibility. Some sense of hope. Some sense of agency. Some sense of resistance in a moment of defeat and disillusionment and a moment of discouragement."[92]

SECTION II

Tragedy and Political Solidarity

CHAPTER 5

Nelson Mandela: Tragedy in a Divided South Africa

[In retirement, I will] do all the things I've missed: be with my children and grandchildren and with my family; the ability to sit down and read what I would like to read. You know, in prison—although it was a tragedy to spend twenty-seven years in prison—one of the advantages was the ability to sit down and think. This is one of the things I miss most.

Nelson Mandela[1]

In the political transformation that South Africans experienced in the decade after his February 10, 1990, release, Nelson Mandela played an indispensable role. Over his 27-year incarceration, Mandela became one of the foremost rallying symbols of the liberation struggle in South Africa. He was instrumental during the late 1980s in helping the leaders of the South African apartheid regime to appreciate the advantages of pursuing a negotiated settlement with their opponents. Once free, Mandela was a central player in the negotiations that led the regime finally to accept elections on the basis of the principle of one person, one vote. After his election in 1994 as the first African President of the Republic of South Africa, Mandela promoted the reconciliation of previously warring factions through his leadership of a government of national unity and through his resort to several symbolic public gestures.[2] With his decision to serve only one term and his subsequent retirement from high state and party offices, Mandela has earned further praise both for seeking to end South Africa's dependence on his charismatic leadership and for setting an example of the orderly, constitutional transfer of power.[3]

It should come as no surprise that Mandela's life, so variable in its private fortunes and so significant in its public consequences, has become the subject of many biographies. In several of these biographies, Mandela's life is explicitly characterized in terms of tragedy. Mandela's reference to the "tragedy" of "spending twenty seven years in prison" concludes the final chapter of Martin Meredith's 1997 biography. In the prologue of his 1999 authorized biography, Anthony Sampson quotes the newly elected Mandela reflecting about the "tragedy" of his past incarceration in similar terms: "It was a tragedy to lose the best days of your life, but you learned a lot. You had time to think—to stand away from yourself, to look at yourself from a distance, to see the contradictions in yourself."[4]

In the discourses generated by Mandela and others in response to the conditions of his life and work, "tragedy" finds use in a variety of contexts, both political and nonpolitical, theoretical and ordinary. Surveying these uses, this chapter will reveal how they can be seen to reflect, if not also to promote, the reconciliatory impulses of Mandela's politics through their promotion of a sense of community based on shared suffering. Mandela's case reveals how these ordinary uses can often be provoked in response to the life and work of notable individuals whose strivings and sufferings become representative of the strivings and sufferings of a community. To be sure, attempts at reconciliation and solidarity evoked through the language of tragedy do not always work, as the dispute between McNamara and his North Vietnamese interlocutors (Chapter One) revealed. Some cases that draw the label of tragedy are just too contentious, while others are too personal. However fragile and limited, the solidarity that is evoked in both tragic theories and colloquial discourse is nevertheless significant enough to merit closer attention.

Examination of Mandela's politics of tragedy reveals a political actor whose uses of tragedy are not as deliberate and systematic as Cornel West's. Nor are Mandela's uses grounded in the sort of professional knowledge of theater possessed by Václav Havel. Drawing upon his long experience as a political activist and leader as well as a subtle appreciation of the theatrical dimensions of political action, Mandela nevertheless managed to enlist the language of tragedy and drama in the service both of his political goal of democratic transformation and of his need to make sense of his own suffering and the suffering of his fellow South Africans.

Further differentiating Mandela's politics of tragedy from versions of the politics of tragedy examined in the previous chapters of this book is the primary place given in it to the goal of solidarity. While the urgent need for promoting, organizing, and coordinating political agency on the part of those who were fighting for a democratic South Africa was always present to Mandela, his uses of "tragedy," and his articulation of political challenges in terms of the dynamics of theater or drama seem primarily to be responses to the suffering and loss generated by the profound cleavages of South African society. The foremost goal was to bring contending factions together in a democratic South Africa. Such an orientation makes sense given the political challenge Mandela and the ANC faced in the last decade or so of the twentieth century: finding a democratic accommodation with a minority regime whose repressive forces remained powerful enough both to ward off an ANC military victory and to brutalize a restive majority population indefinitely. The language of tragedy and drama thus became one of Mandela's rhetorical resources as he sought to foster reconciliation between warring factions (minority regime/ANC, ANC/Inkatha) and build up the level of national solidarity necessary for the achievement of what Philippe-Joseph Salazar has called an "African Athens," a "democracy won at the negotiating table and also won every day in public deliberation."[5]

The Politics of Tragedy in Ordinary Language

Whether serving to close or to introduce the story of Mandela's life, the above-mentioned references to tragedy are deployed by his biographers to convey more or less the same point: Mandela's sense of having gained something worthwhile from his long imprisonment, even if, as a result of that imprisonment he had experienced extreme forms of deprivation and loss. As will become clear from a more systematic survey of Mandela's usage, not all tragic losses can be compensated or offset. Some of the forms of loss to which Mandela applies the label "tragedy" are too severe. There are consistent patterns in the usage, however. For example, "tragedy" and related terms are applied consistently to events, conditions, or situations resulting in suffering and loss that violate a fundamental sense of normalcy. In most instances, those violations which draw the label "tragedy" or "tragic" consist of the premature loss of family members or friends. The political dimensions of these ordinary uses are not immediately apparent until one considers the ways others use "tragedy" and related terms in response to Mandela's life and work. In reflecting on the nature and quality of his response to suffering and loss, Mandela's interlocutors and biographers reach for the language of tragedy and, in doing so, contribute to his political project of reconciliation.

Among the forms of deprivation and loss that apparently counted for Mandela as a significant part of the "tragedy" of his long imprisonment was, being deprived of contact with his family. In his autobiography, Mandela reflects several times on the "inhumane" separations which the apartheid regime imposed on African families. More than once, he chooses explicitly to characterize these separations as tragic. So, for example, the Population Registration Act of 1950, which authorized state officials to classify individuals according to arbitrary racial characteristics, "often resulted in tragic cases where members of the same family were classified differently, all depending on whether one child had a lighter or darker complexion."[6] Another, more personal, case of family separation that Mandela explicitly characterized as tragic was his decision to separate from his wife, Winnie, after he was released from prison. "It was a decision which was in fact tragic. But it had to be taken and I have taken it and I think it was the correct decision to make."[7] Mandela cast the breakup of his marriage against the backdrop of "the pressures of our shared commitment to the African National Congress and the struggle to end apartheid," which made it impossible "to enjoy a normal family life." The neglect of family responsibilities that followed upon his acceptance of the duties of fighting for freedom, regardless of personal cost, remained Mandela's "greatest regret, and the most painful aspect of the choice (he) made."[8]

The term "tragic" had also earlier served Winnie Mandela in characterizing a painful family split. Reflecting on her decision to break with her father over his support of the apartheid regime's Bantu authorities, she concluded that "it was tragic that politically my father and I did not see eye to eye. It left terrible scars in my heart."[9] Mandela family friend and anti-apartheid activist Helen Joseph similarly characterizes the forced separation of family members as a "tragedy." Reflecting on the restrictions that kept Zindzi and Zeni Mandela from having a normal relationship with their father, she writes:

> Zindzi said he still looked young and strong. She had "seen him walk once" and he had walked "like a young man." He must inevitably have seemed a stranger that first meeting, trying to capture some of the lost moments of their childhood, the family life that neither he nor they had ever known, Zindzi had seen her father "walk once"—for me that sums up the searing tragedy which miraculously has not destroyed this family.[10]

In these tragic situations, the state figures significantly either as the agent whose actions (e.g., policies of residential apartheid, incarceration of activists) split families up directly or as the cause of individuals choosing a life of political activism and taking on commitments that supersede claims based on family ties.

The unexpected deaths of family members or friends are also tragedies for Mandela. In recalling the time in 1969 that he was notified of the death of his twenty-five-year-old son, Thembi, in a car accident, Mandela rhetorically asks, "What can one say about such a tragedy?"[11] (It would also occur to Mandela's long-time friend and fellow political prisoner, Walter Sisulu, to refer to this event as a "tragedy" in the foreword he contributed to the 1990 pictorial story of Mandela's role in the anti-apartheid movement, *Mandela: Echoes of an Era*, by Alf Kumalo and Eskia Mphalehle: "But the narrative between the covers of this book, pictorial and verbal, is a record not only of this public figure and his political struggle, but also of a man who experienced personal tragedy, including the death of a son.")[12] Similarly, Mandela notes that "the one tragic note" of a December 1975 visit by his wife, Winnie, and their daughter, Zindzi, was news of the death of Bram Fischer, an old friend and political comrade.[13] (471) In 1985, after having been notified of the death of his sister-in-law, Niki, Mandela wrote a letter to his wife in which he described Niki's death as a "grievous blow, very difficult to bear" and expressed the wish that he "could be there . . . . and remind [her] of all the good things with which [her] name is linked and help [her] to forget about the tragedies which have repeatedly overtaken the family."[14] In response to news of the accidental death of the son of Chief Warrant Officer James Gregory, the jailer who, for many years, personally oversaw the conditions of Mandela's incarceration, Mandela was led to write, "I am deeply shocked to hear of the tragic death of your beloved son, Brent."[15]

In these last instances, tragedies happen in the form of unexpected and fatal losses of family members or close friends caused by accident or other unforeseen circumstances. Additionally, and in contrast to Mandela's references to the "tragedy" of his long imprisonment found in the biographies of Sampson and Meredith, these latter references do not refer to events, conditions, or circumstances brought about primarily by agents or policies of the state or politically active citizens. Furthermore, they are not accompanied by any explicit claim that a tragic loss can promise compensatory rewards or benefits. Thus, the death of Mandela's son "left a hole in my heart that can never be filled."[16] And the only consolation he can offer Winnie in the aftermath of her sister's death is the thought that her good name might cause her to forget the pain of her loss.

In three of the uses of "tragedy" described above, the term marks a sense of loss felt by (or attributed to) fathers in response to the accidental deaths of their adult sons. Tellingly, Mandela does not characterize his mother's death (at an advanced age) as tragic. During her last visit to Robben Island in 1968, he noticed that she "had lost a great deal of weight" and that "her face appeared haggard." He "feared that it would be the last time [he] would ever see her."[17] And although his pain at losing his mother was intensified by the prison authorities' refusing his request to attend her funeral, Mandela's reflections are mostly focused on the question of whether his political commitments led him unjustly to neglect his mother's needs in old age. The unsurprising difference between Mandela's characterizations of these two personal losses most likely had to do with his expectation of outliving his parents and of being outlived by his children. Typically, a parent's loss of a child is more grievous than an adult's loss of an elderly parent; this is so, one might argue, because of a sense that the normal or natural order of things has been violated or disrupted.[18]

Evidence that violations of order or normalcy may be at play in Mandela's application of the term "tragedy" is to be found in his account of a trip he happened to make to Cape Town during his years as a lawyer and ANC activist. While on a walk, he "noticed a white woman in a gutter . . . poor and apparently homeless." Mandela writes that, "I was used to seeing black beggars on the street, and it startled me to see a white one. While I normally did not give to African beggars, I felt the urge to give this woman money." Mandela draws a lesson from the feeling of pity evoked in him by the sight of a poor white:

> I realized the tricks that apartheid plays on one, for the everyday travails that afflict Africans are accepted as a matter of course, while my heart immediately went out to this bedraggled white woman. In South Africa, to be poor and black was normal, to be poor and white was a tragedy.[19]

In the contrast he draws between his typical behavior in the face of homeless Africans and his initial response to a homeless white woman, Mandela counterposes human suffering that is expected and therefore (inappropriately) considered normal and human suffering that violates normal expectations. In this respect, the tragedy of being white and poor in apartheid South Africa is akin to the tragedies of a son's fatal auto accident or the unexpected onset and culmination of a close friend's fatal sickness.

Considerations of normalcy and order also apparently figure in Mandela's evolving response (as reported by Chief Warrant Officer Gregory) to a fatal series of floods. Toward the end of his period of imprisonment, Mandela was secretly permitted to take day trips to the countryside. One of those trips, at Mandela's request, was to

Laingsburg, a small town a few hours drive out of Cape Town. Explaining the reason for his interest, Mandela observes, "I was intrigued by the flash floods which killed so many people in the area some years ago. I'm not sure why the place stayed in my mind, but I always felt I'd like to see it, to try to understand how such a tragedy occurred." After arriving at the site and examining the water marks which reached twelve feet high on some of the town's structures, Mandela concludes, "It's astonishing; it just shows you the might of God. This is a terrible thing, a natural disaster where man cannot be blamed."[20] In his on-site response, use of the adjectival modifier "natural" precludes use of the word "tragedy." The formulation "natural *tragedy*" just wouldn't sound right. The initial resort to "tragedy" seems connected to Mandela's sense of the immense scale of human loss. In his later reflection, responsibility for the heavy loss of lives and property is assigned to an impersonal force working according to a larger-than-human purpose, and the event becomes a "natural *disaster.*"

It is worth considering for a moment whether the survivors of the flash floods at Laingsbourg, who lost loved ones, acquaintances, and livelihoods, would have subscribed to Mandela's linguistic choice. According to the reasoning outlined above, they would not call it a tragedy if they could fit their experience of loss into a divine plan or logic, a theodicy, say. Would Mandela have been less inclined to conclude that some kind of order or rationale underlay the fatal events at Laingsbourg, an order or rationale according to which a divine power occasionally demonstrates its "might," if he had lost a family member or close friend there? After all, the auto accident that claimed his son's life could analogously have been viewed as a sign of divine purpose, but Mandela chose not to view it this way; presumably this loss was too personal, too grievous. This example of Mandela's reasoning about how to characterize the episode of severe loss at Laingsbourg, fits the pattern of his usage. To the extent that he can understand an episode of loss to be in accord with a larger order or framework of purpose or meaning (for example, the death of his mother in her old age), his tendency is to resort to terms other than tragedy. Losses that violate a fundamental sense of order or a basic framework of meaning are tragedies.

In respect to the notion of tragedy's link to unexpected loss, Mandela's usage is consistent with the uses made of "tragedy" and its cognate "tragic" by those who have chosen to write about Mandela. In the 1986 edition of her book, *Nelson Mandela: The Man and the Movement*, Mary Benson includes a foreword by Anglican Archbishop of South Africa Desmond Tutu, in which the churchman asks why Mandela remains a hero after so many years of incarceration and official bans on the publication of his words or image. "Nelson Mandela is the power that he is because he is a great man— about that there can be no doubt. Our tragedy is that he has not been around to help douse the flames that are destroying our beautiful country."[21] In this instance, South Africans suffer from being deprived of someone whose leadership could save a nation from ongoing processes of destruction. The back cover copy of another of Benson's books on Mandela concludes with the claim that Mandela's release from prison "is widely regarded as the essential first step toward averting catastrophe in that tragic land."[22] In the body of this latter book, Benson cites a similar characterization of South Africa offered by the conservative *Sunday Telegraph* in a 1961 editorial published in anticipation of a judge's decision whether to impose the death penalty on Mandela and his co-defendants after their guilty verdicts in the Rivonia trial: "The essence of the South African tragedy is that men like Mandela find themselves on the wrong side of the law."[23]

Introducing an edition of Mandela's writings and speeches, E. S . Reddy suggests that a full understanding of Mandela's significance cannot be achieved without placing him in the context of, "the tragedy of South Africa," which has been "that the European minority was able to appropriate the land and the resources of the country and institute an inhuman system of racist domination to exploit, humiliate, and oppress the great majority of the people."[24] In this formulation, the tragedy inheres in the deprivation of resources, rights, and human dignity suffered by members of a nation's majority at the hands of a minority. As with the descriptions of accidental or premature loss or natural catastrophe analyzed above, these characterizations of the deprivation and suffering of South Africa or the South African majority as tragedies seem to depend on a sense that a situation or set of circumstances is out of order (a "great man" kept in prison, a minority depriving a majority of fundamental rights, "men like Mandela on the wrong side of the law") and that the resultant suffering is undeserved (a "beautiful country" in "flames"). It is also worth noting that, in these examples, Mandela's tragedy becomes a symbol for a larger, collective tragedy: the tragedy of South Africa.

The exemplary significance of a tragic individual is evoked as well in *Mandela: Naissance d'un destin* by Jean Guilloineau. The second of the book's two epigrams consists of an excerpt of Sophocles's verse from the tragedy, *Antigone*, which Guilloineau notes had already found use in Mandela's autobiography:

> Of course you cannot know a man completely, his character, his principles, sense of judgment, not till he's shown his colors, ruling the people, making laws. Experience, there's the test.[25]

In Mandela's autobiography, the quote from Sophocles is occasioned by Mandela's recollection of his "one memorable role" in the theatrical productions put on by the Robben Island prisoners' drama society. From his experience performing the role of Creon in *Antigone*,[26] Mandela writes, he drew the important lesson that political leaders must beware of letting their sense of right degenerate into an attitude of self righteousness: "[Creon's] inflexibility and blindness ill become a leader, for a leader must temper justice with mercy."[27]

Guilloineau's epigrammatic use of Sophocles' verse evokes the various literary representations and dramatic enactments of human suffering and loss that have come to be categorized as "tragedies" in English language use. A sense of tragedy as

theatrical drama operates together with a notion of tragedy as the occasion of collective suffering and violative loss in Ronald Harwood's *Mandela*, a book that interpolates excerpts of a movie screenplay in a biographical narrative:

> There is no final act in the saga of Nelson and Winnie Mandela. While he remains
> in prison and the present system of government of his country continues, they are
> trapped in the circumstances of a tragic history, participants in an unfolding
> drama, symbolic figures in a struggle for human dignity.[28]

Harwood concludes his book with a statement Mandela composed in response to
P.W. Botha's January 31, 1985, offer to release him on the condition that he renounce
violence. The statement includes the prefatory remarks spoken by Mandela's daughter, Zindzi, at a mass meeting in Soweto's Jabulani Stadium: "My father and his com-
rades at Pollsmoor Prison send their greetings to you, the freedom-loving people of
this, our tragic land."[29]

The Politics of Tragedy in Theory

If the multiplicity of ways in which Nelson Mandela's life is framed by, as, or with
tragedy is noteworthy, it is not because any of these attempts at applying tragic
frameworks are unusual or inappropriate. After all, situations or circumstances or
episodes of extreme and unexpected loss or deprivation do fall under the rubric of
tragedy as that term is commonly used. So, for example, air and car crashes, ship col-
lisions and sinkings, terrorist bombings, shooting sprees, and other unexpected
events have commonly been referred to as tragedies by news reporters, journalists,
public officials, and others who are asked to comment on or reflect upon what
has happened. In these and other instances, "tragedy," and its cognate, "tragic," seem
to serve as markers for the suffering produced by extreme and violative loss or deprivation. Similarly, it is common to find citations of Greek tragedy and references
to other literary tragedies used to reflect on lives afflicted by terrible misfortune.
In short, characterizations of Nelson Mandela's life and of South Africa's condition
of government repression and civil unrest in terms of any of the various and related
meanings of tragedy considered above seem mostly ordinary and not especially worthy of theoretical attention.

There are, however, good theoretical reasons to consider the use of notions of
tragedy in accounts of Mandela's life more closely. In the first place, there is Mandela's
tendency to look upon human and political affairs from a theatrical perspective, to
envision "the world [as a] stage and the actions of all [of its] inhabitants [as] part of
the same drama."[30] This use of theatrical metaphors by Mandela is neither casual nor
isolated. In important texts and speeches composed during his time in prison and
after his release, Mandela returns time and again to a notion of life as a kind of
drama in which characters enact their parts. So, for example, in an unpublished
manuscript on the Black Consciousness Movement written while he was in prison,

Mandela recommends an approach to human affairs more akin to playwriting than to conventional narrative.

> It is often desirable for one not to describe events, but to put the reader in the atmosphere in which the whole drama was played out right inside the theatre, so that he can see with his own eyes the actual stage, all the actors and their costumes, follow their movements, listen to what they say and sing, and to study the facial expressions and the spontaneous reaction of the audience as the drama unfolds.[31]

On the occasion of an historic speech to a joint session of the U.S. Congress shortly after his release, Mandela addressed his hosts in similarly theatrical terms, with an apparent nod to Shakespeare:

> It is a fact of the human condition that each shall, like a meteor—a mere brief passing moment in time—flit across the human stage and pass out of existence. Even the golden lads and lasses, as much as the chimney sweepers, come and tomorrow are no more.[32]

As noted in an earlier chapter, dictionary entries for "tragedy" typically distinguish between what can broadly be characterized as literal and figurative meanings of the term. The term can refer to a performative or narrative genre or work, or it can characterize an event, circumstance, or situation. This semantic segregation generally characterizes ordinary usage as well; writers and speakers of the term usually intend it to convey either a literal or a figurative meaning, and readers or listeners usually have little problem understanding which kind of tragedy is meant. So, for example, Mandela fully expects his readers not to be confused about which meaning he has in mind when he writes of the "tragedy" of his son's death. In at least one important respect, Mandela's usage is extra-resistant to semantic confusion since he seems to use "tragedy" in his published speeches and writings exclusively in reference to unhappy or fatal events or circumstances, reserving "drama" and "play" as labels for performative or narrative tragedies.

It is against the backdrop of the semantic segregation usually operative in ordinary uses of "tragedy" that Mandela's assumption of a theatrical perspective on human affairs stands out as theoretically interesting. This is because Mandela's theatrical perspective on life rests on the integration of the literal and figurative meanings rather than their segregation. Of course, in likening "events" or the "human condition" to a "drama" enacted in a "theater" or a moment passed on a "stage," Mandela does not actually use the word "tragedy." In these and other instances, he prefers "drama," "theater," or "play." However, on the "human stage" Mandela evokes in his speech to the U.S. Congress, the downward movement toward death, which he traces in the lives of both "golden lads" and "chimney sweepers," is implicitly tragic. To the extent that Mandela sees human affairs as a kind of dramatic or theatrical phenomenon, his notions about the nature and purposes of human affairs might reasonably be expected to be related to his notions about the nature, purpose, and effect of (tragic) drama or theater.

Literary critics and philosophers have long been engaged in the project of establishing authoritative criteria for identifying and evaluating works of tragedy in terms of the relationship between narrative form or conditions of performance, on the one hand, and intended effect on an audience's or readership's understanding of, or attitude toward, human existence, on the other. Aristotle's famous definition of tragedy in *Poetics* has decisively shaped subsequent discussion:

> Tragedy . . . is a representation of an action that is worth serious attention, complete in itself, and of some amplitude; in language enriched by a variety of artistic devices appropriate to the several parts of the play; presented in the form of action, not narration; by means of pity [*eleos*] and fear [*phobos*] bringing about the purgation [*kartharsin*] of such emotions.[33]

Of the many modern participants in this tradition of theorizing tragedy, Hegel is perhaps the only one to rival Aristotle in terms of influence on subsequent theorists. He found the drama *Antigone* to be a paradigmatic aesthetic expression of how progress is built on accepting the pain, and recognizing the necessity, of human conflict and suffering. Dissenting from Aristotle, Hegel identified tragedy's characteristic emotional effect as reconciliation; "Over and above mere fear and tragic sympathy, we have therefore the feeling of reconciliation, which tragedy affords in the vision of eternal justice."[34] In its most compelling examples, Greek tragedy merely dramatized the sometimes-difficult-to-discern logic of progressive change constantly operative in human affairs. On this view, historical events such as the trial and condemnation of Socrates could have tragic resonance; "the fate of Socrates is . . . really tragic, not in the superficial sense of the word and as every misfortune is called tragic." Hegel explains that Socrates's death manifested the tragic conflict at the heart of classical Athenian civilization between "divine right" and "self creative reason" and portended the transition of that civilization to a "higher consciousness."[35]

While Mandela's deliberate conflating of theatrical drama with life and the theatrical stage with human affairs does not, in and of itself, indicate his participation (alongside Hegel) in a theoretical tradition reaching back at least to Aristotle's *Poetics*, it does invite closer consideration of his ordinary uses of "tragedy" and his references (under the labels "drama" and "theater") to notions and phenomena associated with tragedy in its literal meaning. Such closer consideration reveals that Mandela has proved himself to be more than ordinarily reflective about the nature and significance of Greek tragedy. In a January 1976 letter written at the beginning of his second decade in prison, Mandela recalled reading a "review of the works of Euripides, Sophocles and other Greek scholars," in which it was claimed that "one of the basic tenets we have inherited from Greek philosophy was that a real man was one who could stand firmly on his feet and never bend his knees even when dealing with the divine."[36] Reflecting in his autobiography on his performance in one of the

Robben Island prisoners' production of *Antigone*, Mandela was led to observe how "enormously elevating" he found the experience of reading the "classic Greek plays in prison." They taught him, he writes, that "character was measured by facing up to difficult situations and that a hero was a man who would not break even under the most trying circumstances."[37]

Mandela's familiarity with tragic drama extended to the writings of Shakespeare, an edition of which secretly circulated among the prisoners of Robben Island.[38] Each political prisoner marked his favorite passage. Affirming the power of tragedy to inspire people to bear up under the most adverse circumstances, Mandela chose a passage from *Julius Caesar* that conveys a stoic acceptance of individual mortality as a condition of human life:

> Cowards die many times before their deaths;
> The valiant never taste of death but once.
> Of all the wonders that I have yet heard,
> It seems to me most strange that men should fear death;
> Seeing that death, a necessary end,
> Will come when it will come.[39]

These examples of Mandela's engagement with tragic drama endorse the heroic striving of individuals who stand up to adverse circumstances. However, other of Mandela's references to the classical literary heritage of tragic drama seem less driven by a sense of the importance of promoting heroic individuality than by a concern to promote solidarity. So, for example, in a speech to a gathering of South African business executives in May, 1990, Mandela quoted at length the famous words of Shylock from *The Merchant of Venice* in order to encourage the executives to recognize the humanity they shared with the masses of South Africa's dispossessed people: "Hath not a Jew eyes? Hath not a Jew hands, organs, dimensions, sense, affections, passions?"[40]

If the world of human affairs appears to Mandela in the form of a play or drama enacted on a stage, the material of his life has analogously appeared to several of his biographers in the form of a drama presented on a stage for the benefit of a world audience. To screenwriter and biographer Ronald Harwood, whose hybrid book has already been mentioned, one can add Anthony Sampson, who, in reference to the passion displayed for Shakespeare by Mandela and his fellow prisoners, concludes that Shakespeare's "deeper understanding of human courage, suffering and sacrifice reassured the prisoners that they were a part of a universal drama."[41] Sampson's evocation of the prisoners' self-understanding in terms of drama is not off-handed or casual; he adopts this notion of drama as a framing idea for his account of Mandela's long period of imprisonment:

> Mandela's prison story has a unique value to a biographer, with its human intensity and tests of character, providing an intimate play rather than a wide-ranging pageant; and Mandela's relationships with his friends and warders became a universal drama, with a significance that transcended African politics.[42] (xv)

In this passage, Sampson suggests that the materials of Mandela's life in prison existed in the form of a play or drama independently of, and prior to, any narrative intervention. Is this play or drama to be understood as unfolding in a specifically *tragic* mode? Sampson does not say so directly. He does follow up the reference of the "universal drama of Mandela's relationships" by identifying the distinctiveness of the approach that he, as biographer, has taken:

> The prison years are often portrayed as a long hiatus in the midst of Mandela's political career; but I see them as the key to his development, transforming the headstrong activist into the reflective and self-disciplined world statesman.[43]

Analyzing Mandela's character development in terms of a polarity between activism and reflectiveness, Sampson seemingly borrows a framework made famous by Nietzsche in *The Birth of Tragedy*. In that book, Nietzsche affirmed the distinctive significance of the Greek tragic chorus as the audience's bridge to a redemptive experience of universal oneness. In combining this redemptive experience of choral song and dance with a drama of individuated heroic striving, Greek tragedy, on Nietzsche's view, brought into creative interplay the (Dionysian) impulse to relax the boundaries of the self and adopt a holistic perspective on existence in which the boundaries between individuals fall away and the (Apollonian) impulse to fortify the boundaries of the self and promote one's individuality. In its distinctive power to "make[e] one feel fiery *and* contemplative at the same time," Greek tragedy consti-tuted for Nietzsche the paradigmatic expression of art's capacity to redeem human existence from its heavy burdens.[44]

In another apparent parallel with Nietzsche's theory of Greek tragedy (in particu-lar, its depiction of Greek tragedy's Dionysian aspect), Sampson follows up his tran-scription of Mandela's remarks about the "tragedy" of "los[ing] the best days of [his] life" by noting how the experience of long imprisonment had endowed Mandela with a kind of "philosopher's detachment" even as it fostered in him the ability to "relate to all kinds of people."[45] Of course, Sampson's appreciation of the power of tragedy to foster contemplation probably derives not from a reading of *The Birth of Tragedy* but from Mandela's own recognition of how his long imprisonment had forced him to appreciate the advantages of being able "to sit down and think," "to stand away from yourself [and] to look at yourself from a distance."[46] Already in 1976, Mandela acknowledged that his time in prison had given him, "advantages my compatriots outside jail rarely have. Here the past literally rushes to memory and there is plenty of time for reflection. One is able to stand back and look at the entire movement from a distance."[47]

Meredith, another post-apartheid Mandela biographer, also shapes his narrative in ways that invite comparison with theories of Greek tragedy. In addition to con-cluding his biography with Mandela's reference to the "tragedy" of his long impris-onment, among the "advantages" of which he includes "the ability to sit down and think,"[48] Meredith wraps up his description of inaugural ceremonies of President

Mandela in apparently Aristotelian terms. Describing how, at the conclusion of Mandela's inaugural speech, "squadrons [of South African military aircraft] passed overhead in a final affirmation of white loyalty to black rule," Meredith highlights the emotional response evoked in many of those present: "[T]he crowds below erupted with an outpouring of enthusiasm. Many who witnessed that moment of national catharsis were moved to tears."[49] If Meredith's use of the term "catharsis" brings to mind Aristotle's theory of Greek tragedy, this use is not dependent on knowing that theory. After all, "catharsis" has been available in written English to convey the notion of "a purging of emotions" at least since 1872.[50]

The parallels between the ordinary uses of the term, "tragedy," "tragic," "drama," or "catharsis" to characterize burdensome events or circumstances in Mandela's life or in South Africa and the more conceptually weighted findings of theorists of tragedy (e.g., catharsis, reconciliation, Dionysian contemplation) suggest that these words can, even in ordinary usage, reflect and promote politically relevant notions of affiliation. While terms referring to destructive events, conditions, or situations such as "calamity," "disaster," and "catastrophe" are sometimes listed by dictionaries or thesauri as synonyms for "tragedy,"[51] at least one aspect of the ordinary uses of tragedy in this figurative sense sets the use of this word apart. "Tragedy" often seems not only to refer to a severe or painful loss but also to suggest or assume the possibility of the achievement of a sense of reconciliation to this loss on the part of a reader or listener. The distinction to be drawn here parallels a distinction Hanna Pitkin makes between the labeling and signaling functions of words in her study of Ludwig Wittgenstein's language philosophy.[52] Like "calamity," "disaster," and "catastrophe," the term, tragedy, can be used to refer to a certain kind of condition or circumstance or event. However, "tragedy" additionally seems to signal a particular way of responding to the condition or event. This "quasi-performative" aspect of tragedy[53] is typically on display in comments uttered on the occasion of ceremonies commemorating untimely deaths. At the groundbreaking ceremony of the Oklahoma City bombing memorial, a survivor noted that, "a lot of us want to get along with our lives and forget the tragedy but not the people inside. This is what we want to remember."[54] At the opening ceremony of the Oklahoma City National Memorial Center, President George Bush, after affirming the power of memorials to "'tell the value of what was lost,'" was reported to have "made several glancing references to ways in which tragedies like the Oklahoma City bombing might be avoided in the future."[55]

In their frequent placement of the term, tragedy, at the end of a report on a fatal event, journalists and editors seem implicitly to recognize a distinctive capacity of the word and its cognate both to signal *and* settle powerful emotions of the sort occasioned by suffering and loss. So, for example, an article reporting the fatal crash of a military transport on a routine training mission concludes with the transcription of a joint statement in which the Army and Air Force "extend their heartfelt sympathy and condolences to the families and friends who lost loved ones in this tragedy."[56] And, in a report about the ease with which a mentally ill person in Utah was able to purchase a handgun later used in a fatal shooting spree, the final word is given to a Connecticut law enforcement officer who had been empowered by his state to confiscate weapons from a depressed person who had threatened his coworkers; "We can't prove how many lives we may have saved . . . . But in our eyes, this case had all the telltale signs. As a police department, we usually don't get to see the signs till after a tragedy has happened."[57] As a concluding utterance in these and other instances[58], tragedy, one might say, signals an attempt to acknowledge a sense of loss which, because it is shared, might be borne more easily.

The use of "tragedy" as an invitation to share a sense of reconciliation with a difficult loss is especially manifest during those instances when that invitation is rejected. Take, for example, the objection political scientist Chalmers Johnson implicitly lodges against a U.S. government official's use of "tragedy" in *Blowback: The Costs and Consequences of American Empire* (2000), a book arguing against U.S. efforts to preserve a military sphere of influence in East Asia. He reports that the idea for the book arose, "as the result of a visit to Okinawa in 1996, after the rape incident of September, 1995 . . . . I was frankly shocked by the sight of the then-42 American bases. And I was equally shocked that after a 12-year-old was raped by two marines and a sailor, the United States sought basically to spin the issue. To call it a unique tragedy. To claim that such things are not a common occurrence."[59] Johnson's use of the adjective, unique, to modify, tragedy, is telling. It reveals his sense that the U.S. government had abdicated its responsibility for the costs imposed on Okinawans by the pervasive U.S. military presence. Given the extent of that presence, the continued occurrence of fatal or burdensome events (e.g., the rape of Okinawans by U.S. servicemen) has become both foreseeable and preventable. For Johnson, the U.S. government's decision not to take preventative action renders inappropriate its resort to a word that implicitly invites listeners or readers to share a sense of reconciliation over a purportedly unforeseen loss.[60] Sharing a sense of loss and disavowing culpability seem to be the implicit aims of a statement Mandela offered in reference to a 1983 car bomb attack by the ANC's military arm, Umkhonto, on South Africa's Air Force headquarters, in which nineteen people were killed and more than 200 people were wounded. Mandela seems to be thinking of the family members and friends of the many civilian victims of that attack, when, in a 1985 interview, he says that, "It was a tragic accident . . . . We aim for buildings and property. So it may be that someone gets killed in a fight, in the heat of battle, but we do not believe in assassination."[61] Almost ten years later, in his autobiography, Mandela repeated his original formulation ("The killing of civilians was a tragic accident.") and followed up this resort to tragic rhetoric with a consideration of the difficulties in preventing unforeseen and unintended suffering in wartime.

> I knew that such accidents were the inevitable consequence of the decision to embark on a military struggle. Human fallibility is always a part of war, and the price for it is always high. It was precisely because we knew that such incidents would occur that our decision to take up arms had been so grave and reluctant.[62]

If, at the time of his earlier comment, Mandela could only anticipate the damage that the escalating military struggle would do to later prospects of national reconciliation, by the time of his later reference, he knew from experience the degrees of mistrust and hatred that had been raised between groups over years of armed struggle. Tellingly, in both instances, consideration of the difficult challenge of fostering a sense of reconciliation calls forth tragic rhetoric.

Disagreements about the propriety of characterizing certain events or conditions as tragedies highlight the stakes involved in using the word and its cognates. Characterizing a fatal or unhappy event or condition as "tragic" signals an effort not only to manage the emotions aroused by loss but also to enlist these emotions in promoting a sense of community based on a shared response to suffering. The significance of this effort is all the greater in cases where conflict has given rise to significant and pervasive suffering and loss. In this regard, it is worth noting that President Mandela's reference to the "tragedy [of] los[ing] the best days of your life" followed immediately upon his recollection of a turning point in his life: his realization "in prison that the warders could be good or bad, like any other people."[63] Remembering this recognition that he shared a common humanity with his warders leads him to a word, "tragedy," that signals his own coming to terms with the deprivations he suffered as a result of his experience in prison.

Mandela's apparent appreciation of the reconciliatory promise of "tragedy" was also evident in the words he chose to describe repeated episodes of political violence in the period between his release from prison in 1990 and South Africa's first free elections in 1994. During this time, the process of constitutional negotiation was accompanied, and occasionally interrupted, by politically motivated attacks mostly carried out by members of the Zulu organization Inkatha, often in collusion with the security forces of the minority government. These attacks were directed against ANC members and their families. In choosing to characterize as "tragedies" the deliberate killing by Inkatha militants of thirty people at Sebokeng on July 22, 1990, and the later, bloody expulsion of ANC people from a squatter camp outside of Gemison by Inkatha, Mandela seems intent on promoting reconciliation and solidarity among black South Africans.[64] Even when caught up in difficult events, as when he gave a speech at King's park in Natal on February 26, 1990, to a mixed audience of ANC and Inkatha members, Mandela seemingly chooses his words with an eye to his ultimate goal of reconciliation: "I call on the people of Inandi. Join hands. All of you from Clermont, join hands . . . . Residents of Durban and Pietermaritzburg, it is your turn. Those from strife-torn Unlazi and tragic KwaMashu, join hands also."[65]

In the two decades since the democratic transformation of South Africa, the initial hopes of millions of South Africans for significant improvements in their conditions of life have been mostly disappointed. While many of the dispossessed majority have experienced upgrades in basic services—electrification, potable water, paved roads—prices for necessities have increased, at the same time that rates of unemployment, crime and AIDS infection rates have remained at, or climbed to, devastatingly high levels. In the face of South Africa's present troubles, questions have been raised about the acceptance by Mandela and the ANC leadership of neoliberal terms of democratic transformation, which undermined the state's powers to intervene in the economy and prevented any significant redistribution of the private capital amassed during the apartheid era.[66]

Nowadays, the language of tragedy is as likely to be applied to sufferings consequent on the failures, real or perceived, of ANC leadership as it is to the legacy of apartheid rule. So, for example, South African AIDS activist Zackie Achmet, who went on a highly publicized campaign against the Mbeki Administration's considered refusal to acknowledge the science of AIDS diffusion and pursue effective treatment policies, offered this assessment: "I am still officially an ANC member. But this is a tragedy. Many, many have died. It's difficult to think of forgiveness."[67] The rhetoric of tragedy also marked Winnie Mandela's criticism of South African media and public authorities for blaming a May, 2008, outbreak of anti-immigrant violence in South African townships on xenophobia rather than on the government's failure to deliver on its promises: "It is most tragic that xenophobia should be used as an explanation for the crisis. It is an explosion caused by lack of delivery. People say the conditions under which they live are conducive to this kind of violence."[68]

The pattern of political significance detected in the ordinary uses of "tragedy" and related terms by Mandela and his biographers invites us to consider whether the post-transition invocations of tragic rhetoric by Achmet and Winnie Mandela are doing similar political work. It is noteworthy in this regard that Achmet's invocation of "tragedy" follows up a presumably reluctant declaration of shared ANC membership with leaders whose AIDS policies had so miserably failed South Africans. And it can plausibly be argued that Winnie Mandela's choice of "tragic" rather than "outrageous" or "self-serving" to describe the official ANC line on the township violence of 2008 serves to mark her own continued sense of solidarity with the ANC.

To the extent both that society is formed of a plurality of self-seeking individuals and that the state disposes of a "very special means, namely, power backed up by violence,"[69] conflict and suffering are necessary conditions of domestic political life, especially in times of constitutional and societal crisis. Under these conditions, promotion of a sense of community becomes a significant political task. Past theorists of Greek tragedy, Nietzsche among them, have distinguished the institution of *tragōidíā* for its not insignificant ("Dionysian") role in supporting that task in the ancient polis. While no strict equivalent of the institution of Greek tragedy in this aspect exists in our day, ordinary uses of English language descendants of *tragōidíā* seem to serve similar reconciliatory and community-fostering functions (albeit at levels much reduced in their effect) as that ancient institution presumably performed in its time. If Nelson Mandela or his biographers (or Zackie Achmet or Winnie Mandela, for that matter) are not theorists of tragedy in the strict sense, then, they are beneficiaries of the politically relevant possibilities opened up by ordinary (English language) uses of "tragedy." Obviously, the widespread and terrible losses and sufferings borne by the South African majority under apartheid rule (and afterward) merit the use of "tragedy" as a descriptive label. What is less obvious is how use of this label, however casual or diffuse, implicates the user in an appeal to others to transform a sense of loss into the basis of a shared feeling of reconciliation. That this appeal might have relevance in politics is suggested by some interesting word choices made by Nelson Mandela, whose personal experience of suffering and loss and whose powerful ambition to found a new national community on the basis of reconciliation found at least one appropriate means of expression in "tragedy."

CHAPTER 6

9/11: Tragedy and Theodicy as American Responses to Suffering

We have come together with a unity of purpose because our nation demands it. September 11, 2001, was a day of unprecedented shock and suffering in the history of the United States. The nation was unprepared. How did this happen, and how can we avoid such tragedy again?

The 9/11 Commission Report[1]

I've learned that God is good. All the time.

Pres. George W. Bush[2]

One of the first officials to utter the term, tragedy, in reference to the events of 9/11 was Mayor Rudolf Giuliani at a press conference hastily convened at the New York City Police Academy in the early afternoon of that day. Thousands were feared dead but no reliable estimate could be made at the World Trade Center because of uncertainty about who had come to work and who had managed to escape and because the site, heaped high with the still smoldering wreckage of the fallen towers, was largely inaccessible. At his news conference, the mayor acknowledged that the day was "obviously one of the most difficult days in the history of the city and the country." Giuliani went on to say, "the tragedy that we are all undergoing right now is something that we've had nightmares about—probably thought wouldn't happen. My heart goes out to all of the innocent victims of this horrible and vicious act of terrorism."[3] Shortly after six in the evening, he held another press conference. With the family and friends of the missing apparently foremost in mind, Giuliani spoke of remaining hopeful in the wake of the "tragedy" while being prepared for the worst. By this time, newscasters on the major networks were also using the term in reference to the shocking events of that day.

Mayor Giuliani's uses of "tragedy" fall into a pattern made recognizable by our previous consideration of the rhetoric of Nelson Mandela and others. In response to an unprecedented and unexpected instance of large-scale suffering, a political leader reaches in an immediate and somewhat unreflective way for words that might promote solidarity with, and among, the survivors, the families of the missing and the dead, and members of the afflicted community. This chapter takes a different approach than the previous one in illuminating the solidarity-fostering aspects of the politics of tragedy. It does not focus on the tragic rhetoric of any one figure but considers the responses to the events of 9/11 elicited from an ensemble of inter-locutors—journalists, public officials, citizens. In doing so, this chapter brings out with greater clarity the political dimensions of the vernacular uses of "tragedy" and related terms.

Casual uses of "tragedy" by journalists or the "man (or woman) on the street" in reference to such fatal events as car wrecks or air crashes have typically been dispar-aged by theorists of tragedy who characterize those uses as indiscriminate and cli-chéd. Although this criticism holds in some cases, systematic attention to the rhetoric of responses to 9/11 reveals that ordinary language uses are more diverse and more significant than academics and literati realize. Consideration of post-9/11 discourses further reveals how uses of "tragedy" are also more convergent than at first appears with the sorts of political effects (e.g., the promotion of solidarity) that academics have traditionally associated with Greek and other forms of performative and narrative tragedy. This chapter will show how academic theorizing about the nature of tragedy and vernacular uses of the term, tragedy, and related terms form different but related facets of a larger discourse about suffering that can come into play, in politically significant ways, in response to traumatic events like those that occurred on 9/11.

If the method of the first part of this chapter is to illuminate the politics of trag-edy by revealing similarities between academic and non-specialist uses of "tragedy", the method adopted in the second part works by sharpening a key contrast between the discourse of tragedy generated in response to 9/11 and a rhetoric of religious consolation rooted in forms of mainstream theodicy[4], on which many Americans apparently relied in their response to the suffering unleashed by the attacks of that day. As will become clear, differences in rhetorical approach to public suffering cor-respond to differences in the kind of solidarity aimed at. The rhetoric of theodicy fosters solidarity on the basis of members' mutual acceptance of transcendental truth claims. The community of sufferers to which an appeal is made is thereby restricted to a circle of doctrinal believers. By contrast, tragic modes of response base their consolatory effects on more diffuse appeals to intuitions or tastes and thereby remain open to a larger potential audience.

Responses to 9/11 in Expert and Ordinary Languages

Like everyone else, I keep using the phrase the events—*the only other word that seems to work is* tragedy.[5]

Judging from the frequency with which the word appears in daily news stories or is spoken on television broadcasts, "tragedy" has become an indispensable part of news journalism's stock of ready-to-use descriptive terms. It should come as no surprise, then, that journalists made liberal use of "tragedy" after the events of 9/11, which were unexpected and fatal to an unprecedented extent. So, for example, a September 15 *New York Times* article entitled, "Clergy of Many Faiths Answer Tragedy's Call," discusses in its lead paragraph how, "members of the clergy . . . [a]lthough hardly as visible as the rescue workers sifting through the debris in New York and at the Pentagon . . . have been deeply involved in the aftermath of the tragedy."[6] Broadcast journalists had occasion to use the term and its cognate, as well. In a compilation of their "eyewitness accounts of what happened in New York, Washington and Pennsylvania . . . that tragic day," a variety of appropriate terms were pressed into service—"catastrophic," "disastrous," "awful," "horrific"—but none more frequently than tragedy and its cognate.[7] Joining in this journalistic usage was the bystander who frequently resorted to "tragedy" or its cognate when asked to articulate a response to 9/11. This was true immediately after the events—"We're living a national tragedy and now we've suffered a personal loss as well," as the one year anniversary approached—"It's a shame that it happened and it's a tragedy but you can't let it affect your world," as well as in responses over two years later to final designs for a ground zero memorial—"[T]hey seem saccharine and feel-good, not memorials in the sense that they evoke some of the enormity of a tragic day."[8] Among the many books about 9/11 soon on offer, John Duffy's *Triumph Over Tragedy: September 11 and the Rebirth of a Business* (2002), co-authored with Mary Schaeffer, stands out for its early and unabashed use of tragic rhetoric. A top executive at Keefe, Bruyette & Woods, a boutique investment banking firm, Duffy lost 67 work colleagues, including one of his sons, in the South Tower. The first part of the book, entitled "Tragedy," recounts the history of the firm up to and including the events of 9/11. The second part ("Triumph") takes up the recovery efforts of the firm's surviving employees. While in the first part "disaster" seems to be the preferred label—"Like everyone else, Mitch stood by helplessly and watched the disaster unfold."—it is eventually supplanted by "tragedy" and "tragic" as the text becomes more retrospective: "Emotionally, that day and I would say for the balance of that week, it was extremely difficult to comprehend that what was happening was real. Who could have imagined anything even close to this in terms of the scope of this tragedy."[9]

The uses made of "tragedy" and "tragic" by journalists, their interview subjects, and people writing letters to the editor in the wake of 9/11 were ordinary, so ordinary, in fact, that they could easily pass unnoticed. In at least one instance, an instance that is particularly revealing, they did pass unnoticed. In a review of Terry Eagleton's book, *Sweet Violence: The Idea of the Tragic* (2002), David Simpson claimed that "in the United States the language of tragedy was not invoked in describing 9/11." He offered several reasons for the absence of a "rhetoric of tragedy": a presumed difficulty in identifying an exemplary or preeminent figure of suffering in an event that left masses of people dead, the mistaken sense that the word could not measure up to the enormity of suffering, and a tendency to substitute a "language of evil" for the "language of tragedy."[10]

Simpson was obviously wrong about the absence of a rhetoric of tragedy in U.S. responses to 9/11 and, within a month of the publication of his review, the *London Review of Books* printed a letter from a reader who reported conducting a Google search in which he cross-referenced "tragedy" and "September 11" and received 853,000 hits.[11] Acknowledging this counterevidence, Simpson nevertheless insisted on underplaying its significance by suggesting that, "few if any of [the 853,000 websites] propose a serious definition or theory of tragedy."[12] Simpson's offhanded dismissal of colloquial usage for its lack of theoretical seriousness is ironic since in his review he had sympathized with Eagleton's argument that literary critics and academic theorists of tragedy, in general, have too often tended to affirm elitist notions of tragic heroism, fate, and suffering, according to which the struggles and burdens of ordinary folk count for little, if anything. So, for example, Eagleton deplores how, among academics and literati, the notion of tragedy tends to become "reified to a spiritual absolute which presides impassively over a degraded everyday existence."[13] To be fair to Simpson, he does not write that the suffering of ordinary folk is unworthy of notice, only that the way in which ordinary folk articulate the nature and meaning of that suffering through the "rhetoric of tragedy" is. It may well be that mundane uses of "tragedy" can be so superficial as to diminish the effectiveness of the term as a meaningful response to suffering. So, for example, folklorists in the U.S. engaged in a project to establish a record of responses to, and impressions of, the events of September 11 found that some people they interviewed were consciously seeking new ways of describing those events because of their feeling that the term, tragedy, had been trivialized by overuse.[14]

Simpson's judgment follows a pattern of academic criticism of ordinary uses of tragedy for being superficial, if not also wrongheaded, in any case, useless to those engaged in understanding the true nature and significance of tragedy. Thus, in a forum organized to gather the views of theatre and performance scholars about the status of tragedy in the aftermath of 9/11, one contributor wrote that, "the term has been devalued into a generic word for calamity," while another warned against "succumbing to popular notions of the tragic."[15] The conclusions of specialists who conform to this pattern of criticism are highly suspect, not least because they are not usually based on a nuanced understanding of how "tragedy" and related terms function in ordinary language. In forming their theories of the nature and significance of tragedy, literary critics have typically drawn their criteria from works of literary criticism, of which Aristotle's *Poetics* has been a particularly influential example. Critics rely, in addition, on works of literature that are thought to portray tragic deeds and sufferings or otherwise to exemplify tragic notions of fate and heroism. One immediately thinks of the importance of *Antigone* for the development of Hegel's dialectical perspective on philosophy and history. Of course, when measured against the theoretical sophistication of this tradition of critical discourse or against the aesthetic craftmanship of enduring works of literature, ordinary uses are bound to seem insignificant. After all, a newscaster's characterization of a fatal drunk driving incident as a tragedy seems premised more on a simple recognition of that event's sad consequences than on a theoretically considered or aesthetically informed understanding of the nature of the tragic.

A sense of the problematic nature and significance of ordinary uses of words such as "tragedy" and "tragic" informs some noteworthy journalistic assessments of the events of 9/11 and their aftermath. Take, for example, William Langewiesche's book, *American Ground: Unbuilding the World Trade Center* (2002). A correspondent for *The Atlantic Monthly*, Langewiesche enjoyed unlimited access to the ruins of the Trade Center and used it to tell a story of how organizers and workers surmounted the challenges of stabilizing the site and clearing away its immense heaps of wreckage. In describing the events that led to the total destruction of the two towers and the deaths of thousands of people, Langewiesche resorts to terms that in ordinary usage and from the standpoint of dictionary definitions and thesaurus entries are interchangeable: tragedy, calamity, apocalypse, disaster. Sometimes the use of a term in one or another instance seems driven by the understandable journalistic need for variety of expression.

> The truth is that people relished the experience [of stabilizing and clearing the site]. It's obvious that they would never have wished this calamity on themselves or others, but inside the perimeter lines and beyond the public's view it served for many of them as an unexpected liberation—a national tragedy, to be sure, but one that was contained, unambiguous, and surprisingly energizing.[16]

Here, September 11 could just as easily have been referred to as a national *calamity* but the use of that term twice in one sentence simply would not do from the standpoint of good style. Similarly, after noting that, "within hours of the collapse, as the rescuers rushed in and resources were marshaled, the disaster was smothered in an exuberant and distinctly American embrace," Langewiesche opts in the very next sentence for the adjectival modifier "apocalyptic" rather than "disastrous" to describe the "nature of the scene" to which rescuers responded: "Despite the apocalyptic nature of the scene, the response was unhesitant and almost childishly optimistic."[17]

Langewiesche's word choices in these and other instances are appropriate and apparently unremarkable. He seemingly chooses terms in the way that any journalist might when faced with the task of writing about an unexpectedly painful or burdensome event, situation, or circumstance. Even if "apocalypse" or its cognates are not your run-of-the-mill terms, they do not seem out of place in a discussion of an event in which the destruction was so sudden and its scale so immense.

Closer consideration of Langewiesche's multiple resorts to the term, tragedy, and its synonyms reveals a not altogether obvious pattern, however. "Tragedy" seems to be the exclusive term of choice on those occasions when Langewiesche is intent on highlighting what he considered to be the unfortunate role of emotionalism in the recovery efforts at the World Trade Center. In particular, he opts for the term or its cognate whenever reference is made to the passionate claims made by, or on behalf of, New York City firefighters to continue occupy the pile and recover the remains of their fallen colleagues ("brothers"). So, for example, "nearly two months after the tragedy, with no conceivable justification for continuing to jump into voids or clamber across unstable cliffs, there were still firefighters running wild." In the lead-up to the "emotionally charged demonstration" by New York City firemen opposed to calls for reducing their numbers at the Trade Center site, Langewiesche notes that, "resentments and jealousies among the various groups had been mounting for weeks, as the initial rush to find survivors had transmuted into a grim search for the dead, and as territoriality and the embrace of tragedy had crept in." In reference to a brawl in the hole that broke out between New York City firemen and policemen over the firemen's demand for a show of respect during the removal of the remains of one of their own, Langewiesche concludes, "the uniformed groups especially seemed sometimes to be clinging to their tragedies." After a highly charged meeting between city officials and the widows of the 9/11 firemen in which the widows characterized the management of the clearing operation as heartless, two managing engineers who had been shaken by the accusations went to a bar and reflected on why issues of loss did not affect them emotionally in the same way that it had affected so many others. As Langewiesche tells it, the two men finally agreed that having become so wrapped up in the engineering challenge of clearing the Trade Center site, "they simply did not have time to dwell on the tragedy."[18]

Langewiesche's uses of the cognate, tragic, are similarly patterned, linking the events of 9/11 to powerful emotional reactions on the part of Americans at large, who respond to "the powerful new iconography that was associated with the disaster— these New York firemen as tragic heroes . . . these smoking ruins as America's hallowed ground," as well as on the part of the firemen, few of whom could resist this "new external idea of themselves as tragic characters on a national stage." The effect on these latter was so powerful that, "the image of 'heroes' seeped through their ranks like a low-grade narcotic."[19]

Langewiesche's presentation of the firefighters as a problematic element in the post-rescue engineering and deconstruction effort and his offhanded references to possible episodes of looting by some of them has given rise to heated criticisms of his book. While the issue of whether Langewiesche was fair-minded in his treatment of New York City firefighters does not directly bear on this discussion, it is clear that his belief that, "the emotionalism surrounding the site, though at its origins genuine and necessary, had grown into something less healthy—an overindulgence,"[20] finds expression, in an important way, in his selective uses of the terms, tragedy and tragic. Time and again, these words mark instances of media hype, hero worship by the public, and self indulgence on the part of firemen. It isn't so much that Langewiesche "resists the urge to turn tragedy into melodrama," as one of the reviewer blurbs (from a review by J. Peder Zane in *The Raleigh Observer*) reprinted in the book suggests, as that he resists the urge to deploy the language of "tragedy" because it has become a means for melodramatic utterance. One might express the import of Langewiesche's pattern of usage in Aristotelian terms; while "tragedy" stirs up emotions, it fails to purge or purify them.

A similar sense of the low worth of tragic rhetoric informs the word choices of Jim Dwyer and Kevin Flynn in their powerful and harrowing account, *102 Minutes: The Untold Story of the Fight to Survive Inside the Twin Towers* (2005). Nowhere in the book except on the book jacket blurb (where reference is made to "tragic flaws") is there any use of tragic rhetoric. To the extent that the book restricts itself to a reconstruction of the events from the time of the crash of the first jetliner until the collapse of the second tower the absence of tragic rhetoric is understandable. "Tragedy" or "tragic" are labels usually applied retrospectively, after the danger of an event has passed and an opportunity to grasp the scale of loss first presents itself. (In this regard, it is worth recalling the pattern of usage in the aforementioned book by John Duffy.) In the retrospective accounting provided by the book's epilogue, however, where one might expect "tragedy" to be used, one reads instead "calamity" and "disaster."[21]

As it turns out, the absence of tragic rhetoric in *102 Minutes* is not coincidental; it is the result of the deliberate choice of at least one of the authors. The crux of the matter for Dwyer is that "tragedy," which once referred to significant suffering that is the "ruinous outcome of a fundamental flaw in someone," has come to be used as shorthand for suffering of any sort. To the extent that, "the word, tragedy, pins some of the responsibility for calamitous events on the victim or the victim's basic human makeup," Dwyer felt that it did not apply to the "broad sweep of events . . . at the trade center," which were instigated by "killers who were attacking the buildings as symbols of America, globalism, secularism," and who took no account of the victims. Conceding that the deficient working of the emergency response system and the actions of some few individuals inside the buildings could fit his definition of trag- edy, Dwyer nevertheless avoided the term altogether partly because of his sense that the word had become "debased."[22]

One might extend Dwyer's criticism of the debasement of "tragedy" to identify a form of rhetorical misuse at a pole opposite to the hyper-emotionalism criticized by Langewiesche, a form indicative of an inappropriate lack of emotional involvement. Here, the indiscriminate or clichéd use of "tragedy" would register or promote only superficial kinds of attentiveness to the suffering of others, kinds of attentiveness that do not promote genuine understanding or inspire corrective action. Using Aristotelian language, one might say the flaw in such usage consists in the failure to provoke the appropriate emotions (pity and fear, say) whose later catharsis or purga- tion presumably constitutes the very basis of tragedy's value in human affairs. The two sorts of journalistic responses to 9/11 considered at length so far raise the pros- pects of two kinds of ordinary language abuse, then. On the one hand, "tragedy" or "tragic" can stir emotions to an extent or in a way that distorts one's perspective or prevents one from thinking clearly. On the other hand, these words can prevent the activation of emotions so that the attention needed to form a perspective or to focus one's thought is absent from the start.

Against the backdrop both of Dwyer's criticism of the indiscriminate ("debased") use of "tragedy" and its cognate and of Langewiesche's implicit association of the terms with a kind of emotionalism that prevents people from taking a clear-eyed and sober view of life and its challenges, what is one to make of the copious use of tragic rhetoric made by Duffy in *Triumph Into Tragedy*? One could dismiss it. After all, Duffy isn't a professional writer. Or one could excuse it; a person who suffers the loss of a son (as well as of several close friends) is entitled to a larger degree of emotional involvement. Excusing Duffy's use of tragic rhetoric as the entitlement of a grieving father or friend belies the tone of detachment that pervades the book he composed (with help from Mary Schaeffer) so soon after the events of 9/11, however. The text performs many functions: besides memorializing the individuals who were lost, it celebrates Keefe, Bruyette & Woods' past achievements, it reassures present employees and clients of the firm's survival, and it advertises the firm's future viability to prospective employees and clients. What the text decidedly does not do, is express the author's personal grief in too direct or unmediated a way. It may even be that, *pace* Langewiesche's approach to ordinary uses of "tragedy" and "tragic," the language of tragedy served Duffy as a means of acknowledging loss without giving in to it, of permitting an appropriately intermediate level of emotional involvement. What else is one to make of a parent being able to classify the violent and painful death of one of his children as a "tragedy"[23] other than as a tribute to the power of language and, in particular, the rhetoric of tragedy to signal some degree of mastery over powerful feelings of grief?

Or might Duffy's uses of "tragedy" be seen as manifesting a problematic, if understandable, form of emotional detachment from loss? The terrible losses of a son and close friends constituting too great an emotional burden, on this view, Duffy distances himself from the events he recounts by reaching for terms that through indiscriminate use have lost their power to activate, and give cathartic release from, powerful emotions. Opting for terms that skim over the surface rather than plumb the depths, so to speak, would be all the more attractive to someone accustomed to taking risks, to taking action without dwelling overmuch on the past, as one might expect in the case of a successful investment banker. The impulse to favor action over reflection would be all the greater here given Duffy's pledge to use the financial means of his firm to ensure a modicum of financial security to the many families who had lost breadwinners. The different views one can plausibly take on the meaning of Duffy's uses of "tragedy" suggest the not-so-apparent complexity of ordinary usage.

In general, it may be that neither theoretical sophistication nor writerly detachment is a prerequisite for being discriminating in one's use of tragic rhetoric. The people interviewed for the aforementioned 9/11 folklore project, some of whom we can presume to have been non-specialists, seem also to have come to the conclusion that the use of terms other than "tragedy" was called for in the wake of 9/11. One can easily imagine several ways in which disapproval of the cheap emotional effect of "tragedy" and "tragic" can be signaled in ordinary language use. Someone trying to calm a needlessly overwrought friend might say, in mock consternation, "How tragic!" Or, with a similarly deflating purpose in mind, one might respond to a hard luck story, "It's an inconvenience, not a tragedy." And one can cite plenty of instances of ordinary usage that are not debased, that seem to strike just the right note of attentiveness to one's own or another's suffering. So, for example, after a funeral service for a young woman who was deliberately pushed into the path of a New York City subway train, one person described the ceremony as "moving" and then reflected that "tragedy is always around us, and it makes us appreciate life."[24]

One does not need to study Aristotle's discussion of catharsis in *Poetics* or Hegel's discussion of reconciliation to recognize that opting for "tragedy" rather than "disaster" or "calamity" invites a special sort of attentiveness to suffering in which emotions are intensively engaged and, as a paradoxical result, a contemplative mood is fostered. The spectator or reader of tragedy or "tragedy" is drawn to an instance of suffering only to take a larger, more reflective view of its meaning. Similarly, one does not need to consult Friedrich Nietzsche's famous argument in *Birth of Tragedy* about the distinctive existential and political significance of the Greek tragic chorus as the audience's bridge to a Dionysian experience of redemptive wholeness and unity to be aware that "tragedy" invites solidarity with the afflicted. This is true of non-specialists responding to 9/11—"We are living a national tragedy."—as well as tragedy "experts," including the theatre and performance scholar, who, invited to participate in a roundtable on tragedy and 9/11, affirmed that, "tragedy yokes the communal and the personal, linking the individual to the group, the tribe, the nation through the force of its monumental destructiveness."[25]

The solidarity-promoting effect of vernacular uses of "tragedy" is also apparent if one imagines the word choices of al-Qaeda plotters after they learned of the success of their attack plan against American cities. English-language expressions like, "This has been a *disaster* for America!" or "The losses to America have been *catastrophic!*" seem more plausible choices than "This has been a great *tragedy* for America!" or "We have inflicted *tragic* losses on our enemy!" Significantly, tragedy did become the label of choice (at least in translation) for the al-Qaeda leadership in relation to a different instance of suffering. A month after the 9/11 attacks, just as U.S. forces began military operations against the Taliban, Osama Bin Laden released a video-taped statement, which also included a presentation by Ayman Al-Zawahiri, a leading Egyptian Jihadist and his top assistant. Al-Zawahiri's statement included an assertion, which, translated into English, read: "We will not accept that the tragedy of Al Andalus will be repeated in Palestine." Surely, his use of an Arabic term whose English equivalent is "tragedy" in reference to the ending of Islamic rule in the Iberian peninsula was aimed not at his American enemies but at an imagined audience of people who might share his regret at the suffering of Islamic people, whether in a distant time and place ("Al Andalus") or in the present day ("Palestine").

In addition to reconciliation and solidarity, specialized treatments of tragedy and ordinary language uses of "tragedy" converge in their concern with, or indirect commentary on, the nature of agency and responsibility in a conditioned world. A woman who faces sentencing after pleading guilty to drunk driving and vehicular homicide charges apologizes, characterizing the fatal event as a "tragic accident."[26] A U.S. ambassador announces that he is "deeply saddened" by "the tragic loss of innocent life" after a U.S. air strike mistakenly kills nine children in Eastern Afghanistan.[27] In either case, one might argue that the speaker of tragic rhetoric is seeking inappropriately to evade responsibility for avoidable suffering. Similarly, when a letter-to-the-editor writer takes issue with an anniversary report which (in his view) took a "political" view of 9/11 and played the "blame game," he resorts to the rhetoric of tragedy in order to absolve U.S. presidents of responsibility for the catastrophic lapse in U.S. defenses: "I have a feeling that (my friend, the New York City firefighter who has played the bagpipes at several funerals in the weeks after 9/11) has not thought too much about Bush, Clinton or anybody else who [sic] we can blame this tragedy. 9/11 should not be remembered as something political."[28] In the same vein, one might argue, the 9/11 Commission adopts the language of tragedy at the very beginning of its report—"How did this happen, and how can we avoid such tragedy again?"—to convey a bipartisan consensus not to play the blame game. What makes such rhetorical moves attractive in the first place is the etymological link between that rhetoric and the world of *Oedipus Rex* and other classical tragedies in which it so often seems the case that no one is completely in control of the conse- quences of his or her actions and where the line demarcating the zone of personal responsibility is unclear. It is this same world that J. -P. Vernant evokes with his notion of Greek tragedy as occupying a "border zone" between human and divine affairs in which "human action becomes the object of reflection and debate while still not being regarded as sufficiently autonomous to be self sufficient."[29]

What the specialist and vernacular responses to 9/11 reveal is that whether one is a scholar of Greek tragedy or a historian of the ancient Greek polis or a theorist of tragedy or even just an English language speaker faced with choosing the *right* word when confronted with an instance of suffering and loss, one is knowingly or unknow- ingly working within, and from, a cluster of related notions whose origin and point of reference (to greater and lesser extents) is *tragōidía*. For the ancient Athenians, the term referred to the dramas subsidized by order of polis officials, conceived and performed in large part by polis citizens, evaluated by polis representatives sworn to impartiality on pain of death, and witnessed en masse by polis inhabitants as the centerpiece of civic-religious festivals.

Much has been made of the fact that *tragōidía* developed coevally with democ- racy in ancient Athens. The establishment of periodic competitive performances of *tragōidía* as a central feature of Athenian public life and the end of the aristocratic monopoly of power in Athens are both traced to the rise of the Peisistratid tyrants in the middle of the sixth century. Toward the close of that century, after the fall of the tyrants, when Cleisthenes institutionalized democratic political power through his reform of the Athenian tribes, reorganization of the council, extension of mili- tary service, and establishment of the practice of ostracism, Aeschylus was in his late teens. Some scholars argue that *tragōidía* became an important means by which newly empowered democratic citizens could become practiced in politically relevant forms of judgment.[30] Others emphasize *tragōidía*'s role as an institution of self reflec- tion and critique by which democratic citizens could submit their newly won free- dom of action to an authority seemingly beyond (and yet somehow also originating from) themselves.[31] Still others mainly see the enactment of *tragōidía* as part of a process whereby the democratic polis invented its own civic-religious tradition through the appropriation and refiguration of heroic myths and cult rituals.[32] *Tragōidía*'s significance in promoting solidarity between polis citizens has also been duly noted.

To be sure, compared with *tragōidía*'s multifaceted impact on the civic culture of the ancient Athenian polis, the contemporary discourse of tragedy in the United States exercises far less of an obvious civic influence. However weak the contemporary effects of tragedy or "tragedy" are, they do bear a family resemblance to the strong effects of *tragōidía* in ancient Athens. In seeing these awful events against the backdrop of theories of tragedy or in attaching the label, "tragedy," to these events, people responding to 9/11 effectively, if not always deliberately, prepare the ground for judgment or invite solidarity with the afflicted or highlight the conditioned nature of human affairs.

Discourses of Evil and of Tragedy

> *At 8:30 [the] evening [of September 11], President Bush addressed the nation from the White House. After emphasizing that the first priority was to help the injured and protect against any further attacks, he said: "We will make no distinction between the terrorists who committed these acts and those who harbor them." He quoted Psalm 23—"though I walk through the valley of the shadow of death." No American, he said, "will ever forget this day." (The 9/11 Commission Report)*[33]

The difference presumed by literati to exist between academic theories and ordinary uses of tragedy is one issue raised by rhetorical responses to the 9/11 attacks. On more careful consideration, that difference seems less important than the similar ways in which both tragedy and "tragedy" functioned as resources for specialists and nonspecialists alike as they struggled to respond to a terrible blow. Another issue raised by rhetorical responses to 9/11 is the extent to which the discourse of tragedy, whatever its source, was in competition with other discourses adopted by Americans as they sought to make sense of the events of that day. Here again, Simpson's remarks in his review of Eagleton's book on tragedy provide a convenient point of departure, particularly his claim that Americans preferred the "language of evil" over the "language of tragedy" in the aftermath of September 11. If the anecdotal evidence from print journalism and the Web suggests otherwise when it came to U.S. journalists, their interview subjects, and bloggers, Simpson's claim can perhaps be vindicated in relation to the public statements of President Bush, who did often refer to "evil" and "evildoers" in the aftermath of 9/11. What one finds upon examining his speeches and pronouncements, however, are plenty of references to the "tragedy" of the circumstances. So, for example, in his September 13, 2001, address at a service in the National Cathedral on the National Day of Prayer and Remembrance, the president remarked that, "God's signs are not always the ones we look for. We learn in tragedy that His purposes are not always our own." A week later, in his Special Address before Congress, Bush noted that, "all of America was touched on the evening of the tragedy to see Republicans and Democrats join together on the steps of the Capitol singing, 'God Bless America.'" Further on in the speech, he invited Americans to "continue to support victims of this tragedy" with their contributions. At a Pentagon ceremony on the one year anniversary of the attacks, Bush intoned, "the murder of innocents cannot be explained, only endured. And though they died in tragedy, they did not die in vain."[34]

In some respects, Bush's resort to the rhetoric of tragedy was consistent with ordinary language. So, for example, he refers to "tragedy" in a sentence that invokes an unusual display of unity across party lines ("God Bless America" on the steps of the Capitol). As previously noted, ordinary uses of "tragedy" often implicitly function as expressions of anticipated solidarity. Notwithstanding this convergence, one might nevertheless wonder to what extent his vernacular uses of "tragedy" reflected a distinctively tragic sensibility. After all, if Bush was known for anything in the wake of 9/11, it was for his tendency to envision the world in pervasively religious, morally absolutist terms. Such a tendency seems, at least on first look, to be at odds with habits of tragic thinking that tend to emphasize the ironies of human agency and the pitfalls of human pride. Hubris, a notion associated with the overreaching hero of ancient Greek tragedy, did become an issue in relation to the Bush administration's policies but it was an issue raised by administration critics. So, for example, Bush's war policy in Iraq seemed, to some, driven by impulses so at odds with the basic lessons of tragedy that at least one commentator felt impelled to invoke the tragic texts of ancient Athens as a corrective.[35] Concerned about the dire effects of Bush's "Manichean" mode of thinking about Iraq and other issues on democratic values and institutions, another commentator entitled his book, "A Tragic Legacy", to evoke the president's failure to put the country's post-9/11 sense of national purpose to positive use.[36]

Even granting that some of Bush's offhanded references were perfectly consistent with ordinary usage, there were occasions on which his references to the "tragedy" of 9/11 seemed curious. What made them unusual was their being nested in other than tragic contexts. So, for example, the affirmation of the tragic divergence between human and divine purposes in his National Cathedral address was eventually followed up with the claim that, "this world He created is of moral design. Grief and tragedy and hatred are only for a time. Goodness, remembrance, and love have no end. And the Lord of life holds all who die, and all who mourn." In affirming a limit to tragic suffering and in evoking so explicitly the consolatory vision of a divinely ordained afterlife, the president effectively substituted a consolatory Christian vision for a tragic one. In offering a truth claim about the existence and nature of an afterlife, this notion of religious consolation manifested a sensibility at odds with tragedy in which the mode of response to unbearable suffering is not to alleviate that suffering by claims to transcendental truths. Tragedy seeks instead to transfigure suffering aesthetically in the uncertain hope of provoking cathartic or reconciliatory or redemptive forms of relief from it. The special character of tragedy in this regard can be likened to the distinctive promise of storytelling modes of political theory, as described by Judith Shklar in her book, *Ordinary Vices*: "the great intellectual advantage of telling stories is that it does not rationalize the irrationality of actual experience and of history. Indecision, incoherence, and inconsistency are not ironed out or put between brackets. All our conflicts are preserved in all their inconclusiveness."[37]

On another occasion, during a televised speech on the eve of the U.S. invasion of Iraq, Bush situated a reference to the tragedy of 9/11 in a framework of assumptions and aims that are arguably untragic. In the speech, he declared that, while "the United States and other nations did nothing to deserve or invite this threat . . . we will do everything to defeat it. Instead of drifting along toward tragedy, we will set a course toward safety. Before the day of horror can come, before it is too late to act, this danger will be removed." The speech was significant in the way in which it instrumentalized "tragedy," enlisting it as a justification for a policy that seemed to its detractors to be so *un*tragic, so lacking in a basic recognition of the tragic limits of human knowledge and action. For a president who reportedly reads the Bible every day and who has made a point of asserting that, as a wartime leader, he draws personal strength, not from his biological father, but from "a higher father,"[38] there is little apparent incentive to mull over the nature and significance of tragedy or to exploit the cathartic or reconciliatory or redemptive potential of ordinary language uses of "tragedy." Even if gestures are made to the rhetoric of tragedy, the dominant sensibility seems to be one informed by a kind of "eschatological or recompense theodicy . . . based on the conviction that human life transcends personal death and that the righteous eventually receive their full reward."[39]

Suffering, especially when it comes unexpectedly and on an unprecedented scale, tends to provoke efforts to find meaning and consolation in religious symbols, rituals and beliefs. In the aftermath of the 9/11 attacks, churchgoing increased among Americans, according to a Pew survey, and some observers speculated whether the country was undergoing another "Great Awakening."[40] Public recourse to religious symbols, rituals, and beliefs so proliferated that Gustav Niebuhr, a *New York Times* religious affairs columnist, was led to comment that, "symbols of America's culture of civil religion have gained a new prominence. 'God Bless America' has been sung so often that it might as well be the national anthem. 'In God We Trust' can be found on many billboards." One question he raises about this post-9/11 phenomenon is whether it signals the intensification of patriotic feeling or an upsurge of theological fervor. In other words, is it a phenomenon of American *civil* religion or *religion* plain and simple?

The notion of civil religion became a focus of debate in academic circles in the United States in the 1960s and 1970s largely in response to the work of Robert Bellah. In his work, the label came to refer to the various ways that the distribution of power in a given society found effective sanction in beliefs about a divine or suprahuman order. For example, in relatively undifferentiated primitive societies, what hierarchy there is tends to be "simultaneously religious and political." Archaic societies exhibit more political differentiation and centralization with an established "hierarchy of religious specialists" whose role it is to attest to the ruler's divine or divinely ordained status.[41]

Bellah conceptualized the problem of civil religion as one of legitimacy and he considered as a special case the sort of civil religion necessitated by republican self government. Defined by the absence of a divinely ordained royal bloodline and characterized by a wide diffusion of political power, republics depend on citizens who feel solidarity with each other and are willing to control their personal wants to a degree that makes collective self government possible. Feelings of solidarity and self discipline are effects oftentimes associated with religious belief and practice.

> A republic must attempt to be ethical in a positive sense and to elicit the ethical commitment of its citizens. For this reason it inevitably pushes toward the symbolization of an ultimate order of existence in which republican values and virtues make sense. Such symbolization may be nothing more than the worship of the republic itself as the highest good, or it may be, as in the American case, the worship of a higher reality that upholds the standards the republic attempts to embody.[42]

The form republican symbolization of a higher order took in the U.S. was fundamentally shaped by periodic waves of Protestant revivalism starting with the Great Awakening of the 1740s. Bellah described the American civil religion which resulted as "formal in the sparsity of its tenets," "marginal in [its lack of] official support in the legal and constitutional order," "though very securely institutionalized" in the vigorous church life of many U.S. citizens.[43]

Bellah's description provides ready-made criteria by which Niebuhr could have assessed whether the post-9/11 upsurge in religiously toned ritual and symbol manifested civil or theological tendencies. Instead of offering his own assessment, Niebuhr refers his readers to Thomas W. Flynn, editor of *Free Inquiry*, a quarterly published by the Council of Secular Humanism, whose own position is unequivocal: the proliferation of religious pronouncements and ceremonies in the public square is mainly driven by religious belief. This state of affairs is very worrying to Flynn and to his fellow secularists who, he reports, feel excluded from the post-9/11 community of grief. Adding to their discomfort is the fact that, unlike religious believers, secular humanists cannot console themselves with a belief in the afterlife: "If anything, our loss is greater, since we envision no next-worldly existence in which victims might be made whole from what was torn from them." In calling for the inclusion of nonbelievers in national mourning, Flynn resorts, significantly enough, to the rhetoric of tragedy: "The nonreligious feel no less devastated by this national tragedy than other Americans."[44] Flynn's invocation of a "national tragedy," coming as it does in an account of the exclusively religious nature of post-9/11 ceremonies of mourning, is suggestive. Might he implicitly be posing a secular, *tragic* alternative to the sort of eschatological theodicies typically on offer in Christian churches, as an alternative basis for a shared sense of national reconciliation? If so, what would qualify tragedy as such an alternative? One thing that apparently qualifies it in Flynn's mind is its promise of being a more inclusive community of grief, in which membership is not determined by a commitment to a belief in the existence of a deity or of an afterlife.

The notion of religious consolation and tragic reconciliation (or catharsis or Dionysian redemption, to cite other well-known notions from the tradition of theorizing tragedy) as alternative responses to suffering is implied as well by the heading—"Church, State and Tragedy"—given to the section in which Niebuhr raises the question about whether the post-9/11 environment of mourning in the United States is shaped more by patriotism or by religious fervor. The heading can be reformulated as a question: To what extent ought the citizenry ("State") come to terms with a serious loss by opting for modes of religious consolation ("Church"), to what extent by opting for modes of tragic catharsis or reconciliation or redemption ("Tragedy")? The evidence of relevant passages from President Bush's speeches suggests that he prefers the former over the latter as his mode of response to suffering. Psalm 23's anticipation of divine protection and the image of the dead in the caring hands of divinity (evoked by Bush in his address to the nation on the evening of September 11 and in his September 13 address at the National Cathedral, respectively) promise to soothe suffering by offering the metaphysical balm of eternal life. In opting for a response shaped more by theodicy, Bush seeks a kind of certainty that tragedy cannot guarantee. To the extent that a tragic vision would stake its cathartic or reconciliatory or redemption promise on more indirect and less certain means, it leaves its audience more exposed to suffering.

President Bush, who has told reporters that he does not agonize over decisions, manages suffering in another characteristic way: by embracing a kind of moral absolutism (what Glenn Greenwald in the aforementioned book, *A Tragic Legacy*, refers to as Manicheanism), whereby policy judgments take on the character of moral decisions made according to an unquestioned and highly polarized framework of right and wrong. Take, for example, a particularly telling exchange with the journalist Bob Woodward over the question of wartime losses in Iraq. The relevant comments came in a December- 2003 interview, after Woodward quoted British Prime Minister Tony Blair's admission that he had suffered doubts about his decision to commit British troops to the Iraq invasion, especially on those occasions when he heard from parents who had lost sons in Iraq.

> "Yeah," President Bush replied. "I haven't suffered doubt."
> "Is that right?" I asked. "Not at all?"
> "No. And I'm able to convey that to the people." To those who had lost sons or daughters, he said, "I hope I'm able to convey that in a humble way."[45]

Implicit in Bush's responses is the view that the grief of those who have lost loved ones in Iraq can be better alleviated by exposure to a president's unconditional sense of the rightness of his decision to commit U.S. troops to war.

Together with the notion of divine care and protection, Bush's moral absolutism is consistent with a theodicy featuring a just god. Bush's preference for morally absolutist rhetoric ("the language of evil" as Simpson puts it) manifests a sensibility that prefers to overcome suffering rather than contemplate it in refigured form. In response to situations of loss, proponents of moral absolutism apply simple, uncomplicated categories (good and evil, say) on the basis of which members of an ingroup can rechannel their negative feelings by focusing them on an outgroup. (The twin dynamics of moral absolutism and religious consolation as rhetorical responses to loss are sometimes to be found simultaneously at play during funerals held for victims of violence. And to the extent that these dynamics dominate the tone of such ceremonies, they can crowd out dynamics of reconciliation that are more tragically inflected. Take, for an example, a newspaper report of a funeral held in Georgia for an elderly couple brutally murdered by their teenage granddaughter and her accomplice. It is the kind of storyline that so often invites the use of tragic rhetoric by journalists or their interview subjects. Yet, in the case of this story, one finds no references to the "tragedy" of the situation by participants or the reporting journalist. Instead, there are consolatory references to an afterlife—"'No one could have ever guessed my loving parents would have gone to the Lord in this senseless way.'"—and apportionments of blame—"Our hearts cry out with one question: Why? Why here? Why now? There's one answer: Satan. . . . We cannot blame God."[46] A quite different, more tragic, tone is struck in the previously cited report of the funeral held for the woman deliberately pushed in front of a New York City subway: "tragedy is always around us, and it makes us appreciate life.")[47]

The view that President Bush's approach to situations of loss relies on a theodical notion of religious consolation and a stance of moral absolutism and that that approach constitutes an explicitly nontragic alternative to suffering is additionally suggested by the findings of a group of psychologists who have researched the nature of President Bush's popular appeal using Terror Management Theory (TMT). "TMT posits that popular support for leaders is partly the result of the need to allay a deeply rooted fear of death." At times when issues of mortality become more salient in public consciousness, as, for example, in the wake of the 9/11 attacks, this theory predicts that the public will feel a greater need for leaders able "literally and symbolically to deliver the people from illness, calamity, chaos, and death as well as to demonstrate the supremacy of the worldview [sic]." Finding empirical support for a relationship between "mortality salience" and President Bush's popularity in test subjects across the ideological spectrum, these researchers speculated that the basis of his appeal may "lie in his image as a protective shield against death, armed with high-tech weaponry, patriotic rhetoric, and the resolute invocation of doing God's will to 'rid the world of evil.'" The authority of Bush or other political leaders is enhanced, according to this theory, to the extent that he or they can "assume mastery over nature and tragedy and uphold the cultural meaning system that imbues individual lives with transcendent meaning, order, and permanence."[48]

If President Bush did, in fact, "assume mastery over . . . tragedy" in the wake of 9/11, it may have been in a double sense. In evoking a consolatory vision of the after-life and offering absolutist moral judgments, Bush did work to minimize Americans' suffering in the aftermath of a "tragedy," in the sense of an unexpected and profound loss. One could further argue that, in articulating an eschatological theodicy and assuming a moralistic stance, he mastered tragedy in an additional sense as well; he opted for modes of response that tend to render tragic modes of response to 9/11 suf-fering superfluous. So, for example, while President Bush seemingly adopted a tragic perspective on humanity's ignorance of divine purpose at the National Cathedral service (e.g., "God's signs are not always the ones we look for. We learn in tragedy that his purposes are not always our own."), the dominant tone of his address is non-tragic: "Grief and tragedy and hatred are *only for a time*" (emphasis added). Similarly, while Ray Giunta, a crisis chaplain who spent over two months in the early phases of the clearing operation at the World Trade Center, asserts in *God @ Ground Zero* his belief "that this story, begun on a beautiful September morning, was a tragedy," his perspective remains throughout an "eternal" one, according to which "God wanted to redeem every part." The solace Giunta offers to survivors of the attacks and mem-bers of the work crews at Ground Zero comes almost exclusively in the form of a theodical vision, of, for example, a "God" who "helps the victims go into eternity."[49]

In cases where the rhetoric of loss draws upon plot lines and imagery that are explicitly Christian, considerations of tone and context can be decisive in determin-ing whether that rhetoric is more consistent with tragedy or with theodicy. While the notion of Christian *tragedy* may seem strange on first consideration, plenty of effort has been expended to theorize this possibility. In Louis Ruprecht's persuasive line of argument about the tragic potential of the story of the Passion, greater weight is given to the nature of Gospel accounts of the suffering of Jesus than to the transcen-dentally positive end (resurrection) at which some of these accounts gesture or arrive. "The whole power of [Mark's description of] Gethsemane . . . derives from the fact that we here witness the collision between wills, a tragic struggle for self-definition in which we are invited to participate and which we recognize as our own." By con-trast, John's Jesus "is so heroically self-present, so transparent to the divine will, that there is no tragedy and no real suffering."[50]

Perhaps the most memorable instance of presidential rhetoric in which Christian tropes and imagery were used to express a tragic vision of politics and life was Lincoln's Second Inaugural. "Both [sides] read the same Bible, and pray to the same God; each invokes His aid against the other. . . . The prayers of both could not be answered; that of neither has been answered fully. The Almighty has his own pur-poses." In reference to the Second Inaugural, Robert Bellah explicitly recognizes how Lincoln placed Christian rhetoric in the service of tragedy: "Lincoln incorporated biblical symbolism more centrally into the civil religion than had ever been done before or would ever be done again in his great somber tragic vision of an unfaithful nation in need above all of charity and justice."[51] While the biblically informed language for which Bush opted in the wake of 9/11 bears a marked resemblance to

Lincoln's (and may even have been modeled on it), Bush's tone and the larger context of his confident avowals of a redeeming divinity bespeaks a very different sensibility toward suffering. Lacking that same confidence, Lincoln adopted a tragic perspective that was resistant even to the comfort of a "deferred theodicy," according to which "believers deny that the mystery of suffering can be fully understood" and prefer "to defer comprehension [of suffering] and trust in God's ultimate goodness and sovereignty."[52] It may be that the planners of the September 2002 commemoration of the World Trade Center dead were seeking to appropriate some of the tragic power of Lincoln's rhetoric when they decided to include a reading of the Gettysburg Address in the ceremony. Simon Stow has argued for the tragic (Dionysian") effect of Lincoln's famous oration at Gettysburg, according to which a public act of mourning occasioned a transformative process of national self reflection and critical redefinition. He sees the use of the address in the 2002 ceremony as seriously lacking in tragic resonance and as according more with an uncritical and self-congratulatory patriotism.[53]

Theodicy and tragedy loom as issues (the former in an explicit way, the latter only implicitly) in a book that argues for the post-9/11 relevance of the language of evil for non-theodical (tragic) thinking. In *Evil in Modern Thought: An Alternative History of Philosophy* (2002), Susan Neiman laments the resistance of progressives to applying the language of evil to the terrorist acts of September 11; their intellectual scruples effectively surrendered the field of public judgment to "those whose simple, demonic conceptions of evil often deliberately obscure more insidious forms of it." The point, according to Neiman, is to recognize evils however they manifest themselves, whether they are the result of people "play[ing] small parts in systems that lead to evils they do not want to foresee" or of a premeditated and malicious intent to commit mass atrocity.[54]

In response to the suffering of 9/11, Neiman offers no theodicy of her own or even consolation. Instead, she offers a story, the story of some of the passengers on United Airlines Flight 93:

> Informed via cell phone that other hijacked planes had been flown into the towers, some people determined to fight. They failed to overcome the terrorists but succeeded in assuring that the plane crashed into an empty field. They died as heroes die. Unlike the hypothetical fellow in Kant's example who prefers to die rather than bear false witness, their refusal to become instruments of evil became more than a gesture. We will never know how much destruction they prevented, but we know they prevented some. They proved not only that human beings have freedom; we can use it to affect a world we fear we don't control.[55]

The import of that story we only fully learn later, on the final pages of her book, when she approvingly invokes Kant. For, in her view, it was Kant's great achievement philosophically to have faced up to the discrepancy between the human capacity of reason and the human experience of irrational suffering in a way that preserved the dignity

of human action without fostering any illusions about the true extent of human powers. The details of Neiman's rich and persuasive account of Kant's moral philosophy
are not immediately relevant to this discussion except for the fact that, at one point,
she considers the significance of Kant's work explicitly in terms of tragedy: "Tragedy
is about the ways that virtue and happiness fail to rhyme, for the want, or the excess,
of some inconsiderable piece of the world which happens to be the only thing that
mattered. Kant's work was written in increasing awareness of it . . . . The tragedy is
real. Kant's understanding of the ways that the wish to be God fuels most of our mistakes is as deep as his understanding that only being God would really help."[56] In a
book that aims to retell the history of philosophy as a series of intellectual responses
to the problem of human suffering ("evil"), this rare invocation of "tragedy" is significant. After all, Neiman could well have told the history of modern philosophers'
confrontations with the problem of suffering as a history of how modern philosophers have theorized about the tragic nature of the human condition. Neiman did
not opt for this latter narrative approach; yet, she does go out of her way to articulate
in terms of "tragedy" the legacy of that philosopher who seems to exemplify for her
the best intellectual alternative to theodicy. Kant is the last philosopher mentioned in
her book's final pages and the decision to leave off with him suggests the singular
importance of his (tragic) legacy for her concluding recommendation that one face
the world's challenges in a state of mind at once skeptical and hopeful, with a healthy
but not disabling dose of humility. This larger point, reflected back upon her consideration of the evil of 9/11, suggests that Americans were faced with at least two basic
theoretical responses to the suffering caused that day; explaining it away (a secularist
might argue) by means of a theodicy or tragically accepting the burden of that suffering while appreciating the admittedly small but significant margins in which
human agency can happen.

The Politics of Suffering

On the face of it, an approach that treats eschatological (and other forms of) theodicy
and tragedy as distinct and comparable theoretical responses to 9/11 and suffering,
in general, might well raise questions. The image of a caring and just divinity promising eternal life articulated by Bush after 9/11 is a pervasive and longstanding one in
American life, originating as it does in a widely venerated text (the Bible) and enjoying regular promotion by members of the clergy. On the face of it, the discourse of
tragedy, whether in ordinary language or in academic theorizing, lacks the same
sort of doctrinally defined, devotionally reinforced focus. The mismatch seems even
more decisive on a broader view of the character of American spiritual and intellectual culture. The U.S. remains among the developed world's most religious nations,
while it has long been taken as a settled fact that, "Americans have always been
unequivocally optimistic and bereft of a sense of the tragic."[57] Our most distinctive
contribution to world philosophy, pragmatism, has seemed, especially to its European
detractors, to be utterly and fatally lacking in a sense of the tragic. In a culture of

Sunday services and self help programs, of born-again Christians and rags-to-riches biographies, in which a sense of the guiding hand of a caring divinity and a relatively robust confidence in the self's capacity to choose the right way converge, can the contemporary discourse of tragedy plausibly be seen as contending with theodicy as a significant source of comfort to Americans "when bad things happen"?

On a second look, however, the status of tragedy in American life and culture does not appear so tenuous. In the first place, there is the undeniable readiness of many Americans to use the rhetoric of tragedy as, for example, in the wake of 9/11 (i.e., the 853,000 hits from the Google search). Also worth noting are the many and continuing pedagogical, scholarly, and artistic activities of theorists, interpreters, and performers of tragedy in various academic departments, including drama, philosophy, and literature, not to mention the assignment of such texts as *Oedipus Rex*, *Antigone*, *The Eumenides*, in thousands upon thousands of American high school literature classes. And American pragmatism's blind spot when it comes to tragedy, which Cornel West has sought to remedy,[58] must be balanced against the tragic tone that pervades the writing of so many canonical American authors including Melville, Faulkner, Hemingway and Toni Morrison. Even the fact of church affiliation or Christian belief is no guarantee of the absence of a tragic sensibility in the United States; as we have seen in a previous chapter, Cornel West has argued for the significance of Black churches as crucial purveyors of a life-sustaining tragic sensibility to a people exposed to a history of brutal oppression.

If tragedy and theodicy can be treated as contrasting forms of response to suffering, in general, and to 9/11, in particular, what are the stakes in treating them so? In the first place, one stands to gain a more comprehensive understanding of the resources available to Americans in times of crisis. The suffering consequent on U.S. participation in foreign wars or in a civil war, economic depressions and corporate malfeasance, episodes of mob violence, conditions of majority tyranny, and governmental repression cannot always or fully be made good by material compensation or policy adjustments or political recognition. Religion has typically been seen as the primary, if not exclusive, non-political, non-material source of comfort in bad times. Related to this view is a longstanding and widely held belief that deficits in personal integrity and communal solidarity to which citizens in a liberal constitutional order are prone even in good times can only be made up by the socializing, moralizing influence of religion. As Tocqueville argues in *Democracy in America*, "even if the unbeliever does not admit religion to be true, he still considers it useful. Regarding religious institutions in a human point of view, he acknowledges their influence upon manners and legislation. He admits that they may serve to make men live in peace, and prepare them gently for the hour of death."[59] Eschatological theodicy is here significant particularly for its promise of divine punishment for earthly wrongdoing. Against this backdrop of appreciation for theodicy's consolatory and deterrent functions, the discourse of tragedy stands as an alternative for those secularists who find themselves excluded or alienated when public officials, for reasons of personal belief or political calculation, resort to the language of theodicy.

Abraham Lincoln, who stands as one of the most important promoters and, later, posthumous symbols of national reconciliation in U.S. history, did often avail himself of biblical imagery in his public speeches, especially as the civil conflict wore on and the level of death and injury reached unprecedented heights. In addition to being a close reader of the Bible, Lincoln was, also, however, an avid theatergoer and reader of Shakespeare's political tragedies.[60] It may well be that his powerful consolatory presence in the national imagination had as much, if not more, to do with his promotion of a tragic vision of American history (e.g., the Second Inaugural acceptance of wartime suffering as just repayment from both southern *and* northern whites for the suffering inflicted by slavery) and his seeming enactment of the role of tragic scapegoat (i.e., Lincoln's death understood as a form of symbolic repayment for the outbreak of fratricidal conflict).

Recognizing the discourse of tragedy as an alternative to theodicy also means recognizing the differences in the way each discourse works its consolatory effect. While both the discourse of tragedy and theodicy are responses to suffering, the nature of the response in each case is quite different. In the context of American Christianity, theodicy promises relief from suffering through truth claims authorized by a sacred text and reinforced by institutional practices of religious devotion. By contrast, tragedy offers no promise of relief from suffering. Its characteristic mode is not explanation via textually authorized and devotionally reinforced truth claims about the existence of a divinity or an afterlife nor is its sought-after effect primarily a sense of moral righteousness. To be sure, in its earliest form, *tragōidíā* was performed as part of polis cult worship. Even in its original cultic setting, however, *tragōidíā* did not rely for its civic influence on truths purveyed by a "canonical body of beliefs," a centrally authorized sacred text, or a "professional divinely anointed priesthood."[61] And while one might argue that *tragōidíā* functioned as a "privileged locus of religious exploration"[62] in the ancient democratic polis or as a means of "constru[ing] and defin[ing] the . . . problems of theodicy and piety,"[63] it did not provide any final destination for that exploration or solution to those problems. In any case, for our contemporary purposes, Greek tragedy, theories of tragedy and ordinary language uses of "tragedy" are no longer religiously freighted.

The working of tragedy has been described under a variety of rubrics, including catharsis (Aristotle), reconciliation (Hegel), and Dionysian merger (Nietzsche). Of course, theorists of tragedy have held that tragedy can reveal truths but the nature of these truths is of a different quality than the truths of the King James Bible. One could put the difference this way; where theodicy proclaims, tragedy *intimates*. Or, to evoke a distinction made by Judith Shklar in the context of a discussion of possible modes of political theory, where a theological approach proceeds by "fix[ing] exactly the grounds of praise and blame," a novelistic approach proceeds more indirectly, not only by exemplifying truths in story incidents but also by illuminating truths only vaguely or incompletely known.[64]

What theodicy proclaims is the truth of a higher order. By contrast, the discourse of tragedy intimates what might be called a *broader* order. Theodicy's verticality essentially consists in its reaching for a truth above and beyond human affairs as the basis for its consolatory effect. Tragic rhetoric seeks to muster its consolatory effect through a horizontal appeal to a common sense or intuition or incipient knowledge that works its effect to the extent that this sense or intuition or incipient knowledge is felt to be already implicit in the order of things (even if hitherto unrecognized). One might think in this regard of Martha Nussbaum's depiction of *tragōidíā* as an inductive, egalitarian form of paideia in the ancient polis.[65] A relevant historical contrast to *tragōidíā* particularly understood as a horizontally operative form of paideia would be Platonic political philosophy, with its reliance on a notion of tran-scendental truth accessible to the expertly trained few for use as standards of behav-ior in human affairs. It is no coincidence that a major topic of discussion in Platonic works such as *Republic* and *Laws* is theodicy, particularly its importance in helping to maintain order in the polity. According to some, this consideration weighed heav-ily in Platonism's favor among Church fathers, especially when the Church took on the responsibility of secular rule.[66] For good reason, Nietzsche called Christianity a form of Platonism for the masses.

To what extent differences in the ways that the discourse of tragedy and theodicy operate correspond to different levels of support for democratic politics is an open question. Is one or the other more compatible with democracy? The answer one might give would probably depend in large part on what one believed about the nature of authority in a democracy. To the extent one believed with Tocqueville that democratic politics can most reliably be sustained as long as a critical mass of citi-zens are believers in a transcendental source of authority, one would see eschatologi-cal or other sorts of theodicy as a crucial support for democracy especially in times when citizens are challenged by suffering and loss. To the extent one held that demo-cratic politics does not or should not rely on extrapolitical sources of authority, theod-icy might be seen as an obstacle to a fuller development of the democratic ideal of self-rule. Taking this latter position in her book, *On Revolution* (1963), Hannah Arendt defends the basic autonomy of politics by locating an appropriate *intra*political source of republican authority in the veneration of the act of political founding. Interestingly enough, her book concludes with a lengthy citation of a Greek tragedy, Sophocles' *Oedipus at Colonus*, as if, perhaps, to evoke the significance of tragedy as an alternative to theodicy in fostering and maintaining political authority in republics.[67]

Insofar as the operation of the discourse of tragedy in American political culture has garnered little if any systematic attention, its effects on American politics have not sufficiently been recognized or appreciated. As a result, observers of American politics have too often or too exclusively credited religion for promoting democratic solidarity and authority even when evidence of the positive effects of tragedy is in plain sight. In this regard, Bellah can stand in as a representative example. He ends his influential book, *The Broken Covenant: American Civil Religion in a Time of Crisis* (1974), which focuses its critical energy on the growing individualism and materialism of American culture, with what one might fairly characterize as an ambivalent call for another Great Awakening. However, alongside the implicit endorsement of religious revivalism as the one viable resource available for use in a program of American cultural renewal are scattered acknowledgments of the promise of tragedy to respond to America's crisis of meaning and community. So, for example, Melville and Hawthorne are mentioned as artists who "showed that even in this raw new country tragic understanding was possible." William Faulkner "deepened the Southern sense of defeat into a genuine apprehension of tragedy." And Lincoln's outstanding significance for American civil religion in Bellah's description seems to have as much to do with his "somber tragic vision" as it does with his biblical literacy.[68]

It may be that the discourse of tragedy lacks the theoretical coherence or institutional support or cultural resonance to perform the political role secularists would wish for it. One cannot know for sure, however, until more adequate measure is taken of its past effects on American political culture. In the meantime, tragedy remains a promising point of orientation for those who seek to live decent and meaningful lives in a world that appears irrevocably disenchanted.

SECTION III

Tragedy and Political Identity

CHAPTER 7

Botho Strauss: Goatsong in a Democratic Key?

If Americans conventionally stand as a people whose self conception is hostile or indifferent to a tragic sensibility, Germans have long been represented and have represented themselves as *the* tragic people par excellence. If the American voices arguing for the relevance of tragedy in history and politics have been few, marginal, and/or indirect, tragic voices in Germany have tended to be numerous, central and explicit. Affirmations of tragedy's relevance to social and political life in Germany have been so pronounced that, at times and especially in the wake of catastrophic experiences of war and dictatorship, significant efforts have been expended to lessen or purge the influence of tragic thinking or theorizing about tragedy in German life.

The distinctive engagement of German philosophers and literati with Greek and modern tragedies, theories of tragedy, and notions of *das Tragische* invites consideration of the relationship of tragedy to questions of political identity, another important dimension, along with agency and solidarity, of social and political life. How and why does tragedy become central to the political self definition of a people? What advantages are promised by this sort of self-definition and what dangers might follow from it? In this and the following two chapters, we consider three prominent German engagements with tragedy in public intellectual life and art. In the first, focused on the controversy surrounding dramatist Botho Strauss's publication of *"Anschwellender Bockgesang"* (Goat Song Rising) in 1993, an attempt is made to affirm the value of tragedy and redefine newly reunified Germans as a tragic people. The second chapter, focused on the literary production of (former East) German novelist Christa Wolf over a 15-year period spanning the fall of the Wall, traces both her ambivalent treatment of tragedy and her switch from the role of critic of tragedy for its nefarious effects on German (and Western) culture to the role of aspiring tragedian seeking to activate its politically beneficent effects in German politics. The last chapter on tragedy and identity focuses on a recent cinematic attempt by Michael Schorr to mediate the political and cultural stresses consequent upon the reunification of Germany by importing an African-American tradition of tragic engagement.

* * *

[W]hen people start destroying human beings like vermin ... then they destroy not only six million souls but also, just in passing, the language of the survivors. I observe how the survivors ... are always biting their tongues and how literature tries to get along without metaphors. The language has got the evil eye, whereas the beggar-woman, whom I am passing again, has lost it; she is merely a woman who can be defined with a few adjectives: miserable, tragic, old. (Alfred Andersch, *Efraim's Book*)[1]

Toward the end of 2005, the *New York Times* reported on a public service campaign, produced by one of Germany's leading ad firms, which "aimed at cheering up the presumably gloomy population, nudging Germans toward an unaccustomed optimism." At stake in the "battle" against "national melancholy" was the country's recovery from ballooning budget deficits and high unemployment. Citing survey results indicating half as many Germans as Americans believing in their ability to shape their own fates (30 percent and 60 percent, respectively), one of the ad campaign's creators was quoted as saying, "a lot of (German) people think that their fate is controlled by somebody else, and in our eyes that is a mistake." While identifying the disappointments raised in the aftermath of unification as the proximate cause for the German malaise, the report eventually alludes to an explanation that grounded Germans' sense of fatalism in their national character; "Germans are by nature pessimistic, and that does have something to do with the poor economy."[2]

The notion of a German national character marked by a distinctive form of pessimism or fatalism is a longstanding one, to which critics have often recurred, especially in the wake of Germany's early twentieth century history of moral and political irresponsibility. So, for example, Thomas Mann in a 1946 essay entitled, "The Tragedy of Germany," quoted liberally from 1933–1934 diary entries in which he identified "indifference, fatalism, hopelessness" (rather than "faith and enthusiasm") as the emotional bases of popular support for the newly entrenched Nazi regime. In those early years of National Socialist rule, Mann "saw . . . a people lashed and intoxicated again and again into a nationalistic and falsely revolutionary frenzy, but a people nevertheless depressed, fearful of future ills, fatalistically indifferent." These national qualities explained not only Germans' initial acquiescence to Nazi rule but also their later commitment to support the regime's prosecution of wars of conquest—"to an uncritical people like the Germans, war is simply a challenge to . . . its willingness to sacrifice"—as well as their final determination to fight to the bitter end: "and when they finally did recognize (that the war was lost), then ingrained fanaticism and Gothic pathos in the face of destruction were made to replace the lost faith in victory."[3]

If Mann conspicuously places central explanatory weight on German fatalism or pessimism for the catastrophic outcome that was Nazi rule, he is less directly forthcoming about what means of recovery are now available to "a nation that never knew how to become a nation" and "a people that . . . despairs of ever governing itself . . . ." "The hope remains," Mann concludes, "that, with the cooperation of the German will itself, purified by cruel suffering, a form of government and of life for the German people may be found that will encourage the development of its best powers and educate it to become a sincere co-worker for a brighter future of mankind."[4] One might think Mann's reference to a process of purification through suffering an *inadvertent* echo of the Aristotelian notion of catharsis were it not for the presence of a resonant term in the piece's title, tragedy, whose nuances are apparently meant by Mann to be aesthetic as well as historical. In this regard, it is worth noting that even as Mann composed this essay, he was in the midst of writing *Doktor Faustus*, which he described as a "passionate and telling dramatization of our [i.e., the German] tragedy."[5] The novel relates the story of composer Adrian Leverkühn's efforts to usher in a culturally revitalizing artistic breakthrough by purging his music of any effect of human subjectivity. His single-minded focus on pushing the technical means of musical expression to their logical extreme produces compositions lacking in human appeal and eventually results in the composer's mental and physical collapse. Witness to this tragic story of artistic hubris is the novel's narrator, Serenus Zeitblom, *Gymnasium* teacher and humanist, who reveals himself, for a time at least, to be no less susceptible (than Leverkühn) to the temptation of unburdening the self of moral and political responsibility in accordance with Germany's cultural pattern of "mechanized Romanticism."[6] In Zeitblom's case, the syndrome manifests itself not in the radically apolitical aestheticism of the artist but in the intellectual's dangerous commitment to a notion of Germany as weighed upon by a world historical destiny whose purported necessities included the launch of a preemptive war in 1914.[7]

In suggesting tragedy to be an appropriate means of response to moral and political deficits in German social or civic life, Mann signals his participation in a venerable German philosophical and literary tradition going back to the eighteenth-century philhellene art appreciator Johann Joachim Winckelmann, whose interpretation of the aesthetic significance of the ancient sculpture of Laocoon and his sons under attack by a serpent doing the bidding of a wrathful Apollo became a crucial touchstone of art criticism for generations of German literati. In particular, he formulated the aesthetic achievement of classical Greece under the rubric, *edle Einfalt und stille Grösse* (noble simplicity and serene greatness), by which he meant the Greeks' singular capacity to represent composure under duress: "the expression in Greek figures reveals greatness and composure of soul in the throes of whatever passions. This spirit is depicted in Laocoon's face, and not in the face alone, in spite of the most violent sufferings."[8]

If Mann held to a notion of narrative tragedy, whether in the form of a full-blown novelistic allegory of Germany's fall or in the form of a short essay focused directly on the causes and consequences of that fall, as a means of diagnosing and counteracting Germany's postwar conditions of spiritual demoralization and political apathy, he was not unaware that tragic ideas and rhetoric could sometimes foster the very political and moral dysfunctions against which he was struggling. So, for example, in an address at the Library of Congress held shortly after the fall of Berlin, he disavowed "tragic" as a descriptive term applicable to German history—"It is a melancholy story,—I call it that, instead of 'tragic,' because misfortune should not boast"[9]—in an apparent effort not to encourage further his co-nationals' susceptibility to "Gothic pathos." He was also aware of the possible exculpatory uses of tragedy as when he referred to the "stir" caused by one journalist's report "of German writers, who in their tragic effusions over their fate only revealed their moral flabbiness, their emotional conceit." He called this behavior a "disturbing exposé of the conduct of Inner Emigration"[10] and strongly criticized it in a public letter exchange with writer Frank Thiess, who hadn't emigrated and whose claims to moral and patriotic virtue—silently opposing the Nazi regime while living in solidarity with the German people in their suffering—Mann found self-serving, hypocritical, and false.

When is a use of tragic rhetoric or the experience of a work of tragedy a help in fostering an appropriate sense of individual agency or collective political responsibility, when is it a hindrance? Aware of both the promise and dangers of tragedy, Mann's approach to distinguishing between them is a bit ad hoc and not always entirely consistent. So, for example, in the same Library of Congress address in which he disavows the use of "tragic" because of its association with pernicious tendencies in German culture, Mann concludes by subsuming Germany's fall under the potentially exculpating rubric of "tragedy": "the German misfortune is only a paradigm of the tragedy of human life. And the grace that German so sorely needs, my friends, all of us need it."[11]

Mann's ambiguous postwar treatment of notions of tragedy and the tragic anticipates the emergence of a German intellectual environment relatively more hostile to any sort of overt reference to tragedy or notions of the tragic. So, for example, in the Historians' Controversy or *Historikerstreit* of the mid-1980s, contention over the nature of German history and identity becomes entangled in disagreements over the worth of tragedy as an orienting concept in historical and social scientific discourse. Paying close attention to the use of tragic rhetoric in the *Historikerstreit* (particularly Jürgen Habermas's unconditional rejection of such rhetoric) and analyzing its larger theoretical significance, this chapter proceeds to a consideration of how the experience of German unification, by unsettling postwar definitions of national identity and membership, spurred attempts in public intellectual life at re-engaging tragedy along the lines of earlier German efforts.

In particular, this chapter analyzes the arguments and reception of West German dramatist Botho Strauss's 1993 *Der Spiegel* essay, "*Anschwellender Bockgesang*," which controversially asserted that the prospects for a post-unification revitalization of German political culture would crucially depend on the extent to which Germans regained an authentic sense of the tragic. Navigating between the unconditional rejection of tragic notions and rhetoric expressed by some participants in the *Historikerstreit* and Strauss's one-sided embrace of them, this article concludes by gesturing to some ways in which theories of tragedy and notions of the tragic have been engaged for political effect while avoiding the excesses or dangers that seemed so salient in the aftermath of the catastrophes of Nazi rule.

The Historikerstreit

The *Historikerstreit* of 1986 was set off by an article authored by Jürgen Habermas and published in *Die Zeit*, in which he attacked the claims of several German historians whose works he saw as exemplifying a neoconservative political impulse to normalize the Nazi past and rehabilitate nationalistic definitions of German identity. He took Ernst Nolte to task for minimizing the unprecedented and radical nature of Nazi genocide by casting it as product of, and defensive response to, a history of industrial-era ideologies and movements of class warfare culminating in Bolshevik programs of mass arrest, deportation, and murder. To Michael Stürmer's claim that West German identity ought to be grounded in a sense of German historical continuity, Habermas countered that vital gains in moral and political responsibility attained by West Germans had been premised precisely on recognition of the fundamental historical rupture represented by Nazi-era criminality. Habermas also registered strong disapproval of Andreas Hillgruber's book, *Zweierlei Untergang: Die Zerschlagung des Deutschen Reiches und das Ende des Europäische Judentums* (Twofold Ruin: The Shattering of the German Empire and the End of European Jewry), for what he viewed as both its uncritically sympathetic account of German military efforts to hold the line against advancing Soviet armies in the last stages of the war and its emotionally detached view of the Nazi genocide of the Jews.

Habermas's shot across the bow provoked a series of responses and counter-responses in newspapers, current event magazines, and professional journals from historians, social scientists, and journalists. The merits of the various arguments in the debate are less important to this discussion than the frequency with which interlocutors couched their positions on the issues of German history and identity in terms of the rhetoric of tragedy. For Habermas and for many of his fellow critics, the use of such rhetoric by the historians in question or their adoption of tragic perspectives reflected the problematic nature of the purportedly revisionist notions of German history and identity being propagated. So, for example, at the very outset of the controversy, Habermas criticizes Hillgruber's portrayal of the "tragic-heroic" achievement (*"dem 'tragischen' Heldengeschehen"*) of German military resistance to the Soviet advance, as registering much more emotional commitment on the part of the author than his account of the other major event of that time, the genocidal attack on European Jews. Calling attention to Hillgruber's use of tragic rhetoric, Habermas goes on to characterize it as an example of juvenile bluster (*"nicht-revidierten . . . Klischees eines aus Jugendtagen mitgeführten Jargons"*). One might recall, in this connection, the state of mind Zeitblom (of *Doktor Faustus*) evokes when he and other Germans enthusiastically responded to the mobilization of 1914. The "tragic" nature of Germany's situation—denied the international respect and status that ought to have been forthcoming in light of the empire's power and achievements—becomes an excuse to plunge Europe into war.[12] A similar sense, of how the act of depicting one's situation as "tragic" (as *supposedly* bereft of any obviously good or decent options) can serve to justify all sorts of politically irresponsible actions and policies, seems to animate Habermas's criticism of Hillgruber's rhetoric.

Another instance where Habermas chooses to express his aversion to revisionist arguments through a critical engagement with the rhetoric of tragedy can be found in the concluding passage of his essay. There, a negatively valenced reference is made to Cassandra, a figure from Greek epic and tragedy, whose curse it was to foretell future catastrophes only to have her warnings go unheeded. Habermas invokes Cassandra as a *false* prophetess of doom and likens revisionist warnings about a purported crisis of German identity to her prophecies. These historians' unfounded expressions of pessimism about the future of a West Germany in which its people do not overcome their sense of a discontinuous past or discard their skepticism toward traditional nationalism are, he writes, like the calls of Cassandra (*"Kassandrarufen"*).[13]

Tragic rhetoric becomes a flashpoint for criticisms of so-called neoconservative attempts to reassess the nature and meaning of Nazi rule and the current prospects of German identity for several of Habermas's fellow critics, as well. In the view of Micha Brumlik, for example, casting the German defensive struggle against the Soviet armies as a tragic occurrence (*"tragischen Ereignis"*) served to justify the prolongation of the killing process in the camps as a necessary byproduct of a praiseworthy effort to defend German civilian populations in the East. The tragic mood–inducing rhetoric (*"tragisierende Worthülsen"*) so favored by Hillgruber in his book was therefore blameworthy for its effect of concealing or minimizing the extreme nature of German cruelty. Similarly, the book title's characterizations of Jewish experiences of Nazi extermination policies as an *"Untergang"* (literally, a going down) and as an *"Ende des Europäischen Judentums"* (End of European Jewry) constituted forms of tragic abstraction (*"tragisierende Abstraktifizierung"*) that blurred the harsh contours of individualized suffering.[14]

Relating the historians' dispute to an attempt on the part of Chancellor Helmut Kohl and his conservative government to replace the traditional understanding of World War Two as a war against Hitler's tyranny with a view of the war as an anticommunist crusade, Hans Mommsen, another critic, argued that such a reinterpretation would cast the Third Reich as a "tragic" entanglement made understandable when seen in the light of the threat of Bolshevik aggression (*"erschien das Dritte Reich als eine tragische aber angesichts der Bedrohung durch die bolschewistiche Aggression begreifliche Verstrickung"*). Among the items on this revisionist political agenda mentioned by Mommsen is the *"Dramaturgie des Bitburg-Spektakels"* whereby Ronald Reagan, at the invitation of Kohl, participated in a wreath-laying ceremony at a German military cemetery in Bitburg at which remains of Waffen SS troops also happened to be buried. Also considered worthy of note by Mommsen was a public lecture given by the Reagan Administration's ambassador to Germany in which he urged Germans to liberate themselves from the *"Tragödie der Zeit von 1933–1945"* and focus on the positive, democratic aspects of German history.[15]

Tragic notions and rhetoric become flashpoints for criticizing revisionist historians, one suspects, partly because the critics can only envision tragedy negatively. In general, the prevailing sense is that tragedy distorts or undermines political judgment in at least two ways. In assigning a false sense of necessity to certain events, it inappropriately diminishes the significance of human agency and relieves human agents of responsibility for their acts.

In addition to its potential in fostering a politically problematic sense of fatalism, reflection on tragedy or on the tragic aspects of existence might also lead to forms of aestheticism that interfere with the proper functioning of political or moral judgment. Dramatic and literary tragedies frame enactments or depictions of human suffering within a set of fictive conventions. In instances of real suffering, the temptation is to dodge the full horror of, or full responsibility for, awful situations by seeing them through the screen of fictive tragedy. In tempting us to see a painful historical event as a spectacle or a drama, tragic rhetoric can inappropriately distance us from the reality of human suffering, or so Brumlik seems implicitly to argue.

If Habermas and many of his fellow critics gave systematic and negative attention to revisionist historians' use of tragic notions and rhetoric, these historians were prepared to defend that use as appropriate. Hillgruber and Klaus Hildebrand separately defended *Zweierlei Untergang*'s tragedy-inflected characterization of the final defensive struggle of German troops on the Eastern Front as being entirely appropriate given the unfortunate choice facing German troops; ending their resistance and exposing German populations in the East to the wrath of vengeful Soviet armies or fighting on to give German civilians a chance to evacuate and thereby also *tragically* prolonging the operation of the extermination camps. Their defense essentially rests on a notion of tragedy as a situation that allows no unconditionally good options. Under circumstances like that which purportedly held for the German troops on the Eastern Front in the last stages of the war, every choice entailed serious costs; hence the tragedy.

Not content to limit themselves merely to a defense of the uses of tragic notions and rhetoric, Hildebrand and Hillgruber go on separately to argue that Habermas's aversion to tragedy manifests a serious blind spot in his own thinking, a blindspot caused by the working of a utopian impulse. Citing Andre Malraux's warning about the danger of revolutionaries trying to eliminate tragedy from life, Hildebrand argues that Habermas's "too optimistic trust in social scientific explanation" prevents him from seeing the past in a differentiated and nuanced way.[16] On this view, taking a tragic perspective on history means being more attentive to the irrational and contradictory aspects of human life. Following from this, the true danger to be avoided would be utopian (rather than tragic) thinking because of its tendency to rationalize history to an inappropriate extreme and assess past events according to overly simplistic, ideological worldviews.[17]

Of the 27 disputants whose articles, essays, interviews, or letters to the editor were assembled to form the documentary volume, *Historikerstreit*, published by Piper, at least a third of them self-consciously employ tragic notions and rhetoric (e.g., *Tragödie, Katharsis, Schicksal*) or single them out for critical analysis. Notions of tragedy seem also to figure significantly, if implicitly, in Charles Maier's volume, *The Unmasterable Past: History, Holocaust, and German Identity*, when he characterizes the *Historikerstreit* as "part of a larger conflict [pitting] those for whom history, if hardly a story of progress, is still a summons to enlightenment and to the advance of reason through the analysis of violence and repression" against "those for whom history bears witness to obscure drives, unavoidable suffering, and universal reversions."[18] That the assessments of German history and identity so centrally at issue in this polemic so often incorporate judgments about the nature and worth of tragic notions and rhetoric raises a larger question: Does a German's experience of history or sense of national identity and membership entail a special receptivity to the tragic dimensions of human life and human affairs? Thomas Mann thought so, although his observations of the consequences of Nazi rule apparently led him to recognize (in addition to the promise) the dangers of a German tragic sensibility. In the course of provoking the *Historikerstreit*, Habermas seems to be concerned only with the dangers. As a proponent of Enlightenment universalism and as a leading postwar polemicist against affirmations of German exceptionalism rooted in notions of historical fatality, mythic memory, or aesthetic community, Habermas would be expected to view as highly suspect any tendency in German letters and philosophy in which emphasis is placed on the tragic dimensions of German political or social life.[19]

Botho Strauss

A few short years after the *Historikerstreit*, the monumental political changes associated with the period of Germany's reunification would spark a series of high profile debates about the nature and meaning of German identity and political agency. If notions of tragedy and tragic rhetoric had been drawn into the exchanges between participants in the *Historikerstreit* somewhat as an afterthought, they came to play a more systematic role in at least one highly visible post-unification debate. This resort to tragedy (to be discussed below), far from being an exception in the history of public intellectual gestures, fitted into a larger German pattern. Episodes of radical political discontinuity, of which modern Germany has experienced its share, have often led German intellectuals to generate theories or works of tragedy as a means for rethinking the nature of German identity and community.

As we have seen, Thomas Mann, writing in the immediate aftermath of Germany's ruinous defeat in World War Two, cast the disasters of Nazi rule as products of the regime's cynical exploitation of Germans' susceptibility to attitudes of political fatalism or indifference. Nietzsche composed his first book, *The Birth of Tragedy*, at an earlier nodal point of German history—in the immediate aftermath of the Franco-Prussian War and as a new German *Reich* under the leadership of the Prussian royal house was founded. His unearthing in that book of an archaic Dionysian basis of Attic tragedy was intended not only as a scholarly settling of accounts with antiquarian classicists but also (and more importantly, for Nietzsche) as a public intellectual intervention in an emerging German national culture whose values would increasingly be shaped by middle class moralism and imperial power politics.

Nietzsche held middle class moralism to be one of the fruits of the instinct-stifling Socratic belief that "thought is capable not only of knowing being but even of *correcting* it." Among the pernicious effects he attributed to middle class moralism was the undermining of a culture's capacity to achieve revitalizing contact with potentially chaotic Dionysian energies. Marking this condition of cultural exhaustion in Nietzsche's Germany was the rise of criticism as the dominant mode of cultural production and the emergence of the critic, "without joy and energy, . . . at bottom a librarian and corrector of proofs," as representative bearer of culture.[20]

The second threat, of which Nietzsche took only passing and mostly implicit notice in his book on Greek tragedy, was imperial power politics. Characterizing militaristic and nationalistic Rome, "where the political drives [were] . . . taken as absolutely valid," as a deficient alternative to artistic and tragic Greece, whose "people of the tragic mysteries" did not "exhaust themselves . . . in a consuming chase after worldly power and worldly honor," Nietzsche anticipated the path on which Germany was soon embarked after its victory in the Franco-Prussian War. Roman-style imperialism generated its own characteristic form of instinctual economy whereby Dionysian energies were repressed in lop-sided favor of the Apollonian drive toward self assertion which ultimately found collective expression in a program of nationalistic aggression and world conquest. What the Germans of the new *Reich* stood to lose if these trends won out was the opportunity to be engaged in cultural-aesthetic modes of sublimation that put the impulses of Apollonian proportion and Dionysian instinct, of individuation and communal merger in creative, balanced, and life-affirming interplay.[21] (For a time, Nietzsche held up Wagnerian music drama as the paradigmatic cultural-aesthetic mode of sublimation worth encouraging in contemporary Germany but he eventually withdrew his endorsement.)

In apparent emulation of Nietzsche's declaration of cultural renewal, West German playwright Botho Strauss chose to publish a tragically themed polemic against German mass culture and left-liberal moralism in the aftermath of another critical juncture in German history, the collapse of the postwar division of the country into a U.S.S.R.-aligned East Germany and a U.S.-aligned West Germany. In *"Anschwellender Bocksgesang"* (Goatsong Rising), published in the February 6, 1993, issue of *Der Spiegel*, Strauss affirmed the urgent need for a revitalization of German culture and argued that the prospects for such a renewal would crucially depend on the extent to which newly unified Germans gained an authentic sense of the tragic. In the very title of his polemical broadside, Strauss seemingly gestures to Nietzsche's work in at least two significant respects. In the first place, *Bockgesang*, a literal translation of the compound Greek word, *tragōidía*, which combines *trágos* (goat) and *ōidé* (song), highlights the musical aspect of tragedy. Nietzsche's book, the full title of which is *Die Geburt die Tragödie aus dem Geiste der Musik*, argued for the primary importance of the singing and dancing chorus whose precursor (he suggested) was the circle of Dionysus worshippers engaged in ecstatic ritual. In the second place, Strauss's title, with its reference to a sacrificial animal (*Bock*), evokes a view of the cultic origins of Greek tragedy in ritually organized and communally celebrated acts of bloodletting. This evocation falls squarely within a tradition, among whose earliest and most influential proponents was Nietzsche, of interpreting Greek tragedy as originating in rites of cultic sacrifice.

Similarities with Nietzsche's *Birth* are also to be found in the polemical content of Strauss's argument. In particular, his critique of mass society and intellectual culture in post-unification Germany mirrors Nietzsche's earlier critique of Wilhelmine society and academic culture. Strauss's attack is two-pronged, on the one hand taking mass society to task for its materialism, conformism, and susceptibility to the appeals of an intrusive and superficial mass media, and on the other, attacking German intellectuals for their political correctness and their privileging of critical analysis and abstraction over more poetic modes of understanding.[22] Describing the members of the liberal-left intelligentsia as products of an intellectual Protestantism, he criticizes them for reflexively rejecting the values of community, tradition, authority, and myth and for rendering taboo the sort of conservative position from which such values might constructively be affirmed. The distinction between conservatives and left-liberal intellectuals, he goes on to write, can also be defined in terms of accessibility to notions and manifestations of fate or tragedy; the latter "possess no sense of fate" ("*keinen Sinn für Verhängnis besitzen*") and are "incapable of comprehending manifestations of the tragic."[23]

To be sure, there is a wider context of German cultural critique into which "*Anschwellender Bockgesang*" can be fitted. Whether it is the tendency to "Gothic pathos" evoked by Thomas Mann or the German anti-rationalism studied by Isaiah Berlin or the "Germanic ideology" Fritz Stern criticized, these and similar concerns about the state of modern German culture fall under the same general rubric of concern about spiritual decline and loss of vitality in the face of a one-sided and hegemonic process of rationalization.[24] Also not to be discounted as an influence on Strauss is *The Dialectic of the Enlightenment*, in which Adorno and Horkheimer describe human beings' attempt to escape fate through the rational critique of mythical thinking only to become enthralled, once the new order of reason is institutionalized, to a new myth of rational mastery. What makes Nietzsche's *Birth of Tragedy* a key point of reference for Strauss's manifesto of cultural critique is the central role Greek tragedy (understood in its archaic dimension) plays in both cases. This is particularly evident in Strauss's invocation of the Dionysian, a power or force capable of breaking down structure and routine, abolishing any conventional sense of time, and fostering a mysterious sense of connection between people. It is "some hidden undercurrent that runs through everyone, emanates from everyone, and secretly draws everyone away from the realms of their habitual consciousness."[25] Banished from public forms of expression in German culture or politics by the intolerance of a left-liberal rationalistic hegemony founded in reaction to the experience of Hitler's catastrophic rule, the Dionysian impulse erupts unpredictably and destructively as when neo-Nazi youth attack immigrants, refugees, and other perceived outsiders.[26]

Strauss's analysis of Germany's contemporary cultural and political ills implicitly rests on differently valenced notions of sublimation and repression. The operation of the latter process afflicts German society and threatens to bring about a destructive return of repressed Dionyian impulses; "But we lack the reliable means of defense when Bromios, the deafening horror, crashes into our abstract world and topples our supposedly reality-conquering structures of simulacra and simulations overnight."[27] The value of sublimation, by contrast, rests on a recognition both of the enduring presence of cultic passions ("*Kultleidenschaften*"[28]), human impulses to feel deeply a sense of community, and of the unavoidability of pain and suffering. Strauss implicitly sets as the goal of this sublimation process the channeling of those passions in such a way that sacrifice begets some sort of collective cultural benefit. What is ultimately at stake for Strauss is how suffering is to be experienced: through "tragedy, [which] gave us a measure for the experience of disaster and for learning how to endure it" ("*Die Tragödie gab ein Mass zum Erfahren des Unheils wie auch dazu, es ertragen zu lernen*") or through such modes of intellectual denial as "leftist fantasies that work by aping salvation history" ("*die Linke, Heilsgeschichte parodiende Phantasie*") or through media trivialization ("*das unmenschliche Abmässigen der Tragödien in der Vermittlung*").[29]

It should come as no surprise that an affirmation of tragedy's distinctive role in how humans ought to respond to suffering would be forthcoming from a man of the theater. After all, the formative text of literary criticism, Aristotle's *Poetics*, famously offers a theory of catharsis as a central characteristic of tragedy. Of course, Strauss's notion of tragedy's healing power, with its emphasis on cultic sacrifice, relies more on René Girard (and, apparently, on Nietzsche) than it does on Aristotle. No less surprising, given the longstanding themes of Strauss's dramatic and fictional oeuvre, are the targets of his polemical ire in "*Anschwellender Bockgesang*." As early as 1977 in his novel, *Die Widmung* (translated in 1979 under the title, *Devotion*), Strauss is already casting a critical eye on those very aspects of West German political discourse (e.g., the substitution of unthinking vilification for reasoned political argument[30]) and West German mass culture (e.g., the proliferation of image-driven consumerism[31]) that he would later mark out in his *Der Spiegel* polemic for explicit disparagement. In *Die Widmung*, we also find expressed in the narrator's invidious comparison of novel-reading with the routines of West German life an early yearning for an experience that bears some resemblance to that experience that Strauss eventually comes to associate with Bromios/Dionysus: "Our real life offers us no opportunities to experience satiety. And so a passion ready to be expressed crouches in us after we've read . . . but nothing touches it off. After a while this crouching in a tense, contorted position begins to be painful. We contain more feeling than we may release."[32] Taking notice of the large extent of political and social commentary nested in Strauss's dramatic and fictional works, literary critic Thomas Assheuer did not find too surprising (or commendable) his transition from a poet-diagnostician of societal ills to an aspiring social therapist.[33]

Bearing in mind the history of polemical dispute over the political valence and ramifications of tragedy going back in Germany at least as far back as Nietzsche's publication of *Birth of Tragedy*, it is even less surprising that a claim for tragedy's political significance would come packaged in a polemic avowedly aimed at rehabilitating conservative nationalism in contemporary German intellectual thought.[34] For, as was evident in the *Historikerstreit*, for one example, notions of tragedy and the tragic, associated as they have been with attitudes affirming the role of fate and myth in human life, seem necessarily to invite sympathy with conservative notions of organic community and conservative tendencies to venerate the past and emphasize the pitfalls rather than the promise of robust political agency.

In his essay accompanying *Southern Humanity Review*'s Fall 2004 translation of "*Anschwellender Bockgesang*," Gregory Wolf offers a defense of Strauss's public intellectual intervention premised on a notion of "conservative aesthetics." Wolf suggests that Strauss "is not and never was a 'political' author in the sense of Günter Grass" and that he is "at worst guilty of mixing his social critique (of liberalism, conformity, and materialism) with his aesthetic program."[35] Wolf may well be right to imply that the polemical attacks against Strauss (e.g., "Ist Botho Strauss ein Faschist?"[36]) unfairly extrapolate a *political* position on the extreme right from what is fundamentally a conservative *aesthetics*. Whatever the political merits of Strauss's public intellectual intervention are, our concern is with the political valence of his use of tragic notions and theories of tragedy.

The affinity conservative thinkers tend to feel with notions of tragedy was manifest not only in Strauss's polemic but also in some of the essays gathered in sympathetic response to his polemic in the volume, *Die Selbstbewusste Nation: "Anschwellender Bockgesang" und weitere Beiträge zu einer deutschen Debatte* (1994) (The Self-Conscious Nation: 'Goatsong Rising' and Further Contributions to a German Debate). Among the essays in that volume that specifically address the issue of German identity, filmmaker and longtime proponent of tragic engagement Hans-Jürgen Syberberg's, "*Eigenes und Fremdes: Über den Verlust des Tragischen*" (One's Own and What Is Foreign: On the Loss of the Tragic) announces in its very title a claim about the link between German identity and tragedy. Arguing that German identity had been formed in the course of an especially intense theoretical and literary engagement with "*die Tragödie des Da-Seins*," Syberberg suggests that, in the aftermath of Nazi misdeeds, Germans' "*Trauerarbeit*" or work of mourning had been hindered by a postwar disavowal of the distinctively tragic dimensions of German thought and character.[37] If Gerd Bergfleth, another contributor, does not organize his essay so centrally and conspicuously around a notion of tragedy, tragedy nevertheless plays an important role for him as well. He links German identity to a pronounced sense of metaphysical homelessness ("*metaphysischen Unbehausheit*"), which sense originally formed (he goes on to suggest) in response to northern Germans' experiencing a landscape of nordically dark tragic forest primeval ("*nordisch-düstere tragische Urgewalt*"). As a result of this unique wilderness encounter, they (more than their southern brethren) came to comprehend "*die Tragödie der Erde*," the tendency of humans increasingly to alienate themselves from nature by treating nature as a resource to be exploited.[38]

The Heideggerian echoes in the accounts of Syberberg and Bergfleth are unmistakable. Evoking the tragic nature of German cultural self-understanding in a Heideggerian key, these accounts point toward another relevant episode of German political and social discontinuity, in response to which notions of tragedy were mobilized. While ancient Greek texts had been at the center of Heidegger's philosophical reflections long before the Nazi takeover, Greek tragedy became an especially important touchstone for him in that period when the Nazi Party ascended to power. Initially, he used that touchstone to suggest the promise of Nazi rule, as when he strategically invoked a line of verse from Aeschylus' *Prometheus* in his infamous 1933 Rector's Address, "The Self-Assertion of the German University," given at the University of Freiburg under the auspices of a Nazi program of educational consolidation.[39] Later, as he presumably came to rue his partnership with the movement, the first (*polla ta deina*) choral verse of the *Antigone* became important for him as a way of reflecting on how successful attempts to allow Being (*Dasein*) presence may also lead humans to engage in forms of mastery that block them from the vitalizing presence of Being. Throughout, Heidegger never gave up his sense of the ancient tragic theater as a privileged site of contact with *Dasein*.[40]

Might Jaspers, to whom Heidegger blithely sent a translation of the verse from *Antigone* in July 1935, have had Heidegger, among others, in mind when, under a Nazi publishing ban, he later composed his thoughts about one pernicious form of tragic theoretical engagement, the tendency of some enthusiasts of tragedy to "see the world in terms of grandiose and tragic interpretations: the world is so made that everything great in it is doomed to perish, and it is made for the delight of the unconcerned spectator"?[41] Perhaps. In any case, his concern about some intellectuals' tendency to retreat to a position of tragic wonder about, and Olympian detachment from, political affairs seems significantly to have shaped the terms by which he critically engages Heidegger in a decisive letter exchange after the war. Jaspers' critical response is provoked by an April 8, 1950, letter, in which Heidegger offers an explanation of his actions during the Nazi period, urgently warns about the danger of Stalinism, and declares the crucial, if limited, importance of his activity of philosophizing in the coming metapolitical struggle. Waiting almost two years, Jaspers sent a withering response in which he criticized Heidegger for missing the real political danger (the rehabilitation of anti-communist nationalism), for laying claim to the sort of contemplatively privileged perspective on political life once arrogantly assumed by the self-proclaimed poet-prophets Stefan George and Rainer Maria Rilke, and for implicitly derogating to himself the questionable role of philosopher-savior in a time of crisis. This last move, which Jaspers finds expressed in Heidegger's assertion that, "in this homelessness . . . an Advent conceals itself," Jaspers calls *"reine Träumerei"* (pure daydream).[42]

Jaspers's postwar criticism of Heidegger, particularly insofar as it links dangerously apolitical aspirations for prophetic leadership with a tragic vision of world affairs, provides a helpful backdrop against which one might assess Strauss's own uses of tragedy. His insistence on deploying, in an uncritical, if not also cryptic, fashion, a vocabulary of tragedy—fate, myth, cultic sacrifice—freighted with highly negative historical associations only serves to invite the charge of Nazi sympathy that he anticipates and deplores in advance.[43] Putting aside questions about the nature and worth of Strauss's goal in writing "*Anschwellender Bockgesang*," whether it be to warn against the possible costs of an inflexible postwar German moral and political consensus or to rehabilitate a position of conservative nationalism in German politics or to affirm the importance of maintaining the position of artistic outsider in the face of mass culture, one can find fault with Strauss for how he goes about pursuing his goal. It isn't that his chosen means—notions of the tragic and theories of tragedy—are necessarily or *in toto* faulty or illegitimate. It is rather that they are too narrowly conceived and awkwardly deployed. While there may be value in recognizing the limits of human agency or in acknowledging the enduring power of human aspirations to belong to a group and draw spiritual sustenance from a framework of meaning that transcends individual rationality, that recognition or acknowledgment could be conveyed by means of a more fully developed concept of tragedy, one that goes beyond cryptic invocations of Dionysian passion and "*religiöse oder protopolitische Initiation*."[44] To the extent that the German tradition of engaging the tragic and theorizing tragedy is a rich and multifaceted one, Strauss could have broadened his references to include mention of tragedy's many significant roles in ancient Athenian civic life. Among these was tragedy's power to unsettle convention while also acting as a sponsor of civic solidarity and authority.[45] To put it another way, one might ask of Strauss, Where is the discussion of the polis that might give helpful political context to your polemical resort to tragedy?

Even Nietzsche, whose power in the *Birth* to provoke and unsettle conventional ways of thinking is unrivalled, manages mostly to maintain a sense of the polis context in his ruminations about the healing power of myth. In one of the most famous passages of his book, he places Greece between Buddhist India and nationalistic Rome, arguing that it was by means of tragedy (*tragōidía*) that the Greeks were able to develop forms of cultural experience that served to foster a salutary sense of philosophical detachment from political drives of conquest and mastery[46] Although middle class moralism is the most direct target of Nietzsche's polemical invocations of the Dionysian, it should be remembered that he also had his eye on the dangers of nationalism posed by the second German *Reich*. Writing in a country that had, within living memory, manifested the worst excesses of nationalistic fervor under the third German *Reich*,[47] and for whose intellectual class, the language of tragic fatalism—for example, *Verhängnis, Schicksalkampf, tragisches Geschick* —had become highly suspect politically and morally, Strauss could have been expected to have chosen his tragic means with more nuance and historically informed judgment. As it is, his polemical invocations of ritualistic elements of tragedy too easily lend themselves to notions of agency anchored in communal willfulness rather than individual moral reflection. If the revisionist use of tragic rhetoric targeted by Habermas lent itself too easily to fatalistic views of German actions during the Nazi period or aestheticized views of the suffering of their victims, Strauss's more explicit and full-bore appropriation of Dionysian tragedy invites criticism also for its apparently uncritical affirmation of ritualism.

In collapsing longstanding political boundaries and institutions, the reunification of Germany unsettled previously established ways of thinking and invited more broad and intensive reflection about what it meant to be German. Strauss's response to this new political theoretical environment was to continue the German literary and philosophical tradition of engaging theories of tragedy and notions of the tragic for the purpose of identifying worthy and viable forms of German political agency and identity. The fact that his continuation of that tradition happened to be in the service of a conservative political agenda does not mean that the tradition can serve as a theoretical resource exclusively for anti-liberal or anti-leftist German critics and intellectuals. One might well assume this state of affairs given the pattern of polemical dispute in German intellectual history between thinkers on the Left and Right over the worth of concepts derived from, or otherwise associated with, tragedy. In one notable interwar episode, the "interrelation of affirmation and fate in tragic experience made it a key adversary of critical theory in the thirties." Christoph Menke characterizes both Walter Benjamin, with his "messianic critique of mythical fate," and Horkheimer, with his "critique of fetishistic reification," as having engaged in a "crusade against tragic thinking" during that period. And yet Menke, who has made engagement with tragic thinking from a critical theory perspective a central aim of his own philosophical work, argues that critical theory's "materialistic interpretation of social praxis" implies a tragic acceptance of some degree of tension between the material bases of individual and social life and the moral aspiration to shape those material bases. "The *fragility* of moral praxis consists in the fact that moral demands depend for their realization upon something that is subject to its own 'somatic' necessity that can turn against moral logic."[48]

To vindicate the potential of Germany's tradition of tragic engagement as a touchstone for thinking about issues of identity and agency from liberal or left perspectives, one might begin by proceeding as Menke does and take a broader view of what tragedy promises. For Strauss, who seems most concerned with the integrity of the artist in a culture of mass conformity and media trivialization, on the one hand, and with the legitimation of some form of German nationalism, on the other, engagement with tragedy promises at least two things. It promises to deepen or make more profound Germans' experience of life by intensifying their appreciation of life's inalterable limits ("the sense of fate") and it promises to channel (through forms of sometimes ritual-like experience to which Strauss vaguely alludes) the emotional effects of this intensification in ways that foster a nontrivial sense of fellow feeling between Germans. For other critics, with social or political concerns different than Strauss's, engagement with tragedy can promise things other than a sense of fatality or ritual regeneration of community. As Chapter Four shows, social democratic African-American intellectual Cornel West has argued that a "black sense of the tragic," developed by New World Africans as a result of their exposure to the traumas of slavery and Jim Crow, played a key role in their preserving a meaningful sense of identity and democratic agency. As will be seen in the following chapter, Christa Wolf, a celebrated East German writer who grew increasingly skeptical of the German

Democratic Republic's capacity to live up to its declared ideals, re-imagined Greek tragedy in her best-selling novel, *Kassandra* (1983), in the hope of fostering a community of critical-minded readers whose solidarity would be based not on force or selfish interest but on self knowledge and voluntary commitment to the good of the community. In the aftermath of reunification, continuing concerns about the nature and prospects of social democratic agency and solidarity in the new German order seemed to have impel her to embrace more fully the example of Greek tragedy in *Medea: Stimmen* (1996).

The examples of Wolf, West and others (German and non-German) one might cite, reveal tragedy as a resource for those concerned with fostering forms of political identity, agency, and solidarity in support of centrist or leftist visions of democracy. This should come as no surprise given Greek tragedy's historic role in the unprecedented emergence and development of democracy in ancient Athens. One of the foremost students of the relationship between *tragōidía* and democratic politics in ancient Athens, the German classicist Christian Meier, has gone so far as to claim that, "Attic democracy was as dependent on tragedy as upon its councils and assemblies."[49] These examples raise the prospect that, notwithstanding the shadow cast by the disasters of imperial politics and Nazi misrule upon the legacy of German philosophical and literary engagements with tragedy, this tradition remains a viable resource of democratic thought for German intellectuals in the twenty-first century.

CHAPTER 8

Christa Wolf: Greek Tragedy and German Democracy

The men of that age never felt that the nature and influence of tragedy were purely and simply aesthetic. Its power over them was so vast that they held it responsible for the spirit of the whole state; and although we as historians may believe that even the greatest poets were the representatives, not the creators, of national spirit, our belief cannot alter the fact that the Athenians held (the tragedians) to be their spiritual leaders, with a responsibility greater and graver than the constitutional authority of successive political leaders.

(Werner Jaeger, *Paideia*[1])

Aren't we beyond all proclamations and prophecies, and so beyond tragedy?

(Christa Wolf, *Cassandra*[2])

In times of political or social crisis, issues of identity and affiliation tend to become more salient. In response to the threatened or actual disruption of the routines of material provision, social order, and ideological legitimation, definitions of self and community that had formerly been considered authoritative come under more frequent and more extensive questioning. Responses to this condition of uncertainty and doubt about identity and affiliation are typically forthcoming from many different quarters: party politicians, leaders of social movements, public intellectuals, and religious authorities. Such responses can also be quite varied as was the case, for example, in the aftermath of the fall of the Berlin Wall. Only months after the event and with major questions about the future of the two Germanies in the air, Jürgen Habermas surveyed the various possible sources of German identity that were on offer at that time—economic prestige ("*DM*-nationalism"), cultural inheritance, linguistic unity, ethnic descent, historical fate, aesthetic experience, and constitutional patriotism—and found all but the last seriously wanting.[3] In any given episode of crisis and questioning, most responses will ultimately have little or no effect; the eventual reestablishment of the routines of provision, order, and legitimation usually means that one or another set of definitions of self and community has won out and become authoritative for a critical mass of citizens.

Christa Wolf's promotion of a continued condition of divided sovereignty and the establishment of an authentic social democracy in East Germany can be counted as one of those responses to the collapse of Leninist definitions of self and community in East Germany that had little if any political effect, even if it had a significant personal one. Partly in response to Wolf's outspoken refusal to accept that the absorption of East Germany by West Germany was an unalloyed good, she became the subject of a *"deutsch-deutsche Literaturstreit,"* a heated, at times vituperative, debate among East and West German critics, intellectuals, and artists about the nature of civic and moral responsibility in the postwar German states. The debate was initially framed by one literary critic's two-pronged critique of the moral and aesthetic dimensions of Wolf's life and works. Morally, the charge was that, in the aftermath of the fall of the wall, Wolf did not directly and forthrightly acknowledge the evil nature of the one-party dictatorship under which she had lived. Where moral condemnation of communist dictatorship was to be expected, Wolf had evaded this responsibility by continuing to hew to the antifascist line of the *SED* regime (i.e., capitalism is another form of fascism) and by refusing to give up her longstanding role as victim of history. Aesthetically, the charge was that Wolf's wide acceptance had less to do with the aesthetic worth of her writings than with their evocation of a mood of angst and mourning and general threat that readers sympathetic toward feminism or postmodernism or left-liberal political orthodoxy found congenial.[4]

Rather than engage the polemical attacks on Wolf's civic and moral integrity or the aesthetic worth of her writings in general, this chapter singles out one area of her work—her ambivalent engagement with Greek tragedy and theories of tragedy—and examines the extent to which Wolf tried to understand the challenges of imagining a democratic German identity on this particular ground. This chapter will suggest how Wolf responded to changes in her political situation—from political membership in East Germany's one-party authoritarian state to political membership in a unified country under the auspices of West German political values and institutions—by shifting her attitude toward, and political uses of, Greek tragedy.

Engaging Greek Tragedy from the German Left

The task of reflecting on the nature and limits, the promises and pitfalls of German identity is one that has defined Wolf's writing career, not least because she lived in a country whose history had been so broken up by episodes of radical discontinuity, including wartime defeats, regime transformations, genocidal campaigns, foreign occupations, and territorial partitions. Born in 1929 in a part of Germany that became Polish territory after World War II, Wolf grew to adolescence and began school during a time of increasingly pervasive National Socialist regimentation of German life. With the rollback of German forces and the approach of the Soviet armies in January 1945, she and her family fled westward, eventually settling in what became the territory of the German Democratic Republic. Wolf finished *Gymnasium* in 1949 and joined the ruling Marxist-Leninist party, the *SED* (the Socialist Unity Party), rising to public prominence on the strength of her early novels. From this time onward, her "literary output [was] concerned with plumbing the depths and delineating the outer boundaries of a socialist subject."[5]

The disjunctures between an adolescent sense of identity fostered within the context of Nazi organization and ideology and an adult sense of identity stamped by Leninist socialism came to form the substance of her barely disguised autobiographical work, *Patterns of Childhood* (originally published in 1975 under the title, *Kinderheitsmuster*). In another of her early works, *The Quest for Christa T.* (originally published in 1967 as *Nachdenken über Christa T.*), Wolf sympathetically portrayed characters whose aspirations to a satisfactory sense of self were being frustrated under the conditions of modern East German society. In essays and public statements written or made during and after the dissolution of the GDR, the theme of selfhood under pressure framed Wolf's argument that East German citizens should have been given (and themselves taken) the opportunity to create an authentic social democracy. If the terms of reunification were to be that, "East Germans self-sacrificially devote themselves to trying to fit in, while West Germans act out feelings of superiority and victory," Wolf feared that her fellow citizens would undergo what she referred to as a "process of estrangement," whereby, "East Germany's history is publicly suppressed . . . and is driven back inside the people who made, experienced, and endured it."[6]

In a literary career marked by wide variation in style and setting, Wolf has published two major adaptations of Greek tragedy or tragic myth, the widely translated *Kassandra* (first published in 1983) and *Medea: Stimmen* (1996). *Kassandra* consists of a fictional narrative told mostly from the point of view of Kassandra as she faces the prospect of a violent end upon her arrival at Mycenae with her new master, Agamemnon. A companion volume, *Voraussetzungen einer Erzählung: Kassandra*, published in the same year, is an amalgam of works consisting of a two-part travel diary in which Wolf weaves accounts of her trip to Greece with reflections on the layered meanings of ancient Greek history; a work diary; and an extended critical reflection on gender and literature in epistolary form. *Medea: Stimmen* is a retelling of the tragic myth in the form of character monologues in which the plot deviates substantially from the account given in Euripides's drama (e.g., in Wolf's version, Medea does not kill her children). A companion volume, *Christa Wolfs Medea* (1998), consisting of epistolary exchanges between Wolf and classical scholars, entries from her work diary, interviews, and reviews of *Medea: Stimmen*, has also been published. Wolf's engagement with Greek tragic themes is also evident in her contribution of an afterword to a 1983 edition of Heinrich von Kleist's *Penthesilea: Eine Tragödie*.[7]

On the face of it, the fact that a contemporary German writer chooses to revisit Greek tragedy and tragic myth ought to come as no surprise. As we saw in Chapter 7, since the mid-eighteenth-century publication of Winckelmann's reflections on the significance of the arts in ancient Greece, German intellectuals have been intrigued by the way in which the Greeks acknowledged human suffering and turned that acknowledgment into the material of life-affirming forms of art. Engagement with such art forms as Greek tragedy is seen, time and again, as having crucial importance in resolving contemporary German cultural and political crises. Consistent with the traditional pattern of politically conditioned resorts to Greek tragedy by German philosophers and men and women of letters, Wolf wrote *Kassandra* (1983) with the deployment of a new class of intermediate range, nuclear-armed missiles in Central Europe, and the ratcheting up of Cold War rhetoric between the nuclear superpowers very much in mind.

> At the highpoint of missile deployments in Europe, I asked myself the question when actually this tendency to violence in Western culture began. I looked into the depths of time and established that myth provided some material, for example, the history of the murderous Trojan war. It stimulated me to see this in a new light and to relate it to our own situation.[8]

Many readers of *Medea: Stimmen* (1996) have been struck by the parallels between its portrayal of the oppressive situation in which Medea and her fellow refugees from the eastern city-state of Colchis find themselves in Corinth and Wolf's view of East Germans' burdensome status as historical losers within the new German political and social order.

In general, Wolf's engagement with Greek tragedy is marked by ambivalence. She attacks Greek tragedy, attempting to undermine its status as a model for Western literary imagining, while, at the same time, she uses Greek tragedy as a model for her own literary imagining. She is also seemingly of two minds on whether her engagement with Greek tragedy is motivated by a feeling of political urgency. So, for example, on more than one occasion, Wolf rejects any association of her book, *Medea: Stimmen*, with issues raised by the course of German reunification.[9] However, on other occasions, including in a 1992 letter excerpted below, Wolf provides indirect evidence that she wrote *Medea: Stimmen* partly in response to issues raised by German reunification.

> For more than a year, my thoughts have circled around the character Medea even though, after having worked over the Kassandra motif, I was very sure that I would never again return to this early period of our history. . . . I couldn't foresee that another deeply stirring experience—as then, insight into the destructive nature of our civilization—would drive me to formulate this insight again. It was the theme of colonization, aversion toward outsiders, that appeared to me to be contained in the Medea figure: She was the barbarian from the East.[10]

Wolf's ambivalence may partly have to do with the tensions that seem inherent in trying to reconcile Greek tragedy and tragic themes with socialist commitment to a robust sense of political agency. The legacy of Greek tragedy and tragic myth, in which notions of fate and acceptance of limits on human aspiration and action figure prominently, would seem to offer little of value to someone committed to an ideology of scientific socialism, in which dominant weight is placed on the possibility of progressive social change through rationally directed action. Botho Strauss's full-bore and unhesitating engagement with tragedy and notions of the tragic presents an instructive contrast. His orientation to conservative forms of solidarity based on notions of fatedness, mythic truth, and ritual enactments, seemingly presents no obstacle to his attachment to the tragic. One might expect that if a socialist thinker were to engage Greek tragedy, it would be solely to criticize it, to deplore the fatalistic view of the human condition it so often seems to promote. Yet, as Menke has shown (see Chapter 10), the critical theorist Max Horkheimer backtracked from an unconditional rejection of notions of tragedy for their propensity to foster a fatalistic view of human affairs to an implicitly tragic acceptance of the ironies of human agency.[11]

Other schools of the Marxist tradition permit more explicit acceptance of notions of tragic suffering and limitation, as, for example, "the romantic element of Marxist alienation theory," considered by Heinz-Peter Preusser in his study of East German literature.[12] He sees a concern with the alienating effects of the social division of labor upon the individual's sense of integrity and wholeness as impelling and fundamentally shaping the literary appropriations of Greek tragic myth by some East German writers, notably including Christa Wolf. Ulrich Profitlich's sourcebook of German tragic theory, *Tragödien-Theorie: Texte und Kommentare Vom Barock bis zur Gegenwart* (1999), reveals several tragic scenarios permitted by the censors and favored by East German writers; the source of fatal suffering could be a class enemy, forces of nature resistant to human technological mastery, or human relations in a newly emerging society.[13] Wolf's early novel, *Nachdenken über Christa T*, is mentioned as an example of a tragedy that remains within acceptable political limits; the human fatality in this work is attributed, according to this view, to a subjective defect rather than a flaw in social organization. Resort to mythic themes could also be interpreted in the East German context as an indirect form of social critique adopted by writers facing censorship in a one-party state.[14] Whether East German literatis' unusually pronounced concern with Greek tragedy is explained as a compensation for the limitations of Marxist theory or as an amplification of a Romantic strand of Marxist thought or as disguised critique of East German socialist reality, the focus remains on the theoretical or political context of East German socialism. This chapter places Christa Wolf's tragic Hellenism in a different context, a history of political and social discontinuity and crisis reaching back well before 1945 in response to which German literati came to treat works and theories of Greek tragedy as important means for imagining new forms of German identity and more viable ways of imagining a German form of identity compatible with democracy. Such an approach nevertheless acknowledges that the East German context of one party monopoly and cultural censorship could foster a distinctive sort of crisis atmosphere for East German writers, one in which the search for authentic selfhood was overdetermined.[15]

Christa Wolf as Tragic Playwright

In her two adaptations of Greek tragic myth and in companion works, Wolf vigorously contests the hold that Homer, Aeschylus, and Euripides exercise over the

Western imagination. However, in her contest against the epic and tragic composers, Wolf also indirectly pays tribute to their influence and achievement, especially in her later work, *Medea*. This ambivalence has partly to do with the requirements built in to the task of criticism. In engaging a text, any critic, even a hostile one, risks the possibility of being changed by it. Wolf's susceptibility to being changed by her encounter with Greek tragedy was significantly increased, I will argue, by changes in the political context in which she lived and wrote. In particular, I will suggest that the fall of the Wall and the subsequent dissolution of her political community, the German Democratic Republic, led her, in typically German fashion, to evoke an imaginary community through Greek tragedy.

At the outset, it would be helpful to distinguish between the notions of tragedy operative in Wolf's Greek-themed works. In the first place, Wolf often has occasion to refer both to the works of Aeschylus and Euripides and to the ancient Greek performance practice in which they were involved as dramatic composers or "tragedian(s)." For example, at the outset of the first part of the work diary included in *Kassandra*, Wolf describes how, in the days before her departure for a trip to Greece, a reading of Aeschylus's *Oresteia* put her in imaginative contact with the character Kassandra. "She, the captive, took me captive; herself made an object by others, she took possession of me. . . . I believed every word she said. . . . Three thousand years—melted away. . . . It seemed to me that she was the only person in the play who knew herself." Wolf seems to have tragedy in mind, in the second place, when she discusses literary form or genre. She almost never refers to literary genre under the label, tragedy, preferring instead to invoke tragic form indirectly under other labels such as the "classical aesthetic" or through considerations of such texts as Aristotle's *Poetics*. Thirdly, "tragedy" or "the tragic" serve Wolf as labels for a particular kind of orientation people may have toward difficult or burdensome situations or conditions; the suffering that results from such situations or conditions is taken to be fated or destined because, on a tragic view, there aren't any alternatives. So, for example, Wolf refers to human beings "placing [them]selves in a situation which, because it offers no acceptable alternative, is called 'tragic'" and implicitly laments that such tragic situations are "so favorable to literature."[16]

These notions of tragedy are at play as Wolf considers the challenge of imagining a form of German identity compatible with democracy in at least three contexts: citizenship, vocation, and gender. Wolf has framed the challenge facing Germans of the former East Germany as one of resisting the pressure to repudiate their past entirely and wholly remake themselves according to the individualist model of citizenship promoted by liberal capitalism. The nature of self and community are also in question for Wolf in post unification Germany in relation to her vocation as writer. In particular, she wonders about how creative artists of the former East Germany, whose activities once carried great political weight both for the regime and for society, will adjust to new, post-Cold War conditions of indifference, even hostility, to the arts. "What has happened to art?" she asks a couple of months after the fall of the wall:

The theaters are half empty. Even productions which a short while ago were besieged by audiences who used them to shore up their own protest actions seem deserted now. Sometimes people's feelings of inadequacy lead to a hostile attitude toward art and artists, of a kind which in the past had to be fostered artificially by state and Party machines. . . . We need to ask ourselves if we have really been released from our public responsibility, and, if not, what our future role should be—assuming that it will be more marginal than in the past.[17]

How tragedy might relate to issues of self and community in Wolf's thought is perhaps most immediately seen in the ways in which issues of gender and patriarchy are broached in *Kassandra* and its related texts. To what extent can women express who they are and who they want to be in a world marked by "a deep-seated tradition of contempt for women (and) hostility toward women," and in which, for "the past two thousand years, (they) really have not been able to exert any public influence"?[18]

Wolf traces the roots of modern patriarchy to a time when a pre-existing matriarchal form of social life—more egalitarian, communitarian, and pacifist—was displaced by a male-dominated warrior culture of the sort Homer describes in the *Iliad*.[19] In Wolf's *Kassandra*, Achilles and his fellow Achaeans exemplify this warrior culture in which an individual's ability to slaughter his enemies becomes the standard of heroism. ("As for the *Iliad*, it was the first known attempt to impose a standard of human emotion on a bare chronology ruled by the law of battle and carnage. That standard: the wrath of Achilles. . . . Everyday life, the world of women, shines through only in the gaps between the descriptions of battle.")[20] Under the pressures of war, Troy, a patriarchal society in which the memory and influence of an earlier matriarchy has not been entirely repressed, becomes more and more Greek, that is, patriarchal. (Similarly, in her rewriting of Euripides's *Medea*, Wolf contrasts Corinth, a Greek city-state in which patriarchal institutions and practices have been thoroughly consolidated, with Medea's birth city, Colchis, in which social relations continue to display the influence of a prehistoric matriarchy.)[21] In this process of transformation, the role of Greek tragedy, on Wolf's view, was one of helping to consolidate patriarchy. "The classical Greek dramatist helped create, by aesthetic means, the political-ethical attitude of the free, adult, male citizen of the polis."[22]

Paralleling Wolf's open hostility toward Greek tragedy (which is derivative in significant part from her hostility toward Homeric epic) is her aversion to any form of literary genre or aesthetic framework according to whose conventions "coherent stories [are] held together by war and murder and homicide and the heroic deeds which accrue to them." Taking issue with what she considers to be the simplistic moral dualism of Aristotle's *Poetics*—"The mimetic artist depicts human beings in action. These people are necessarily either good or bad."—and rejecting the Homeric linearity or "one-track-minded" logic of conventional narration, Wolf offers instead a "network" model of writing. She likens her work on Kassandra to a "fabric . . . [not] completely tidy . . . not surveyable at a glance. . . . [with] many of its threads tangled."[23]

One reason Wolf deploys a "network" model of writing against a linear model of classical aesthetics ultimately founded on the examples of Homer's epic poetry and Greek tragedy is to counteract the pernicious effects of a tragic world view or perspective. For her, assuming a tragic perspective on existence means, among other things, accepting the prevailing patriarchal form of social life as an unalterable given. Wolf evokes the fatalism of such a perspective and links it to the classical heritage in an observation she makes of contemporary Greek culture. "A saying like 'In the long run you make your own luck' could not develop among these people. That is why, ever since the time of Homer, of Aeschylus, they have not been able to describe misfortune as guilt." Wolf sees in the transformation of the "female ancestors [of matriarchal prehistory] into the goddesses of fate" of classical Greek culture, a foreshadowing of the cultural pressures modern women will feel to accept their subordinate status in social and political life as necessary or fated. (So, for example, observations of familial relations in the Greek countryside lead Wolf to conclude that, "the deceptive family peace that arises from the women's total attachment to the fate of the men [or rather to the fate of being a woman] . . . erupts again and again in bursts of barbaric behavior.")[24]

In trying imaginatively to recover Cassandra's links to a matriarchal past, Wolf seeks to promote an alternative social reality, "something new we can aim at." In more than one instance, she refers to this alternative social reality as a form of utopia. So, for example, rather than accept the conventional notion of Cassandra as a "tragic" figure fated by the logic of events simply to be murdered in the palace of her captor, Wolf presents her as a link to a utopia of prehistorical matriarchy. And even if this "utopia . . . was no longer valid" because of the Achaeans' destruction of Troy and that "order of peace in the eastern Mediterranean" for which it stood, the creative recovery of Cassandra's utopian background is meant to generate an alternative vision of social and political life for modern times.[25] By means of such a vision, contemporary women might imagine new ways of understanding, and acting on, the world. This, I think, is why Wolf asserts, in a 1983 interview, that "for me, this book [Cassandra], which of all my books goes the furthest back into the past, is the most utopian of my books."[26]

If achieving selfhood as a woman in a man's world seems mostly at stake in the story and materials comprising Cassandra (and, it is as a feminist critique of patriarchy that the work is mainly read), other dimensions of identity—citizen, artist—are not entirely absent from consideration. As presented by Wolf, Cassandra is, after all, "a vivacious person interested in society and politics," entitled, as a member of the royal family, to practice the vocation of "priestess, seeress." Expected to fulfill that role in the traditional way, she becomes instead a teller of politically inconvenient truths; "the visions which overwhelm her no longer have anything to do with the ritual decrees of her oracle. She 'sees' the future because she has the courage to see things as they really are in the present."[27]

Consideration of Wolf's references to a matriarchal utopia in Cassandra suggests that she sees the prospects for women (as well as for citizens and artists) successfully fostering forms of community better suited to the true needs of the self as dependent in significant part on rejecting the hold that tragedy—as art form, as literary genre, and as existential perspective—has upon our thinking. To be sure, the opposition of utopia and tragedy in Wolf's thought is not total nor is it everywhere and in every way consistent. Putting aside legitimate questions that can be raised about the validity of Wolf's readings of Homer and Aeschylus (which, in places, are arguably somewhat facile, polemical, and ungenerous),[28] one notes a certain halfheartedness in Wolf's critical animus toward Aeschylus and Greek tragedy in general as compared to her aversion to Homer. After all, it is a work of Greek tragedy, Aeschylus's *Agamemnon*, that first puts Wolf in contact with the character, Cassandra. Also worth noting is that Wolf finds the character of Cassandra as drawn by Aeschylus to be highly plausible in every respect save one. And Wolf pays indirect tribute to the transformative power of Aeschylus's text when she likens her encounter with his Cassandra "to that decisive change that occurred . . . when [she] first became acquainted with Marxist theory and attitudes; a liberating and illuminating experience which altered [her] thinking, [her] view, what [she] felt about and demanded of [her]self." By contrast, Homer has no such power over her imagination: "To whom can I say that the *Iliad* bores me."[29]

In her later text, *Medea* and its companion volume, Wolf's relative ambivalence toward Greek tragedy is even more pronounced. On the one side, this work represents an extension of Wolf's argument about the role of Greek tragedy in promoting patriarchy. In particular, she finds Euripides's fifth-century portrayal of Medea as a homicidally vengeful mother and partner in his dramatic work to be false, fundamentally at odds with centuries old mythic stories in which no mention is made of Medea as a child killer. For Wolf, Euripides's presentation of Medea as a "witch" rather than as a "healer" answers the anxiety-driven "need of patriarchs to devalue female qualities." It may even be that for Wolf no transformation of a female character of matriarchal myth into a figure of menace and threat by epic poetry or tragic drama is as radical or pernicious as that transformation effected by Euripides on the figure of Medea.[30]

So, on the one hand, the grounds for criticizing Greek tragedy have not apparently changed for Wolf in the thirteen years between the publication of *Kassandra* and *Medea*. On the other hand, however, there are some noteworthy novelties in the narrative style and structure of the later work, ones that suggest that Greek tragedy functions, in some important respects, as a positive model for Wolf. Worth considering at the outset is the German-language title of the work: *Medea: Stimmen*. The English translation of "*Stimmen*" is "voices." Wolf's use of the term surely has partly to do with the unusual narrative structure of the book. It is written as a series of chapter-long interior monologues voiced by Medea, Jason, and other characters from Euripides's drama. Each monologue is prefaced by an epigraph, some of which are drawn from ancient sources (Euripides's *Medea*, Seneca's *Medea*, Plato's *Symposium*, Cato), others from modern sources (Ingeborg Bachmann, Rene Girard's *Violence and the Sacred*, Dietmar Kamper, Adriana Cavarero).

The monologues might easily be taken for dramatic set pieces, an impression further fostered by Wolf's placement of a dramatis personae or list of characters at the beginning of her text. The epigraphs can be seen to function as choral odes, setting the stage on which the monologues are performed. In effect, Wolf assumes the role of a playwright in composing her version of the Medea story. One of her readers has even suggested that Wolf's adoption of the monologue format constitutes a sort of "unwitting homage . . . to one of the most noticeable features of Euripidean drama."[31]

Consistent with signs of Wolf's newfound acceptance of Euripidean tragedy as a literary model are indications of her newfound appreciation of the tragic world view. Formerly, Wolf associated tragic world views with an attitude of fatalistic resignation in the face of a burdensome situation or condition. To accept a situation or condition as tragic was inappropriately to believe that no viable alternative existed. In the early 1980s, the prospect of a new European war with nuclear weapons on the territories of East and West Germany was apparently not enough to push Wolf to adopt a tragic view of the international situation. Nor was the utter lack of prospects for political reform in East Germany enough for her to take a tragic view on domestic affairs. However, in the aftermath of the absorption of East Germany into the West German liberal capitalist order, Wolf seems to have become more open to the notion of the tragic.

On first consideration, this change in orientation should come as no surprise. After all, if the term "tragic" refers to situations in which viable alternatives are lacking, a German leftist in the early 1990s might be forgiven for taking a tragic view of a situation in which "the 'left' has disappeared as a reference point [in German politics], German newspaper columnists [are] bidding farewell to utopia," and the goal of "reshaping West German society into a social and economic commonwealth . . . of reducing the capitalist features and enhancing the democratic features in West Germany's capitalist democracy" has been all but given up.[32] In the months after the fall of the Wall, Wolf had seen and experienced the spontaneous emergence of "citizens' groups, in residential districts, town councils, and committees . . . uncovering the evils of the past, breaking up the structures that caused those evils, working tenaciously on useful projects, and designing concrete blueprints for specific sectors of society." Her hopes that this experience of "grass-roots democracy in action" might lead to the foundation of a new and authentic German social democracy were totally disappointed.[33] In a 1994 lecture in which she takes stock of that disappointment, Wolf conjures up (and implicitly takes issue with) what she takes to be the explicitly anti-tragic views of a German writer from an earlier era of political failure and disappointment:

Have we Germans now come together in a polity that at last is proof against the temptation to think "tragically, mythically, heroically," the kind of thinking Thomas Mann attributed in 1934 to those dear compatriots of his who had succumbed to German myth? Aren't we at last thinking "economically," "politically"—that is, realistically—in what Mann said then was not the German way? Yes, if thinking economically means thinking that the maximization of profit is the highest of all values and if thinking politically means putting the interests of one's own party above everything else.[34]

Further indications of Wolf's lessening aversion to a tragic view are to be found in the admiring portraits she draws of Konrad Wolf (no relation) and Anna Seghers, prominent East German creative artists who inspired her and supported her work. Both of them recognized the highly problematic aspects of East German political and social life without giving up their commitment to make the system live up to its stated ideals. To live in this "field of conflict" between commitment to socialist ideals and commitment to existing socialism as Wolf and Seghers did, was to live "tragically," which, for Wolf, now apparently means to live worthily.[35] Judging from these examples, the valence Wolf gives to the tragic has changed from negative to positive. This raises the question of whether the meaning Wolf attributes to tragedy has also changed. Previously, taking a tragic view of things meant fatalistically accepting an unjust status quo and giving up on the possibility of promoting positive social and political change in the world. Is resignation the state of mind that Wolf wants to evoke with her (now) positively valenced references to tragedy in the aftermath of the collapse of the East German nation and the apparently irrevocable rollback of the reform agenda of the Left?

It may well be that Wolf's changing engagement with Greek tragedy and notions of the tragic marked a retreat from some forms of political agency. Many academic readers of *Medea: Stimmen* argue that the work marks a retreat from the more robust sense of individual sense of agency present in *Kassandra*.

> In *Kassandra*, just as we assume that individuals exercise sovereign control over the myths they circulate, so we have the impression that history results from human agency in accordance with the will of those in power. In *Medea*, Wolf seems more doubtful about the ability of individuals to control events, even those they have caused.[36]

In addition to frustrating Wolf's reformist hopes, the unification of Germany deprived her of important forms of community and undermined a sense of identity that she had painstakenly contructed as a young adult growing up in a Leninist-Marxist regime. The loss of her socialist citizenship (not to mention the frustration of her hopes for citizenship in a new East German social democracy) left Wolf with no political community of which to feel part. Granted, her feeling of belonging to an East German political community before the fall of the wall had been increasingly attenuated as she came more and more to doubt the regime's capacity for reform. So, for example, in a 1981 work diary entry, she mentions the "growing list of people here who are going away," and writes that, "we cannot hope that the used-up institutions, to which many were accustomed, will supply a new direction." However, notwithstanding her apparent pessimism, Wolf remained attached to the ideals those institutions officially embodied. She could therefore remain a citizen of that unfinished

community, however dimly and remotely it was reflected in the ideological pronouncements and institutional practices of East German socialism. As she ambigu-
ously put it at the end of the work diary entry quoted above, "You feel that you are
standing at bay. Australia is not a way out."[37]

In addition to the loss of citizenship, any feeling of being part of a larger German
artistic community must surely have been destroyed by the sustained attacks in the
(West) German press on her ethical and artistic integrity in the early 1990s. "In
Germany . . . the wide open field of art, particularly of fiction, of storytelling has
become a battlefield, slash and stab is the order of the day."[38] These attacks, which
included charges that Wolf had played the role of "*Staatsdichterin*" and "*Staatsdienerin*"
under the old regime,[39] were fundamentally more wounding than the official statements of disapproval she had earlier received from the East German literary
establishment. This was so because such attacks struck directly at her conception of
herself as a beleaguered artist/truthteller searching for the grounds of an authentic
subjectivity.

In response to these deficits of community and in a move characteristic of the
longstanding German tradition of engaging the legacy of ancient Greece,[40] Wolf can
be seen to have relied on the example of Greek tragedy and on notions of the tragic to
evoke an imaginary community. The power of Greek tragedy to evoke community
may have something to do with an appreciation of Greek tragedy's significant role in
fostering a new sense of civic belonging and solidarity in the fledgling democracy
of Athens in the early classical period. In a line of argument dating back to the
nineteenth century and alluded to in this book's first chapter, much significance is
given to the coeval developments of tragedy and democratic self-rule in Athens. On
this view, the publicly supported enactments of mythic stories of the deeds and sufferings of tragic heroes and the dramatization of historical events served to develop
audience members' capacities of judgment as well as their sense of membership in a
newly democratized polity. It should be noted that this imagined audience of democratic citizens of Athens classical era is not quite the one Wolf seeks to evoke as compensation for the loss of her civic community; it is too compromised by its male
definition of individuality.

> German classicists committed an act of self-deception that in historical terms was
> understandable, even necessary, when they viewed Greek classicism as an exam-
> ple of the successful bonding of the individual (male) to the community. . . . This
> encouraged them to smooth over the unharmonious aspects of conditions in
> classical Greece.[41]

She has in mind a pre-classical, matriarchally influenced society, the outlines of
which she learned in part from J. J. Bachoven's influential book, *Mutterrecht*. Unlike
the later, more patriarchal era of classical Greece, in which individuality was defined
in accordance with the self aggrandizing "masculine" values personified by Homer's
Achilles (at least as Wolf reads his character), this earlier stage of social development

presumably permitted forms of individuality more compatible with democratic solidarity and more respectful of the mundane tasks of life sustenance. Thus, for Wolf, Greek tragedy does not function so much as a pediment frieze whose expertly sculpted surface attests to the greatness of classical Greece as an untidy fabric, in whose tangled threads and unfinished patterns traces can be recovered of an earlier, pre- or proto-literate stage of civilization.[42]

In addition to a deficit of civic community, Wolf's renewed engagement with tragic myth may also be driven by her sense of having lost a community of German writers and her attempt imaginatively to become part of that community of German literati and philosophers of the eighteenth and nineteenth centuries who found in Greek tragedy a vantage point from which to make sense of the politically fragmented and socially backward conditions of their time. To be sure, Wolf does not seek the fellowship of all members of that community of German literati; she prefers Heinrich von Kleist and Karoline von Günderrode to the classical giants Goethe and Schiller.[43]

Attention has justly been called to the unusually prominent role of men and women of letters in Central Europe's break with Communism in 1989 and the years following. Essayist Adam Michnik was a leader of the Polish opposition who became a key member of the pro-Solidarity faction of Parliament in Poland's transition to democracy. Playwright and human rights activist Václav Havel went from jail to informal leadership of the democratic opposition to parliamentary election as president of Czechoslovakia and, later, the Czech Republic. Hungarian playwright Arpád Göncz was involved in the events leading to the posthumous rehabilitation of reformist Imre Nagy and the subsequent opening of talks between the government and the democratic opposition and eventually became president of Hungary in 1990, serving until 2000.[44] Philosopher Zhelyu Zhelev was a 1988 co-founder of "one of Bulgaria's first opposition movements."[45] What has often been forgotten in the wake of the controversies over the nature and degree of Christa Wolf's collaboration with the East German authoritarian regime is the fact that she too was offered an opportunity to occupy high political office during this transitional period. Although not a member of the citizens' movement in East Germany, she had spoken out in the last months of Leninist party monopoly for major reforms, including the establishment of a commission to investigate allegations of police brutality against democracy activists. After the wall was breached in November 1989, East German Christian Democratic Union leader Lothar de Maizière offered her the state presidency in the event of a *CDU* victory in the next election, an offer which she refused with dispatch.[46]

In foregoing this opportunity of political leadership, Wolf lost the chance to bring her vision of an East German self fit for a truly democratic community directly to bear on post-Communist German politics. In her return to Greek tragic myth as literary form and subject after reunification, we may nevertheless see a continuing aspiration to exert an influence upon the German "national spirit" akin to the influence of the Greek tragedians (as imagined by Werner Jaeger among many others) upon the political culture of their day. Of course, the political effect one might expect from the publication of a new adaptation of the Medea myth in today's mass media saturated world is negligible, especially when one compares it to the political effect an ancient tragedy, publicly staged as the central part of a civic festival venerating Dionysus, might have had upon the inhabitants of a polis. (Even compared with *Kassandra*, which was a bestseller in the two Germanies and continues to be reissued in German and foreign-language editions, *Medea: Stimmen* has not drawn a large readership and has had little cultural resonance.)[47] The effort of Christa Wolf to return to Greek tragic myth as a source of reflection and creative inspiration is nevertheless noteworthy. In addition to being an aesthetic work in its own right, this effort signalled Christa Wolf's continuing engagement in the shaping of notions of German identity.[48] Her 1996 effort, as well as the effort of Strauss a few years prior, to adapt Greek tragic myth and notions of the tragic to changed political conditions serve as indicators of the extent to which issues of self and community continue to remain unsettled in Germany's post-unification democracy. As will be seen in the next chapter's consideration of director Michael Schorr's hit feature film debut, *Schultze Gets the Blues* (2003), the irresolution of those issues over a decade after unification continues to inspire German creative artists to seek comfort and aid in tragedy. Unusually in the case of Schorr, however, that tragic comfort and aid is sought in New World Africa rather than Old World Greece.

CHAPTER 9

Michael Schorr's *Schultze Gets the Blues*: German Borrowings from the New World African Tragic

The Blues are, perhaps, as close as Americans can come to expressing the spirit of tragedy.
Ralph Ellison, "The World and the Jug"[1]

Schultze Gets the Blues (2003), the critically acclaimed first feature and box office hit from German director Michael Schorr, who also wrote the screenplay, tells the story of a taciturn, rotund, middle-aged bachelor and mineworker living in the small town of Teutschenthal in the eastern German province of Saxon-Anhalt who is sent into early retirement. For Schultze, early retirement means the continuation of a life of routine: solitary meals, meeting his pals, Jürgen and Manfred, over beers at the local pub or fishing with them from a bridge, and playing accordion (as his father had before him) for the town band. While turning the radio dial one evening, he perks up at the unfamiliar sound of Zydeco-style accordion playing. Getting hold of his instrument, he replays the tune from memory. In the following days and weeks, Schultze begins to evince, in his own low-keyed way, an interest in things Cajun—preparing a Jambalaya dinner for his friends, performing his Zydeco tune to uncomprehending audiences at a seniors' home and at the fiftieth anniversary celebration of the town band, eyeing the latest fare specials to New Orleans advertised at a local travel agency. As he stolidly presses against the limits of his musical-cultural imagination, Schultze increasingly finds his daily life populated by offbeat characters including Frau Lorant, a theatrically mannered, hard-drinking resident of his mother's old age home, and Lisa, a flamboyant, flamenco-dancing pub waitress.

Schultze's friends and band colleagues arrange for him to represent the town at a German-American folk festival in New Braunfels, Texas, Teutschental's sister city. Once there, Schultze abandons the festivities and, in a stolen boat, makes his way to the mouth of the Mississippi and thence upriver to the Bayou. During his pilgrimage, he encounters people of all backgrounds, among them, bar locals playing domino, members of a Czech-American polka band, a Cajun fiddler at a backwoods dance club, and the crew of a police patrol boat. Ending up the unexpected guest of an African-American woman and her daughter on their houseboat, he accompanies them to a local club where the band happens to be playing his trademark Zydeco tune. He dances until a coughing spasm forces him to stop. That night, seated under the stars on the deck of the houseboat, he dreams of people dancing in silhouette and breathes his last breath. (Periodic episodes of labored breathing and coughing depicted throughout the film suggest the cause of death is congestive heart failure.) In the film's final scene, a funeral procession delivers his ashes to the Teutschenthal cemetery, after which, Schultze's bandmates, striking up his trademark Zydeco tune, festively lead the funeral party back to town.

In its attention to the details of everyday life, *Schultze* invites consideration in terms of the *Heimat* films of 1950s German cinema, in which domestic routine and local dialect are prominently on display, and the homespun values of rural life find affirmation. Unlike those films, *Schultze's* embrace of homespun values is cosmopolitan, not provincial, extending to a foreign place and people. (In this regard, it is noteworthy that members of his adopted African-American family are conspicuously in attendance at his funeral. As they are integrated into Schultze's community as participant in its rituals of mourning, so the music associated with them—or, better, *through* them to one of its sources, the Blues—is incorporated into the repertoire of that community's musical life.) At the same time, Schorr's somewhat depreciating take on provincial life in eastern Germany lacks the censorious edge of "the critical Heimatfilm of the early seventies, which presented country life as a false idyll, a breeding ground for private and collective neuroses."[2]

In terms of traditional genres, *Schultze's* skillful blending of funny and forlorn moments also resists easy definition. The many understated comic moments of *Schultze* do not add up to the sort of accessible comedy upon which the unexpected international box office success of German cinema was based in the decade after the fall of the Wall. To be sure, *Schultze* invites consideration alongside those German films featuring "male protagonists [who] confront their diminished social or economic status . . . through the affirmation . . . of their class-based otherness in the context of job activities, hobbies, sports and other recreational activities." However, the downward arc of its plot and its moments of quiet melancholy resist categorization in terms of what Sabine Hake has called the "petty-bourgeois comedies of the 1990s" or of their higher higher profile cousins, romantic comedies such as *Abgeschminkt!* (1993) and *Keiner liebt mich* (1994).[3]

If anything, Schorr's multifaceted involvement as writer and director of *Schultze* and his use of a small film crew seem a throwback to the *autorenfilm* associated with the New German Cinema of the 1970s. In a recent consideration of the *autorenfilm* tradition, Ian Garwood has listed, besides the employment of an "'artisanal' aesthetic," "involvement of the filmic with 'higher,' or more established, art forms," and "engagement with nationally specific themes" as major characteristics.[4] While *Schultze's* incorporation of Zydeco music as both plot element and musical accompaniment seems arguably to fit the second criterion, the film's engagement with nationally specific themes is less immediately obvious. In the program notes, the director has suggested that the performance of Horst Krause, who plays the title role, "pays homage to life and actually celebrates it."[5] Probably a significant part of the film's appeal to critics and popular audiences is the understated way in which it affirms life by depicting how a chance encounter with music impels an ordinary guy on a quest for fulfillment. That this fulfillment is preceded by a personal crisis and culminates in the main character's death lends a degree of dramatic gravity to the story and indirectly gestures to its possible political significance as a vehicle for enacting individual and collective quests for integration into community.

Community or, to put it more precisely, the rich associational life of Teutschenthal, seems to be a background theme of no small importance to the film. From one of the earliest scenes, when the mineworkers express their workplace solidarity in song at Schultze's retirement ceremony, images of fellowship and collaborative effort predominate. Among the gatherings or meetings depicted in an unobtrusive documentary-like style are those of the organizing committee for the band's fiftieth anniversary celebration, the local chess club, the town band, a local chorus, celebrants at the anniversary celebration, and Schultze's friends and band colleagues at a surprise party thrown for him before his trip to the United States. The impression one gets (and the director's decision to enlist the local inhabitants and their institutions—e.g., chorus, band—in the making of the film reinforces this impression) is of a community richly and densely populated with voluntary associations whose members are woven together, so to speak, by ties of friendship and joint participation in longstanding practices of common interest.

This backdrop of associational fellowship and collective involvement sets the stage for Schultze's quest for meaning since it is prompted by problems he has integrating himself in a viable community. Expelled from his community of work at the start of the film, he falls back on his friends, who, having also lost jobs at the mine, fall to bickering with each other. It is while he is cut off from his work colleagues and friendship circle that Schultze chances upon the Zydeco tune. Ironically, his passion for the music isolates him all the more as demonstrated by the indifference of the audience of seniors and the outright hostility ("*Scheissnegermusik!*") of at least one listener at the town band's fiftieth anniversary celebration. The crucial, if unremarked upon, backdrop of Schultze's failure to integrate himself into a viable community is the reunification of Germany and the dissolution of the nation, East Germany, of which he formerly had been part. (One German reviewer characterized *Schultze* as the "first German film, that isn't conceivable without reunification, the consequences of which it describes indirectly.")[6] Considered against the backdrop of a new and (for some former East Germans) problematic German national identity, Schultze's decision to leave his native country and pursue his quest in the United States seems especially noteworthy. His life finds its fulfillment and meets its unexpected end *outside* of Germany. Just as noteworthy is the fact that his interment on native ground at film's end becomes an occasion both for the integration of outsiders into the ritual life of his community and his community's integration of an outsider music into its cultural repertoire.

In and of itself, the two-way transfer of a German character's quest for fulfillment to American shores and an American cultural legacy to German shores is not unusual in the history of German film. Eric Rentschler (e.g., "How American Is It: The U.S. As Image and Imaginary in German Film" [1984]) and, more recently, Gerd Gemünden (*Framed Visions: Popular Culture, Americanization, and the Contemporary*

German and Austrian Imagination [1998]) have noted how the intense and highly ambivalent attitudes toward U.S. military, political, and cultural influence in Germany have left their mark on German cinematic treatments of America in such films as Luis Trenker's *The Prodigal Son* (1934), Werner Herzog's *Stroszck* (1977), Wim Wenders' *Alice in the Cities* (1973), and Monika Treut's *My Father Is Coming* (1991). The United States, Rentschler writes in specific reference to the first three of these films, has played "the role of an imaginary (in the Lacanian sense), a set of possibilities one contemplates and toys with . . . as a hall of mirrors one passes through while self-reflecting."[7]

In the decade after the fall of the Wall, as German filmmakers embraced a more genre-oriented and popular cinema and came to rely more on private sources of funding, America's role as cinematic touchstone arguably shifted. Where it had earlier often functioned for West German cinema as a convenient plot destination for "confused, inexperienced, and incomplete" German characters seeking to "gain wisdom and insight," it increasingly came to stand as a viable production model (Hollywood) for how Germans might successfully make and market their films in a privatizing global media economy. Also, in terms of plot preferences, the Hollywood model seemed more in evidence in the 1990s as entertainment values and a disposition to follow genre conventions took precedence over political messages and avant garde artistic gestures.[8] As observed by Sabine Hake, the high profile German films of the 1990s "fostered a new *Erlebniskultur* (culture of diversion)," in which the values of "commercialism," "individual ambition, and self-interest" found powerful expression and validation. These films "sought to accommodate the audience's contradictory desire both for less complicated narratives of Germanness—including in terms of national identity—and for more optimistic visions of a multi-ethnic, multicultural society."[9]

Paying close attention to significant elements of *Schultze*'s avowal of the relevance of an American folk music style to an ex-miner living in the economic backwaters of eastern Germany, this chapter suggests how the film, picking up an earlier cinematic trope of West German encounter with America and incorporating post-unification cinema's embrace of multicultural themes, offers a vision of German identity that navigates between the extremes of a global ideology of consumer individualism associated with the United States and West Germany, on the one hand, and an inward-turned particularism associated with the economically depressed former East, on the other. Of particular help in delineating this vision will be the concept of surrogation proposed by Joseph Roach in *Cities of the Dead: Circum-Atlantic Performance* (1996), as well as Cornel West's theorization of an African-American *tragic* sensibility.

Jazz and German Politics

In its very title, *Schultze Gets the Blues* announces its ambition to cross national-cultural boundaries. Blues music enjoyed a privileged place in German officials' early postwar evaluations of American music, according to Ute Poiger's study of

East and West German Cold War perceptions of African-American music styles and their political significance. In the early 1950s, official concerns about the reputedly pernicious influence of contemporary American music and dance on the sexual mores and social attitudes of German youth led to condemnations of "African American-influenced musical and dance styles, like boogie-woogie and rock 'n' roll, that East and West German adolescents copied from American films." As anxious as East and West German officials were about the influence of African-American forms of musical expression upon the behavior of German youth, they did not take a position of blanket rejection, attempting instead to delineate acceptable from unacceptable musical forms. In the resulting political judgments of music recounted by Poiger, Blues invariably won praise for being "authentic." So, for example, in 1949, "at the height of Soviet attacks on jazz," no less an authority than Paul Robeson had argued, in a Soviet music journal, "that spirituals and blues were the only true Negro music in the United States." Expanding upon Robeson's argument in a 1952 article published in East Germany, an East German musicologist "contrasted what he called 'authentic' jazz, like blues and Dixieland, with those musical forms, like swing, sweet, and rebop, that the American music industry allegedly produced as part of an American imperialist strategy." It was no small irony, according to Poiger, that many of the early attacks on "degenerate" forms of jazz carried over rhetorical tropes from the Nazi era, including implicitly anti-Semitic charges against the "'cosmopolitan' culture industry and 'cosmopolitan' hits."[10] In the contemporary context in which *Schultze* is set, the terminological flashpoint for disagreements over the desirability of outsider presence and influence would more likely be "Multikulti" rather than "Kosmopolit." The differences between multiculturalism and cosmopolitanism as objects of scholarly discourse—for example, the former tending to occasion reflection on the nature of relations between individual citizens or groups of citizens of different races or ethnicities within the nation-state, the latter tending to invite consideration of the nation-state in relation to the global order—are not immediately relevant to my discussion in this chapter.[11]

Poiger notes a liberalizing trend toward the end of the 1950s in West German officialdom's attitude toward jazz, which turned on its head prior assumptions about jazz's influence on the young. In line with the rhetoric of political pluralism and consumer choice that an emerging generation of Cold War liberals increasingly favored, jazz came to be considered a means for sublimating and de-politicizing the rebellious impulses of the young. Tolerance for jazz in all its forms also became a way for the liberal democratic West to promote its ideological commitment to cultural freedom. In line with this newfound view of jazz as a "messenger for liberal democracy," an influential West German jazz expert and radio host praised the music, in a 1958 article, for its proven record in overcoming "differences in status and education ... race, religious denomination, political conviction, and even [nationality]."[12]

The story Poiger relates about the evolution of official East and West German attitudes toward jazz as a catchall category of African-American music provides one historical backdrop against which to assess the political meaning of Schultze's ultimately successful importation of Zydeco into the musical life of his hometown. One could see his townspeople's acceptance of Zydeco as marking their belated post-Cold War acceptance of the pluralist-consumerist version of American-style liberalism with which their new compatriots in the former West Germany had already become aligned starting in the late 1950s. From this perspective, the political meaning of *Schultze*'s use of blues music would mainly derive from its serving as an oblique commentary on (and symptom of) Germany's insertion in an emerging post-Soviet world order of *neo*liberal pluralism and consumerism in which the programmatic embrace of difference or otherness is mainly meant to serve the corporate drive for global sales (i.e., "the United Colors of Benetton"). The theme of cosmopolitan acceptance of an outsider music and people to which the film devotes its final scenes would, taking this view, appear more as a contrivance or instrumentality, an "ersatz multiculturalism," to use a term that Amy Robinson, writing in the early post-Cold War years, uses to denigrate the "virtual industry of black authenticity ranging from Madonna to *White Men Can't Jump* to Vanilla Ice to Bill Clinton."[13]

For Robinson, proponents of ersatz multiculturalism affirm the perspectives and forms of cultural expression of outsider or marginalized groups while ignoring the structural disadvantages under which members of these groups continue to struggle. "Such appropriations [of the cultural cachet of outside groups] have earned these authors the liberal profit of . . . defin[ing] America as a place where (to quote Madonna) 'it makes no difference if you're black or white.' "[14] Sabine Hake alludes to this problematic phenomenon in her account of a "narcissistic" trend in German filmmaking of the 1990s, according to which "retrograde fantasies of family and community" were "combin[ed] with (superficially) liberal attitudes toward alternative sexualities and hybrid identities."[15] Robinson's discussion suggests that one of the criteria for distinguishing between appropriate and inappropriate forms of multicultural engagement is whether some acknowledgment of continuing structural inequities accompanies the "call for communities of common interest."[16] Another, related criterion would be the degree to which the nod to multicultural values is exclusively or mostly motivated by self aggrandizement rather than by concern for a larger or common good.

In support of a view that discounts Schultze's gestures of multicultural tolerance, one might cite the curious way in which the film neglects the Blues as a plot element at the same time that it hypes the Blues in its title and in its program notes: "With a title like *Schultze Gets the Blues* and with a storyline about a laid-off mineworker, audiences might think they're in for a melancholy movie. Yet the fact is that this extraordinary little film packs a big inspirational punch. For Schultze doesn't ever really get blue; he actually gets—or understands—"The Blues" and all the power and passion of music."[17] It is, after all, Zydeco music, not blues music, that captures Schultze's imagination and propels him on his life-changing odyssey.

Associated with the Cajun people of Louisiana, whose New World French forbearers, the Acadians, had been brutally expelled from Canada by the British, Zydeco supposedly got its name from a French expression, *Les haricots sont pas salés*, which folklorist Barry Jean Ancelet has interpreted as referring to those difficult times when the salted meat one normally used to season bean dishes was not available.[18] Musically, Zydeco was formed when Creole music from south-central and southwest Louisiana was crossed with rhythm and blues in the years after World War II. If this genealogy puts Zydeco in an ancestral line traceable back to the Blues, their kinship remains somewhat remote, a fact acknowledged by Schorr. In his commentary on the film, made available on the DVD release, he explained his need for an American music "basically connected to the kind of polka accordion music Schultze plays" and his discovery that Zydeco, like polka, has "the accordion as the lead instrument." In a sketchy account of the sources of Zydeco, Schorr mentions, besides blues music, musette, two step, and polka, which link Zydeco to Old World (e.g., French and German immigrant musical traditions) as well as New World origins: "the accordion is an instrument that represents the great German migration to America in the eighteenth and nineteenth centuries. Many people took their accordions overseas with them . . . and it then became established in the American states, the classic example being Louisiana." Schorr goes on in his commentary to trace his first encounters with Zydeco to a trip he took to Louisiana where he attended impromptu dance gatherings whose vitality and family ambience left a lasting impression upon him.[19]

In spite of his decision to make Zydeco the musical impetus for key plot developments, Schorr chooses not to make Cajuns the cultural interlocutors of his film. That role is reserved for African Americans who occupy strategic places in the film narrative. Notable, in this regard, is the fact that the Zydeco band playing Schultze's tune in one of the film's concluding Louisiana scenes, is composed of African-American players. While the music that accompanies the first American location shot is a Cajun song (one of the first to be mechanically recorded, according to Schorr), the first scene in which Schultze encounters an American is one in which he unexpectedly meets an African-American woman in a parking lot hot tub at the Edelweiss Inn in New Braunfels. When he hesitates to join her, she successfully persuades him to share the hotel's amenity. In the Louisiana houseboat encounter, Schultze arrives unannounced, as the African-American houseboat resident is cooking dinner. Asking for a glass of water, he is invited by her to stay and eat. After the visit to the dance club and while Schultze sleeps on the houseboat deck, she tucks a blanket around him. These arguably maternal gestures on the part of African-American women characters raise the possibility that notions of the nurturing and caregiving "mammy,"[20] broadly circulating among privileged whites of the United States and implicitly supporting ideas of unconditional black service to white needs, may have, in some measure, been at play in Schultze's making. Of course, the relevant scenes invite other, less politically questionable, readings. The hot tub encounter, for example, can be read as an implicit repudiation of a system of racial segregation in the American South that, in the not-so-distant past, strictly prohibited racial mixing in public swimming pools.

It may be that the strategic presence of African-American women reflects an inadvertent appropriation of politically suspect notions of black service from American culture. It may also be that the film's substitution of African Americans as agents of cultural exchange and the avowal of African-American music in the film's title despite the absence of blues music in the film's plot merely reflect the longstanding authority in postwar German culture of the Blues as an "authentic" American folk music. There is, however, another way to read the branding of Schultze as a film about the Blues and its seemingly suspect privileging of African-American characters. On this, more generous, reading, the film will be interpreted as reflecting a substantive agenda of transcultural engagement and multicultural affirmation, one of whose significant effects is the promotion of a post-unification German identity that recognizes the distinctive social-cultural virtues of the inhabitants of each of the former German states, namely, East Germans' appreciation of the advantages of community and West Germans' willingness to engage with, and incorporate, outsider cultures.

Surrogation and Schultze's Jazz Funeral

In the life of a community, the process of surrogation does not begin or end but continues as actual or perceived vacancies occur in the network of relations that constitutes the social fabric. Into the cavities created by loss through death or other forms of departure ... survivors attempt to fit satisfactory alternates. (Joseph Roach, Cities of the Dead)[21]

A student of the encounters and exchanges of the "many peoples along the Atlantic rim . . . [including the] Bambara, Iroquois, Spanish, English, Aztec, Yoruba, and French," Joseph Roach has developed the notion of surrogation in order to describe the hybridity and fluidity of cultural meanings and practices. Holding that a "fixed and unified culture exists only as a convenient but dangerous fiction," Roach's work opens a theoretical space for better understanding how marginalized or oppressed groups maintain a sense of corporate identity, exercise agency, and refashion social meaning through engaging in performance practices.[22] New Orleans serves Roach as a particularly resonant case study of surrogation not only because of its rich traditions of popularly enacted performance traditions, including Mardi Gras float parades and jazz funerals, but also because of Louisiana creole culture's role as "the most significant source of Africanization of the entire culture of the United States."[23]

Among the flamboyant and vibrant performance practices of New Orleans described by Roach are the Mardi Gras Indians, neighborhood-based African-American Indian masqueraders in elaborately crafted beadwork costume, who engage in unscripted running exercises of one-upmanship that are unsanctioned by city authorities. "[T]he extraordinary artistry and craftsmanship of the costumes, which may take a year to build, taken together with the many-layered protocols of Sunday rehearsals, parade-day tactics and strategy, and music-dance-drama performance, make the honor of 'masking Indian' a New Orleanian way of life."[24] While the sources of the practice are not altogether known—but are thought to include

West African traditions of musical performance and traditional African mutual assistance societies—Roach takes up the suggestion of some scholars that the visit of Buffalo Bill's Wild West Show to New Orleans in 1884–1885 was a key catalyst. Of particular note, in Roach's view was "the spectacle of costumed and armed Plains warriors, some of them recent victors over Custer, striding proudly through the streets of New Orleans on the days before Christmas 1884."[25]

The appearance of Plains Indians inside and outside the Wild West Show's arena evoked a "theme of frontier space" that, according to Roach, "illuminates the importance of the border skirmishes and alarums enacted by Mardi Gras Indians."[26] In the setting of modern New Orleans, the performative evocation of frontier space by African-American neighborhood residents helped to preserve a sense of collective agency and fellowship: "On Mardi Gras Day, Indian gangs could claim the space through which they move, like a passing renegade band. . . . They perform a rite of territory repossessed to assert not sole ownership, perhaps, but certainly collective entitlement to fair use."[27] The experience further worked to unsettle flattering self images of the dominant political and social authorities: "the truth that Mardi Gras Indians seem to alter by reenacting African-American memory through the surrogation of Native American identities is the infinitude of Anglo-American entitlement."[28] The practice of Mardi Gras Indians thus marks a dynamic by which one group's history of struggle against oppression can become a resource for another group encountering their own set of challenges through the latter's creative appropriation and reworking of past performance rites.

Roach concludes his book, *Cities of the Dead*, with a descriptive analysis of a jazz funeral held in 1992 for an acclaimed rhythm and blues musician, who was, as the saying goes, "buried with music."[29] In this loosely choreographed event, the musicians, playing in cadenced rhythm, follow in procession after the hearse with family members walking in the lead. When the time comes for "cutting the body loose," the family members embark in limos to accompany the hearse to a distant cemetery while the band breaks into an "uptempo number" and continues the parade along with other celebrants, "some of whom dance, others of whom add counterrhythmic accompaniment on improvised instruments."[30] This account of funereal ritual evokes the meaning of surrogation in a particularly powerful way. Death is, after all, one of the more concrete examples of the sort of "vacancy" or "cavity" in the social network that calls forth attempts at repair in the form of communal rituals which mourn loss at the same time that they affirm community.

> In any funeral, the body of the deceased performs the limits of the community called into being by the need to mark its passing. United around a corpse that is no longer inside but not yet outside of its boundaries, the members of the community may reflect on its symbolic embodiment of loss and renewal.[31]

To be sure, the notion of funereal ritual as an occasion for participants both to mourn loss and to feel a revitalized sense of community is not new. One need only read Pericles' Funeral Oration as transmitted in Thucydides' *History of the Peloponnesian War* or Lincoln's "Gettysburg Address" or recognize their continuing relevance as occasions of political theoretical reflection—for example, Garry Wills's *Lincoln at Gettysburg: The Words That Remade America* (1992)—to appreciate the importance of ritual acknowledgment of the dead in shaping collective identity and self understanding.

Still, New Orleans jazz funerals stand out as remarkable examples of ritual mourning, not least because of the central role played in them by music and move-ment. Other distinctive aspects include the broad and active involvement of partici-pants, and the ritual prominence of celebratory modes of expression. What makes the New Orleans tradition of jazz funerals an especially fitting touchstone of analysis in the particular case of *Schultze* is the fact that the film's concluding enactment of the interment of Schultze's ashes unfolds in the form of a jazz funeral. Thus, one sees the procession of mourners moving onto the cemetery grounds led by the local clergyman and the urn containing Schultze's mortal remains. The African-American daughter stands front row center during the clergyman's eulogy, with her mother a row behind. Band musicians are also present, playing a mournful tune heard in a previous scene when Schultze performed at Frau Lorant's interment. After his ashes are laid to rest with due ceremony, lightened by a moment of comic relief, the procession leaves the cemetery grounds to the musical accompaniment of Schultze's Zydeco tune. In the film's final shot, we see a repeat of the first shot, a bare country-side with a wind turbine to one side. In the opening scene, Schultze had biked across the expanse. In the closing scene, the funeral band parades by, still playing Schultze's Zydeco tune, accompanied by the other mourners-turned-celebrants.

Schultze's mortal end thus becomes the occasion for the transformation and revi-talization of public life through the integration of an outsider form of music and people into his provincial eastern German community. Attesting to the benevolent vitality of Schultze's influence even in death is the comic moment initiated when a cellphone ring-tone interrupts the graveside ceremony. In some embarrassment, Manfred digs his phone out of a coat pocket and puts it to his ear only to utter "Schultze!?" in mock surprise as though the caller at the other end were the departed himself. To the extent that the cell phone has become one of the icons of globaliza-tion, Schultze's "call" evokes his community's newfound capacity to manage the intrusive presence of global technologies and even integrate them into local prac-tices. That it is Manfred's cell phone is no accident. His identification with an American-style self-aggrandizing individualism is indicated in earlier scenes where he encourages his dirt bike-riding son to compete in a U.S.-sponsored motor cross competition with big prize money and attends a motor cross event holding a mini-American flag.

Even more telling in regard to Schultze's role as a benevolent spirit mediating the local and the global, the particular and the multicultural, is the parallel we have drawn between a burial ceremony in a provincial town in former East Germany and the practices associated with New Orleans jazz funerals. This parallel provides an important context for understanding the deeper significance of the strategic presence of African-American characters and the use of the Blues as a brand name for the film. On our interpretation, what Schultze "gets" about the Blues is not merely or primarily a generic sense of the "power and passion of music." More significantly, what he gets about (or, more precisely, achieves in the name of) the Blues is trans-formative contact with a culture of tragic expression that holds out the promise of resisting two sorts of post-unification temptation: the universal "end of history" state of consumerist individualism proffered by cheerleaders of globalization, on the one hand, and the resentment-driven particularism to which some former East Germans were initially drawn as they faced conditions of massive economic, social, and political dislocation.

New World African Tragedy and German Unification

It has long been recognized that African-American styles of music, including the Blues, form part of a larger complex of salutary cultural responses to life under the emergency conditions of slavery and Jim Crow. The terrible conditions experienced by enslaved New World Africans and their exposure, even after formal emancipa-tion, to pervasive discrimination and episodes of mob or state violence called forth various forms of cultural resistance and resilience, among which Cornel West significantly counts a "black sense of the tragic."[32] Folk music forms that developed from within the matrix of African-American Christianity (e.g., Gospel) or outside of it (e.g., blues) conveyed more widely and amplified further the tragic message of endurance and affirmation through which an oppressed people could, in the face of serious setbacks and harsh disappointments, maintain hope in the future advent of a more just state of affairs while remaining open in the present to the joys of existence. In acknowledgment of African-American music's role as a key transmitter of the tragic sensibility, West designates the tenor saxophonist and jazz composer John Coltrane as a significant disseminator of a tragic sensibility, grouping him with more conventional literary and philosophical figures of tragic reflection and expression, including the novelists William Faulkner and Toni Morrison, as well as the author of *The Tragic Sense of Life*, Miguel de Unamuno.

We have already considered in Chapter 4 how issues of political agency and soli-darity and a theory of a New World African tragic sensibility frame West's analyses of the political and psychological challenges facing contemporary middle-class African Americans and African-American members of the underclass. West speaks knowingly of the pressures placed upon members of the black middle class by a formally color blind and rhetorically hyperindividualist majoritarian middle-class culture. For middle-class African Americans, buying in to the "American Dream" means having to hold their anger about, and mute their public criticism of, structural inequalities in American society based on racial identification and class position. It also means having to forego to some extent the sort of collective agency and soli-darity with other African Americans that might result in a societal shift toward greater egalitarianism. Problems of deficient or defective agency plague the African-American underclass as well, only in this case the costs are more dire. In a 1987 interview, West thus laments the varieties of self-destructive behaviors afflicting the inner city black underclass: drug addiction, alcoholism, homicide, and suicide.[33]

If it is, in general, the work of tragedy to acknowledge and channel the existential dread or anxiety people feel as they contemplate the fundamental fragility of mortal life, it is no wonder, given the prevailing social conditions in which they have historically found themselves, that African Americans have evolved a rich culture of tragic expression. In that culture, West sees one important means by which African-American individualities have been fostered and maintained, husbanded for collective deployment during those rare moments in American history when political and social arrangements have been open to major change. If the conditions of social life facing the new eastern citizens of Germany after the fall of the wall were not nearly so drastic, they were challenging enough, especially for a population accustomed to the working of a comprehensive (if increasingly corrupt and inefficient) state system of welfare paternalism.

In a key early scene, Schultze and his friends collect their personal belongings from work and go on to attend, in uncomfortable silence, a peremptory ceremony of farewell organized by their workmates. Judging from their state of befuddlement at the tacky retirement gifts, these men did not choose to retire early—they had to accept early retirement from company managers presumably interested in cutting labor costs. The same calculus of economic rationalization had in the early years of unification resulted in the shedding of hundreds of thousands of jobs in the East. These conditions of social disorientation and newfound economic dependence on the financial largesse of West Germany were alienating to many former citizens of the German Democratic Republic, some of whom likely felt pressure to assimilate on the sort of humiliating psychological terms that, according to West, have long held for middle-class African Americans—expressing unconditional and cheerful acceptance of, and attachment to, all of the values and practices of mainstream (in the German context, West German) society. As we saw in the previous chapter, among those who appreciated the psychological cost of those humiliating terms was Christa Wolf, who had initially hoped that the collapse of the German Democratic Republic might lead to the founding by her eastern co-nationals of a genuinely participatory social democracy, expressed her sense of the psychological toll entailed by West Germany's assimilation of the East in a parallel way. If the terms of post-unification adjustment were to be that "East Germans self-sacrificially devote themselves to trying to fit in, while West Germans act out feelings of superiority and victory," the likelihood was that her fellow citizens would undergo a "process of estrangement" whereby "East Germany's history is publicly suppressed . . . and is driven inside the people who made, experienced, and endured it."[34] For people living in areas of mass unemployment and feeling deep uncertainty about future prospects, the temptation would have been great to retreat to a stance of defensive parochialism and resentment-ridden nostalgia for the old order.

In *Schultze*, moments when the harsher legacies of unification are felt and expressed are few. Arguably, the dispute between the newly pensioned Manfred and Jürgen over a chess game, which results in the hot-headed Manfred sweeping the pieces off the board and angrily stalking off, is one. The argument is set off when Manfred tries to take back a bad move and Jürgen insists on abiding by the rules, declaring, "This isn't the Wild West, after all!" The larger, more significant game the two men (and their fellow East German ex-nationals) are arguably engaged in playing is how to adapt to the "Wild West" conditions of the new post Cold War order, in which the expectation increasingly is that individuals will fudge the rules in pursuit of their narrow self interest. One might think here of the breathtaking financial success of many Communist apparatchiks, who did very well for themselves in the post-Communist transition. In any case, after Jürgen announces his disgust with the situation and also departs, Schultze is left sitting uncomfortably alone at the table, chess pieces scattered before him. Neither of the responses to post-unification pressures enacted by his friends in this scene—Manfred's aping of neoliberal individualism, Jürgen's stubborn insistence on sticking by the rules of pre-unification life—will ultimately determine his path.

Another, more significant reference to post-unification social quandaries occurs in the film's one scene of physical menace. The moment comes after Schultze performs his Zydeco tune at the town band's fiftieth anniversary celebration. In the lead up to his solo accordion performance, Schultze is uncharacteristically anxious and self-doubting. As it turns out, he has reason to be. For when he finishes his performance, audience members, seated at two long tables in front of the stage, remain mostly silent. His colleagues had been expecting a tried-and-true traditional polka from the stalwart Schultze—instead, they hear something unexpected and unfamiliar and seem stunned by it. As Schultze's friends at one table begin to applaud supportively, a man from the other table cries out in a tone of aggressive contempt: "*Scheissnegermusik!*" In response, Manfred, at the other table, stands up as if to intimidate the naysayer into silence. Whereupon he is, in turn, challenged by someone at the first table who rises menacingly and glowers at Manfred until he backs down. The tension is then broken when Lisa, the flamenco-dancing pub waitress, suggests a toast to "*Negermusik*," which is heartily taken up by the rest of Schultze's friends.

In his film commentary, Schorr makes nothing of this symbolic scene of communal rupture. (He is more interested in describing the complexity of the camera movement in the shot of Schultze's performance, which stands out in a film whose scenes are mostly filmed with a single stationary camera.) From our perspective, which foregrounds issues surrounding the German reception of African-American music, this scene is a critical one for our understanding of the film's larger political meaning. Simply put, the confrontation frames Schultze's idiosyncratic change of musical taste within a larger public context of contention over multiculturalism. That public dispute pits those in Teutschenthal who are willing to welcome foreign influences on local cultural practices against those who are not. And, judging from the flare up of tempers, the disagreement is one that is deeply felt.

It is no small irony that even as they disagree in their responses to Schultze's performance of Zydeco, the two "factions" share a misapprehension about its character—namely that it is an African-American music. Strictly speaking, its ties to blues music are distant and derivative. Yet, if we take the inclusion of African Americans in key places in the film as reflecting an insistence on their role as U.S.-German cultural interlocutors, this misapprehension can point toward an interpretation of what plausibly is the film's larger political theoretical meaning. The promise of the film's title invites us to consider the significance of African-American tragic culture to post-unification German social and political challenges.

Considered from the perspective of Roach's work, the history of African-American life and struggle reveals a powerful national dynamic of surrogation. Notwithstanding systematic attempts to segregate or close off ("white") American culture from New World African participation and influence, American culture has been subject to the effects of hybridization as substantial cavities or vacancies in American social relations worked by slavery and Jim Crow invited efforts at compensation. Following West, we would see as one of the more significant results of New World African compensatory efforts to be forms of tragic expression—for example, the Blues—that had the capacity to challenge major aspects of mainstream American culture, including its dogmatic market-driven individualism.

To the radically individualistic self-perception of mainstream Americans, the African-American tragic sensibility has urged a greater recognition of the limits of individual agency, a finer appreciation for the vulnerability felt by members of marginalized and oppressed groups, and increased sensitivity to the merits of alternative ways of envisioning social life. In short, the African-American tragic sensibility has brought the example of a socially minded, subaltern, self-critical perspective to bear on a dangerously narrow and smug form of individualism. The influence of this example has arguably become all the more urgent in a post Cold War ideological environment in which the institutions of global capitalism have been assiduously promoting a consumerist ethos of American-style individualism as the only worthy or viable goal of societal development.

On a cursory viewing, Schultze's engagement with outsider music and cultures might appear simply to be a manifestation of "ersatz multiculturalism," of Schorr's knowing or unknowing attempt to cash in on the cachet of the Blues or Zydeco or pre-Katrina New Orleans as a travel destination by uncritically and self-interestedly offering appropriations of outsider culture for consumption by German and international movie audiences. A closer look at the film reveals something different and more valuable. In so conspicuously gesturing to the Blues background of Zydeco and choosing African-American characters rather than Cajun as cultural interlocutors, it achieves critical distance on its multicultural sympathies.

Schultze adopts a multicultural message that is specifically responsive to the challenges of provincial life in the economic backwaters of unified Germany. Its response is grounded in real parallels between challenges facing members of post-unification eastern German society and middle-class African Americans. For members of both groups, assimilation into the mainstream comes at the cost of forgetting or repressing a painful history and foregoing the benefits of solidarity with one's in-group. The point of the Blues references and the surrogation of African-American identities in this film is not merely to avoid the danger of permitting a Heimat-like parochialism to morph, under the disorienting and stressful social conditions of post-unification eastern Germany, into a resentment-driven particularism that is reflexively hostile to outsider people and cultures. The point is also to acknowledge the virtues of noninstrumental social ties and devotion to the collective good in a world where the champions of neoliberalism have instrumentalized the rhetoric of multiculturalism in the service of a global ideology of consumer individualism.

In his unexpected encounter and life-changing engagement with Zydeco music, Schultze finds personal compensation for the vacancy opened in his own life by an unwelcome retirement. In presenting Schultze as the subject of a quest for fulfillment that results in his becoming the subject of a communal form of compensation (Teutschenthal's first jazz funeral), Schultze gestures to the presence of a larger, regional vacancy in post-reunification Germany, a vacancy opened by the German Democratic Republic's longstanding abuse of the ideals of democratic egalitarianism and social solidarity and held open by western pressure to dismiss the East German political and social experience *in toto* (including the stated ideals according to which it was officially measured) in favor of a narrow definition of freedom as consumer individualism. Schultze also gestures to an African-American culture of tragic expression that remains available for surrogation by Germans interested in maintaining a vision of democracy and freedom that acknowledges the legitimate claims of solidarity as well as individuality, of localism as well as globalization. In this regard, Michael Schorr's *Schultze Gets the Blues* indicates a third option available to those who would continue Germany's public intellectual tradition of engaging tragedy: not the embracing of a tragic politics of fatality and nationalist collectivism (Strauss), nor the withdrawal into a democratic socialist politics of tragic utopianism (Wolf), but an open-eyed and sympathetic enlistment of a tragic sensibility from outside for use within Germany.

CHAPTER 10

Conclusion: Anticipating a Different Kind of Sixties Tragedy

In an essay on the legacy of her friend Walter Benjamin, whose peculiar form of relating to the ideas and texts of past writers she likened, via Shakespeare's image of "a sea-change into something rich and strange," to pearl diving, Hannah Arendt wrote of the lasting potential of words to evoke past experiences whose nature and significance have been forgotten. "The Greek *polis* will continue to exist at the bottom of our political existence—that is, at the bottom of the sea—for as long as we use the word 'politics.'" For Arendt, the word "politics" served as a link to a mode of human experience in the democratic *polis* of ancient Athens not fully or seriously appreciated in contemporary times: the regular manifestation of a public space (what Arendt often referred to as a "space of appearance") in which citizens of even the most modest means and obscure backgrounds could speak to, debate, judge and (in concert) decide issues of importance. Arendt's aim in inviting her readers to rethink the *polis* whenever they encountered the word "politics" was not to resurrect that particular historical experience. After all, the fullest experience of polis life in the Athenian democracy was restricted to native, free-born, adult males of Athenian descent whose political activity was supported, in part, by coerced labor. The aim, rather, was to unsettle contemporary notions of politics by retrieving from the depths of historical forgetfulness, so to speak, the "thought fragment" of an early experience of broad and active citizenship.[1]

This book grew out of an appreciation for the richness of politically relevant experience evoked, consciously or inadvertently, directly or remotely, whenever the word, "tragedy," or its cognate are spoken or written or when Greek and other tragedies are referenced and discussed. While Arendt never explicitly considered how the *tragōidía* of ancient Athens might lie at the bottom of certain of our contemporary experiences for as long as we use the word "tragedy," the many, if scattered, references to tragedy in her writings, prompted my own investigation into how a "thought fragment" formed from the linguistic remnants of that earlier experience might serve to provoke critical reflections on the state of politics in contemporary times. In particular, "tragedy" seemed to me to evoke dimensions of that "space of appearance" constituted, according to Arendt, by the speech and actions of citizens gathered in each other's presence to deal with issues of importance in their individual and collective lives. My book, *Hannah Arendt and the Politics of Tragedy* (2001), considered in detail the various aspects of what I considered to be a strategically important, if under-articulated, dimension of her thought: a theory of the political significance of tragedy. Among those aspects were glosses of Aristotelian concepts related to Greek tragedy (e.g., *katharsis, pathos, peripeteia, drama*), appropriations of characters and verse from Greek tragedy and epic (e.g., Odysseus, Achilles, choral verse from *Oedipus at Colonus*), and invocations of German literati and philosophers known for their strategic theoretical engagement with the legacy of Greek tragedy (e.g., Lessing, Hegel).[2] Read with these features particularly in mind, Arendt's writing appeared to me to manifest the working of a politics of tragedy.

Never fully acknowledged or systematically articulated by Arendt, her politics of tragedy was nevertheless discernible in the patterned ways in which she related tragedy, on the one hand, and active citizenship or what she also referred to throughout her works as political freedom, on the other. First, there was her tendency to label an event marking the loss of political freedom as a "tragedy," as when she so characterized the lost opportunity to institutionalize township democracy in the American constitutional order or the repression of revolutionary councils in Hungary after the Soviet invasion of 1956. These characterizations seemed aimed at supporting freedom by rescuing from historical oblivion instances of autonomous action that had seemingly come to nought. This pattern in Arendt's writings formed a helpful framework for understanding why Havel, living under a sclerotic Communist dictatorship and reflecting back upon the heady days of Prague Spring, also resorted to the rhetoric of tragedy. Clearly, his intent was to keep hope alive for a return to the days of autonomous political mobilization. Arendt's way of linking tragedy and losses of freedom also opened a perspective from which to recognize the similar political significance of neorealist films and Greek tragedy and to hear the unappreciated political resonances of the tragic rhetoric used by neorealist film directors and critics. Thus, Chapter 3 recasts that cinematic inheritance as a memorial to the efforts undertaken and sacrifices suffered (including the author's maternal grandfather who fell in ambush in early 1944 guiding escaped British POWs back to Allied lines) for a more participatory and egalitarian Italian democracy.

A second pattern discernible in Arendt's treatment of freedom is her building a notion of the tragic into her understanding of the phenomenon of freedom. For her, freedom was by its very nature tragic as a result of the unintended and unforeseen consequences that inevitably follow upon someone taking initiative or acting. "Because the actor always moves among and in reaction to other acting beings, he is never merely a 'doer' but always and at the same time a sufferer."[3] In making suffering the flip side of acting, Arendt established a basis for recognizing another dimension of the politics of tragedy: the promotion of solidarity. Here, as we have seen, ordinary usage, which academic theorists of tragedy typically dismiss as politically irrelevant or pernicious, is a good guide, especially in cases such as 9/11 or Nelson Mandela's long imprisonment when the rhetoric of tragedy comes to serve efforts at fostering fellow feeling.

Arendt's scattered references to the political role of Greek tragedy in ancient Athenian polis life constituted a third dimension of her politics of tragedy. While she never systematically considered the relationship between the institution of Greek

tragedy and the democratic political life of ancient Athens, occasional references—
for example, "Athenians attended the theatre for the sake of the play, its mythological
content and the grandeur of its language, through which they hoped to become the
masters of their passions and molders of their national destiny"[4]—make clear that
Arendt thought of that relationship as both robust and significant. As the chapters
on Havel, Strauss, and Wolf have shown, the politics of *tragōidía* continues to serve
as a conceptual resource for thinking through episodes of democratic crisis even
when this service goes mostly unrecognized.

The fourth way in which Arendt connected freedom and tragedy was by conceptualizing the realm of political freedom as a kind of theatrical stage on which citizens
appear and act. Theatrical metaphors become one of the major linguistic means by
which Arendt tried to convey the distinctive qualities of her participatory conception
of political freedom. No less striking, if less systematic, has been the resort to theatrical
metaphors by Mandela and Botho Strauss among others considered in this book as
they have sought to reflect on the political challenges faced by their respective
societies.

Any prospect of Arendt relying upon a theory of tragedy in order theoretically to
work out responsible and worthwhile forms of political community and action was
seriously jeopardized during the war and immediately afterward by the possibility
that forms of tragic engagement had facilitated German citizens' moral collapse and
their abdication of political responsibility under Nazi rule. In seeming recognition of
this problem, Arendt chose her words carefully in her wartime essays and apparently
preferred such terms as "catastrophe," "annihilation," or "destruction" to "tragedy"
when referring to the awful consequences of Nazi rule.[5] Her caution is additionally
evidenced by her decision in the early 1950s to organize the translation and publication (under the title *Tragedy Is Not Enough*) of her mentor Karl Jaspers's critique
of the "philosophy of nothing-but-tragedy" whereby "the arrogant nihilist can ele-
vate himself to the pathos of feeling himself a hero" and "set free the turmoil of dark
impulses."[6] How and why positively valenced references to tragedy and Greek tragic
verse come to proliferate in the work she published later, toward the close of the 1950s
into the early 1960s and what this change meant for her political thought are subjects
that I have already considered at length in my earlier book. The turn to Arendt in this
book's concluding pages serves in part as an acknowledgment of how that earlier
encounter with her work oriented my later thinking about the modes and possibilities of democratic theory in a powerful and lasting way.

From a perspective organized around the notion of a politics of tragedy, Arendt's
work can be seen as an important guide both for recovering what is best from a tradition that has served what is worst and for transporting the best of Germany's tradition of tragic engagement to a culture that remains (as Cornel West has reminded us)
mostly indifferent or oblivious to some important lessons of tragedy. Considered
against the backdrop of Arendt's achievement, Michael Schorr's cinematic gesture
of bringing a New World African tragic sensibility to bear on Old World German

political quandaries constitutes a return journey of sorts, one whose irony *and* promise Arendt might well have appreciated. In instructive contrast, she would in all likelihood have found much less promising the very different response to post-unification quandaries worked out by Botho Strauss. Even granting that Strauss offered his more full-throated and provocative call for engaging tragedy from the vantage point of a stable democratic German polity almost 50 years removed from the atrocities of its Nazi past, Arendt would certainly have questioned the narrow basis of that call, as well as its stated aim of rehabilitating a conservative nationalist position in German politics.

In choosing to revisit Arendt at the conclusion of this book, I am not merely acknowledging an intellectual debt. It is also my aim to bring into final focus that subject on which Arendt spoke so powerfully and for which "tragedy" is such a vital signpost: the conditions and meaning of active citizenship in today's democracies.

Today, with the exception of moments of populist activism of the sort that helped transform the governments and polities of Central and Eastern Europe in 1989–1990, examples of active citizenship in developed countries mostly exist on the margins of large-scale bureaucratic systems of public and private administration and representative systems of self-government. In this context of bureaucratic domination and representational politics, political agency, solidarity, and identity can seem hollowed out realities to the modern democratic citizen. As participation in elections becomes, more or less, the full content of political agency, democratic agency appears even more diminished by the influence on the legislative process of special interest money and lobbying. If sharing a passport or a party affiliation constitutes the full content of political solidarity, claims of democratic solidarity are bound to lose credibility in a globalizing world where national political institutions have increasingly less say about how corporations shape local economic and social conditions. A political identity that has been reduced to the accident of one's birth in a given national territory is one that in times of crisis can be easily hijacked by movements based on ethnic or religious homogeneity. (In relation to this last point, one need only note the calls in the United States that have grown in some circles to deny citizenship to native-born children of illegal immigrants.)

Arendt made the crisis of democratic forms of agency, solidarity, and identity a central focus of her thought as she formulated the arguments of those publications that would later form the basis for her breakthrough work, *The Origins of Totalitarianism* (first published in 1951). So, for example, a sense of that crisis underlay the account of the rise to power of totalitarian movements in interwar Europe that she gave in her 1946 essay, "The Moral of History."

> The moral of the history of the nineteenth century is the fact that men who were not ready to assume a responsible role in public affairs in the end were turned into mere beasts who could be used for anything before being led to the slaughter. Institutions left to themselves without control or guidance by men, turned into monsters devouring nations and countries.[7]

For Arendt, fulfilling a "responsible role in public affairs" did not merely mean periodically voting for party candidates in contested elections. It meant active citizenship, direct involvement in public affairs as had been the case, however fleetingly, in the initial stages of the French Revolution when Frenchmen entered the public square and, in their new role as citizens, gave content to the idea of government by and for the people. The example set by citizen action in the "popular societies" (where, as Arendt informs us in her 1963 work, *On Revolution*, there was "an enormous appetite for debate, for instruction, for mutual enlightenment, and exchange of opinion")[8] did not stick, however, and among the factors Arendt cites is the influence of capitalist institutions and mores whose effect was to promote self-seeking individualism at the expense of public-minded citizenship. "The general history of Europe, from the French Revolution to the beginning of World War I, may be described in its most tragic aspect as the slow but steady transformation of the *citoyen* of the French Revolution into the *bourgeois* of the pre-war period."[9]

In many ways, Arendt's critique of bourgeois individualism parallels Marx's argument in *On the Jewish Question*. In that essay, Marx casts early nineteenth-century European demands for equal citizenship regardless of religious affiliation as a demand for political emancipation. Political emancipation or equal citizenship promised people genuine equality and solidarity. The problem for Marx was that political emancipation could not deliver on its promises because giving people equal citizenship rights did not eliminate the power exercised by money in civil society. The factory owner and factory worker might be equal in a formal way, each having one vote during a given election, but where it counted for the material conditions of their lives, like access to food, shelter, safe working conditions, medicine and a doctor's care, they were vastly unequal. In Marx's eyes, then, while political emancipation or liberal democracy constituted a step forward in the emancipation of human beings to the extent that it affirmed in politics the ideas of equality and solidarity, it failed to give real content to those ideas. Liberal democracy was a way station on the road to communism, a system that would not only affirm the ideas of equality and solidarity, but also make them real.

Arendt, like Marx, criticized capitalism for its atomizing effects on human solidarity and its enervating effects on human agency. However, while she was also, as he was, a harsh critic of liberal democracy, she did not agree that it was necessarily a sham. In Arendt's view, while the institutions of liberal democracy did raise major structural and conceptual obstacles to regular and consequential citizen participation—that is, party bureaucracies that seek to monopolize political action and reduce the scope of citizen aspiration to a defense of negative liberty—they did keep open avenues of concerted political action and effective dissent through their guarantees of certain freedoms such as press and assembly. Citizenship in a liberal democracy became a sham in part because people did not take political participation seriously enough. So, for example, too many enfranchised citizens of Western European polities in the late nineteenth and early twentieth centuries had internalized the dog-eat-dog mentality of capitalism and, as a result, had stopped taking the ideas of civic virtue and the public good seriously enough.

As Arendt recounts it in *The Origins of Totalitarianism*, the nineteenth century declines in the quality of political participation and in the credibility of parties and parliamentary leaders were punctuated by two events that tipped the situation into severe crisis: the Great War and the Great Depression. In the wake of the war, with millions dead and millions more terribly wounded in body and spirit, cynicism about the worth of liberal democratic institutions was raised to new levels. After the Great Depression wiped out the livelihoods of millions, liberal democratic elites seemed at a loss for what to do. It was in this context of declining trust in politics and accelerating economic dislocation that Arendt situates the emergence of masses of people who were politically alienated, socially isolated, economically vulnerable, and indifferent to the calls of traditional religion.[10] These "mass men," whom Arendt calls the true descendants of the nineteenth-century bourgeois, go on, she argues, to become the crucial constituency of totalitarian movements like Nazism.

> [I]t became clear that for the sake of his pension, his life insurance, the security of his wife and children, (the family man) was ready to sacrifice his beliefs, his honor, and his human dignity. . . . The Only condition he put was that he should be fully exempted from responsibility for his actions. Thus, the very person, the average German, whom the Nazis notwithstanding years of the most furious propaganda could not induce to kill a Jew on his own account . . . now serves the machine of destruction without opposition. In contrast to the earlier units of the SS men and Gestapo, Himmler's over-all organization relies not on fanatics nor on congenital murderers, nor on sadists; it relies entirely upon the normality of job holders and family-men.[11]

To be sure, Arendt's analysis of pre- and post-World War I Europe is by no means the last word in explaining the sources of democratic collapse or the bases of Nazism's emergence as a world power. Whether or not it remains a perspective worthy of serious consideration by historians of that period is not germane to this study. What is germane is how that analysis formed the impetus for her later thinking about the nature and meaning of political participation.

Theoretically focused in the early postwar years upon the catastrophic effects of interwar crises of political agency, solidarity and identity, Arendt came, by the early 1960s, increasingly to engage in a politics of tragedy. Taking into account the pattern we have traced of political thinkers and activists engaging tragedy during instances of democratic opening, the coincidence of Arendt's turn to a theory of tragedy and the emerging salience in the United States of social movements demonstrating the effectiveness and virtues of direct political participation is suggestive. The coincidence not only demonstrates Arendt's foresight in anticipating major challenges to conventional understandings of representation as the exclusive mechanism for citizen involvement in politics but also complicates the common perception of the 1960s as a tragic era. So, for example, referring to memories of the JFK assassination, the first moon walk, Martin Luther King Jr.'s "I Have a Dream" speech, "a naked girl in Vietnam running, screaming, burning with napalm," David Farber, the author of *The Age of Great Dreams*, asserts that Americans continue to be emotionally invested in "the possibilities, the grandeur, and *always* the tragedy" of the 1960s.[12] As the final term in a sequence that starts with "possibilities," tragedy as it is evoked here is seemingly equated with instances of unredeemed failure or unredeemable suffering. It is perhaps his awareness of a tendency to see the 1960s through a prism of tragic failure that led Todd Gitlin in his notable study, *The Sixties: Years of Hope, Days of Rage*, studiously to avoid the term in one of his concluding summations of that era's significance: "Disappointment too eagerly embraced becomes habit, becomes doom. Say what we will about the Sixties' *failures, limits, disasters*, America's political and cultural space would probably not have opened as much as it did without the movement's delirium."[13]

Lest one feel tempted to limit the meanings of "tragedy" to suffering or fate, it would do well to remember the timing of Arendt's turn to tragedy as an explicit conceptual resource: the beginning of the 1960s. If the ingredients of that turn—Greek verse, notions of catharsis (Aristotle) and reconciliation (Hegel), evocations of the role of Attic tragedy in ancient Greek politics—originated from an intellectual training in a venerable, if also democratically suspect, German philosophical tradition, her reconfiguration of them into a participatory democratic politics of tragedy was almost certainly conditioned by exposure to her adopted country's participatory traditions and surviving practices of active citizenship. In light of the mostly minimal, though variable, presence of those traditions and practices, one might well ask what the use is of reflecting on active citizenship or of holding it up as a standard against which the nature and worth of the modern politics of representation and administration might be measured. The aim of this book has been to suggest that we are appropriately called to that sort of reflection and assessment not only by the theories of tragedy's political significance and the evocations of Greek and other tragedy on offer from notable political actors and public intellectuals and engaged artists responding to urgent political challenges of our times but also by the language of tragedy, however offhandedly or inexpertly it comes to be deployed in our daily lives.

Notes

Chapter 1

1. Arthur Schlesinger, *Robert Kennedy and His Times* (Boston, MA: Houghton Mifflin, 1978), 618.
2. Quoted by Evan Thomas from an interview with Adam Walinsky in *Robert Kennedy: His Life* (New York: Simon & Schuster, 2000), 367.
3. Ibid., 394.
4. Schlesinger, 619.
5. Quoted in Thomas, 453. Thomas's book indicates "1953" as the relevant date but this is likely a misprint.
6. The source of the Greek reference is Edith Hamilton: "An old Greek inscription states that the aim of mankind should be 'to tame the savageness of man and make gentle the life of the world.'" *The Ever-Present Past* (New York: Norton, 1964), 34.
7. *Make Gentle the Life of This World: The Vision of Robert F. Kennedy* (New York: Harcourt Brace, 1998), xvii.
8. Ronald Steel, *In Love With Night: The American Romance With Robert Kennedy* (New York: Simon & Schuster, 2000), 95.
9. "On Black Nationalism" and "Prophetic Christian as Organic Intellectual: Martin Luther King, Jr.," *The Cornel West Reader* (New York: Basic Civitas Books, 1999), and 427–521, respectively.
10. "Pragmatism and the Tragic," *Prophetic Thought in Postmodern Times* (Monroe, ME: Common Courage Press, 1993), 34.
11. Simon Schama, "The Unloved American," *The New Yorker* (March 10, 2003), 35.
12. Kenneth E. Morris, *Jimmy Carter: American Moralist* (Athens, GA: University of Georgia Press, 1996), 5.
13. Jack Newfield, *Robert Kennedy: A Memoir* (New York: Bantam, 1970), 40–1.
14. Robert McNamara, *In Retrospect: The Tragedy and Lessons of Vietnam* (New York: Random House, 1995), xv, xvi.
15. McNamara, xvii.
16. Ibid., 107.
17. Robert McNamara et al., *Argument Without End: In Search of Answers to the Vietnam Tragedy* (New York: Public Affairs, 2000), xi.
18. Ibid., 19.
19. Two recent examples include David Kaiser, *American Tragedy: Kennedy, Johnson, and the Origins of the Vietnam War* (Boston, MA: Belknap, 2000) and Lewis Sorley, *A Better War: The Unexamined Victories and Final Tragedy of America's Last Years in Vietnam* (New York: Harcourt Brace, 1999).
20. McNamara, 280.

21. Ibid., xvii. A more literal translation would be, "knowledge through suffering."
22. David Halberstam, *The Best and the Brightest* (New York: Random House, 1972), 219, 248, 514.
23. Ibid., 258–9.
24. Ibid., 215, 668.
25. Mary McCarthy, *The Seventeenth Degree* (New York: Harcourt Brace Jovanovich, 1974), 17, 422.
26. Newfield, 262.
27. McNamara et al., 24.
28. Interview segment in Errol Morris, *The Fog of War* (2004).
29. See McNamara's introduction to Robert Kennedy's *Thirteen Days: A Memoir of the Cuban Missile Crisis* (New York: Norton, 1969), 13–16.
30. Among the passages he underlined in his copy of *The Greek Way* was the following verse from Agamemnon's *Persians*: "All arrogance will reap a harvest rich in tears. God calls men to a heavy reckoning for overweening pride." Thomas (2000), 22.
31. See Jerome Groopman, "The Grief Industry," *The New Yorker* (January 26, 2004) and Richard M. Valelly, "What's Gone Right in the Study of What's Gone Wrong," *The Chronicle Review* (April 16, 2004).
32. The earliest surviving use of "tragedy" in this last sense in English cited by the Oxford English Dictionary is by Chaucer, who, in a 1374 manuscript translation of Boethius's *De Consolatione Philosophie*, offered the following gloss ("glose"): "Tragedie is to seyn, a dittee (ditty) of a prosperitee for a tyme, that ended in wrecchedness." Chaucer's definition is occasioned by the following passage from the *Consolatione*: "*Quid tragoediarum clamor aliud, nisi indiscreto ictu fortunam Felicia regna vertentum*"? ("Notes to the Canterbury Tales," *The Complete Works of Geoffrey Chaucer* [Oxford: Clarendon, 1963] 226). Etymological dictionaries trace the Middle English *tragedie* to an Old French word identically spelled except for an acute accent over the second "e". It entered Old French as a learned borrowing from *tragoedia*, a Latin derivation of the ancient Greek *tragōidíā*. This Greek ancestor term referred to verse dramas performed by actors on the occasion of civic-religious festivals, the most notable of which was the City Dionysia. Uses of *tragedie* and other Middle English variants of the word in literary references to Greek and Latin lyric and dramatic works are recorded as early as 1430. Even earlier, in 1412, an English writer had applied the term more generally to describe a category of works elevated in style and sorrowful in theme. "Tragedy," *The Oxford English Dictionary*, 2nd edn. (Oxford: Clarendon, 1989), 360.
33. Ibid., 360.
34. Excerpts of Myer's testimony from *New York Times* (May 8, 2004), A6. For Bush Administration questioning of the Geneva Convention, see, for example, Secretary of Defense Donald Rumsfeld's remarks at a February 8, 2002, press conference: "The reality is that the set of facts that exist today with respect to Al Qaeda and Taliban were not necessarily the kinds of facts that were considered

when the Geneva Convention was fashioned some half a century ago." Tara McKelvey, *Monstering: Inside America Policy of Secret Interrogations and Torture in the Terror War* (New York: Carroll & Graf, 2007), 33.

35. "Woman gets 15 years in fatal wreck," *Savannah Morning News* (March 4, 2001), 1A.
36. *Sweet Violence: The Idea of the Tragic* (Malden, MA: Blackwell, 2003), 44.
37. Cited by Cornel West in *The American Evasion of Philosophy* (Madison, WI: University of Wisconsin Press, 1989), 24.
38. "The Social Role of the Intellectual," *Power, Politics, and People: The Collected Essays of C. Wright Mills* (New York: Ballantine Books, 1944), 294, 300.
39. See note 21 above.
40. "Noble simplicity and serene greatness." See, for example, M. S. Silk and J. P. Stern, *Nietzsche on Tragedy* (Cambridge: Cambridge University Press, 1987 [1981 first edition]), 5.
41. Václav Havel, "New Year's Address to the Nation," *The Art of the Impossible: Politics as Morality in Practice*, trans. Paul Wilson et al. (New York: Fromm International, 1998), 6.
42. M. I. Finley writes that the "interests of the mass of citizens fell into two broad areas. One was their power (in a formal sense) to defend themselves and their rights at law. . . . The second broad area of interests that political gains were expected to advance [were] debt and land hunger." *Politics in the Ancient World* (Cambridge: Cambridge University Press, 1983), 108.
43. The foreign policy challenges posed to Athens' fledgling democracy are concisely listed by Gerald Else: "In the years immediately following 510, after the expulsion of the Pisistratids, Athens became a democracy . . . . [T]he young democracy promptly faced severe trials. It had to fight hard against oligarchic neighbors, Thebes, Aegina, Megara, Corinth. Then came the Ionian revolt against the Persian Empire, (499–494), conspicuously encouraged and supported by Athens. Its collapse was followed very shortly by the first invasion of Greece under Darius, in 490, and ten years later by that of Xerxes. Then, at Marathon and at Salamis, Athens suddenly emerged as the moral champion and leader of the Greek nation. It was a peripety for which other Greeks were not prepared and which some of them found hard to accept, then and afterward." *The Origin and Early Form of Greek Tragedy* (Cambridge, MA: Harvard University Press, 1965), 79. See, also, Christian Meier in *The Political Art of Greek Tragedy*, trans. Andrew Webber (Baltimore, MD: Johns Hopkins University Press, 1993), 34–43.
44. See, for a dissenting view, W. R. Connor, who argues that the City Dionysia was inaugurated after Athens' transition to democracy, around 508BCE. "City Dionysia and Athenian Democracy," *Classica et Mediaevalia* XL, 7–32.
45. *Paideia, Volume 1* (Oxford: Oxford University Press, 1974), 248.
46. Meier, 219.
47. "But let us ask by means of what remedy it was possible for the Greeks during their great period, in spite of the extraordinary strength of their Dionysian and

political instincts, not to exhaust themselves either in ecstatic brooding or in a consuming chase after worldly power and worldly honor, but rather to attain that splendid mixture which resembles a noble wine in making one feel fiery and contemplative at the same time." *The Birth of Tragedy and The Case of Wagner*, trans. Walter Kaufmann (New York: Vintage, 1967), 125.

48. Else, 43, 44.
49. Among the major scholarly works of the last generation or two to be consulted in the following chapters are Jean-Pierre Vernant and Pierre Vidal-Naquet's, *Myth and Tragedy in Ancient Greece* (1988, original French editions 1972 and 1986), Christian Meier's *The Political Art of Tragedy* (1993, original German edition 1988) and M. S. Silk's edited volume, *Tragedy and the Tragic: Greek Theatre and Beyond* (1996). Works of political philosophy or theory that have drawn insightfully on studies of *tragōidíā* and from which the argument of this book has drawn include Karen Hermassi's *Polity and Theatre In Historical Perspective* (1977), Martha Nussbaum's *The Fragility of Goodness: Luck and Ethics in Greek Tragedy and Philosophy* (1986), J. Peter Euben's *The Tragedy of Political Theory: The Road Not Taken* (1990), Louis Ruprecht's *Tragic Posture and Tragic Vision* (1994), and Dennis J. Schmidt's *On Germans and Other Greeks: Tragedy and Ethical Life* (2001).

Chapter 2

1. Timothy Garton Ash, *The Magic Lantern: The Revolution of '89 Witnessed in Warsaw, Budapest, Berlin, and Prague* (New York: Vintage, 1993), 78, 79.
2. See Havel's December 21, 1992, address at Wroclaw University. Václav Havel, *The Art of the Impossible* (New York: Fromm International, 1998), 111.
3. "Address to a Joint Session of the U.S. Congress: February 21, 1990," Ibid., 19.
4. "The Power of the Powerless" in *Open Letters: Selected Writings, 1965–1990* (New York: Knopf, 1991), 161.
5. "The Intellectual in the Post Modern Age: East/West Contrasts," *Philosophy Today* (Winter 1990), 292.
6. Martin J. Matustik, *Postnational Identity: Critical Theory and Existential Philosophy in Habermas, Kierkegaard, and Havel* (New York: The Guilford Press, 1993), vi, xi.
7. "The Seer of Prague," *The New Republic* (July, 1, 1991), 37. Calling attention to ambiguous phrasings in consecutive letters sent by Havel to his wife from prison, Rorty does admit to a degree of uncertainty about whether Havel agrees or disagrees with Patočka's Socratic position.
8. *Truth and Progress* (Cambridge: Cambridge University Press, 1998), 231, 236, 239. Thanks to Helena Schmidt for this reference.
9. "Address to a Joint Session of Congress: February 21, 1990," in Havel, 19.
10. "Havel on Political Responsibility," *The Political Science Reviewer*, 35.
11. "Attempts to Escape the Logic of Capitalism," *The London Review of Books*, 7.

12. "A Man For This Season: Václav Havel on Freedom and Responsibility," *Perspectives on Political Science*, 21 (4) (Fall 1992), 202, 206.
13. Aviezer Tucker, *The Philosophy and Politics of Czech Dissidence from Patočka to Havel* (Pittsburgh, PA: University of Pittsburgh Press, 2000), 156 and 162. See also, ibid., 248.
14. "Classical Ethics and Postmodern Critique: Political Philosophy in Václav Havel and Jan Patočka," *The Review of Politics*, 426, 437.
15. Ibid., 404, 409–10, 422.
16. Petr Lom, "East Meets West—Jan Patočka and Richard Rorty on Freedom: A Czech Philosopher Brought into Dialogue with American Postmodernism," *Political Theory* (August 1999), 456.
17. Havel, *Disturbing the Peace*, trans. Paul Wilson (New York: Knopf, 1990), 26.
18. As recounted by Paul Wilson in his introduction to Havel's *Letters to Olga* (New York: Holt, 1989), 18.
19. Ibid., 18–19.
20. Ibid., 154, 270.
21. Tucker, 116, 118.
22. "Václav Havel's Construction of a Democratic Discourse: Politics in a Postmodern Age," *Philosophy Today* (Summer 1995), 127.
23. The "I"/"we" phrasing is borrowed from Hammer, who puts it to a different use. See ibid., 124. Theoretically formulating the problem of agency in this way, we do not forget the peculiar political valence that the "I"/"we" distinction gained as a result of the official rhetoric of Communist regimes in Central and Eastern Europe. Use of the "I" became ideologically suspect, while the "we" was invested with positive notions of class solidarity and regime support. Padraic Kenney also makes this point in *The Burdens of Freedom: Eastern Europe Since 1989* (Nova Scotia: Fernwood, 2007), 12, citing Slavonka Drakulić's discussion in her 1996 book, *Café Europa*.
24. Tucker, 248.
25. Jane Perlez, "For the Czechs, The Fairy Tale Is All Over Now," *New York Times* (December 1, 1997), 1, 8.
26. Paul Wilson's introduction to his translation of Havel's address, "The State of the Republic," *The New York Review of Books* (March 5, 1998), 45. For the quote which heads this article, see Ibid., 42.
27. Michael Simmons, *The Reluctant President: A Political Life of Václav Havel* (London: Methuen, 1991), 201.
28. Havel, "The State of the Republic," *The New York Review of Books* (March 5, 1998) 43, 45.
29. Cases for the centrality of Greek tragedy to the thought of Martin Heidegger are persuasively made in George Steiner *Antigones* (Oxford: Oxford University Press, 1984) and Josef Chytry *The Aesthetic State: A Quest in Modern German Thought* (Los Angeles, CA: University of California Press, 1989), 391–2.

30. For Patočka as student of Heidegger, see Erazim Kohák, *Jan Patočka: Philosophy and Selected Writings* (Chicago, IL: University of Chicago Press, 1989), xi. For Heidegger's turn to Greek tragedy in 1933, see Dennis Schmidt, *On Germans and Other Greeks: Tragedy and Ethical Life* (Bloomington, IN: Indiana University Press, 2001), 237.

31. John Keane, *Václav Havel: A Political Tragedy in Six Acts* (London: Bloomsbury, 1999), 16.

32. *Disturbing the Peace* trans. Paul Wilson (New York: Knopf, 1990), 40.

33. *Letters to Olga* trans. Paul Wilson (New York: Henry Holt, 1989), 250.

34. "Second Wind" (December, 1976), trans. Paul Wilson, *Open Letters* (New York: Knopf, 1991), 6.

35. "The Power of the Powerless," 135, 143.

36. In one of his letters to Olga, Havel distinguishes three interrelated ways in which the theater experience fosters a sense of community. There is, first, the "short-term communal feeling in a specific audience" aroused in response to a per-formance event. As people come to frequent theater, they come to establish a second, more durable kind of community based on shared tastes and sensibili-ties and common linguistic references. With emergence of a theater-going public, one can expect "an impact on the awareness and self-esteem of society as a whole." *Letters to Olga,* 260–2.

37. *Disturbing the Peace,* 40.

38. *Letters to Olga,* 250, 252, 256.

39. Ibid., 250. Apparently, Havel's sense of the continuing relevance of the polis for thinking about contemporary politics was influenced by Václav Benda's concep-tualization of dissident movements as a form of "parallel polis." See Havel's essay, "The Power of the Powerless," trans. Paul Wilson and collected in *Open Letters* (1991), 193–6, 204, 213.

40. "It Always Makes Sense to Tell the Truth" (1975), interview with Jirí Lederer trans. Paul Wilson, *Open Letters,* 98.

41. *Dálkovy Vyslech,* 174.

42. *Disturbing the Peace,* 199, 200, 201.

43. *Disturbing the Peace,* 201. Bracketed word from *Dálkovy Vyslech,* 174.

44. *Čištĕni* is also used in the Czech language to refer to catharsis.

45. *Disturbing the Peace,* 105–6. Czech phrases from *Dálkovy Vyslech,* 94–5.

46. *Dálkovy Vyslech,* 95.

47. *Disturbing the Peace,* 105.

48. *Disturbing the Peace,* 106. Bracketed word from *Dálkovy Vyslech,* 96.

49. "The Power of the Powerless," trans. Paul Wilson, *Open Letters,* 151.

50. *The Journal of Politics* (Vol. 20), 5, 7.

51. For an example of an ordinary use of the term, tragedy, in reference to Havel, one need only consider John Keane's recent biography, *Václav Havel: A Political Tragedy in Six Acts* (London: Bloomsbury, 1999), which begins with the state-ment, "Time can be a cruel despot. Acting on a whim, it sometimes pounces on

particular lives, pushing them into custody, dragging them to a destination of suffering and unhappy endings. Such has been the fate of Václav Havel." Although Keane notes several interesting ways by which Havel sought in his first presidency to aestheticize republican politics, he does not link these attempts with any notions of tragedy held by Havel. For Keane, the only relevant meaning of tragedy is a story with a sad ending.

52. A comprehensive study of the uses of tragedy in Arendt's thought is undertaken in Robert Pirro, *Hannah Arendt and the Politics of Tragedy* (Dekalb, IL: Northern Illinois University Press, 2000).

53. In his essay, "Masaryk, Patočka and the Care of the Soul," Roger Scruton has suggested that, "the writings of Arendt have been as influential in post-war Czech philosophy as those of Patočka." Josef Novak ed. *On Masaryk: Texts in German and English* (Amsterdam: Rodopi, 1988), 125. If Havel has read Arendt, he has left nothing in the way of a direct reference to her or to her works in his writings published in English, to my knowledge. In any case, Havel can certainly be said to fit the profile of a theorist of the "Great Republic," what Agnes Heller has described as a Central European model of politics different in important ways from liberalism, conservatism, and socialism, among whose proponents she counts Hannah Arendt. "The Great Republic," *Praxis International* (Oxford) 5 (1) (April 1985).

54. *Disturbing the Peace*, 109, 138.

55. "Farce, Reformability, and the Future of the World" (1987), trans. A. G. Brain, *Open Letters*, 355.

56. *Disturbing the Peace*, 173, 177. Bracketed words from *Dálkovy Vyslech*, 152.

57. "It Always Makes Sense to Tell the Truth," interview with Jiří Lederer trans. Paul Wilson, *Open Letters*, 98.

58. "[I]t bothered me that Kundera—and he was far from being the only one—began to explain the Soviet occupation and the Czechoslovak accomodation to it as part of our national lot, as though the Soviets had come here not to renew their version of order in a disobedient dominion but simply to fulfill the ancient Czech destiny . . . ." *Disturbing the Peace*, 179.

59. *Letters to Olga*, 152.

60. Ibid., 230.

61. "Genuine conscience and genuine responsibility are always, in the end, explicable only as an expression of the silent assumption that we are observed 'from above' (in what I have called the 'memory of Being'), that everything is visible, nothing is forgotten, and so earthly time has no power to wipe away the sharp disappointments of earthly failure: our spirit knows that it is not the only entity aware of these failures." *Summer Meditations* trans. Paul Wilson (New York: Vintage, 1992), 6. This sense of Being as a guarantor of permanence is reiterated by Havel in his 1996 address at Trinity College in Dublin. *The Art of the Impossible*, 245.

62. *Summer Meditations*, 6.

63. "The Salzburg Festival," trans. Káca Poláckóva-Henley, *The Art of the Impossible*, 50.
64. *Classical Literary Criticism*, trans. T. S. Dorsch (London: Penguin), 38–9.
65. "Anatomy of a Reticence," trans. Erazim Kohák, *Open Letters*, 309.
66. Ibid., 301–2.
67. Ibid., 300.
68. Ibid., 302.
69. "Thinking About Frantisek K.," trans. A. G. Brain, *Open Letters*, 363, 364, 366.
70. Ibid., 367, 368.
71. *Hegel on Tragedy* ed. Anne and Henry Paolucci (Garden City: Anchor Books, 1962), 51, 68, 237.
72. For an interesting analysis of a tragic genre of Bolshevik-era literature which propagated a Leninist version of Hegel's "cunning of reason," see Dariusz Tolczyk, *See No Evil* (Hartford, CT: Yale University Press, 1999), 65–78. Havel's tragic rendering of Kriegel's life bears no important resemblance to works in this genre.
73. "Thinking about Frantisek K.," 372.
74. Ibid., 372.
75. "The Co-responsibility of the West," originally published in *Foreign Affairs* (December 22, 1993), *The Art of the Impossible*, 134. In his February 8, 1994 address on receiving the Indira Gandhi prize, Havel referred to the end of the "pseudo-order" of Cold War bipolarity and characterized the post-Cold War world as "going through a transitional phase." (156) In a 1995 address to the Australian National Press Club, Havel agrees that, "the Western world is suffering from a crisis of authority." (198)
76. *Art of the Impossible*, 162, 163.
77. "October 4, 1996 address to Academy of Performing Arts in Prague," ibid., 250, 251, 252.
78. "The State of the Republic," *The New York Review of Books*, 42.
79. This contrast should not be overstated. After all, Havel well understood both that post-totalitarian Communism provided ample motive and opportunity for individualistic plundering and that capitalism promoted inappropriate levels of consumerist conformity. We are talking about differences in the emphasis Havel places on the use of tragic catharsis.
80. *Art of the Impossible*, 138, 139.
81. "New Year's Address to the Nation," ibid., 6.
82. Ibid., 4, 5.
83. Ibid., 8.
84. It may alternatively be that such a burden is intensified as a result of the release of revolutionary passions. See, for example, Artemy Magun's interesting analysis of Arendt's *On Revolution*: "Similarly, a revolution—be it the French Revolution or the recent fall of socialist regimes in Eastern Europe—turns into a crisis when the oppressive regime (absolute monarchy or Communist Party rule) that was

relatively alien to society is gone, while the contradictions and the negative revolutionary thrust remain. In these circumstances, the negative energy, left without an object, is re-directed against society itself, against the subject itself, which can lead to fratricidal terror, or to self-inhibition and symbolic self-destitution." "The Double Bind: The Ambivalent Treatment of Tragic Passions in Hannah Arendt's Theory of Revolution," *History of Political Thought,* 28:4.

85. "Thinking about Frantisek K.," 371.

86. So, for example, in an address given on the occasion of a memorial concert in Prague for Jewish victims of Nazi genocide in Czechoslovakia, Havel considers the Jewish people as a "scapegoat, as a substitute sacrifice," "chosen to arouse the conscience of humanity through their suffering." The "tragic meaning" he attributes to their suffering seems dangerously compatible with Hegel's "cunning of reason." *Art of the Impossible,* 75, 76, 77.

87. *To the Castle and Back,* trans. Paul Wilson (New York: Knopf, 2007), 14, 64, 277, 286.

Chapter 3

1. For consideration of Havel's involvement in a circle of student intellectuals in Prague who discussed philosophy and literature, attended the theater, and went to the cinema, see John Keane's *Václav Havel: A Political Tragedy in Six Acts* (New York: Basic Books, 2000), 105. For discussion of the influence of Italian neorealist films on the Czech cinema, see Mira Liehm, *Passion and Defiance: Film in Italy from 1942 to the Present* (Berkeley, CA: University of California Press, 1984), 131.

2. Lubica Učník, "Aesthetics or Ethics? Italian Neorealism and the Czechoslovak New Wave Cinema," *Italian Neorealism and Global Cinema,* Laura Ruberto and Kristi Wilson, eds (Detroit, MI: Wayne State University Press, 2007), 59, 60, 66.

3. Author's translation of a Zavattini interview response republished in *Cesare Zavattini Neorealismo ecc.,* Mino Argentieri, ed. (Milan: Bompiani, 1979), 82.

4. Liehm, 130.

5. According to Tag Gallagher, the April and June 1948 issues of the Italian journal *Bianco e Nero* and the May 1948 issue of the Paris-based *La Revue du Cinéma* were the first print sources in which the new Italian cinema was characterized in terms of neorealism. "Neorealism=mc2," *The Adventures of Robert Rossellini* (New York: Da Capo, 1998), 268.

6. Gallagher, 272.

7. Liehm, 135.

8. Cited by Mario Cannella, "Ideology and Aesthetic Hypotheses in the Criticism of NeoRealism," *Screen* 14 (Winter 1973), 9, 40.

9. Liehm, 135. By contrast with Liehm, Mario Cannella argues that the problem with leftist interpretations of neorealism was their being too broad rather than too narrow. By his account, Communist critics, in following the Italian Communist Party line of alliance with bourgeois democratic parties in the

mid-1940s, tended to interpret neorealist films in terms of the politically conservative principles of humanitarianism and populism rather than the radical
(and more authentically Communist) principle of class struggle. Cannella,
32–6.

10. Liehm, 134.
11. André Bazin, "An Aesthetic of Reality," *What Is Cinema I*, ed. and trans. Hugh
Gray (Berkeley, CA: University of California Press, 1971), 21.
12. Bazin, "De Sica: Metteur en Scène," Ibid., 74.
13. Peter Bondanella, *Italian Cinema: From Neorealism to the Present* (New York:
Continuum, 1990), 130, 34.
14. Of this fact, Bazin was also aware: "One is compelled to choose between one
kind of reality and another." Ibid., 29. To be fair, Bazin's understanding of
neorealism is a rich one, encompassing a recognition of its sociohistorical and
aesthetic, as well as humanist dimensions. It nevertheless remains true that, in
his understanding, predominant explanatory weight is placed on neorealism's
humanistic significance. Similarly, Bondanella is here made to stand for aestheticist approaches not because he is unmindful of the socio-historical or
humanistic dimensions of neorealism—he isn't—but because he places major
emphasis on the aesthetic.
15. Taking a Lacanian approach, film scholars explain the positive reception of
neorealist films by critics and audiences as resulting from Italians' psychological
need to organize a coherent and satisfactory sense of subjectivity in the aftermath of twenty years' experience of fascism. So, for example, Vincent Rocchio
interprets occasions of narrative disruption and displacement in *Open City* as
devices that helped Italian cinemagoers preserve a satisfactory sense of self by
obfuscating the unpleasant reality of their portion of responsibility in accepting
and supporting fascist rule. Rocchio, *Cinema of Anxiety: A Psychoanalysis of
Italian Neorealism* (Austin, TX: University of Texas Press, 1999), 41–51. For
another example of a Lacanian approach to neorealism, see chapter 2 of Angelo
Restivo, *The Cinema of Economic Miracles: Visuality and Modernization in the
Italian Art Film* (Durham, NC: Duke University Press, 2002).
16. "Bicycle Thieves: A Re-reading," *Cinema Journal* 21 (2) (Spring 1982), 5, 9.
17. See, for example, Millicent Marcus, *Italian Film in the Light of Neorealism*
(Princeton, NJ: Princeton University Press, 1984), 42–4.
18. For a comprehensive survey of the immense variety of notions of tragedy and the
tragic, see Richard H. Palmer, *Tragedy and Tragic Theory: An Analytical Guide*
(Westport, CT: Greenwood Press, 1992).
19. "A Thesis on Neorealism," *Springtime in Italy: A Reader on Italian Neo-Realism*
ed. and trans. David Overbey (Hamden, CT: Archon Books, 1978), 68, 70. In the
same vein, Roberto Rossellini writes that, "the subject of neorealist film is the
world; not a story or narrative. It contains no preconceived thesis." "A Few Words
about Neo-realism," ibid., 90.
20. Peter Bondanella notes the criticisms lodged against Rossellini for relying in
Open City "upon traditional devices of melodrama" in his book, *The Films of*

Roberto Rossellini (Cambridge, MA: Cambridge University Press, 1993), 62. The technical observations about the *Bicycle Thieves* film script and shot structure are from Tomasulo, 4, 6.

21. Peter Bondanella, *Italian Cinema: From Neorealism to the Present* (New York: Continuum, 1990), 31–4.

22. Ibid., 130.

23. See Angela Dalle Vacche's argument that neorealist cinema manifested a form of "'comedic' microhistory" derived from the tradition of *commedia dell'arte* in *The Body in the Mirror: Shapes of History in Italian Cinema* (Princeton, NJ: Princeton University Press, 1992), 6.

24. John Hay, *Popular Film Culture in Fascist Italy: The Passing of the Rex* (Bloomington, IN: Indiana University Press, 1987), 8. More recently, Mark Shiel has singled out one aspect of modernization—urbanization—as a key variable in the analysis of neorealism. See "Chapter 3: Neorealism and the City," *Italian Neorealism: Rebuilding the Cinematic City* (London: Wallflower, 2006).

25. Hay, 248.

26. Hermasi, xi.

27. Roger Manvell, *"Paisá"*: How It Struck Our Contemporaries," *The Penguin Film Review* 9 (London: Penguin, 1949), 53–4, 56, 58. In *Il Popolo*'s September 25, 1945, review of Rossellini's, *Open City*, the film was described as depicting, "the harsh and tragic life lived during the imprisonment of Rome." Carlo Trabuco's words quoted (in translation) by David Forgacs, "Space, Rhetoric and the Divided City," in *Roberto Rossellini's Rome Open City*, ed. Sidney Gottlieb (Cambridge: Cambridge University Press, 2004).

28. Chiarini, "A Discourse on Neo-Realism," *Springtime in Italy: A Reader on Italian Neo-Realism* (Hamden, CT: Archon Books, 1978), 139, 144, 151. In the Italian language original, the last quote reads as follows: "[C]'era rispecchiata tutta l'Italia con la sua tragedia, le sue miserie . . . " Discorso sul neorealismo," *Sul neorealismo: testi e documenti, 1939–1955* (Pesaro: 10a Mostra Internazionale del Nuovo Cinema, 1974), 173.

29. Liehm , 39, 60, 135, 317.

30. Marcus, 44, 46, 69, 71, 89, 115.

31. Bondanella, 37, 38, 39, 53, 55, 69, 73.

32. *Paideia, Volume 1,* trans. Gilbert Highet (Oxford: Oxford University Press, 1974), 231.

33. Mary Ann Frese Witt, *The Search for Modern Tragedy: Aesthetic Fascism in Italy and France* (Ithaca, NY: Cornell, 2001), 19. Mabel Berezin considers Italian fascism's robust sponsorship of public spectacle under the rubric, "festival state," in "The Festival State: Celebration and Commemoration in Fascist Italy," *Journal of Modern European History*.

34. Witt, 23.

35. Hay, 12.

36. H. Stuart Hughes, *The United States and Italy* (Cambridge: Harvard University Press, 1979), 48.

37. Paul Ginsborg, *A History of Contemporary Italy: Society and Politics, 1943–1988* (New York: Palgrave, 2003), 12.

38. So, for example, Palmiro Togliatti, leader of the Communist resistance in Italy, committed his party to the establishment of a new sort of parliamentary democracy, "a form of state that involved more direct popular participation than did a normal parliamentary democracy." Second in numerical strength to the Communists, members of the "Justice and Liberty" Brigades, "were committed to establishing a new democracy based on greater local autonomies" and concerned to correct the "distortions and injustices" of the capitalist order (ibid., 43 and 15). The Popular Front position of the Italian Communists was dictated in part by a Soviet interest not to alienate their British and American allies, whose cross-channel invasion of Occupied France was urgently awaited by Soviet forces battling a still potent German military machine in the East.

39. Ibid., 36 and 60.

40. To frame the challenge facing Greek society in the sixth–fifth centuries BCE as one of mediating an older religious conception of collective life and a newer legalistic one is to rely on J. P. Vernant's path-breaking work in *Tragedy and Myth in Ancient Greece*, which was co-written with Pierre Vidal-Naquet (Atlantic Highlands, NJ: Humanities Press, 1981), 4.

41. Ibid., 19.

42. Noted by Simon Goldhill, "Collectivity and Otherness—The Authority of the Tragic Chorus: Response to Gould," *Tragedy and the Tragic: Greek Theatre and Beyond*, ed. M. S. Silk (Oxford: Clarendon Press, 1998), 251.

43. Goldhill in Silk, 250.

44. John Gould, "Tragedy and Collective Experience," *Tragedy and the Tragic: Greek Theatre and Beyond*, ed. M. S. Silk (Oxford: Clarendon Press, 1998), 233.

45. Goldhill in Silk, 255.

46. "A Few Words about Neorealism," *Springtime in Italy: A Reader on Italian Neo-Realism* (Hamden, CT: Archon Books, 1978), 90.

47. P. Adams Sitney, *Vital Crises in Italian Film* (Austin, TX: University of Texas Press, 1995), 31.

48. Citing a review by Michelangelo Antonioni of a 1940 pro-Franco film, *L'assedio dell'Alcazar* (*The Siege of Alcazar*), Bondanella notes the importance of *coralitá* as a concept of film criticism among fascist-era film critics. Peter Bondanella, "The Making of *Roma Citta Apertá*," in *Roberto Rossellini's Rome Open City*, ed. Sidney Gottlieb (Cambridge: Cambridge University Press, 2004), 49.

49. John Ayto, *Dictionary of Word Origins* (New York: Arcade, 1990), 526.

50. Rune Frederiksen, "The Greek Theatre: A Typical Building in the Urban Centre of the *Polis*?", in *Even More Studies in the Ancient Greek Polis*, ed. Thomas Nielsen (Stuttgart: Franz Steiner Verlag, 2002), 92. Thanks to Josef Chytry for this reference.

51. H. C. Baldry, *The Greek Tragic Theatre* (Norton: New York, 1971), 81.

52. Hay, 15.

53. "Audience Figures," *The Companion to Italian Cinema*, eds Geoffrey Nowell-Smith et al. (London: Cassell and the British Film Institute, 1996), 161.

54. Issues of direct political import were, on occasion, raised and decided in the theater; "in Athens, meetings of the *ekklesia* [assembly] and other secular activities sometimes took place in the theatre immediately before or after the dramatic performances." Frederiksen, 81.

55. Hermassi, 7. J. P. Vernant writes that, "perhaps the essential feature that defines (Greek tragedy) is that the drama brought to the stage unfolds both at the level of everyday existence, in a human, opaque time made up of successive and limited present moments and also beyond this earthly life, in a divine, omnipresent time that at every instance encompasses the totality of events." *Tragedy and Myth in Ancient Greece*, with Pierre Vidal-Naquet, 10.

56. Liehm, 134. For background on Bazin's formative influences, see Dudley Andrew, *André Bazin* (New York: Columbia University Press, 1978), chapter 1.

57. "An Aesthetic of Reality," *What Is Cinema I*, ed. and trans. Hugh Gray (Berkeley, CA: University of California Press, 1971), 19–20.

58. Bazin, "Bicycle Thief," *What Is Cinema I*, 49–50.

59. Bazin, "De Sica: Metteur en Scène," *What Is Cinema I*, 66.

60. Bazin, "Bicycle Thief," *What Is Cinema I*, 50; "Umberto D," *What Is Cinema I*, 81.

61. Bazin, "Bicycle Thief," *What Is Cinema I*, 53, 59.

62. Zavattini, "A Thesis on Neo-Realism," *Springtime in Italy: A Reader on Italian Neo-Realism* (Hamden, CT: Archon Books, 1978), 67, 69, 76.

63. Ibid., 67.

64. *Sweet Violence: The Idea of the Tragic* (Malden, MA: Blackwell, 2003), 72 and 75, respectively.

65. C. Wright Mills, *Power, Politics, and People* (New York: Ballantine Books, 1963), 294.

66. Zavattini, "A Thesis on Neorealism," 68.

67. Ibid., 76.

68. "*Il Cinema, Zavattini, e la Realtà,*" Zavattini interview (*La Fiera Letteraria*, December 9, 1951) by Pasquale Festa Campanile, republished in *Cesare Zavattini Neorealismo ecc.*, ed. Mino Argentieri (Milan: Bompiani, 1979), 82.

69. Marcus, 59, 62.

70. Bazin, "Bicycle Thief," 54–5.

71. Phillip Lopate, "The Images of Children in Films," *Totally, Tenderly, Tragically: Essays and Criticism from a Lifelong Love Affair with the Movies* (New York: Doubleday, 1998), 326.

72. "*In questa scena conclusiva, dopo aver creato una congruenza perfetta tra lo sguardo dei ragazzi e quello degli spettatori, Rossellini mette in prospettiva, lungo lo stesso asse visivo, gli spettatori, I protagonisti dell'azione e lo spazio urbano.*" Gian Piero Brunetta, *Cent'anni di cinema italiano: Dal 1945 ai giorni nostri II* (Rome: Editori Laterza, 1998), 29.

73. Rossellini, "Why I Directed Stromboli," *My Method: Writings and Interviews* (New York: Marsilio, 1992), 29.

74. "Neo-Realism: Yesterday," *Springtime in Italy: A Reader on Italian Neo-Realism* (Hamden, CT: Archon Books, 1978), 202.

75. Sitney, 11.

76. Ibid., 42.

77. Marcia Landy offers a parallel analysis of the appeal of Rossellini's landmark film under the rubric of "cliché." She argues that *Roma Citta Apertá* offers clichés about womanhood, the Catholic Church, and other venerable institutions of Italian life in ways that both attract and unsettle the viewer: "The young boys, after viewing the death of Don Pietro, march solemnly toward St. Peter's. . . . The film spectator's gaze follows the movement of the young boys but the images viewed do not yield a determinate meaning but rather uncertainty about their role. The familiar becomes unfamiliar. The spectator views St. Peter's as a distant image and nothing more than an image—as a historical landmark and as a visual cliché, but as a cliché invested with a different source of power. . . . In the *Open City*'s final sequence, the cliché is subjected to a cinematic gaze that undermines an automatic response and instead invites reflection." "Diverting Clichés: Femininity, Masculinity, Melodrama, and Neorealism in *Open City*," in *Roberto Rossellini's Rome Open City*, ed. Sidney Gottlieb (Cambridge: Cambridge University Press, 2004), 100–1.

78. Paolo Spriano, quoted in Paul Ginsborg, *A History of Contemporary Italy: Society and Politics, 1943–1988* (New York: Palgrave, 2003), 71.

79. Ginsborg, 105–10, 122–31.

80. Named after Giulio Andreotti, the Christian Democratic Undersecretary of Public Entertainment and protégé of Prime Minister De Gasperi. Bondanella (1990), 87. David Overbey, "Introduction," *Springtime in Italy: A Reader on Italian Neo-Realism*, 28–9.

81. Shiel, 5.

82. It would be interesting to examine whether the link developed between democratization and tragic cinema in the case of wartime and postwar Italy holds for non-Western countries as well. So, for example, to what extent might China's Fourth or Fifth generation directors, working in a similar context of political opening and democratic aspiration before the post-Tianenmen repression, also be seen as developing a cinematic aesthetic of tragedy? Film historian Yingjin Zhang notes the influence of Italian neorealism and André Bazin on Zhang Nuanxin and Li Tuo's 1979 article, "On the Modernization of Film Language," which came to be considered the "artistic manifesto of the fourth generation." Yingjin Zhang characterizes the general aim of Fourth Generation films as the "indict[ment of] (past) historical tragedies." *Chinese National Cinema* (New York: Routledge, 2004), 231, 235. Thanks to Karen Fang for suggesting an application of my model to the case of China's Fifth Generation film directors.

Chapter 4

1. "The Unloved American," *The New Yorker*, 35.
2. "America and the World," *The New York Review of Books* (L/6), 31. Thanks to David Allen for this reference.
3. David Simpson quoting from Terry Eagleton in his review of Eagleton's recently published book, *Sweet Violence: The Idea of the Tragic*. "It's not about cheering us up," *London Review of Books*, 17. Thanks to Geoff Gershenson for this reference.
4. *The Fragility of Goodness: Luck and Ethics in Greek Tragedy and Philosophy* (Cambridge: University of Cambridge Press, 1986), 1–21.
5. *The Birth of Tragedy/The Case of Wagner*, trans. Walter Kaufmann (New York: Vintage, 1967), 124.
6. "Pragmatism and the Tragic," *Prophetic Thought in Postmodern Times* (Monroe, ME: Common Courage Press, 1993), 32.
7. Foreword to Part Three, *The Cornell West Reader* (New York: Basic *Civitas* Books, 1999), 141.
8. *The American Evasion of Philosophy: A Genealogy of Pragmatism* (Madison, WI: University of Wisconsin, 1989), 229, 235. "On Black-Brown Relations," *The Cornell West Reader* (New York: Basic *Civitas* Books, 1999), 511.
9. "On My Intellectual Vocation," *The Cornell West Reader*, 25.
10. "Afterword," *Cornel West: A Critical Reader*, ed. George Yancy (Malden, MA: Blackwell Publishers, 2001), 356–7. In addition to the seven references to "tragicomic darkness" (347, 351, 352, 357), the 16-page-long Afterword also refers to "tragicomic blues" (352, 356), "tragicomic laughter" (362), the "tragicomic character of the flowering of radical democracy" (353), the "tragicomic character of a commodified and bureaucratized world" (357), and the "tragicomic voices and viewpoints within African-American culture" (356).
11. Ibid., 353.
12. Eduardo Mendieta and Lucius T. Outlaw, Jr. *Critical Reader*, 99 and 276–7, respectively.
13. Jennifer Greenstein Altmann, "West spends first fall back on campus with first-year students," *Princeton Weekly Bulletin* (92/8), http://www.princeton.edu/pr/pwb/02/1104/1b.shtml, 1..
14. "A Moment with Cornel West *80," *Princeton Alumni Weekly* (November 6, 2002), http://princeton.edu/~paw/archive_new/PAW02-03/04-1106/moment.html, 2.
15. "Afterword," *Cornel West: A Critical Reader*, , 348.
16. "A World of Ideas," *The Cornell West Reader*, 294.
17. "The New Cultural Politics of Difference," *The Cornell West Reader*, 136.
18. *All Things Considered*, radio broadcast July 24, 2002.
19. *American Evasion*, 129.
20. Ibid., 130.

21. Ibid., 128.
22. "The New Cultural Politics of Difference," *The Cornell West Reader*, 132.
23. "On the 1980s," *The Cornell West Reader*, 346.
24. *American Evasion*, 227.
25. Ibid., 180.
26. Ibid., 227, 230.
27. *Prophesy Deliverance!: An Afro-American Revolutionary Christianity* (Philadelphia, PA: The Westminster Press, 1982), 18.
28. "Pragmatism and the Tragic," *Prophetic Thought in Postmodern Times*, 34.
29. *American Evasion*, 227.
30. "Subversive Joy and Revolutionary Patience in Black Christianity," *The Cornell West Reader*, 438.
31. See, for example, Peter Euben, *The Tragedy of Political Theory* (Princeton, NJ: Princeton University Press, 1990) and Karen Hermassi, *Polity and Theatre in Historical Perspective* (Berkeley, CA: University of California Press, 1977).
32. Jennifer Greenstein Altmann, "West spends first fall back on campus with first-year students," *Princeton Weekly Bulletin* (92/8).
33. "A World of Ideas," *The Cornell West Reader*, 296.
34. *Prophesy Deliverance!*, 151.
35. "Race and Modernity," *The Cornell West Reader*, 59.
36. "Prophetic Christian as Organic Intellectual: Martin Luther King, Jr.," *The Cornell West Reader*, 427.
37. *Prophesy Deliverance!*, 35.
38. "On Black Nationalism," *The Cornell West Reader*, 521.
39. "Subversive Joy and Revolutionary Patience in Black Christianity," ibid., 437. West also notes that, "in biblical stories, one can capture the grandeur, the sublime and tragedy among ordinary people." "Pragmatism and the Tragic," *Prophetic Thought in Postmodern Times*, 34.
40. *Prophesy Deliverance!*, fn #9, 151.
41. *Tragedy Is Not Enough* (Boston, MA: Archon Books, 1969), 38.
42. See, for an interesting and recent example, Louis A. Ruprecht, Jr., *This Tragic Gospel: How John Corrupted the Heart of Christianity* (San Francisco, CA: Jossey Bass, 2008), chapter 2.
43. *Prophesy Deliverance!*, fn#9, 151, 152.
44. Ibid., 20, 151, 152.
45. In Greek tragedy, "some transcendent knowledge of what it is to be human . . . is the only saving grace for the hero, who is crushed by the intractable limits of his or her situation." The modern tragic viewpoint rejects "any end or aim of human existence"; it "tends to presuppose luxury in that it may stimulate the ironic consciousness of a declining petite bourgeoisie, but it spells suicide for the downtrodden." "Subversive Joy and Revolutionary Patience in Black Christianity," *The Cornell West Reader*, 438.
46. Ibid.

47. Ibid.
48. Ibid.
49. Ibid., 435, 439.
50. "Black Strivings in a Twilight Civilization," *The Cornell West Reader* , 105. The particular context of this statement is a discussion of W. E. B. Du Bois's analysis of the challenges which the "Veil" poses to Black self respect in the era of Jim Crow. West believes the analysis has continued relevance in contemporary times.
51. "The Political Intellectual," Ibid., 284.
52. "Black Strivings in a Twilight Civilization," ibid., 105.
53. "The Political Intellectual," ibid., 284, 293.
54. "The Role of Law in Progressive Politics," ibid., 272.
55. See, for example, Peniel E. Joseph's critique, " 'It's Dark and Hell Is Hot': Cornel West, the Crisis of African-American Intellectuals and the Cultural Politics of Race," *Cornel West: A Critical Reader*, 295–311.
56. "A World of Ideas," *The Cornell West Reader*, 300. See, also, "Afterword," *Cornel West: A Critical Reader*, 358.
57. *American Evasion*, 228.
58. See, for example, the discussion of how, "the interrelation of affirmation and fate in tragic experience made it a key adversary of critical theory in the thirties," in Christoph Menke, "Critical Theory and Tragic Knowledge," in *Handbook of Critical Theory*, ed. David Rasmussen (London: Blackwell, 1996), 58. In the case of Horkheimer, Menke shows that initial hostility to the idea of tragedy eventually gave way to a grudging acceptance of a notion of tragic limits.
59. "The Political Intellectual," in *The Cornel West Reader*, 280.
60. "The Indispensability Yet Insufficiency of Marxist Theory," ibid., 215.
61. *American Evasion*, 229.
62. John Farrell, *Revolution as Tragedy: The Dilemma of the Moderate from Scott to Arnold* (Ithaca, NY: Cornell University Press, 1980), 19. Max Weber's deflationary account of the promise of revolution in his famous lecture, "Politics as a Vocation," constitutes another example of this "revolution as tragedy" viewpoint. Responding in 1919 to Germany's postwar condition of political turmoil and to the revolutionary enthusiasms of some of his students, Weber argued that the psychological and material requirements of radical political mobilization place inexorable limits on the idealistic promise of revolution. "The following can be harnessed only so long as an honest belief in his person and [revolutionary] cause inspires at least part of the following, probably never on earth even a majority. This belief, even when subjectively sincere, is in a very great number of cases really no more than an ethical 'legitimation' of cravings for revenge, power, booty, and spoils. We shall not be deceived about this by verbiage; the materialist interpretation of history is no cab to be taken at will; it does not stop short of promoters of revolutions." *From Max Weber*, eds H. H. Gerth and C. Wright Mills (New York: Oxford University Press, 1958), 125. Although Weber does not

use the German language equivalents of the words, "tragedy" or "tragic," his perspective betrays a deeply tragic sensibility signaled, in part, by the curious appearance of Shakespearean verse at the end of a public lecture on the nature of modern politics. For further elaboration of the tragic dimensions of Weber's thought, see John Diggins, *Max Weber: Politics and the Spirit of Tragedy* (New York: Basic Books, 1996).

63. See, Robert Pirro, *Hannah Arendt and the Politics of Tragedy* (Dekalb, IL: Northern Illinois University Press, 2001), 86–9, 136–42.

64. *American Evasion*, 229.

65. "The Legacy of Raymond Williams," *Prophetic Thought in Postmodern Times*, 173.

66. In his subtle understanding of "culture as a crucial component of class capacity" or the power of community and tradition to generate resistance to capitalist hegemony, Williams earns a place in a tradition powerfully exemplified by the work of Antonio Gramsci. "Like James Connolly before him and Raymond Williams in our own time, Gramsci examined the ways in which cultural resources enabled (and disenabled) political struggle among the exploited and excluded in capitalist societies." "Religion and the Left," *The Cornell West Reader*, 374. One thing that distinguishes Williams from Gramsci, at least as far as West's interest is concerned, is the former's explicit engagement with notions of tragedy.

67. "The Legacy of Raymond Williams," *Prophetic Thought in Postmodern Times*, 173.

68. Williams' formulation as quoted by West in "The Political Intellectual," *The Cornell West Reader*, 293.

69. "Race and Social Theory," *The Cornell West Reader*, 263.

70. West suggests that this need found satisfaction through acceptance of Christian ideology and practice for a time but that with the Western decline of religious belief, "human immortality quests were channeled into secular ideologies of science, art, nation, profession, race, sexuality and consumption," ibid., 264.

71. "The Legacy of Raymond Williams," *Prophetic Thought in Postmodern Times*, 171.

72. "On Black-Brown Relations," *The Cornell West Reader*, 510.

73. *The American Evasion of Philosophy: A Genealogy of Pragmatism*, 111.

74. See, for example, Robert Gooding-Williams, "Evading Narrative Myth, Evading Prophetic Pragmatism: Cornel West's *The American Evasion of Philosophy*," *The Massachusetts Review*, 517–42.

75. *American Evasion*, 187.

76. Ibid., 226, 35.

77. Ibid., 113–14, 171, 172.

78. Ibid., 163, 226, 228.

79. Ibid., 143, 147, 178.

80. "Black Strivings in a Twilight Civilization," *The Cornell West Reader*, 90.

81. Ibid., 92.

82. "The Political Intellectual," ibid., 285.
83. *American Evasion*, 229.
84. "The Future of Pragmatic Thought," *Prophetic Thought in Postmodern Times*, 75.
85. "Evading Theory and Tragedy?: Reading Cornel West," *Praxis International* 13: 1, 39.
86. "Theodicy, Tragedy and Prophesy: Comments on Cornel West's *The American Evasion of Philosophy*," *APA Newsletter on the Black Experience* 90: 3, 22.
87. "Introduction," in *The Cornel West Reader*, p. xv, and "The Making of an American Radical Democrat of African Descent," in ibid., 13.
88. "On My Intellectual Vocation," ibid, 33.
89. "Black Strivings," ibid., 92.
90. For West's view of Greek tragedy, see above. For criticisms of West's treatment of the relative merits of Kafaka, Chekhov, and Du Bois, see Lucius T. Outlaw, Jr., "On Cornel West on W. E. B. Du Bois," in *Cornel West: A Critical Reader*, 276–7.
91. So, for example, in response to one critic, West concedes that, "Outlaw correctly takes me to task for not specifying the criteria for my desirable tragicomic viewpoint." "Afterword," ibid., 357.
92. "Pragmatism and the Tragic," *Prophetic Thought in Postmodern Times*, 32.

Chapter 5

1. Martin Meredith, *Nelson Mandela: A Biography* (London: Penguin, 1997), 554.
2. For example, his courtesy visit to the 94-year-old widow of Hendrik Verwoerd, ideological and political founder of the South African apartheid state (see Anthony Sampson, *Mandela: The Authorized Biography* (New York: Knopf, 1999), 514. For other examples, see Meredith, 526–31.
3. Allister Sparks, "Mandela's South Africa—And After: The Status of the Dream," *The Wilson Quarterly* (XXIII, 2), 89. Jim Hoagland, "South Africa Moves Forward Into Routine Democracy," *International Herald Tribune* (June 14, 1999).
4. In remarks to Anthony Sampson, as quoted in Sampson, xxvi.
5. Philippe-Joseph Salazar, *An African Athens: Rhetoric and the Shaping of Democracy in South Africa* (Mahwah, NJ: Lawrence Erlbaum, 2002), xix.
6. Nelson Mandela, *Long Walk to Freedom* (Boston, MA: Little, Brown and Company, 1995), 121–2.
7. *Mandela*, dir. Angus Gibson and Jo Menell, Island Pictures.
8. Mandela, *Long Walk to Freedom*, 597, 598; see also 623.
9. Winnie Mandela quoted in Mary Benson, *Nelson Mandela: The Man and the Movement* (New York: Norton, 1986), 78.
10. Helen Joseph, *Side by Side: The Autobiography of Helen Joseph* (London: Zed, 1986), 216.
11. Mandela, *Long Walk to Freedom*, 446.

12. Walter Sisulu, foreward, *Mandela: Echoes of an Era*, by Alf Kumalo and Es'kia Mphahlele (New York: Penguin, 1990), 3.

13. Mandela, *Long Walk to Freedom*, 471.

14. Winnie Mandela, *Part of my Soul Went with Him*, ed. Anne Benjamin (New York: Norton, 1985), 149.

15. James Gregory, *Goodbye Bafana: Nelson Mandela, My Prisoner, My Friend* (London: Headline Book Publishing, 1995), 328.

16. Mandela, *Long Walk to Freedom*, 447.

17. Ibid., 444.

18. In a parallel way, Helen Joseph refers to the deaths of another anti-apartheid activist's wife (in a car accident) and son (through sickness) as "tragedies." *Side by Side*, 160, 176.

19. Mandela, *Long Walk to Freedom*, 187.

20. Gregory, 279.

21. Nelson Mandela: *The Man and the Movement*, 7.

22. *Nelson Mandela* (London: Penguin, 1989), back cover.

23. Benson, *Nelson Mandela: The Man and the Movement*, 162.

24. *Nelson Mandela: Symbol of Resistance and Hope for a Free South Africa*, ed. E. S. Reddy (New Dehli: Sterling Publishers, 1990), vii.

25. *Long Walk to Freedom*, 456. the epigram, as it appears, opposite the first page of Guilloineau's biography, reads as follows: "*Mais comment pourrait-on juger l'âme d'un homme, ses sentiments, ses intentions, tant qu'il n'a pas connu l'épreuve du pouvoir ni édicté ses lois*. Sophocle, *Antigone*, traduction de Jacques Lacarrière, cité par Nelson Mandela dans *Un long chemin vers la liberté*," *Mandela: Naissance d'un destin* (Paris: Editions Autrement, 1998), 6.

26. In a 1973 letter, Mandela's fellow prisoner Ahmed Kathrada remembers the play as being Jean Anouilh's version of *Antigone*. He notes Mandela's outstanding performance as Creon. Ahmed Kathrada, *Letters from Robben Island: A Selection of Ahmed Kathrada's Prison Correspondence, 1964–1989* (East Lansing, MI: Michigan State University, 1999), 64.

27. Mandela, *Long Walk to Freedom*, 456.

28. *Mandela* (Scarborough, Ontario: The New American Library, 1987), 127. Similarly, Walter Sisulu, in the previously mentioned foreward to *Mandela: Echoes of an Era* by Alf Kumalo and Es'kia Mphahlele, refers to the "Kumalo-Mphahlele stage" whose "chief actor [is] Nelson Mandela," 3.

29. A similar characterization of South Africa was offered by Zindzi Mandela on the occasion of a mass meeting in Soweto in February, 1985; Reprinted in *Nelson Mandela: The Struggle Is My Life* (New York: Pathfinder Press, 1990), 195.

30. Mandela, *In the Words of Nelson Mandela*, ed. Jennifer Crwys-Williams (Secaucus, NJ: Carol, 1998), 40.

31. From Mandela's unpublished 1978 manuscript, "Black Consciousness Movement," as quoted in Sampson, 277.

32. Nelson Mandela, Address to U.S. Congress, June 27, 1990; *Nelson Mandela Speaks: Forging a Democratic, Nonracial South Africa* (New York: Pathfinder,

1993), 35. The last sentence of the passage is a paraphrase of a line from Shakespeare's *Cymberline* (Mandela, *Nelson Mandela Speaks* 270, n7).

33. *Aristotle/Horace/Longinus: Classical Literary Criticism*, trans. and ed. T. S. Dorsch (New York: Penguin, 1965), 39.

34. "Tragedy as Dramatic Art," *Hegel on Tragedy*, eds Anne and Henry Paolucci (Garden City, NY: Anchor, 1962), 51.

35. Paolucci, 364, 365.

36. Fatima Meer, *Higher than Hope: The Authorized Biography of Nelson Mandela* (New York: Harper & Row, 1988), 409.

37. Mandela, 456. See, Fatima Meer, 409.

38. Even before his imprisonment, Mandela took note of Shakespearean verse, especially when it was deployed to political effect. So, for example, after 36 years, he recalled seeing a political cartoon of British Prime Minister Harold MacMillan, who had criticized the apartheid system during a 1959 trip to South Africa, with a caption taken from Julius Caesar: "O! pardon me, thou bleeding piece of earth,/ that I am meek and gentle with these butchers" (Sampson, 128).

39. Ibid., 231.

40. Reddy, 49–50. "Many a time the martingales and deprived people whom we represent have posed the same bitter questions that Shylock posed in Shakespeare's *Merchant of Venice*: 'Hath not a Jew eyes? Hath not a Jew hands, organs, dimensions, sense, affections, passions? Fed with the same food, hurt with the same weapons, subject to the same diseases, healed by the same means, warmed and cooled by the same winter and summer, as a Christian is? If you prick us, do we not bleed? If you tickle us, do we not laugh? If you poison us, do we not die? And if you wrong us, shall we not revenge? If we are like you in the rest, we will resemble you in that . . . the villainy you teach me, I will execute; and it shall be so hard, but I will better the instruction.'"

41. Sampson, 231.

42. Ibid., p. xv.

43. Ibid.

44. Friedrich Nietzsche, *The Birth of Tragedy and The Case of Wagner*, ed. Walter Kaufmann (New York: Vintage, 1967), 125, sec. 21. Emphasis added.

45. Sampson, xxvi. For the full transcription, see the second extended quote on page one.

46. Meredith, 554, and Sampson, xxvi.

47. From Mandela's 1976 unpublished manuscript, "National Liberation," as quoted in Sampson, 268.

48. Meredith, 554.

49. Ibid., 521.

50. Robert Barnhardt, ed., *The Barnhardt Dictionary of Etymology* (New York: Wilson, 1988), 151.

51. For some examples, see the relevant entries in *Roget's College Thesaurus*, rev. edn (New York: Signet, 1978), 513 and the *Oxford American Dictionary* (New York: Avon, 1980), 728.

52. *Wittgenstein and Justice: Of the Significance of Ludwig Wittgenstein for Social and Political Thought* (Berkeley, CA: University of California Press, 1972), 71.

53. Pitkin, 39.

54. Patrick Casey, "Thousands Gather for Groundbreaking of Oklahoma City Bombing Memorial," *Savannah Morning News* (October 26, 1998), A9.

55. Frank Bruni, "Bush Dedicates Museum at Site of Oklahoma Bombing," *New York Times* (February 20, 2001), A12.

56. Elliott Minor, "Military Plane Crash Kills 21," *Savannah Morning News* (March 4, 2001), A3.

57. Fox Butterfield, "Hole in Gun Control Law Lets Mentally Ill Through," *New York Times* (April 11, 2000), A23.

58. In a newspaper report of Pope John Paul II's visit to a mosque in Damascus (the first such visit by a pope), a contrast is drawn with his earlier visit to a Roman synagogue. In the article's concluding paragraph, final word is given to a high-ranking church official: "'This [the visit to the mosque] is a major event, but it is certainly not comparable,'Cardinal Jean-Marie Lustiger, the archbishop of Paris, who, born a Jew in Poland, was taken in by French Catholics during the German occupation, and converted after the war. This is a courteous dialogue, but it is not the joint re-examination of a tragic history.'" Alessandra Stanley, "Pope, in Damascus, Goes to a Mosque in Move For Unity," *New York Times* (May 7, 2001), A8.

59. Chalmers Johnson, interview, "Verbatim," *The Chronicle of Higher Education* (April 7, 2000), A30.

60. In the aftermath of an incident in which a young man (apparently) deliberately plowed the car he was driving into a crowd of people, killing four of them, his father told the press that, "I just want to say how devastated and heartbroken we are for everybody who's been affected by this very horrible tragedy." See, "Film Director Apologizes In 4 Pedestrian Deaths," *New York Review of Books* (February 28, 2001). One can imagine that the appeal of this statement to friends and family of the dead would depend in significant part on the extent to which the father is seen by them to be responsible for his son's deed. If, in their eyes, he willfully ignored or carelessly overlooked signs of his son's homicidal intent, the father's invitation to share a sense of loss would have little appeal.

61. Lord Nicholas Bethell, "An Interview with Nelson Mandela," *Apartheid in Crisis*, ed. Mark Uhlig (New York: Oxford University Press, 1986), 196–7.

62. Mandela, *Long Walk to Freedom*, 518.

63. Sampson, xxvi.

64. Mandela, *Long Walk to Freedom*, 588.

65. Mandela, "One Nation, One Country," Occasional Papers of the Phelps-Stokes Fund (May 4, 1990), p. 14.

66. For a well-documented and vigorously critical view of the neoliberal dimensions of South Africa's transition to democracy and their human costs, see Naomi Klein, *The Shock Doctrine: The Rise of Disaster Capitalism* (Los Angeles, CA:

Metropolitan Books, 2007). For a similarly critical South African assessment, see Andrew Nash, "Mandela's Democracy," *Monthly Review*(April 1999).

67. Quoted in Alec Russell's, *Bring Me My Machine Gun: The Battle for the Soul of South Africa from Mandela to Zuma* (New York: PublicAffairs, 2009), 206.

68. Ibid., 84.

69. Max Weber, "Politics as a Vocation," *From Max Weber: Essays in Sociology*, eds H. H. Gerth and C. Wright Mills (New York: Oxford University Press, 1958), 119.

Chapter 6

1. *The 9/11 Commission Report* (New York: W. W. Norton, 2004), xv.

2. Kimberley Strassel, "Bush on His Record," *The Wall Street Journal* (December 20, 2008) WSJ.com.

3. Andrew Kirtzman, *Rudy Giuliani: Emperor of the City* (New York: Perennial, 2001), 302.

4. Theodicies are attempts to square the suffering of innocents with belief in a divinity considered to be both all powerful and absolutely good. First coined in French (*théodicée*) by Gottfried Leibniz, in the late seventeenth century, the term takes up issues that have been of concern since at least the dawn of monotheistic religion. In his extensive contribution to Mircea Eliade's *Encyclopedia of Religion* (1987), Rodney M. Green identifies four general approaches to reconciling the suffering of innocents with belief in an all-powerful god of absolute goodness. "Free-will theodicies" generally conclude that, "God must expose the world to suffering and evil if he chooses to create beings who are genuinely free." Of course, to the extent this conception emphasizes that suffering is merited by poor choices, it leaves the realm of theodicy whose main concern is the explanation of unmerited suffering. "Educative theodicies" argue that suffering exists to "enrich human experience, to build moral character, or to develop human capacities." "Eschatological or recompense theodicies" justify earthly suffering by reference to an afterlife of rewards or punishments. "Communion theodicies" view unmerited suffering as an "occasion for direct relationship, collaboration and even communion with God." Green also notes that a believer can choose to bear suffering by giving up the attempt to explain it. This is not theodicy, strictly speaking, but "theodicy deferred," according to which one chooses "to defer comprehension and to trust in God's ultimate goodness and sovereignty." See Rodney M. Green, "Theodicy," *Encyclopedia of Religion: Volume 14*, ed. Mircea Eliade (1987), 432–4.

5. W. B. Worthen, "A Forum on Theatre and Tragedy in the Wake of September 11," in David Román (ed.) *Theatre Journal* 54 (2002), 100.

6. Gustav Niebuhr, "Clergy of Many Faiths Answer Tragedy's Call," *New York Times* (September 15, 2001), B10.

7. Allison Gilbert et al., *Covering Catastrophe: Broadcast Journalists Report September 11*, xii, 117, 158, 206. Of the 133 journalists whose comments are

recorded, 13 refer directly or indirectly to the aftermath of the attacks as a "tragedy" or "tragic." See 6, 43, 63, 85, 88, 130, 208, 221, 228, 239, 247, 250.

8. Sam Howe Verhovek, "2 Disasters Lead a Cruise Ship into Nights of Vigils and Prayers," *New York Times* (September 15, 2001), B10. Jim Yardley, "Smaller but Heartfelt Ceremonies Around the United States", *New York Times* (September 7, 2002). James Mechalakos, "Letter to the Editor," *New York Times* (December 2, 2003), A30.

9. John Duffy and Mary Schaeffer, *Triumph Over Tragedy: September 11 and the Rebirth of a Business* (New York: John Wiley & Sons, 2002), 45, 48. For other references to "disaster," see 40, 42, 79. For other references to "tragedy" and "tragic," see 77, 87, 91, 100, 102, 159, 166, 185.

10. David Simpson, "It's Not About Cheering Us Up", *London Review of Books* 25 (7) (April 3, 2003), 19.

11. Martin Harris, "Letter," *London Review of Books* 25 (9) (May 8, 2003).

12. David Simpson, "Letter," *London Review of Books* 25 (10) (May 22, 2003).

13. Terry Eagleton, *Sweet Violence: The Idea of the Tragic* (Malden, MA: Blackwell, 2003), 44.

14. Debra Schifrin, "Report," *Morning Edition*. National Public Radio (October 4, 2001).

15. Alice Raynor and Harry J. Elam, Jr., "A Forum on Theatre and Tragedy: A Response to September 11, 2001," *Theatre Journal* 2002; 54 (1), 95–138.

16. William Langewiesche, *American Ground: Unbuilding the Trade Center* (New York: North Point Press, 2003), 10.

17. Ibid., 8.

18. Ibid., 145, 162, 169, 199.

19. Ibid., 10, 158.

20. Ibid., 207.

21. Jim Dwyer and Kevin Flynn, *102 Minutes: The Untold Story of the Fight to Survive Inside the Twin Towers* (New York: Times Books, 2005), 249.

22. March 2, 2005 e-mail communication with Dwyer.

23. Duffy and Schaeffer, 100, 102.

24. David W. Chen, "Subway Victim's Funeral Is Intimate Look at Close-Knit Family," *New York Times* (January 8, 1999), A17.

25. Janelle Reinelt, "A Forum on Theatre and Tragedy: A Response to September 11, 2001," *Theatre Journal* 2002; 54 (1), 134.

26. "Woman Gets 15 Years in Fatal Wreck," *Savannah Morning News* (March 4, 2001), 1A.

27. Aijaz Rahi, "U.S. Strike Mistakenly Kills 9 Children," *AOL News* (December 7, 2003).

28. Howard Dewey, Jr., "Letter to the Editor," *Connect Savannah* (September 11, 2002).

29. Jean-Pierre Vernant and Pierre Vidal-Naquet, *Tragedy and Myth in Ancient Greece* (Atlantic Highlands, NJ: Humanities Press, 1981), 4–5.

30. See, for two examples, Christian Meier, *Die politische Kunst der griechischen Tragödie* (Beck: Munich and Ober, 1988); Josiah and Barry Strauss, "Drama,

Political Rhetoric, and the Discourse of Athenian Democracy," in *Nothing to Do with Dionysos? Athenian Drama in Its Social context*, eds John Winkler and Froma Zeitlin (Princeton, NJ: Princeton University Press, 1990).

31. See, for two examples, Vernant and Vidal-Naquet and "Public Mourning," *American Political Science Review* 101 (2) (May 2007), 195–208.

32. See, for example, Christiane Sourvinou-Inwood, *Tragedy and Athenian Religion* (New York: Lexington, 2003).

33. *The 9/11 Commission Report*, 326.

34. Dan Barry, "A Day of Tributes, Tears and the Litany of the Lost," *New York Times* (September 12, 2002), A1.

35. Daniel Mendelsohn, "Theatres of War", *The New Yorker* 79 (42) (January 12, 2004), 84.

36. Glenn Greenwald, *A Tragic Legacy: How a Good vs. Evil Mentality Destroyed the Bush Presidency* (New York: Crown Publishers, 2007).

37. Judith Shklar, *Ordinary Vices* (Cambridge, MA: Belknap Press, 1984), 230.

38. Bob Woodward, *Plan of Attack* (New York: Simon & Schuster, 2004), 421.

39. Rodney Green, "Theodicy", in *Encyclopedia of Religion*, ed. Mircea Eliade (New York: Macmillan, 1987), 433.

40. For reference to the Pew Survey, see Pippa Norris and Ronald Inglehart, *Sacred and Secular: Religion and Politics Worldwide* (Cambridge: Cambridge University Press, 2004), 76. For reference to media speculations about a new "Great Awakening," see Ray Giunta with Lynda Rutledge Stephenson, *God @ Ground Zero* (Nashville, TN: Integrity Publishers, 2002), 109.

41. Robert Bellah and Phillip Hammond, *Varieties of Civil Religion* (San Francisco, CA: Harper & Row, 1980), viii.

42. Ibid., 12–13.

43. Ibid.

44. Cited by Gustav Niebuhr, "Religion Journal: In Devastation's Shadow, a Renewal," *New York Times* (November 3, 2001).

45. Woodward, 420.

46. Kristen Wyatt, "Hope, Helplessness Present at Grandparents' Funeral", *Savannah Morning News* (August 10, 2004), 3B.

47. Perhaps the differences in tone had something to do with the different criminal circumstances—in the latter instance, a mentally unbalanced perpetrator impulsively attacking a stranger, in the former, a rebellious teenager acting with some premeditation against family members—of the two cases or with the different cultural contexts of the funerals—in the latter instance, Catholic ritual in the northeast, in the former, a Baptist ceremony in the Bible Belt.

48. Mark J. Landau et al., "Deliver Us From Evil: The Effects of Mortality Salience and Reminders of 9/11 on Support for President George W. Bush", *Personality and Social Psychology Bulletin* 30 (9) (September 2004), 1138–9.

49. Giunta with Stephenson, 175.

50. Louis Ruprecht, Jr. *Tragic Posture and Tragic Vision* (New York: Continuum, 1994), 223–4. For further discussion of this contrast, see chapter 2 of Ruprecht's

This Tragic Gospel: How John Corrupted the Heart of Christianity (San Francisco, CA: Jossey Bass, 2008).

51. Bellah and Hammond, 15.

52. Green, 432.

53. Simon Stow, "Pericles at Gettysburg and Ground Zero: Tragedy, Patriotism, and Public Mourning", *American Political Science Review* 101 (2) (May 2007), 195–208.

54. Susan Neiman, *Evil in Modern Thought: An Alternative History of Philosophy* (Princeton, NJ: Princeton University Press, 2002), 285, 286.

55. Ibid., 288.

56. Ibid., 75.

57. Kenneth E. Morris, *Jimmy Carter: American Moralist* (Athens, GA: University of Georgia Press, 1996), 5.

58. See Chapter 4.

59. Alexis de Tocqueville, *Democracy in American Volume I*, trans. Henry Reeve (Cambridge, MA: Sever and Francis, 1863), 400.

60. David C. Mearns, "Mr. Lincoln and the Books He Read", in *Three Presidents and Their Books: Jefferson, Lincoln, F.D. Roosevelt* (Urbana, IL: University of Illinois Books, 1963), 79–80.

61. Christiane Sourvinou-Inwood, *Tragedy and Athenian Religion* (New York: Lexington, 2003), 12.

62. Ibid., 12.

63. William F. Zak, *The Polis and the Divine Order* (Lewisburg, PA: Bucknell University Press, 1995), 13.

64. Shklar, 229.

65. Lisa Disch, *Hannah Arendt and the Limits of Philosophy* (Ithaca, NY: Cornell University Press, 1994), 111–12.

66. Hannah Arendt, 'What is Authority?', *Between Past and Future* (New York: Penguin, 1978), 128–33.

67. For elaboration of this point, see Robert Pirro, *Hannah Arendt and the Politics of Tragedy* (Dekalb, IL: Northern Illinois University Press, 2001). From a different theoretical standpoint, Cornelius Castoriadis offers a defense of the autonomy of politics in which Greek tragedy finds a prominent place. Consider, for example, the following remarks: "Although its many different effects can by no means be reduced simply to its political aspect, tragedy also possessed a very clear-cut political signification: the constant reminder of self-limitation. For tragedy was also and especially the exhibition of the effects of *hubris* and, more than that, the demonstration that contrary reasons can coexist (this was one of the 'lessons' of the tragedy *Antigone*) and that it is not in obstinately persisting in one's own reasons (*monos phronein*) that it becomes possible to solve the grave problems that may be encountered in collective life (which has nothing to do with the watery consensus of contemporary times). Above all else, tragedy was democratic in this, that it was a constant reminder of mortality, that is, of the radical

limitation on human beings." "The Greek and the Modern Imaginary," *World in Fragments: Writings on Politics, Society, Psychoanalysis, and the Imagination,* ed. and trans. David Ames Curtis (Stanford, CA: Stanford University Press, 1997), 93–4.

68. Robert Bellah, *The Broken Covenant: American Civil Religion in Time of Trial* (Chicago, IL: University of Chicago Press, 1992), 145, 150, 179.

Chapter 7

1. *Efraim's Book*, trans. Ralph Mannheim (New York: Penguin, 1984), 67. Here is the original text from Alfred Andersch's, *Efraim* (Zürich: Diogenes, 1967): "[W]enn man anfängt Menschen zu vernichten wie Ungeziefer... dann vernichtet man nicht nur sechs Millionen Seelen, sondern, ganz nebenbei, auch die Sprache der Überlebenden. Ich beobachtete, wie die Übriggebliebenen . . . fortwährend damit beschäftigt sind, sich auf die Zunge zu beissen, und wie Literatur versucht, ohne Metaphern auszukommen. Die Sprache hat den bösen Blick bekommen, während die Bettlerin, an der ich wieder einmal vorbeigehe, ihn verloren hat; sie ist nicht weiter als eine Frau, die man mit ein paar Adjektiven definieren kann: elend,tragisch, alt"* (102).

2. Richard Bernstein, "Germans Told to Cheer Up. 'Why Should We?' Some Say." *New York Times* (December 6, 2005), A3.

3. Thomas Mann, "The Tragedy of Germany," *Treasury for the Free World*, ed. Ben Raeburn (New York: Arco Publishing, 1945), 186, 187.

4. Ibid., 187, 188.

5. Thomas Mann, *The Story of a Novel* (New York: Knopf, 1961), 73.

6. Mann, "The Tragedy of Germany," 188.

7. Zeitblom gives expression to this notion of fate in recollecting his service on the Western Front in chapter XXX of *Doctor Faustus*. Reflecting on Germany's geopolitical situation in the era leading up to the outbreak of the Great War, he offers the sort of apologia for preemptive military action that then counted as conventional wisdom for the educated classes of Wilhelmine Germany. Significantly, this apologia finds expression in an explicitly tragic key: "We were already long a great power, we were quite used to it, and it did not make us as happy as we had expected. The feeling that it had not made us more winning, that our relation to the world had rather worsened than improved, lay, unconfirmed, deep in our hearts. A new breakthrough seemed due: we would become a dominating world power—but such a position was not to be achieved by means of moral "homework." War, then, and if needs must, war against everybody, to convince everybody and to win; that was our lot, our "sending" [*Schicksal*] (the very word is Germanic, the idea pre-Christian, the whole concept a tragically mythological, musical-dramatic motif [*ein tragisch-mythologisch-musikdramatisches Motiv*]; that was what fate [*Schicksal*] had willed and we-only we!—enthusiastically responded and set forth." *Doctor Faustus* (New York:

Vintage, 1971), 301. Bracketed words from *Doktor Faustus* (Frankfurt-am-Main: Fischer, 1967 [original edition 1947]), 401.

8. M. S. Silk and J. P. Stern, *Nietzsche on Tragedy* (Cambridge: Cambridge University Press, 1987), 5.

9. "Germany and the Germans," *Thomas Mann's Addresses* (Washington, DC: Library of Congress, 1963), 64.

10. Mann, *Story of a Novel*, 191.

11. Mann, "Germany and the Germans," 66.

12. Thomas Mann, *Doctor Faustus*, trans. H. T. Lowe-Porter (New York: Vintage, 1971), 300–1.

13. Jürgen Habermas, *"Eine Art Schadensabwicklung: Die apologetischen Tendenzen in der deutschen Zeitgeschichtsschreibung,"* *Historikerstreit* (Munich: Piper, 1987), 66, 75.

14. Micha Brumlik, *"Neuer Staatsmythos Ostfront: Die neueste Entwicklung der Geschichtswissenschaft der BRD,"* *Historikerstreit* (Munich: Piper, 1987), 78, 80–1.

15. Hans Mommsen, *"Suche nach der 'verlorenen Geschichte': Bemerkungen zum historischen Selbstverständnis der Bundesrepublik,"* *Historikerstreit* (Munich: Piper, 1987), 163–7.

16. Klaus Hildebrand, *"Der Zeitalter der Tyrannen,"* *Historikerstreit* (Munich: Piper, 1987), 88.

17. Ibid, 88–9. Andreas Hillgruber, *"Jürgen Habermas, Karl-Heinz Janssen und die Aufklärung Anno 1986,"* *Historikerstreit* (Munich: Piper, 1987), 343.

18. *The Unmasterable Past: History, Holocaust, and German Identity* (Cambridge: Harvard University Press, 1988), 171. Interestingly, in his opening discussion of the controversy, Maier sometimes seems uncritically to take over neoconservative uses of tragic rhetoric, while other times criticizing it. So, for example, he adopts Hillgruber's formulation of the Wehrmacht's role on the Eastern Front toward the end of the war as the "tragic task of defending the German population," but later takes Hillgruber to task for "build[ing] his argument upon mood music and tragic atmospherics." (20, 48) Maier also pointedly refers to, and critically assesses, the notions of tragedy underlying the Kohl government's invitation to Reagan to participate in the wreath-laying ceremony at Bitburg; "Intended as a ritual of reconciliation[, in which] the sacrifices of both sides [were] to be hallowed as historical 'tragedy'[, the event ended up being] catharsis manqué." (9, 10) I am grateful to William Astore for calling my attention to this book.

19. See, for example, his critical survey of the menu of proposed bases of German identity on offer in the wake of reunification, "Yet Again: German Identity in a Unified Nation of Angry DM-Burghers?", *New German Critique* 52 (Winter 1991), 84–101.

20. *The Birth of Tragedy and The Case of Wagner*, ed. and trans. Walter Kaufmann (New York: Vintage, 1967), 95, 114.

21. Ibid., 124–5.

22. Strauss, "Goat Song Rising," trans. Thomas Ringmayr, *Southern Humanities Review* 38 (4) (Fall 2004), 328–30.

23. Ringmayer, 331, 332. Botho Strauss, "*Anschwellender Bockgesang*," *Deutsche Literature 1993: Jahresüberblick*, eds Frank Görtz, Volker Hage and Uwe Wittstock (Stuttgart: Phillip Reclam, 1994), 261.

24. See, respectively, the previously cited works by Mann, Berlin's *Against the Current: Essays in the History of Ideas* (Princeton, NJ: Princeton University Press, 1979), and Stern's *The Politics of Cultural Despair: A Study in the Rise of the Germanic Ideology* (New York: Doubleday Anchor, 1965).

25. Ringmayer, 340.

26. Ibid., 339.

27. Ibid., 341.

28. Strauss, 263.

29. Ringmayer, 340, 331. Strauss, 262, 259, 267.

30. Consider, for example, the narrator's censorious recollection of his father: "Long after the Hitler state is smashed, his father finds relief in expressing contempt for humankind every time he can say that some man had been a Nazi. He writes 'Nazi pig!' in the margins of book pages on which an author has convicted himself of harboring 'brown ideas.'" Botho Strauss, *Devotion*, trans. Sophie Wilkins (New York: Farrar Straus Giroux, 1979), 6.

31. "People are all face. Everybody's too much, a personal supermarket overflowing with special sales, eye-catchers, attention-getters, you an hardly get through all that to the actual merchandise. . . . We keep enhancing our image. Impenetrable layers of appearances covering persistently simple motives. Never once does the *character* let himself be simply himself—when shall I ever see his irreducible, incorruptible seriousness?" Wilkins, 29.

32. Wilkins, 64. Also worth noting is an observation of Bernard, a character from his 1978 drama cycle, *Gross und Klein* (translated in 1979 under the title, *Big and Little*), which seems to anticipate the sense of embattlement Strauss would come to feel in the wake of the deliberate provocation performed by "*Anschwellender Bockgesang*": "The belief in the goodness of man holds people together everywhere. It unites. But once you're a skeptic, once you see a dark future for mankind, in general, then you experience bit by bit how your best friends draw away from you. Though you haven't offended anyone personally. People are afraid of a pessimistic thought in and of itself, the truth, finally. Personally you can be the nicest guy in the world, a pessimist is always left alone. Too bad. It is conceivable once could be a pessimist without being a misanthrope at the same time. One should be allowed to be a pessimist and to be socially desirable, too." Botho Strauss, *Big and Little*, Trans. Anne Cattaneo (New York: Farrar Straus Giroux, 1979), 135.

33. "*Schon länger gab es Warnzeichen, dass die Medusa das Unheils, die der Autor in die Kammer liess, nun als politisierte Heilsgöttin zurückkehrt: Der Dichter*

und sein Schrifttum als Retter im geisstigen Raum der Nation." Assheuer, *"Was ist rechts? Botho Strauss blässt ins Bockshorn,"* *Deutsche Literatur* 1993, eds F. J. Görtz, V. Hage, and U. Wittstock (Stuttgart: Philipp Reclam, 1994), 270.

34. To be sure, Strauss does not explicitly endorse nationalism in his essay. However, his attacks on leftist "derision of eros, derision of the soldier, derision of the church, tradition and authority" and his affirmation of, "a collective memory that envelops the entire being," are very compatible with an agenda of revitalizing German nationalism. Ringmayer, 329, 330.

35. "Botho Strauss and Conservative Aesthetics: An Introduction to 'Goatsong Rising.'" *Southern Humanities Review* 38 (4) (Fall 2004), 319, 323.

36. *Taz.* February 13, 1996 issue, p. 16.

37. Heimo Schwilk and Ulrich Schacht, eds. (Berlin: Ullstein, 1994), 129–33.

38. *"Erde und Heimat: Über das Ende der Ära des Unheils,"* *Die selbstbewusste Nation,* 117.

39. See chapter 6 of Dennis Schmidt's *On Germans and Other Greeks: Tragedy and Ethical Life* (Bloomington, IN: Indiana University Press, 2001).

40. Josef Chytry expresses the importance of the tragic theater for Heidegger's thought this way: "As aesthetic state the Heideggerian polis reaches its apogee with the public artwork of tragedy." Chytry, *The Aesthetic State: A Quest in Modern German Thought* (Berkeley, CA: University of California Press, 1989), 391.

41. *Tragedy Is Not Enough,* trans. H. Reiche, H. Moore, and K. Deutsch (Hamden, CT: Archon, 1969 [first edition 1952]), 88.

42. *Martin Heidegger, Karl Jaspers: Briefwechsel, 1920–1963,* eds. Walter Biemel and Hans Saner (München: Piper, 1992), 210–11.

43. *"Die Botschaft, die uns Botho Strauss mit seinem blutigen Geraune mitteilen will, ist weder neu noch originell: Was da aufdämmert—Blutopfer, Mythos, Tiefenerinnerung, Initiation, Verhängnis, Schicksal, Opfergesänge—,hat vor 60 Jahren Hitler und seiner Partei zur Macht verholfen."* Cornelia Benz, letter to the editor, *Der Spiegel* (February 22, 1993), 12.

44. Strauss, 259.

45. For a comprehensive study of the significance of *tragōidíā* for the polis that would have been available to Strauss, see Christine Meier's *Die politische Kunst der griechischen Tragödie* (Beck: Munich, 1988).

46. Kaufmann, sec 21, 124–5.

47. Certainly, a case can be made that Hitler's vision was fundamentally racist and therefore, in some respects, non- or anti-nationalistic. However, his ability to rally key institutions (e.g., the Wehrmacht), political forces (the old-line aristocracy), and popular sentiment in support of the prosecution of a genocidal war in Europe depended in significant part on his cultivation and stimulation of nationalistic sentiment.

48. Christoph Menke, "Critical Theory and Tragic Knowledge," in *Handbook of Critical Theory,* ed. David M. Rasmussen (London: Wiley-Blackwell, 1996), 58, 71, and 70. Menke notes his borrowing of the notion of "fragility" from Martha

Nussbaum's work, *The Fragility of Goodness: Luck and Ethics in Greek Tragedy* (Cambridge: Cambridge University Press, 1986).
49. *The Political Art of Greek Tragedy*, trans. Andrew Webber (Baltimore, MD: Johns Hopkins Press, 1983), 219.

Chapter 8

1. Werner Jaeger, *Paideia: The Ideals of Greek Culture* (Volume 1), trans. Gilbert Highet (New York: Oxford University Press, 1962), 247.
2. Christa Wolf, *Cassandra: A Novel and Four Essays*, trans. Jan Van Heurck (New York: Farrar, Straus and Giroux, 1984), 164. The German language original reads: "Sind wir nichts jenseits aller Verkündigungen und Prophezeiungen, also jenseits der Tragödie?" Christa Wolf, *Voraussetzungen einer Erzälung: Kassandra* (Darmstadt: Luchterhand, 1983), 27.
3. Jürgen Habermas, "Yet Again: Germany Identity—A Unified Nation of Angry *DM-Burghers?*", *New German Critique* 52 (Winter 1991), 84–101.
4. Ulrich Greiner's review article of Wolf's *Was Bleibt* (1990), which appeared in the June 1, 1990, edition of *Die Zeit* and Frank Schirrmacher's review article, "*Auch eine Studie über den autoritären Charakter: Christa Wolf's Aufsätze, Reden und ihre jüngste Erzählung,*" which appeared in the June 2, 1990 edition of *Frankfurter Allgemeine Zeitung*, set off the debate. See Karl Deiritz and Hannes Krauss, eds, *Der deutsche-deutsche Literaturstreit oder "Freunde, es spricht sich schlecht mit gebundener Zunge"* (Hamburg: Sammlung Luchterhand, 1991).
5. Benjamin Robinson, "Santa Monica of the Turn: Catastrophe and Commitment in an Autobiography of Collaboration," *New German Critique* 84 (Fall 2001), 110.
6. Wolf, "Momentary Interruption," in *Parting from Phantoms: Selected Writings, 1990–1994*, trans. Jan van Heurek (Chicago, IL: University of Chicago Press, 1997), 9.
7. Heinrich von Kleist, *Penthesilea: Ein Tragödie* (Berlin: Buchverlag Der Morgen, 1983).
8. *Christa Wolfs Medea: Voraussetzungen zu einem Text* (München: Deutscher Taschenbuch Verlag, 2000), 76.
9. Ibid., 90, 163.
10. Ibid., 31.
11. Christoph Menke, "Critical Theory and Tragic Knowledge," in *Handbook of Critical Theory*, ed. David M. Rasmussen (London: Blackwell, 1996), 58, 71, and 70. Menke notes his borrowing of the notion of "fragility" from Martha Nussbaum's work, *The Fragility of Goodness: Luck and Ethics in Greek Tragedy* (Cambridge, MA: Cambridge University Press, 1986).
12. Heinz-Peter Preusser, *Mythos als Sinnkonstruktion: Die Antikenprojeckte von Christa Wolf, Heiner Müller, Stefan Schütz und Volker Braun* (Köln: Böhlau Verlag, 2000), 33.

13. Ulrich Profitlich's sourcebook of German tragic theory, *Tragödien-Theorie: Texte und Kommentare Vom Barock bis zur Gegenwart* (Hamburg: Rohwolt, 1999), 283–6.

14. Wolfgang Emmerich, *Kleine Literaturgeschichte der DDR* (Frankfurt am Main: Sammlung Luchterhand, 1989), 342.

15. "[T]he use of the first-person plural 'we' in the GDR is a good example of the way language, collective identity and the problematic of the autonomous subject intersect. What Katja Lange-Müller called 'this strange use of the plural in the GDR' points to a kind of national narcissism that functioned on many different levels . . . . This undefined solidarity . . . undoubtedly contributed, for example, to the discourse of subjective authenticity and self-realization that appeared in GDR literature and essays beginning in the 1970s and then dominated writing in the 1980s. The attempt to find the self through language was articulated as the process of learning and re-learning to be an autonomous subject against the official and officious notions of the socialist personality in the socialist state." Marc Silberman, "Speaking with Silence: The GDR Author in the New Germany," *German Politics & Society* 29 (Summer 1993), 95.

16. Wolf, *Cassandra: A Novel and Four Essays*, 164, 144–5, 175, 226, 278–82. The German terms Wolf uses and for which "tragedy," "tragedian," "tragic" are translations all share the Greek stem, *trag*, with their English counterparts. See Wolf, *Voraussetzungen einer Erzälung: Kassandra*, 27, 38.

17. "Momentary Interruption," *Parting From Phantoms: Selected Writings, 1990–1994*, trans. Jan Van Heurck (Chicago, IL: University of Chicago Press, 1997), 12.

18. Wolf, "Illness and Love Deprivation: Questions for Psychosomatic Medicine," *The Author's Dimension: Selected Essays*, trans. Jan Heurck (New York: Farrar, Strauss and Giroux, 1993), 74. "A Conversation With Grace Paley," (1993), 275.

19. See, for example, Wolf, "Illness and Love Deprivation," (1993), 74.

20. Wolf, *Cassandra*, 233.

21. *Christa Wolfs Medea*, 75.

22. Wolf, *Cassandra*, 226.

23. Ibid., 142, 262, 278, 287.

24. Ibid., 164, 209, 291.

25. Ibid., 230, 235. For Wolf's evolving view of Cassandra see the following passage: "I can no longer view Cassandra as a tragic figure. I do not think she saw herself that way," ibid., 264. See, also: "The character continually changes as I occupy myself with the material; the deadly seriousness, and everything heroic and tragic, is disappearing; accordingly, compassion and unilateral bias in her favor are disappearing, too. I view her more soberly, even with irony and humor. I see through her. Than her environment crowded in on me: her women friends, her family," ibid., 247–8.

26. Wolf, "A Conversation with Grace Paley," 275.

27. Wolf, *Cassandra*, 238.

28. For criticisms of *Kassandra* and *Medea: Stimmen* as ideologically driven polemics see, respectively, Stephanie West, "Christa Wolf's Kassandra: A Classical Perspective," *Oxford German Studies* 20/21 (1991/92), 164–85 and Glenn Most, "*Eine Medea im Wolfspelz*," *Mythen in nachmythischer Zeit: Die Antike in der deutschsprachigen Literatur der Gegenwart*, eds Bernd Seidensticker and Martin Voehler (Berlin: Walter de Gruyter, 2002), 348–67. Hanz-Peter Preusser considers both of Wolf's Greek-themed works as examples of what he unsympathetically characterizes as the fusion of a romantic impulse with a conservative cultural anthropology in East German literature in his book, *Mythos als Sinnkonstruktion: Die Antikenprojekt von Christa Wolf, Heiner Müller, Stefan Schütz, and Volker Braun* (Köln: Böhlau, 2000).
29. Wolf, *Cassandra*, 144–56, 236, 278,
30. *Christa Wolfs Medea*, 78, 79, 92.
31. Glenn Most, 361.
32. "Heinrich Böll on the Occasion of His Seventy-Fifth Birthday," *Parting From Phantoms: Selected Writings, 1990–1994*, trans. Jan Van Heurck (Chicago, IL: University of Chicago Press, 1997), 201. "Parting from Phantoms: On Germany," ibid., 296.
33. "Momentary Interruption," ibid., 12.
34. "Parting from Phantoms: On Germany," ibid., 297.
35. "Those among us who were closely acquainted with Konrad Wolf know how greatly he strained in this field of conflict. In the life and death of Konrad Wolf I see tragic elements. It would be unforgivable of us to let lives like his be sucked into the dark hole with the rest." "Two Letters," ibid., 58. "I never again saw the expression of shock that I observed on the night of the dinner. But I did not forget it, and I often seemed to see it glimmering through her everyday face, a signal I could not interpret at first and that I only gradually understood bore witness to a life whose tragic features she wished to hide. . . . I saw her at times when she looked perplexed, suspicious, haggard, and disappointed—disappointed in me too, incidentally, when I no longer saw a possibility of mediating between irreconcilable opposites. She was afraid we might put at risk the thing she couldn't help but value the most: the continued existence of our commonwealth, where she thought she could see possibilities, however buried, that were worthy of human beings and could develop further, given more favorable conditions." "The Faces of Anna Seghers," ibid., 176, 182.
36. Helen Bridge, "Chista Wolf's Kassandra and Medea: Continuity and Change," *German Life and Letters* 57 (1) (January 2004), 33.
37. Wolf, *Cassandra*, 239.
38. Christa Wolf, "From Cassandra to Medea," trans. John Cullen (1998), www.randomhouse.com.
39. Greiner, op cit., and Marcel Reich-Ranicki, "*Tante Christa, Mutter Wolfen*," *Der Spiegel* (April 14, 1994), 197, respectively.

40. H. Strich writes that, "Classicism has usually been the product of corporate feeling, but German classicism looked upon it as its mission to call this corporate feeling into existence through art." Quoted in W. H. Bruford, *Germany in the Eighteenth Century: The Social Background of the Literary Revival* (Cambridge: Cambridge University Press, 1968), 324.
41. Wolf, *Cassandra*, 286–7.
42. For the pediment and fabric metaphors, ibid., 142 and 292, respectively.
43. Wolf, *Cassandra*, 286–7.
44. Timothy Garton Ash, *The Magic Lantern: The Revolution of '89 Witnessed in Warsaw, Budapest, Berlin and Prague* (New York: Vintage, 1993), 11, 40, 54, 60, 158.
45. Padraic Kennedy, *The Burdens of Freedom: Eastern Europe Since 1989* (Nova Scotia: Fernwood Publishing, 2006), 105.
46. Jörg Magenau, *Christa Wolf: A Biographie* (Berlin: Kindler, 2002), 378–9, 390.
47. For the reception of *Kassandra*, see Christine Schmidjell, *Erläuterungen und Dokumente: Christa Wolf Kassandra* (Stuttgart: Philipp Reclam, 2003), chapter III.
48. This reading of the significance of *Medea: Stimmen* in Wolf's oevre goes against the grain of the majority view of critics who tend to see the book as marking an abdication of any ambition to exercise a leading role in fostering a new sense of German identity or community. See, for a recent example, Jörg Magenau, who argues in the previously cited biography of Wolf that, "The intellectual who dealt in ideologies instead of in religion now [with the publication of *Medea*] stands before us empty-handed." As quoted by Julia Hell, "Loyal Dissidents and Stasi Poets: Sascha Anderson, Christa Wolf, and the Incomplete Project of GDR Research," *German Politics & Society* 65 (Winter 2002), 99. See, for another recent example, Charity Scribner, who, in noting that, "images of solidarity, images of a working circle all but disappear from *Medea*," argues that Wolf has given up on a coherent vision of community. *Requiem for Communism* (Cambridge: The MIT Press, 2003), 148.

Chapter 9

1. "The World and the Jug," *Shadow and Act* (New York: Vintage, 1966), 140.
2. Anton Kaes, *From Hitler to Heimat: The Return of History as Film* (Cambridge: Harvard, 1989), 167.
3. Sabine Hake, *German National Cinema* (London: Routledge, 2002), 184.
4. Ian Garwood, "The *Autorenfilm* in Contemporary German Cinema," *The German Film Book*, eds Tim Bergfelder, Erica Carter and Deniz Göktürk (London: bfi, 2002), 203.
5. http://72.14.207.104/search?q=cache!5QxnBzYuHncT:Media.movieweb.com
6. *Berliner Zeitung*. April, 21, 2004 www.Schultzegets theblues.de/en/downloads/BerlinerZeitung210404.pdf

7. "How American Is It: The United States As Image and Imaginary in German Film," *Perspectives on German Cinema*, eds Terri Ginsberg and Kirsten Moana Thompon (New York: G. K. Hall, 1996), 287.

8. Randall halle, "German Film, *Aufgehoben*: Ensembles of Transnational Cinema," *New German Critique* 87 (Fall 2002), 11.

9. Hake, 180, 182.

10. Ute Poiger, *Jazz, Rock and Rebels: Cold War Politics and American Culture in a Divided Germany* (Berkeley, CA: University of California Press, 2000), 85, 153–4, 158.

11. Robert Fine and Vivienne Boon, eds, "Special Issues: Cosmopolitanism: Between Past and Future," *European Journal of Social Theory*, 10 (1) (2007), 5–16—offers a fine survey of the contemporary agenda of cosmopolitan thought. Thanks to Steve Engel for this reference. For a historical analysis of cosmopolitan thought in Germany see Pauline Kleingeld's "Six Varieties of Cosmopolitanism in Late-Eighteenth Century Germany," *Journal of the History of Ideas* (1999), 505–24.

12. Poiger, 163, 165.

13. Amy Robinson, "It Takes One to Know One: Passing and Communities of Common Interest," *Critical Inquiry* 20 (Summer 1994), 735.

14. Robinson, 735.

15. Hake, 182.

16. Robinson, 735.

17. http://72.14.207.104/search?q=cache!5QxnBzYuHncT:Mdedia.movieweb.com, 8.

18. http://www.bme.jhu.edu/~jrice/NewFiles/beginners.html

19. Director commentary, *Schultze Gets the Blues* DVD (Paramount Pictures, 2005).

20. Recent additions to the voluminous literature on cinematic images of "mammy" and their political significance include Donald Bogle, *Toms, Coons, Mulattoes, Mammies & Bucks: An Interpretive History of Blacks* (New York: Continuum, 2001) and Patricia Turner, *Ceramic Uncles and Celluloid Mammies: Black Images and Their Influence on Culture* (New York: Anchor Books, 1994).

21. Joseph Roach, *Cities of the Dead: Circum-Atlantic Performance* (New York: Columbia University Press, 1996), 2.

22. Ibid., 5.

23. Ibid., 22.

24. Ibid., 194.

25. Ibid, 203.

26. Ibid., 205.

27. Ibid.

28. Ibid., 207.

29. Ibid., 277.

30. Ibid., 278–9.

31. Ibid., 14.

32. Cornel West, "On Black Nationalism," in *The Cornel West Reader* (New York, 1999) 521.

33. Cornel West, "The Political Intellectual" in ibid., 284.
34. Christa Wolf, "Momentary Interruption," in *Parting From Phantoms: Selected Writings* trans. Jan van Heurek (Chicago, IL: University of Chicago Press, 1997), 9.

Chapter 10

1. "Walter Benjamin: 1892–1940," *Men In Dark Times* (New York: Harvest/HBJ, 1968), 204, 205.
2. For a fuller accounting of Arendtian passages relating to tragedy see Robert Pirro, *Hannah Arendt and the Politics of Tragedy* (DeKalb, IL: Northern Illinois University Press, 2001), 38–9, 46–9, 86–9, 128–50.
3. *The Human Condition* (Chicago, IL: University of Chicago Press, 1958), 190.
4. "Portrait of a Period (October 1943)", *The Jew As Pariah*, ed. Ron Feldman (New York: Grove Press, 1978), 117.
5. See Arendt's essays, "We Refugees" and "The Moral of History," reprinted in *The Jew As Pariah*, 62, 107, 109.
6. *Tragedy Is Not Enough*, trans. H. Reiche, H. Moore, and K. Deutsch (Hamden, CT: Archon, 1969), 97.
7. See note 9, p. 110.
8. *On Revolution* (New York: Penguin, 1979), 246.
9. See note 9, p. 109.
10. See "Chapter Ten: The Masses" of *The Origins of Totalitarianism*.
11. "Organized Guilt and Universal Responsibility," *The Jew As Pariah*, 232.
12. David Farber, *The Age of Great Dreams*, 3. Emphasis added.
13. Todd Gitlin, *The Sixties: Years of Hope, Days of Rage* (New York: Bantam Books, 1993), 435. My emphases.

Select Bibliography

The 9/11 Commission Report (New York: W.W. Norton, 2004).

Andersch, Alfred. *Efraim's Book*, Ralph Mannheim, tr. (New York: Penguin, 1984).

Arendt, Hannah. *On Revolution* (New York: Penguin, 1979).

—. *Between Past and Future* (New York: Penguin, 1978).

—. *The Jew as Pariah*, Ron Feldman, ed. (New York: Grove Press, 1978).

—. *The Origins of Totalitarianism* (New York: Harvest/HBJ, 1973).

—. "Walter Benjamin: 1892–1940," *Men In Dark Times* (New York: Harvest/HBJ, 1968).

—. *The Human Condition* (Chicago: University of Chicago Press, 1958).

Aristotle, Horace, Longinus. *Classical Literary Criticism*, T. S. Dorsch, tr. (London: Penguin, 1965).

Ash, Timothy Garton. *The Magic Lantern: The Revolution of '89 Witnessed in Warsaw, Budapest, Berlin, and Prague* (New York: Vintage, 1993).

Ayto, John. *Dictionary of Word Origins* (New York: Arcade, 1990).

Baldry, H.C. *The Greek Tragic Theatre*, (New York: Norton, 1971).

Barnhardt, Robert, ed. *The Barnhardt Dictionary of Etymology* (New York: Wilson, 1988).

Bayard, Carolyn. "The Intellectual in the Post Modern Age: East/West Contrasts," *Philosophy Today* (Winter 1990).

Bazin, André. *What Is Cinema I*, Hugh Gray, ed. and tr. (Berkeley: University of California Press, 1971).

Bellah, Robert. *The Broken Covenant: American Civil Religion in Time of Trial*. (Chicago: University of Chicago Press, 1992).

Bellah, Robert and Hammond, Phillip. *Varieties of Civil Religion* (San Francisco: Harper & Row, 1980).

Benson, Mary. *Nelson Mandela: The Man and the Movement* (New York: Norton, 1986).

Berezin, Mabel. "The Festival State: Celebration and Commemoration in Fascist Italy," *Journal of Modern European History* (2006).

Bergfleth, Gerd. "Erde und Heimat: Über das Ende der Ära des Unheils," in *Die selbstbewusste Nation*, Heimo Schwilk and Ulrich Schacht, eds. (Berlin: Ullstein, 1994).

Berlin, Isaiah. *Against the Current: Essays in the History of Ideas* (Princeton: Princeton University Press, 1979).

Bethell, Lord Nicholas. "An Interview with Nelson Mandela," *Apartheid in Crisis*, Mark Uhlig, ed. (New York: Oxford University Press, 1986).

Bondanella, Peter. "The Making of *Roma Citta Apertá*," *Roberto Rossellini's Rome Open City* Sidney Gottlieb, ed., (Cambridge: Cambridge University Press, 2004).

—. *The Films of Roberto Rossellini* (Cambridge: Cambridge University Press, 1993)

—. *Italian Cinema: From Neorealism to the Present* (New York: Continuum, 1990).

Bridge, Helen. "Christa Wolf's Kassandra and Medea: Continuity and Change," *German Life and Letters* 57:1 (January 2004).

Bruford, W. H. *Germany in the Eighteenth Century: The Social Background of the Literary Revival* (Cambridge: Cambridge University Press, 1968).

Brumlik, Micha. "*Neuer Staatsmythos Ostfront: Die neueste Entwicklung der Geschichtswissenschaft der BRD*," *Historikerstreit* (Munich: Piper, 1987).

Brunetta, Gian Piero. *Cent'anni di cinema italiano: Dal 1945 ai giorni nostri* II (Rome: Editori Laterza, 1998).

Cannella, Mario. "Ideology and Aesthetic Hypotheses in the Criticism of Neo-Realism," *Screen* 14 (Winter 1973).

Castoriadis, Cornelius. *World in Fragments: Writings on Politics, Society, Psychoanalysis, and the Imagination*, David Ames Curtis, ed. and tr. (Stanford: Stanford University Press, 1997).

Chytry, Josef. *The Aesthetic State: A Quest in Modern German Thought* (Los Angeles: University of California Press, 1989).

Connor, W. Robert. "Civil Society, Dionysiac Festival and the Athenian Democracy," in *Dēmokratia*, Josiah Ober and Charles Hedrick, eds. (Princeton: Princeton University Press, 1996).

—. "City Dionysia and Athenian Democracy," *Classica et Mediaevalia* 40 (1989).

Dalle Vacche, Angela. *The Body in the Mirror: Shapes of History in Italian Cinema* (Princeton: Princeton University Press, 1992).

De Tocqueville, Alexis. *Democracy in America, Volume I*, Henry Reeve, tr. (Cambridge: Sever and Francis, 1863).

Diggins, John. *Max Weber: Politics and the Spirit of Tragedy* (New York: Basic Books, 1996).

Disch, Lisa. *Hannah Arendt and the Limits of Philosophy* (Ithaca: Cornell University Press, 1994).

Duffy, John and Schaeffer, Mary. *Triumph over Tragedy: September 11 and the Rebirth of a Business* (New York: John Wiley & Sons, 2002).

Dwyer, Jim and Kevin Flynn. *102 Minutes: The Untold Story of the Fight to Survive Inside the Twin Towers* (New York: Times Books, 2005).

Eagleton, Terry. *Sweet Violence: The Idea of the Tragic* (Malden: Blackwell, 2003).

Elam, Harry J. Jr. "A Forum on Theatre and Tragedy in the Wake of September 11," David Román, ed. *Theatre Journal* 54 (2002).

Ellison, Ralph. "The World and the Jug," in *Shadow and Act* (New York: Vintage, 1966).

Else, Gerald. *The Origin and Early Form of Greek Tragedy* (Cambridge: Harvard University Press, 1965).

Elshtain, Jean Bethke. "A Man For This Season: Václav Havel on Freedom and Responsibility," *Perspectives on Political Science* 21:4, 92.

Emmerich, Wolfgang. *Kleine Literaturgeschichte der DDR* (Frankfurt am Main: Sammlung Luchterhand, 1989).

Euben, J. Peter. *The Tragedy of Political Theory: The Road Not Taken* (Princeton: Princeton University Press, 1990)

Farber, David. *The Age of Great Dreams* (New York: Farrar, Strauss & Giroux, 1994).

Farrell, John. *Revolution as Tragedy: The Dilemma of the Moderate from Scott to Arnold* (Ithaca: Cornell University Press, 1980).

Findlay, Edward. "Classical Ethics and Postmodern Critique: Political Philosophy in Václav Havel and Jan Patočka," *The Review of Politics* (Summer, 1999).

Finley, M.I. *Politics in the Ancient World* (Cambridge: Cambridge University Press, 1983).

Forgacs, David. "Space, Rhetoric and the Divided City," in *Roberto Rossellini's Rome Open City*, Sidney Gottlieb, ed. (Cambridge: Cambridge University Press, 2004).

Frederiksen, Rune. "The Greek Theatre: A Typical Building in the Urban Centre of the *Polis*?" in *Even More Studies in the Ancient Greek Polis*, Thomas Nielsen, ed. (Stuttgart: Franz Steiner Verlag, 2002).

Gallagher, Tag. *The Adventures of Robert Rossellini* (New York: Da Capo, 1998).

Garwood, Ian. "The *Autorenfilm* in Contemporary German Cinema," in *The German Film Book*, Tim Bergfelder, Erica Carter and Deniz Göktürk, eds. (London: British Film Institute, 2002).

Gibson, Angus, and Jo Menell, dirs. *Mandela* (London: Island Pictures, 1996).

Gilbert, Allison, et al. *Covering Catastrophe: Broadcast Journalists Report September 11* (Chicago: Bonus Books, 2002).

Ginsborg, Paul. *A History of Contemporary Italy: Society and Politics, 1943–1988* (New York: Palgrave, 2003).

Gitlin, Todd. *The Sixties: Years of Hope, Days of Rage* (New York: Bantam, 1993).

Giunta, Ray, with Lynda Rutledge Stephenson. *God @ Ground Zero* (Nashville: Integrity Publishers, 2002).

Goldhill, Simon. "Collectivity and Otherness—The Authority of the Tragic Chorus: Response to Gould," in *Tragedy and the Tragic: Greek Theatre and Beyond*, M. S. Silk, ed. (Oxford: Clarendon Press, 1998).

Gould, John. "Tragedy and Collective Experience," in *Tragedy and the Tragic: Greek Theatre and Beyond*, M. S. Silk, ed. (Oxford: Clarendon Press, 1998).

Green, Rodney M. "Theodicy," *Encyclopedia of Religion, Volume 14*, Mircea Eliade (New York: Collier, 1987).

Greenwald, Glenn. *A Tragic Legacy: How a Good vs. Evil Mentality Destroyed the Bush Presidency* (New York: Crown Publishers, 2007).

Gregory, James. *Goodbye Bafana: Nelson Mandela, My Prisoner, My Friend* (London: Headline Book Publishing, 1995).

Groopman, Jerome. "The Grief Industry," *The New Yorker* (January 26, 2004).

Guiloineau, Jean. *Mandela: Naissance d'un destin* (Paris: Editions Autrement, 1998).

Habermas, Jürgen. "Yet Again: German Identity in a Unified Nation of Angry DM-Burghers?" *New German Critique* 52 (Winter 1991).

—. *"Eine* Art Schadensabwicklung: Die apologetischen Tendenzen in der deutschen Zeitgeschichtsschreibung," *Historikerstreit* (Munich: Piper, 1987).

Hake, Sabine. *German National Cinema* (London: Routledge, 2002).

Halberstam, David. *The Best and the Brightest* (New York: Random House, 1972).

Halle, Randall. "German Film, *Aufgehoben*: Ensembles of Transnational Cinema," *New German Critique* 87 (Fall 2002).

Hamilton, Edith. *The Greek Way* (New York: Norton, 1993).

—. *The Ever-Present Past* (New York: Norton, 1964).

Hammer, Dean. "Václav Havel's Construction of a Democratic Discourse: Politics in a Postmodern Age," *Philosophy Today* (Summer, 1995).

Havel, Václav. *To the Castle and Back*, Paul Wilson, tr. (New York: Knopf, 2007).

—. *The Art of the Impossible: Politics as Morality in Practice*, Paul Wilson et al., tr. (New York: Fromm International, 1998).

—. *Summer Meditations*, Paul Wilson, tr. (New York: Vintage, 1992).

—. *Open Letters: Selected Writings, 1965–1990*, various translators (New York: Knopf, 1991).

—. *Disturbing the Peace*, Paul Wilson, tr. (New York: Knopf, 1990).

—. *Letters to Olga*, Paul Wilson, tr. (New York: Holt, 1989).

Hay, John. *Popular Film Culture in Fascist Italy: The Passing of the Rex* (Bloomington: Indiana University Press, 1987).

Hegel, G. W. F. *Hegel on Tragedy*, Anne and Henry Paolucci, eds. (Garden City: Anchor Books, 1962).

Hell, Julia. "Loyal Dissidents and Stasi Poets: Sascha Anderson, Christa Wolf, and the Incomplete Project of GDR Research," *German Politics & Society* 65 (Winter 2002).

Heller, Agnes. "The Great Republic," *Praxis International* 5:1 (April 1985).

Hermassi, Karen. *Polity and Theatre in Historical Perspective* (Berkeley: University of California Press, 1977).

Hildebrand, Klaus. "*Der Zeitalter der Tyrannen*," in *Historikerstreit* (Munich: Piper, 1987).

Hillgruber, Andreas. "*Jürgen Habermas, Karl-Heinz Janssen und die Aufklärung Anno 1986*," in *Historikerstreit* (Munich: Piper, 1987).

Hughes, H. Stuart. *The United States and Italy* (Cambridge: Harvard University Press, 1979).

Jaeger, Werner. *Paideia, Volume 1*, Gilbert Highet, tr. (Oxford: Oxford University Press, 1974).

Jaspers, Karl. *Tragedy Is Not Enough*, Harald Reiche, Harry Moore, and Karl Deutsche, trs. (Boston: Archon Books, 1969).

Joseph, Helen. *Side by Side: The Autobiography of Helen Joseph* (London: Zed, 1986).

Kaes, Anton. *From Hitler to Heimat: The Return of History as Film* (Cambridge: Harvard University Press, 1989).

Kaiser, David. *American Tragedy: Kennedy, Johnson, and the Origins of the Vietnam War* (Boston: Belknap, 2000)

Kathrada, Ahmed. *Letters from Robben Island: A Selection of Ahmed Kathrada's Prison Correspondence, 1964–1989* (East Lansing: Michigan State University, 1999).

Keane, John. *Václav Havel: A Political Tragedy in Six Acts* (London: Bloomsbury, 1999).

Kennedy, Maxwell Taylor. *Make Gentle the Life of This World: The Vision of Robert F. Kennedy* (New York: Harcourt Brace, 1998).

Kennedy, Robert. *Thirteen Days: A Memoir of the Cuban Missile Crisis* (New York: Norton, 1969).

Kenney, Padraic. *The Burdens of Freedom: Eastern Europe since 1989* (Nova Scotia: Fernwood, 2007).

Kirtzman, Andrew. *Rudy Giuliani: Emperor of the City.* (New York: Perennial, 2004).

Klein, Naomi. *The Shock Doctrine: The Rise of Disaster Capitalism* (Los Angeles: Metropolitan Books, 2007).

Kumalo, Alf, and Es'kia Mphahlele. *Mandela: Echoes of an Era* (New York: Penguin, 1990).

Landau, Mark J., et al. "Deliver Us from Evil: The Effects of Mortality Salience and Reminders of 9/11 on Support for President George W. Bush," *Personality and Social Psychology Bulletin* 30:9 (September 2004).

Landy, Marcia. "Diverting Clichés: Femininity, Masculinity, Melodrama, and Neorealism in *Open City*," in *Roberto Rossellini's Rome Open City*, Sidney Gottlieb, ed. (Cambridge: Cambridge University Press, 2004).

Langewiesche, William. *American Ground: Unbuilding the Trade Center* (New York: North Point Press, 2003).

Lawler, Peter Augustine. "Havel on Political Responsibility," *The Political Science Reviewer* (1993).

Liehm, Mira. *Passion and Defiance: Film in Italy from 1942 to the Present* (Berkeley: University of California Press, 1984).

Lom, Petr. "East Meets West—Jan Patočka and Richard Rorty on Freedom: A Czech Philosopher Brought into Dialogue with American Postmodernism," *Political Theory* 27:4 (August 1999).

Lopate, Phillip. *Totally, Tenderly, Tragically: Essays and Criticism from a Lifelong Love Affair with the Movies* (New York: Doubleday, 1998).

Magun, Artemy. "The Double Bind: The Ambivalent Treatment of Tragic Passions in Hannah Arendt's Theory of Revolution," *History of Political Thought*, 28:4 (Winter 2007).

Maier, Charles. *The Unmasterable Past: History, Holocaust, and German Identity* (Cambridge: Harvard University Press, 1988).

Mandela, Nelson. *In the Words of Nelson Mandela*, Jennifer Crwys-Williams, ed. (Secaucus: Carol, 1998)

—. *Long Walk to Freedom* (Boston: Little, Brown and Company, 1995).

—. *Nelson Mandela Speaks: Forging a Democratic, Nonracial South Africa* (New York: Pathfinder, 1993).

—. *Nelson Mandela: Symbol of Resistance and Hope for a Free South Africa*, E. S. Reddy, ed. (New Dehli: Sterling Publishers, 1990).

—. *Nelson Mandela: The Struggle Is My Life* (New York: Pathfinder Press, 1990).

Mandela, Winnie. *Part of My Soul Went with Him*, Anne Benjamin, ed. (New York: Norton, 1985).

Mann, Thomas. *Doctor Faustus*, H.T. Lowe-Porter, tr. (New York: Vintage, 1971).

—. "Germany and the Germans," *Thomas Mann's Addresses* (Washington D.C.: Library of Congress, 1963).

—. *The Story of a Novel* (New York: Knopf, 1961).

—. "The Tragedy of Germany," *Treasury for the Free World*, Ben Raeburn, ed. (New York: Arco Publishing, 1945).

Marcus, Millicent. *Italian Film in the Light of Neorealism* (Princeton: Princeton University Press, 1984).

Martin Heidegger, Karl Jaspers: Briefwechsel, 1920–1963 Walter Biemel and Hans Saner, eds. (München: Piper, 1992)

Matuštik, Martin. *Postnational Identity: Critical Theory and Existential Philosophy in Habermas, Kierkegaard, and Havel* (New York: The Guilford Press, 1993).

McCarthy, Mary. *The Seventeenth Degree* (New York: Harcourt Brace Jovanovich).

McKelvey, Tara. *Monstering: Inside America's Policy of Secret Interrogations and Torture in the Terror War* (New York: Carroll & Graf, 2007).

McNamara, Robert. *In Retrospect: The Tragedy and Lessons of Vietnam* (New York: Random House, 1995).

McNamara, Robert, with James G. Blight, Robert K. Brigham, Thomas J. Biersteker, and Herbert Y. Schandler. *Argument without End: In Search of Answers to the Vietnam Tragedy* (New York: Public Affairs, 2000).

Mearns, David C. *Three Presidents and Their Books: Jefferson, Lincoln, F.D. Roosevelt* (Urbana: University of Illinois Books, 1963).

Meer, Fatima. *Higher Than Hope: The Authorized Biography of Nelson Mandela* (New York: Harper, 1988).

Meier, Christian. *The Political Art of Greek Tragedy*, tr. Andrew Webber (Baltimore: Johns Hopkins University Press, 1993).

Mendelsohn, Daniel. "Theatres of War," *The New Yorker* 79:42 (January 12, 2004).

Menke, Christoph. "Critical Theory and Tragic Knowledge," Rasmussen, David, ed. *Handbook of Critical Theory* (London: Blackwell, 1996).

Meredith, Martin. *Nelson Mandela: A Biography* (London: Penguin, 1997).

Mills, C. Wright. *Power, Politics, and People: The Collected Essays of C. Wright Mills* (New York: Ballantine Books, 1944).

Mommsen, Hans. "Suche nach der 'verlorenen Geschichte': Bemerkungen zum historischen Selbstverständnis der Bundesrepublik," *Historikerstreit* (Munich: Piper, 1987).

Morris, Errol, dir. *The Fog of War* (New York: Sony Pictures, 2004).

Morris, Kenneth E. *Jimmy Carter: American Moralist* (Athens: University of Georgia Press, 1996).

Most, Glenn. *"Eine Medea im Wolfspelz,* " *Mythen in nachmythischer Zeit: Die Antike in der deutschsprachigen Literatur der Gegenwart,* Bernd Seidensticker and Martin Vöhler, eds. (Berlin: Walter de Gruyter, 2002).

Nash, Andrew. "Mandela's Democracy," *Monthly Review* (April 1999).

Neiman, Susan. *Evil in Modern Thought: An Alternative History of Philosophy* (Princeton: Princeton University Press, 2002).

Newfield, Jack. *Robert Kennedy: A Memoir* (Bantam: New York, 1970).

Nietzsche, Friedrich. *The Birth of Tragedy and The Case of Wagner,* Walter Kaufmann, tr. (New York: Vintage, 1967).

Norris, Pippa, and Ronald Inglehart. *Sacred and Secular: Religion and Politics Worldwide* (Cambridge: Cambridge University Press, 2004).

Nowell-Smith, Geoffrey, et al. *The Companion to Italian Cinema* (London: Cassell and the British Film Institute, 1996).

Nussbaum, Martha. *The Fragility of Goodness: Luck and Ethics in Greek Tragedy and Philosophy* (Cambridge: Cambridge University Press, 1986).

Ober, Josiah and Barry Strauss. "Drama, Political Rhetoric, and the Discourse of Athenian Democracy," in John Winkler and Froma Zeitlin, eds. *Nothing to Do with Dionysos? Athenian Drama in its Social Context* (Princeton: Princeton University Press, 1990).

Overbey, David. *Springtime in Italy: A Reader on Italian Neo-Realism* (Hamden: Archon Books, 1978).

Palmer, Richard H. *Tragedy and Tragic Theory: An Analytical Guide* (Westport: Greenwood Press, 1992).

Patočka, Jan. *Jan Patočka: Philosophy and Selected Writings,* Erazim Kohák, ed. (Chicago: University of Chicago Press, 1989).

Pirro, Robert. *Hannah Arendt and the Politics of Tragedy* (Dekalb: Northern Illinois University Press, 2000).

Pitkin, Hanna. *Wittgenstein and Justice: Of the Significance of Ludwig Wittgenstein for Social and Political Thought* (Berkeley: University of California Press, 1972).

Poiger, Ute. *Jazz, Rock and Rebels: Cold War Politics and American Culture in a Divided Germany* (Berkeley: University of California Press, 2000).

Preusser, Heinz-Peter. *Mythos als Sinnkonstruktion: Die Antikenprojeckte von Christa Wolf, Heiner Müller, Stefan Schütz und Volker Braun* (Köln: Böhlau Verlag, 2000).

Profitlich, Ulrich. *Tragödien-Theorie: Texte und Kommentare Vom Barock bis zur Gegenwart* (Hamburg: Rohwolt, 1999).

Raynor, Alice. "A Forum on Theatre and Tragedy in the Wake of September 11," David Román, ed. *Theatre Journal* 54 (2002).

Reinelt, Janelle. "A Forum on Theatre and Tragedy in the Wake of September 11," David Román, ed. *Theatre Journal* 54 (2002).

Rentschler, Eric. "How American Is It? The U.S. as Image and Imaginary in German Film," *Perspectives on German Cinema,* Terri Ginsberg and Kirsten Moana Thompon, eds. (New York: G. K. Hall, 1996).

Restivo, Angelo. *The Cinema of Economic Miracles: Visuality and Modernization in the Italian Art Film* (Durham: Duke University Press, 2002).

Roach, Joseph. *Cities of the Dead: Circum-Atlantic Performance* (New York: Columbia University Press, 1996).

Robinson, Amy. "It Takes One to Know One: Passing and Communities of Common Interest," *Critical Inquiry* 20 (Summer 1994).

Robinson, Benjamin. "Santa Monica of the Turn: Catastrophe and Commitment in an Autobiography of Collaboration," *New German Critique* 84 (Fall, 2001).

Rocchio, Vincent. *Cinema of Anxiety: A Psychoanalysis of Italian Neorealism* (Austin: University of Texas Press, 1999).

Rorty, Richard. *Truth and Progress* (Cambridge: Cambridge University Press, 1998).

—. "The Seer of Prague," *The New Republic* (July 1, 1991).

Rossellini, Roberto. *My Method: Writings and Interviews* (New York: Marsilio, 1992).

Ruprecht, Louis. *This Tragic Gospel: How John Corrupted the Heart of Christianity* (San Francisco: Jossey-Bass, 2008).

—. *Tragic Posture and Tragic Vision* (New York: Continuum, 1994).

Russell, Alec. *Bring Me My Machine Gun: The Battle for the Soul of South Africa from Mandela to Zuma* (New York: Public Affairs, 2009).

Salazar, Philippe-Joseph. *An African Athens: Rhetoric and the Shaping of Democracy in South Africa* (Mahwah: Lawrence Erlbaum, 2002).

Sampson, Anthony. *Mandela: The Authorized Biography* (New York: Knopf, 1999).

Schama, Simon. "The Unloved American," *The New Yorker* (March 10, 2003).

Schlesinger, Arthur. *Robert Kennedy and His Times* (Boston: Houghton Mifflin, 1978).

Schmidt, Dennis J. *On Germans and Other Greeks: Tragedy and Ethical Life* (Bloomington: Indiana University Press, 2001).

Schorr, Michael, dir. *Schultze Gets the Blues* (Paramount Pictures, 2005).

Scribner, Charity. *Requiem for Communism* (Cambridge: The MIT Press, 2003).

Scruton, Roger. "Masaryk, Patočka and the Care of the Soul," in Josef Novak, ed. *On Masaryk: Texts in German and English* (Amsterdam: Rodopi, 1988).

Shiel, Mark. *Italian Neorealism: Rebuilding the Cinematic City* (London: Wallflower, 2006).

Shklar, Judith. *Ordinary Vices* (Cambridge: Belknap Press, 1984).

Silberman, Marc. "Speaking with Silence: The GDR Author in the New Germany," *German Politics and Society* 29 (Summer 1993).

Silk, M.S. and J. P. Stern, *Nietzsche on Tragedy* (Cambridge: Cambridge University Press, 1987).

Simmons, Michael. *The Reluctant President: A Political Life of Václav Havel* (London: Methuen, 1991).

Simpson, David. "It's Not about Cheering Us Up," *London Review of Books* 25:7 (April 3, 2003).

Simpson, Lorenzo. "Evading Theory and Tragedy? Reading Cornel West," *Praxis International* 13:1 (April 1993).

Sitney, P. Adams. *Vital Crises in Italian Film* (Austin: University of Texas Press, 1995).

Sorley, Lewis. *A Better War: The Unexamined Victories and Final Tragedy of America's Last Years in Vietnam* (New York: Harcourt Brace, 1999).

Sourvinou-Inwood, Christiane. *Tragedy and Athenian Religion* (New York: Lexington, 2003).

Sparks, Allister. "Mandela's South Africa–and After: The Status of the Dream," *The Wilson Quarterly* 23:2 (Spring 1999).

Spelman, Elizabeth. "Theodicy, Tragedy, and Prophesy: Comments on Cornel West's *The American Evasion of Philosophy*," *APA Newsletter on the Black Experience* 90:3 (1991).

Steel, Ronald. *In Love With Night: The American Romance with Robert Kennedy* (New York: Simon & Schuster, 2000).

Steiner, George. *Antigones* (Oxford: Oxford University Press, 1984).

Stern, Fritz. *The Politics of Cultural Despair: A Study in the Rise of the Germanic Ideology* (New York: Doubleday Anchor, 1965).

Stow, Simon. "Pericles at Gettysburg and Ground Zero: Tragedy, Patriotism, and Public Mourning," *American Political Science Review* 101:2 (May 2007).

Strauss, Botho. "Goat Song Rising," Thomas Ringmayr, tr., *Southern Humanities Review* 38:4 (Fall 2004).

—. *"Anschwellender Bockgesang,"* in *Deutsche Literature 1993: Jahresüberblick,* Frank Görtz, Volker Hage, and Uwe Wittstock, eds. (Stuttgart: Phillip Reclam, 1994).

—. *Big and Little,* Anne Cattaneo, tr. (New York: Farrar Straus Giroux, 1979).

—. *Devotion,* Sophie Wilkins, tr. (New York: Farrar Straus Giroux, 1979).

Sul neorealismo: testi e documenti, 1939–1955 (Pesaro: 10a Mostra Internazionale del Nuovo Cinema, 1974).

Thomas, Evan. *Robert Kennedy: His Life* (New York: Simon & Schuster, 2000).

Tolczyk, Dariusz. *See No Evil* (Hartford: Yale University Press, 1999).

Tomasulo, Frank. "Bicycle Thieves: A Re-Reading," *Cinema Journal* 21:2 (Spring 1982).

Tucker, Aviezer. *The Philosophy and Politics of Czech Dissidence from Patočka to Havel* (Pittsburgh: University of Pittsburgh Press, 2000).

Učník, Lubica. "Aesthetics or Ethics? Italian Neorealism and the Czechoslovak New Wave Cinema," *Italian Neorealism and Global Cinema,* Laura Ruberto and Kristi Wilson, eds. (Detroit: Wayne State University Press, 2007).

Valelly, Richard M. "What's Gone Right in the Study of What's Gone Wrong," *The Chronicle Review* (April 16, 2004).

Vernant, Jean-Pierre, and Vidal-Naquet, Pierre. *Myth and Tragedy in Ancient Greece* (1988, original French editions 1972 and 1986).

Weber, Max. *From Max Weber,* H. H. Gerth and C. Wright Mills, eds. (New York: Oxford University Press, 1958).

West, Cornel. *The Cornel West Reader* (New York: Basic *Civitas* Books, 1999).

—. *Prophetic Thought in Postmodern Times* (Monroe: Common Courage Press, 1993).

—. *The American Evasion of Philosophy* (Madison: University of Wisconsin Press, 1989).

—. *Prophesy Deliverance! An Afro-American Revolutionary Christianity* (Philadelphia: The Westminster Press, 1982).

West, Stephanie. "Christa Wolf's Kassandra: A Classical Perspective," *Oxford German Studies* 20/21 (1991).

Witt, Mary Ann Frese. *The Search for Modern Tragedy: Aesthetic Fascism in Italy and France* (Ithaca: Cornell, 2001).

Wolf, Christa. *Christa Wolf's Medea: Voraussetzungen zu einem Text* (München: Deutscher Taschenbuch Verlag, 2000).

—. *Parting from Phantoms: Selected Writings, 1990–1994,* Jan van Heurek, tr. (Chicago: University of Chicago Press, 1997).

—. *The Author's Dimension: Selected Essays,* Jan Heurck, tr. (New York: Farrar, Strauss and Giroux, 1993).

—. *Cassandra: A Novel and Four Essays,* Jan Van Heurck, tr. (New York: Farrar, Straus and Giroux, 1984).

Wolf, Gregory H. "Botho Strauss and Conservative Aesthetics: An Introduction to 'Goatsong Rising'." *Southern Humanities Review* 38:4 (Fall 2004).

Woodward, Bob. *Plan of Attack* (New York: Simon & Schuster, 2004).

Worthen, W. B. "A Forum on Theatre and Tragedy in the Wake of September 11," David
　　Román, ed., *Theatre Journal* 54 (2002).
Yancy, George, ed. *Cornel West: A Critical Reader* (Malden: Blackwell Publishers, 2001).
Zak, William F. *The Polis and the Divine Order*. (Lewisburg: Bucknell University Press,
　　1995).
Zavattini, Cesare. *Cesare Zavattini Neorealismo ecc.*, Mino Argentieri, ed. (Milan: Bompiani,
　　1979).
Zhang, Yingjin. *Chinese National Cinema* (New York: Routledge, 2004).
Žižek, Slavoj. "Attempts to Escape the Logic of Capitalism," *The London Review of Books*
　　(October 28, 1999).

Index